PETER REES has been a journalist for forty years, working as a federal political correspondent for the *Melbourne Sun*, the *West Australian* and the *Sunday Telegraph*. He is author of *The Boy from Boree Creek: The Tim Fischer Story* (2001), *Tim Fischer's Outback Heroes* (2002), and *Killing Juanita: A true story of murder and corruption* (2004), which was a winner of the 2004 Ned Kelly Award for Australian crime writing, as well as *Desert Boys: Australians at war from Beersheba to Tobruk and El Alamein* and *Lancaster Men: The Aussie heroes of Bomber Command*. He lives in Canberra and is currently writing a biography of Charles Bean.

# ANZAC GIRLS

## The Extraordinary Story of our World War I Nurses

### PETER REES

ALLEN&UNWIN

First published in Australia and New Zealand by Allen & Unwin as *The Other Anzacs* in 2008

This edition published in 2014

Allen & Unwin
83 Alexander Street
Crows Nest NSW 2065
Australia
Phone:      (61 2) 8425 0100
Email:      info@allenandunwin.com
Web:        www.allenandunwin.com
Cataloguing-in-Publication details are available
from the National Library of Australia
www.trove.nla.gov.au
ISBN 9781743319826
Set in 11/17pt Minion MT by Midland Typesetters, Australia
Printed and bound in Australia by Griffin Press

20 19 18 17 16 15 14 13

*For Sue, who has shared this journey.*

# CONTENTS

# THE MARQUETTE

# THE WESTERN FRONT

# AUTHOR'S NOTE

I have attempted to tell the story of the war through the eyes of particular women, using their diaries and letters to show the conflict's effect on them professionally and personally. This book is not intended as a definitive history but more as a representative account, in the context of the unfolding war as it was seen by a few representing the many in Egypt, Lemnos, the hospital ships and the Western Front.

Throughout the war, staff nurses and sisters were addressed as Sister, with matrons generally being called Miss. The staff nurses did not like being referred to as such, preferring to be called Sister. I have mostly used Sister in titles, but Nurse and Staff Nurse are used where necessary. I have also standardised spelling and capitalisation for readability.

*While men fight one another, women tend the wounded, and there can be no doubt at all but that theirs is the nobler part. Naturally enough the eyes of the world are on the firing line and sometimes the work of the nurses, from the very firing line to the hospitals is overlooked. It was ever thus. Those who scar the tree of life, a great thinker once said, are remembered by the scars, but those who water its roots have nothing by which they may be known. But theirs is the tree.*

—Christchurch *Star*, 3 November 1915

# INTRODUCTION

As nurses in Australia and New Zealand saw it, the issue in 1914 was quite simple. They wanted to be there, with their boys, when they went to war. And the Anzac boys wanted the women there, too, with them on the other side of the world. It was not only their nursing expertise, they were a link to home. As one Australian sister at a hospital in France noted, they always knew when wounded Anzacs arrived: 'If they are not too ill they generally call out "Hullo Australia" or some such remark, they know our uniform from the English sisters. How we do love our dear brave boys.'

Another sister captured it this way in a letter home from a hospital on Malta: 'You don't know [how] these boys of ours love to come across an Australian woman, and then when they saw us they were nearly too shy to come and speak to me . . . poor dears, I would do any mortal thing for them.' Like so many of her boys from the bush, Narelle Hobbes, the former matron of Brewarrina Hospital in far western New South Wales, died on active duty before the war ended.

The Great War was the first test of the fledgling Army nursing services of Australia and New Zealand. More than forty Australian civilian nurses had served officially in the 1899–1902 Boer War in South Africa, together with several more from Australia and New Zealand who went either individually or in independent units. But the Great War was the first time nurses were part of dedicated Army services—the Australian Army Nursing Service (AANS) and the New Zealand Army Nursing Service (NZANS).

The AANS was a trained civilian reserve of the Australian Army Medical Corps. It was established when the various state nursing services joined together. The nurses had done their training in rural and urban hospitals. As civilians, they had limited knowledge of military matters when war was declared.

The NZANS was not fully established until shortly after the Great War began, by which time Australian nurses were already in the field. New Zealand nursing leaders told the government on New Year's eve 1914 that, as with Australia, 'if the sons of New Zealand were serving the Empire in the field it was only right that her daughters, who were able and willing, should be allowed to do so too.'[1] In the years ahead, New Zealand and Australian nurses would often work side by side in military hospitals tending their wounded compatriots, and soldiers from other countries as well.

A wave of patriotism swept Australia and New Zealand when war was declared on 4 August 1914. Anti-German sentiment was strong. Men walked long distances to enlist in the Australian Imperial Force (AIF), and women's voluntary organisations were soon established to assist the war effort in any way they could. In New Zealand, men joined the New Zealand Expeditionary Force (NZEF) with similar enthusiasm. In Melbourne, an over-zealous mob attacked the German Club and Consulate. German citizens were quickly rounded up and interned. A year later, the town of Germanton, in the New South Wales Riverina, would change its name to Holbrook. By 1918, from a population of fewer than five million Australians, 331,781 men would serve overseas, of whom nearly 62,000 would be killed and 153,500 would be wounded or gassed. In New Zealand, with a population of 1.1 million, more than 128,000 enlisted. Of these, more than 16,000 would be killed and 41,300 become casualties.

The declaration of war brought an immediate surge of volunteers among trained nurses keen to become military nurses. Waiting lists were so long for overseas postings that at least 130 nurses chose to sail to England to join the Australian Army Nursing Service's British equivalent, Queen Alexandra's Imperial Military Nursing Service, a recognised body within the Army. Several New Zealand nurses joined the same service. The Australians who left soon found that transferring to their own country's nursing service would not be easy. Other Australian nurses and some women doctors joined private medical units in Europe and Britain, such as the Scottish Women's Hospital Unit, which worked under dreadful conditions in Serbia.

Research by historian Dr Kirsty Harris shows that considerably more than the generally accepted figure of 2139 Australian nurses served overseas. At least 2498 nurses served overseas with the AANS, with around 720 other trained Australian nurses and masseuses serving overseas with various allied services in addition to the AANS. This means that nearly as many Australian nurses served overseas in World War I as in World War II. [2]

In New Zealand, historian Sherayl McNabb has upgraded the number of New Zealand nurses who served overseas with the NZANS from around 550 to at least 610, with about a hundred more serving in other overseas nursing bodies, including Red Cross units and the Queen Alexandra's Imperial Military Nursing Service. Again, it appears that the World War II figures for New Zealand nurses who did overseas service were similar. [3]

In all, sixty-five Military Medals were awarded to military nurses from all World War I nursing services. Also, some forty-four Australian Army nurses received the highly sought after Royal Red Cross and 143 the Associate Royal Red Cross, while fourteen New Zealand nurses were awarded the Royal Red Cross and seventy-two the Associate Royal Red Cross.

To be accepted into the Army nursing services in Australia and New Zealand nurses had to have completed at least three years' training in an approved hospital. Australian military nurses had to be aged between twenty-one and forty and either single or widowed, but in New Zealand they could be aged up to forty-five. If they married, resignation was mandatory for Australian nurses, although this rule does not appear to have been rigidly enforced in the early days of the war. For New Zealand nurses, marriage was first allowed, then banned, and finally allowed again.

The question of whether the nurses were members of the AIF was unclear. Legally, the nursing service could not be part of the AIF since its personnel could not be members of the armed forces. In 1932, the Crown Solicitor provided an opinion that Australian Army Nursing Service members were not enlisted within the meaning of the Australian Defence Act, so appointments to the service were made by the Governor-General. This meant that the AANS was 'not a part of the Defence Force'.[4] In 1943 the AANS changed from an auxiliary service to an incorporated part of the Australian Military Forces, but its status would not finally be clarified until the change from service to corps in 1951.

The issue of rank would become a burning question as the AANS sought to consolidate its organisational structure. A report by the Director-General of Australian Army Medical Services, Lieutenant General R.H.J. 'Bertie' Fetherston, found that in the Australian hospitals on the island of Lemnos there were soldiers who paid no respect to orders issued by women. Noting that Canadian nurses on the island had had military rather than honorary rank since 1901, he recommended, in his reorganisation of the AANS, that Australian nurses should wear badges of rank. Fetherston believed this would improve the nurses' status and authority, especially in the eyes of non-commissioned officers and orderlies.

The change of nurses' status to Army officers rather than civilians took effect in May 1916, even though the nurses were not in favour of the use of badges. The matron-in-chief wore a crown badge, and ranked as a major. The principal matron or matron had three stars, the same as a captain. A sister, with two stars, was equivalent to a 1st lieutenant, and a staff nurse, with one star, the equivalent of a 2nd lieutenant. But their pay was not made commensurate. A matron, for example, earned twelve shillings and sixpence a day, just over half a captain's wage.

A similar situation existed with the New Zealand Army Nursing Service. Although it was officially part of the NZEF, only men could legally be members of the armed forces. An amendment was proposed to the New Zealand Defence Act in 1915 to regularise the NZANS's legal status, but it was never made. Nurses' status remained unclear, and they were refused permission to wear badges of rank. In 1916 a directive went out to all New Zealand camps and hospitals that the military status of matrons, sisters and nurses was that of officers, and that they were to be 'accorded the usual courtesy salute'. But not all officers complied. To compound the insult, the nurses were paid less than male orderlies.

Australian and New Zealand nurses soon saw service in their own backyard as the shadow of the conflict spread into the Pacific. The Allies feared Germany would take over Samoa, which had been a British–German condominium, as a potential base for its Pacific naval squadron. Immediately after war was declared New Zealand was asked to send troops to Samoa to seize the German wireless station there. With six nurses aboard, a troopship sailed on 15 August. A fortnight later, a German takeover of Samoa was prevented when the islands were secured without incident and the Union Jack raised in the capital, Apia. New Zealand nurses took over the running of the Apia hospital.

The German-held colony of New Guinea was also seen to pose a threat. Australia was given the urgent mission of seizing a powerful wireless station that the Germans had installed near Rabaul. On 11 September 1914 a small Australian force landed in the area, but unlike in Samoa, the Germans resisted. Attending to a wounded German during the fighting, a captain in the Australian Army, Dr Brian Pockley, was shot and killed. He became the second Australian casualty of the Great War, an able seaman having been killed earlier in the same operation, which also claimed the life of another Australian soldier. As malaria and dysentery soon began to take their toll on the occupying Australians, medical reinforcements, including nurses, were quickly sent from Sydney aboard the hospital ship *Grantala*.

Also in September 1914, the first Australian nurses saw service in Europe. Sisters Claire Trestrail, Caroline Wilson and Catherine Tully were in the middle of the fighting in Antwerp, Belgium, working at a makeshift 120-bed British Red Cross hospital. By a quirk of fate, the three nurses had been in England when war broke out a few weeks earlier. Separately, each joined the Queen Alexandria's Imperial Military Nursing Service and, with a Red Cross party, sailed to Antwerp to set up the hospital. The nurses were needed more urgently than they knew, for the nursing profession in Europe had yet to make the advances that Florence Nightingale had inspired in English-speaking countries. Another nurse in Antwerp would later assert that the reason for the neglect was that 'nuns were not allowed to attend to men patients below the waist'.[5] Untrained orderlies did most of the work.

Within hours of the nurses' arrival in Antwerp, the roar of the guns could be heard continually, 'till at last we became so used to the sound that we slept peacefully', Sisters Wilson and Trestrail recounted in an article in *The Australasian Nurses' Journal*.[6] Published in December 1914, this was the first account of the experiences of Australian nurses in the Great War. 'No words can describe the awfulness of the wounds,' they wrote. 'Bullets are nothing. It is the shrapnel that tears through the flesh and cuts off limbs, and makes gashes that one cannot possibly describe.' Perhaps earlier than anyone else, they also came face to face with what would come to be known as shell shock. 'The noise, too, shatters the nerves of men, and even deafens and maddens them.' When Belgium fell, the sisters were evacuated. Only troops came after them.

The residents of Boorowa, in southwestern New South Wales, learned of the heroic deeds of the three nurses when the *Burrowa News* published an account of the drama involving the sisters. The paper proudly pointed out that Catherine Tully came from the area and had trained at Goulburn Hospital. For the farming folk of the district, her experiences were their first tangible link to the war.[7]

Like the soldiers, AANS nurses left Australia with little idea of their destination. The war was being waged in vast and varied theatres: Egypt, Turkey, Greece, France, England, India, Mesopotamia, Africa, Italy, Serbia and Russia. The first group of Australian nurses to go overseas—twenty-six in all, including four matrons—were aboard the troopships when the first convoy of 29,000 Australian and New Zealand servicemen left Australia on 1 November 1914. A second, larger contingent of nurses left a month later.

They departed believing they were bound for England and ultimately France to prepare for the establishment of hospitals to be staffed by Australian Army nurses. However, as British military leaders discussed mounting a possible campaign against Turkey at the Dardanelles, the nurses on board were diverted to nearby Egypt. Gallipoli was their introduction to a casualty load that rarely lightened for the duration of the war.

Often they worked in appalling physical conditions, as was the case on the island of Lemnos in the Aegean Sea, or at primitive medical facilities on the Western Front in France. In 1916–17, in France's coldest winter for a century, operating theatres with free-standing fuel heaters exemplified the hardships of working at casualty clearing stations. In the spring of 1917, a sister at No. 3 Australian Casualty Clearing Station, Gertrude Doherty, noted that when she arrived there were no mattresses or pillows, only stretchers and blankets. 'As soon as a patient was operated on and put back on the stretcher, it gradually sank in the mud.'[8]

Sister Ida O'Dwyer, who worked at the same station, was exposed to the full horror of wounds straight from the battlefield only a few kilometres away. Mostly the wounded arrived with the first field dressings still on, 'or perhaps a tourniquet still on a limb that is almost blown off and the wounds still full of mud and clothes and pieces of metal . . . He may be a man with not one wound but perhaps ten or more in which there may be two fractures and a head wound,' she said. 'Then there are the abdominal wounds which appear nothing 'till they are opened and there will be found perhaps the bowel torn in from six to twelve places.'[9]

Sister Elsie Eglinton saw different injuries at No. 2 Australian General Hospital at Wimeraux, near the Somme, in a ward where there were many disfigured faces. 'We never even have time to take a bandage off, it is just cut off,' she recounted. 'It's quite common for a piece of shrapnel the size of a marble to drop out of the jaw whilst you are syringing it.'[10]

And then there was the sheer volume of wounded. In three years at Rouen, more than 90,000 patients passed through No. 1 Australian General Hospital. Most were not Australian—only slightly more than eleven per cent of all admissions to Australian hospitals on the Western Front were AIF members, the rest being Allied troops and even German prisoners of war.

Many of the nurses were away so long that a sprig of wattle sent from home would become a cherished keepsake, a reminder of a long-ago life before war. These women were pioneers in the advancement not just of nursing as a profession but of women's place in society. But many would lose brothers or lovers, or their own health; and some would pay with their lives.

# GALLIPOLI

# 1

# THE BIG ADVENTURE

―――※※―――

Street peddlers jabbered and gesticulated, proffering postcards, figs, Turkish delight and beads. Beggars and urchins pleaded for money. The scene at Port Said, on the Suez Canal, could not have been in starker contrast to the measured pace of life back in Australia. After six weeks at sea, the women from the Australian Army Nursing Service had arrived in Egypt, ready for the serious business of war. But for now they were sitting around a table at the Savoy Hotel. There was a feeling of excitement and anticipation despite the mayhem around them. Sister Elsie Eglinton had seen nothing like it in Adelaide. There were 'merchants of every description so thick around us that we could scarcely give our order to the waiter who kept trying to flick them away with his towel'.

A boy was pulling one of my boots on one side of my chair and another boy on the other side was tugging at my other boot and yet I had them tucked as far under my chair as I could get them. They were beautifully polished before I left the ship and did not require cleaning. I had to keep shouting at them to be off.[1]

3

Another of the women was trying to ward off the attentions of a fortune teller and two annoying bootblacks on their knees who were trying to polish her shoes. Snake charmers, bead sellers and yet more bootblacks added to the pandemonium unfolding before Elsie's eyes.

> Then up came a conjuror, head corks and tins and started pulling chickens out of his shirt front, then began some marvellous tricks. Then the whole crowd started begging for money. I'd as soon go hungry any day as try to enjoy a cup of tea under such circumstances.[2]

The city was at once mesmerising and bewildering. On board the Australian hospital ship *Kyarra*, anchored at Port Said, Sister Elsie Cook was discomforted for different reasons from her colleagues lunching in town. Elsie was in a state of high anticipation, preparing to meet her husband, Lieutenant Syd Cook, an architect and the son of conservative politician Joseph Cook, leader of the Liberal Party. Prime Minister when the war had started in the middle of a federal election campaign, Cook Snr had announced that 'If the Old Country is at war, so are we'. Labor leader Andrew Fisher had promised Great Britain 'our last man and our last shilling' in any conflict with Germany. On 5 September 1914, Cook was defeated and Fisher became Prime Minister for the third time.

On the declaration of war, Elsie had immediately started a scrapbook. The second newspaper story she pasted inside the cover was from the Sydney *Sunday Times* of 9 August. Headed, 'NURSES TO VOLUNTEER', it stated:

> One of the first nurses in New South Wales to volunteer from [*sic*] active service was Nurse Shephard [*sic*], of the Prince Alfred Hospital. She is just completing her term of training, and is a member of the ATNA [Australasian Trained Nurses' Association]. She is also the fiancée of Lieut. Cook, son of the Prime Minister, who has also volunteered for active service.

Elsie and Syd's marriage six weeks later was a high point on Sydney's social calendar. The honeymoon that followed was short, as Syd, a platoon commander in the 2nd Battalion, was already in camp. He sailed for Egypt at the start of November.

Elsie and Syd had not seen each other for nearly three months, and they were both excited at the prospect of meeting. 'Up early and dressed waiting to go ashore, as I thought to meet Syd, who was at the Anzac camp outside Cairo,' Elsie wrote.[3] A telegram arrived with the news that Syd had been denied leave to travel to Port Said. A disconsolate Elsie went ashore, her normally warm smile replaced by a frown. She later harrumphed that Port Said was 'the dirtiest, nastiest place imaginable'. The *Kyarra* left Port Said that evening and a day later docked at Alexandria, Egypt's main port on the Mediterranean.

Everyone was restless and eager to leave the ship, not least Elsie, who was 'fairly dying to get ashore' to see Syd. 'It is a very wearing thing to be tied up in port and not allowed ashore in a new and untrodden part, all its novelties and mysteries still untasted, more especially desirable is it when one's brand new husband is contained therein,' she wrote. When they were finally permitted to disembark, the nurses were captivated by cosmopolitan Alexandria, with its wide avenues, fine buildings, French tea rooms and bohemian culture. After the filth of Port Said, the ancient city's cleanliness and order were a relief.

Elsie travelled by train the 225 kilometres across the flat Nile delta to Cairo. With her were her colleagues from Royal Prince Alfred Hospital in Sydney, Kath King and Ursula Carter. Ursula's brother, Lieutenant Herbert Gordon Carter, of the 1st Battalion, was based, like Syd Cook, at Mena Camp outside Cairo. The three nurses took a taxi there.

Ursula had not seen her brother since he left with the first Anzac convoy. Kath King may well have known Gordon from her life in Sydney, and they all got on famously that day, catching up with each other's news. Gordon hired donkeys and took Kath and Ursula to the Sphinx. Kath fell off her mount, much to everyone's amusement.

Upset to find that Syd was away on a route march in the desert, Elsie stood waiting at his tent. A passing colonel sensed her melancholy and sent his groom to fetch Syd back. 'Soon on the horizon came two galloping specks. I watched them thro' the glasses get nearer and nearer. Syd arrived looking very well and fit. Strange it seemed to meet him away there in a desert camp, after saying goodbye at Kensington [Sydney].'4 Meeting again in an Egyptian desert camp with the ancient Pyramids looming nearby was the stuff of romance for a nurse born and bred on the other side of the world.

They drove into Cairo, through strange narrow streets, and found their way to the opulent Shepheard's Hotel, the social mecca of British Army officers, where they took rooms. After dinner, they drove around Cairo, where the scent of incense gave a 'weird oriental touch and feeling'. Returning to the hotel, they listened enchanted to the orchestra in the lounge before having supper at another popular venue, Gaults. They were in love and their senses were alive to the wonders of Egypt.

Shepheard's was a vibrant centre of European life in Cairo, a city now buzzing with the rapidly expanding presence of the military. The elegant hotel had long been the place to be seen. Its great dining room overflowed during the social season with people of all nationalities and pursuits. The Australian nurses were awestruck. For clergyman's daughter Daisy Richmond, who had trained at Sydney Hospital and worked for the Bush Nursing Association near Boorowa, New South Wales, the hotel was a 'most glorious place', with its magnificent drapes and a head waiter in flowing Egyptian robes. Elsie Cook loved the Victorian-era hotel's broad stairways and wide halls, resplendent with divans, cushions and palms. 'Dark Arabs gliding noiselessly about dressed in white, red fez and sash, the whole so different and fascinating and impressive to my Australian eyes.'5 To Elsie, who had grown up in the leafy and wealthy Sydney suburb of Burwood and attended the local Methodist Ladies College, where she had excelled in physiology, these early days in Cairo were like living a fantasy.

Another Australian nurse, awed by the ancient history surrounding her, wrote home after visiting the Pyramids and the Sphinx, 'It seemed almost incredible that we were there gazing at these wonderful works which we read of and viewed in pictures all our lives and never dreamt of seeing. I can't tell how it makes you feel, that calm, wise face, gazing out over the desert, watching the passage of the centuries as we do the days of the week. It conveys such a sense of understanding everything.'[6]

Six weeks earlier, 160 nurses had boarded the *Kyarra* in Australia, excitement and trepidation running high among them and those who had come to farewell them. While a small advance party of sisters had left with the first convoy of Australian and New Zealand troopships on 1 November, Elsie's group was the first to leave on a hospital ship. The former coastal freighter—hurriedly requisitioned for war service and painted white, with a wide green band round its hull and a large red cross amidships—held two complete general hospitals, fully equipped to accommodate 1640 patients. Troops were also on board.

Elsie boarded the *Kyarra* at Woolloomooloo in Sydney, after it arrived from Brisbane. It was a sultry day, and 'terrific claps of thunder echoed through the ship', the *Australasian Nurses' Journal* reported on 15 December.

We all thought of the more deafening thunder of the guns which roar unceasingly along the battle front, and we remembered that, notwithstanding the bright and festive air which surrounded us, we were bidding farewell not to an ordinary ship, carrying an ordinary body of Australians on pleasure bent, but a band of earnest trained men and women, who in a few weeks' time would be at work in circumstances of hardship, and even perhaps of danger, and surrounded by pain and suffering indescribable.

Kath King noted prosaically in her diary: 'The last of Sydney for a while. I had a crowd of friends see me off. Had a very rough night, three sailors were nearly washed overboard and were injured, one seriously, our first patients.'[7] The *Kyarra* sailed to Melbourne, where the remainder of the contingent boarded, among them Alice Ross King. The Melbourne surgeon she worked for had wanted to enlist but told Alice he would only go if she joined too. Alice agreed. The surgeon failed the medical checks. Alice, who passed, went anyway.

As the ship pulled away from the dock amid singing of *Auld Lang Syne*, streamers of red, white, rose, green and mauve were unfurled, joining passengers with the big crowd on shore. The sinuous ribbons strained and snapped, leaving family and friends waving and shouting as the ship steamed out into Port Phillip Bay. From the deck, Elsie Cook watched her father, Michael Sheppard, grow smaller. 'Last sight of Father was to see him waving his handkerchief on his umbrella.'[8]

For Elsie Eglinton, the streamers 'made me feel very sad as I saw them all snapping as our ship got further and further from land'. She and several others had travelled to Melbourne by train to join the *Kyarra*. Their first farewell had been in Adelaide, where nursing colleagues organised 'a beautiful tea-party and gave each a small gold swashtika [*sic*] for a mascot of Good Luck'.[9] Such charms were deeply appreciated and kept close. 'Father came in to say "Goodbye" this morning,' Elsie wrote of the group's departure from Adelaide, 'but I hurried him off as I was afraid of breaking down and going away red-eyed. We are all ever so happy, Maggie Hay is my chum, we seem to pair off you know.' Best mates would acquire special importance for the nurses during the years ahead.

As their train travelled through the countryside, Elsie and her colleagues were treated like heroines. 'We are having a glorious time so far,' she wrote. 'Our carriages were simply piled with sweets, flowers [and] flags. At one station women and children came on to the platform with hot tea, cakes and flowers. Oh! They did give us a good send off.' Her friend Sister Olive Haynes noted that the carriage was full of gifts. They had supplied themselves with tea but forgot the milk. Drinking black tea from a vacuum flask would soon be the smallest of their inconveniences. Sister Ethel Peters (known as Pete) was upset because she didn't kiss Olive's brother, Dal, and 'she mightn't get another chance'.[10]

On board the *Kyarra*, Olive and Pete were Elsie's cabin mates. 'We get along nicely together we take it in turns to get dressed as there is only room for one at a time,' Elsie wrote. She wondered what the principal matron, Jane Bell, would make of the various state uniforms. 'The girls say that she is most particular. I'm wondering what she will think of the hobble skirts which a few of the NSW and Tasmanians are wearing, anyway they are not the thing for Active Service for they could never run if occasion occurred.'[11] Hobble-skirted uniforms that narrowed at the ankles would be one of the first items to go.

Though well educated, these nurses came from fairly narrow backgrounds. Many had become nurses against their parents' wishes. At the time, nurses had not long emerged from their 19th-century image of drunken promiscuity. The revolution in nursing that Florence Nightingale began during the Crimean War had been taken to Australia by Nightingale's disciple Lucy Osburn in 1868. The young women on the *Kyarra* were all beneficiaries of the new system of nurse training, as were their New Zealand counterparts, who would soon follow.

But their position in society was still confined. Many had never travelled. Kath King, from Orange in New South Wales, displayed the same parochialism as the South Australians, caustically observing after her visit to the Melbourne bayside suburb of St Kilda, 'Melbourne folk think a lot of St Kilda but it really is not any better than Botany Bay.' But for girls with a sense of adventure, the war was a chance to visit places that they had only read about. As with the men, going to the war seemed the chance of a lifetime.

The excitement was palpable in the sea of new faces at dinner that first night after leaving Melbourne. The officers and sisters dined together, the sisters wearing grey frocks, white muslin caps and scarlet capes that contrasted with the officers' navy and scarlet uniforms. But next morning seasickness brought an end to their delight. When Elsie Eglinton awoke she 'heard groans all round our cabin . . . The others were all ill. So down I got and produced my flask of brandy and started to give each one a dose, but I don't remember finishing for my legs seemed to give way under me and I had to lie on the floor as the ladder to the top berth was impossible for a time.'[12] No one got up that day.

Elsie Cook fared just as badly. 'Very fed up with sea life and silently vow never to put foot on a boat again and never to go forth to a war again,' she wrote.[13] But a few days later she was able to breakfast in the saloon, where the troops were rehearsing for an afternoon concert. 'Efforts sounding rather more energetic and persevering than musical, but very entertaining,' she observed.[14] For vibrant young women in the first innocent days of the war, life on a troopship could be fun.

Soon the nurses were getting their sea legs and coming to terms with the overcrowding and poor food, and preparing for a shipboard Christmas. When the *Kyarra* left Fremantle on 13 December, Elsie Cook 'stayed on deck and sadly watched the very last bit of Australia vanish into the night, wondering how long, and what lay before me, before I should see Australian shores again'.

Amid deck games and dances, French classes and boat drills, spirits were high. At the fancy-dress ball on New Year's Eve, Daisy Richmond dressed as a grandmother and thought the festivities 'really splendid considering the material we had to hand'. Elsie Cook went as a mermaid, wrapped in shimmering green-grey silk. 'Wore my hair loose with a wreath of seaweed [and] pineapple leaves from the dinner table on my head,' she noted. The party ended at midnight with a rendition of *Auld Lang Syne*.

And so ended 1914. What an eventful year! My engagement, marriage, finishing my training and old life at Prince Alfred Hospital, the outbreak of the Great War, my joining the Army Nursing Service and leaving home and Australia for the first time! Very eventful. As we stood and watched the old year die and vanish, I regretted to part with it, and hated to see it go. New Year's Day dawned as we stood and watched the old year out and New Year in on the deck of the *Kyarra*. A gloriously moonlit morning. Calm and beautiful, everyone bright and happy and so begins 1915. It seems a good omen.[15]

------

In Bernay, France, New Zealand Sister Ella Cooke was having a very different New Year. On the Western Front, soldiers were shivering in frozen trenches, many stricken with trench foot. In the past few weeks Ella had seen enough to know that the war that was stirring Britons and their allies to patriotic fervour held horrors that not even a Christmas card from King George V to every soldier, sailor and nurse could hide.

Fate had dealt Ella a strange hand. Six months earlier, at the age of twenty-nine, she and her twin sister had left Auckland for Canada and the United States en route to England. But then Britain declared war on Germany. Ella had grown up among people who called England 'Home', and once there she offered her services as a nurse. Not needed, she crossed the Channel in November to serve as a volunteer with the French Flag Nursing Corps. She was paid no salary, merely a sufficient allowance for board and lodging.

Ella saw men with sickening wounds, deep and long, from the bullets, bombs and shrapnel that tore to the bone. No one back home could possibly comprehend what the war meant, she wrote in a letter to the New Zealand nurses' journal, *Kai Tiaki*;[16] they would have to see 'these poor suffering men' to understand. Many had been in the trenches for weeks, and some had not had their boots off since the war began four months earlier in the warmth of summer. 'You can imagine the state they are. Many have swollen feet and frozen up to the ankles; most I am afraid, will lose both feet, and many the legs up to the knee,' she wrote.

Wounded Arab soldiers, fighting for the French, brought the war right into Ella's ward. 'Unless they kill a man outright and cut off his head they don't believe he is really dead. One Arab travelled all the way from the firing line with a German's head in his possession. One day there was an awful smell in his room, and a German's head was found under his bed!'

New Zealand nurse Zillah Jones was working with British Army nurses on the hospital ship *Carisbrook Castle*, sailing between France and England. Along with English soldiers, she tended some German wounded. Despite the news of German atrocities in Belgium, Zillah saw unusual camaraderie among the men, regardless of nationality. 'Our men are most awfully good to [the Germans] on the boat. I have seen them shave them, help them off with their boots, and give them cigarettes.'[17]

A story she heard from a wounded German sniper underlined the poignancy of that first festive season of the war. British infantrymen were astonished on Christmas Eve to see Germans erecting Christmas trees with candles and paper lanterns on the parapets of their trenches. A truce was declared and there was much singing of carols, hymns and popular songs, and even meetings in some areas. The German soldier told Zillah about meeting British troops on this extraordinary Christmas Day. He said one of them had told him that 'the Kaiser was done for now'. The German had just laughed and shaken his head as both sides went about collecting and burying their dead in no man's land. He described how tokens and addresses had been exchanged in an oddly relaxed atmosphere. In a letter home, Zillah recounted what she had learned of the Christmas truce.

Some of the men had been exchanging Woodbines [cigarettes] with the Germans for rank cigars on Christmas Day, and some of them had even taken tea with the enemy, but they took good care that the Germans drank some first—they were taking no risks. One said:

'When are you going to pack up and go home. We are fed up. I live in London and want to get back.' And another said: 'Can't think why you don't go home; you know you are beaten.' They then shook hands, wished each other a Merry Christmas, went back to their trenches, and started shooting at each other.[18]

The reality of the war—which in the next four years would bring a death toll of 20 million troops and civilians—was not yet grasped by anyone, whether in a lounge room in Australia and New Zealand, a trench or hospital in France, aboard a hospital ship, or in an Anzac camp in Egypt.

# 2

# RELATIVE RELATIONS

---

Sister Alice Ross King had always wanted to be a nurse.[1] Perhaps it was because she had seen tragedy in her own family. She was a toddler when her storekeeper father moved the family from Ballarat to Perth in search of a better life in the late 1880s. It was there that he and two brothers drowned in a fishing accident on the Swan River. Alice returned to Melbourne with her mother and completed her education at the Presbyterian Ladies' College.

Not old enough to start nursing training, she worked for some time assisting the matron of the Austin Hospital, but moved to the Alfred Hospital when a typhoid epidemic caused a shortage of nurses. After completing her training, Alice moved back to the Austin Hospital, where she became night superintendent. Further experience as a theatre sister and then matron of a private hospital meant that at twenty-seven, she brought a wealth of experience to the Australian Army Nursing Service.

As they left Australia, Alice and her fellow nurses on the *Kyarra* thought they were going to England and France, but their arrival in Egypt coincided with a shift in war strategy. By the start of 1915, a stalemate had developed on the Western Front, the opposing sides facing each other along a line of trenches stretching through France from Switzerland to the Belgian coast.

In the Middle East, the dynamics were also changing. The Turkish-ruled Ottoman Empire, which was an integral part of the European balance of power, had joined Germany. Russia, aligned with the Allies, was struggling to keep Turkish forces from invading through the Caucasus. The Russians appealed to Britain to mount a diversionary attack to draw the Turks away.

On 15 January 1915, the War Council convened a meeting in London that was to immediately affect the lives of Anzac nurses and troops in Egypt. The First Lord of the Admiralty, Winston Churchill, proposed a naval attack on the forts guarding the Dardanelles, the fifty-kilometre strait linking the Aegean Sea to the inland Sea of Marmara. Control of the Dardanelles and conquest of the Turkish capital of Constantinople would break the stalemate that had developed in the war, Churchill argued. Despite some reservations, the council gave the plan the go-ahead.

Word travelled quickly to Cairo, where the next day Elsie Cook recorded in her diary, 'Strong rumours that we are to stay in Egypt.' At lunch, the nurses were told officially that they were. No. 1 Australian General Hospital would be established at the luxury, four-storey Heliopolis Palace Hotel in the Cairo suburb of Abbassia. No. 2 Australian General Hospital would be set up at Mena House, a former hunting lodge that had recently been turned into another luxury hotel. 'Couldn't be a better arrangement,' Elsie wrote approvingly, clearly not interested in travelling to England when her husband Syd was nearby. That afternoon, Elsie walked down the newly made 'Canberra Road' to Mena Camp and met up with Syd. They walked over the hill to the Pyramids before riding donkeys down to the Sphinx.

Elsie observed that the majority of nurses were pleased to be staying, 'for most of us have someone in Camp'. Not only did the nurses want to be where they could be of most help to their soldiers, but they also wanted to be close to those they cared for. And the men wanted them there. 'Wherever our men were they cheered us and we them,' Daisy Richmond noted.[2] From the time they arrived in Egypt, the sisters and the men sought each other out. With the call to battle imminent, the troops were happy to have the women of their homeland there to socialise with and, all too soon, to tend them in hospital.

> It did not matter how ill they were, whenever they saw a strange Sister, their first question was, 'What part of Australia do you come from?' They all seemed to crave so for the company of some one who might know something of home.[3]

And often this turned to flirting. Alice Ross King captured the mood in her earliest diary entries. While noted for her nursing skill and strength of character, the slim twenty-seven-year-old was also vivacious, and her brown eyes expressed a ready sense of humour. Freed from the social confines of Edwardian Melbourne, she took happily to the heady atmosphere of Cairo.

A keen observer of people, Alice noticed both real and imagined fraternisation between nurses and officers. On 17 January 1915 she wrote that she was 'very interested' in a particular captain, but she believed his eyes were for someone else. Two days later she noted that her 'conjectures' had been mistaken. But by then, she had promised to go on a drive with another officer, 'a nice fresh youth'. Alice's attentions soon drifted again. 'Capt. S. attentions becoming noticed. [Sister] Connolly given me several digs about it today. Went up town with Sister Cuthbert—met an awfully nice man attached to our unit on the return trip. Wrote letters and dodged Capt. S. all the evening.'[4]

Mixing duty with romance in this exotic yet dangerous new environment became a focus for many of the nurses. It helped to have brothers and cousins, male friends and boyfriends in Egypt. In Cairo on 21 January, Kath King, Elsie Cook, Grace 'Tom' Thompson and several of their colleagues from Sydney's Royal Prince Alfred Hospital were invited by two officers to join them on a camel ride to the Step Pyramid at Sakkara and the great necropolis of Memphis. Kath was gregarious and enjoyed the company of the officers. Two days later, at a 'bonser dinner' at the Continental Hotel, she,

Tom and two officers listened to music until late. 'The boys were great and were jolly pleased to see Tom and me again,' she enthused. They were spending as much time as they could with the officers, who were likewise eager to issue invitations and visit them at No. 2 Australian General Hospital, often unannounced, in the hope of a chat and a cup of tea. The officers came to see Kath and Tom, 'but we were both on duty'.

Kath, Ursula and Tom worked in tents in the camp, Kath observing that it was 'quite tricky nursing on the sand'. Managing the flow of invitations was equally tricky. A colonel invited the three women to the mess for dinner one night. They had a 'ripping time, met such a crowd of officers and of course they made a great fuss of us as they had not seen an Australian woman for ages', Kath noted.[5] Not surprisingly, Ursula's brother Gordon Carter was one of the three officers who escorted them home.

One Saturday evening he and two officers called at the nurses' quarters to escort the three women on a donkey ride to the Sphinx and Pyramids. 'Sphinxing', as such outings were known, became a favourite pastime for off-duty officers and sisters. Another of the Mena House sisters, Olive Haynes, spent a day in bed with tonsillitis and noted that 'Col. Springthorpe said it must have been the moonlight Sphinxing.'[6]

For Kath, the ride to the Sphinx was magical. 'It was full moon, one of the most glorious nights I ever remember, as clear as day. Gordon escorted me everywhere.'[7] He described the trip in a letter to his parents, saying the Sphinx 'was made to smile for us by the Arabs. This is done by burning a piece of magnesium wire close up under the head and the shadow thrown up makes the Sphinx appear to smile.'[8]

Gordon became a frequent caller on Kath. One evening she and Ursula went to Mena Camp for tea and stayed for dinner. 'Afterwards the whole crowd of us went to the Picture Show, Gordon chaperoned me; Carter and I were the only two women in a hall full of men, too many for my liking.'[9] Life continued in this pleasant manner for the next few weeks, with Gordon arranging trips around Cairo along with dinners at the Continental and

Shepheard's hotels, visits to the Pyramids and the zoo, horse rides and trysts in the garden at Mena.

Among the sisters, it was common knowledge that Elsie Sheppard and Syd Cook were married. That placed Elsie in breach of AIF Standing Orders, which stated that 'the appointment of any member of the Australian Army Nursing Service who marries will cease from the date of marriage.' Official files are confusing, but it appears that efforts were made to circumvent the regulations to enable Elsie to serve overseas, a crucial part of the subterfuge being a statement that she had been mobilised out of Hobart instead of Sydney. A Minute Paper suggests that she joined under her maiden name, adding that she was 'mobilised in Tasmania, but embarked 2nd Military District [NSW] in the *Kyarra* 24/11/14'. Another document states that 'Nurse Cook enlisted in Melbourne in November 1914 . . . being part of Tasmanian Quota'. However, Army authorities in Hobart later categorically denied that she was part of the Tasmanian contingent.

Elsie's diary seems to confirm that she boarded the *Kyarra* in Sydney, but there is no explanation of why her father was in Melbourne to farewell her eleven days later. However, as a former prime minister and defence minister, her father-in-law had strong military connections, and it is possible that strings were pulled to allow Elsie to sail. Clearly, Elsie was determined to play her part and not be deterred by sexist rules.

After their reunion and trip to the Pyramids, Elsie and Syd had tea at the 'Sydney' tea room, which she noted was a recent 'Egyptian innovation since the advent of Australians at Mena'. Later that evening, Syd went to Mena House to spend more time with her. 'I took him to what I was told to be the sitting room, but [Matron] Miss Gould came along and found us and explained shortly that it wasn't for mere men to intrude there, so Syd soon departed.'[10]

In the weeks that followed, the couple spent as much time as they could together, at Syd's camp, sightseeing, or dining in Cairo with other officers. Matron Nellie Gould—who had worked at the same hospital where Elsie trained—was placed in a difficult situation. In mid-February Elsie was suddenly stricken with pleurisy, but when Syd came to see her, the matron told him off 'for not being properly chaperoned to the sick Sisters quarters'.[11] Syd got the message and, returning next day with red roses and Sydney newspapers, 'was properly escorted and announced by Miss Gould'. A week later, Elsie wrote, 'Miss Gould desires me to take my proper name Cook . . . "to avoid complications". So henceforth I'm to be known as Sheppard Cook. I'm very pleased, it is funny to be called Sheppard when you're Cook and one's friends outside hospital are in a dilemma. Sheppard whilst in hospital and Cook outside is rather confusing and muddley. So exit Sheppard.'[12]

Clearly, there was no secret about Elsie's status as a married woman, or any doubt that her superiors were prepared, however reluctantly, to turn a blind eye to the breach of regulations. Elsie's colleagues, and Syd's, were never in any doubt. 'On duty tonight,' Elsie wrote at the start of February, 'I had one of Syd's sergeants admitted as a patient . . . Sgt Peasey, who was one of our guard of honour. I foresee a bright and much indulged time in hospital ahead of Sgt Peasey.'[13] On Elsie's twenty-fifth birthday, 2 February, Syd sent over an orderly with a 'nice box of chocolates and a note . . . Some blessed night march on, and he will come up later.'

Against the backdrop of a troop build-up, bayonet drills, the steady tramp of feet and clatter of horses' hoofs, and the strains of battalion marching bands, the off-duty events created an air of gay unreality. Gordon and Kath joined a party of ten one carefree afternoon on a houseboat on the Nile. There were yet more dinners at the officers' mess. The social whirl, the flirting and courting went on innocently even as the drums of war quickened their beat.

# 3

# DIFFERENT RULES

———————⊷⊶⊷———————

Kath King found Lieutenant Colonel William Ramsay Smith to be 'a perfect horror'. Alice Ross King was equally unimpressed by the commanding officer of No. 1 Australian General Hospital, commenting acidly that he had 'a most unfortunate way of delivering himself'. Equally difficult to get on with was Principal Matron Jane Bell. Gimlet-eyed, thin-lipped and wearing steel-rimmed glasses, she was not easy to like, yet she was fiercely protective of her nurses' interests. That embroiled her in a bitter power struggle, precipitated by unclear lines of responsibility between the nurses and the Army hierarchy.

Not long after the arrival of the Australian nurses in Cairo, Bell was angered to discover that Ramsay Smith had demoted her from principal matron of the No. 1 hospital to house matron of No. 2 Australian General Hospital. She appealed to the British Director of Medical Services in Egypt, Surgeon-General Sir Richard Ford, who ran the Australian medical services in Egypt but knew little about them. Ford reinstated her, setting the scene for constant tension between her and Ramsay Smith.

One morning, Ramsay Smith ordered a group photograph taken. Alice Ross King, on night duty, was annoyed at having her sleep interrupted.

General William Williams, a 'big fat splodgy thing', sat in the middle of the group. 'I got in the back row and sat down with my back to the camera—we were so annoyed about it. They kept us standing about for 1½ hrs. We asked if we might have a cup of tea before going to bed and were told "Yes if we went without our supper that night" but we could not have both.'[1] This incident typified the level of petty control that military commanders sought over the nursing staff.

The tension began to show. Ramsay Smith refused to cooperate with Matron Bell, not even informing her when nursing reinforcements were to arrive. Despite her support for the nurses, Bell did not endear herself to them. After Kath King was found talking to a certain captain in the nurses' lounge she noted peevishly, 'Miss Bell lectured me the next morning for doing so.'[2] Alice Ross King was alarmed as she watched the matron go 'on the warpath properly . . . She is really the limit there is no mistake about it.'[3]

It is clear that Bell was a disciplinarian and made little allowance for personal issues affecting the nurses. Alice saw her as a martinet. When another sister, 'poor little Clarrie Green', learned by telegram that her mother had died in Australia, and letters from the mother kept arriving, Bell showed no sympathy. Alice was outraged. 'Miss Bell was such a brute to her. Would not give her any time off duty although she had a nurse to spare and went around growling at her. Miss B. is intolerable.'[4]

If the struggle between Bell and Ramsay Smith complicated life at the hospital, work in the wards could also be politically tricky, as Alice experienced one night when Ramsay Smith conducted an inspection. 'Are all your men in bed?' he demanded. 'Yes, Sir!' she answered, 'All except those on light duties.' 'Then what is that man doing sitting by his bed playing patience? You go this instant and send them all to bed.' 'Poor me!' Alice recorded, clearly irritated by Ramsay Smith's high-handedness.[5]

Over the next several months the situation continued to fester. Stories reached the Australian press, and the government agreed to a War Office inquiry. Ramsay Smith and Bell were recalled to Australia to appear before it. The inquiry found that the friction at the hospital arose from Ramsay Smith trying to impose a 'system of command in an arbitrary and tactless manner' on a group of women unaccustomed to military discipline. A review of the matron's role and responsibilities followed, leading to the establishment of the position of Matron-in-Chief of the Australian Army Nursing Service. Alice Ross King had her own thoughts on the affair: 'We feel Miss B has been badly treated but it will be a happier unit without her.'[6]

---

Shortly after arriving in Cairo, and amidst the conflict between Bell and Ramsay Smith, Alice was among twenty nurses who volunteered to set up a clearing hospital at Port Said, five hours away by train. Thousands of Turkish troops were already massed not far from the Canal. The nurses were just ten kilometres from the firing line, where Indian troops were stationed with orders to hold the Canal. It was not safe to go out in Port Said unless under escort, with locals throwing stones and spitting at the nurses. 'Sometimes I feel just a little bit nervous—not for myself though. I seem to think that the dear old mater's prayers will help me along,' Alice noted.[7]

Alice was appointed theatre sister at the hospital, which was set up in a vacant French convent orphanage. The nurses unpacked equipment, prepared the operating theatre, and waited for it to be painted. Everything in the convent was filthy, and her bed was flea-ridden. Alice busied herself scrubbing and cleaning with strong phenol until she could scarcely bear the pain in her hands, and spent a morning sterilising the theatre. That afternoon, the first of the 2nd AIF Contingent came off the Canal, and Alice and several other sisters went to greet them. 'How the men cheered and cheered us. They were delighted to see some of their own women again.'[8] Another troopship arrived two days later. 'As soon as the Boys saw us in the street they hailed us loudly. So we went over and had a talk to them. They are the nicest crowd we have struck yet.'[9]

Heavy fighting erupted at the Canal, with the Turks preparing to cross the waterway before they were driven back. They suffered heavy casualties, some of whom were taken to Alice's hospital for treatment. It was her first contact with enemy wounded. The nurses also treated wounded Indians, who were 'delighted to be dressed by Australian ladies and some who had already been dressed presented themselves for dressing again'. One soldier had had the fingers of his left hand blown off. 'The stumps were in very bad condition and the dressings badly stuck as they had not been dressed since first aid on the field.'[10] The operating theatre opened with an appendicectomy. 'The theatre was crowded with onlookers. I was very nervous but everything went without a hitch.'[11] But the nurses' stay at Suez was brief. Without warning, Alice and her colleagues were recalled to their hospital at the Heliopolis Hotel, arriving back in Cairo in mid-February.

As Alice returned from Port Said, the official Australian war correspondent, Charles Bean, travelled to Ismailia, where he met sisters at the No. 1 Australian Stationary Hospital, which had also been set up to cater for casualties from the Turkish attack on the Canal. They told Bean how they were near the fighting and had been woken by the booming of the big artillery. Bean wrote:

One sister from Melbourne told me that she lay in bed listening to the sound in a dreamy sort of way without in the least realising that it was battle they were listening to—the firing of huge projectiles and the bursting of shell not so very far away. Later in the day some of them walked down to a position from which they could see some of our guns and the huge geysers of white spray shot up by the enemy's projectiles as they fell in the water. They could not bring themselves to believe, as one Tasmanian sister told me, that the guns were being fired into the midst of bodies of men only a little way over the sandhills there.[12]

Bean noted that two nurses had strolled out for a walk after a Turkish attack to be told on their return that they had well been within the

Turkish field of fire 'and in a particularly good place to be hit if the attack had been renewed' with their guns.

In Port Said, Alice Ross King had lamented the difficulty in finding books, noting that she was 'missing my books more than anything'. But there was little time for reading. The nurses' company was frequently sought by the AIF officers. While they were free of many of the moral constraints of home, the sisters still kept an eye on each other. Alice was rather flattered when a convalescing officer felt well enough to single her out for a chat. But the conversation of only a few minutes sparked 'some scathing remark' from another sister, stirring Alice's wrath. 'He seemed rather a nice boy and invited me over to the camp. I said I would go then wondered if I did right.'[13] She thought he might have misunderstood her.

Alice found herself the focus of quite some attention from the officers. Among them was Lieutenant Frank Smith. 'Saw F.S. this a.m. The Lieut. off 4he 2nd Contingent boats. Can't quite make him out.'[14] Frank sent flowers that looked 'as though they might have been picked out too—not just ordered from the florist . . . I got them just as I was going on duty. It cheered me up. I'm beginning to think a good lot about that young man. Expect I shall wake up soon.' But she enjoyed the attention.

The workload began to pick up during February, with actions that included an Allied attack on the forts at the entrance of the Dardanelles. The wounded were shipped to Cairo. The sisters had to consciously separate their private lives from their professional duties. When Frank sent her a telegram, 'coolly expecting me to meet him in Cairo', she wrote: 'He takes things very much for granted.'[15] She did not go. After meeting him again, she was disappointed and decided it was 'just as well not to be falling in love' with him. However, when a young South Australian Lighthorseman invited her out, she decided she 'wanted one more nibble' at Frank. They met at 'a shabby little place' for afternoon tea, the discreet venue chosen, Alice decided, because of 'awkwardness and not meanness'.

One day she accepted an invitation from another officer before realising she had double-booked with Frank. She wrote to the officer, putting him off. 'I'm sorry now because they may be going away to fight any day and goodness knows who will come back again. The nearer it comes the less I can bear to think of our boys being wounded. They are such dear things. Of course we see the best of them because they are always so pleased to see us. Already they are tired of the French Girls.'[16] The 'French Girls' were prostitutes and bar girls in Cairo's red-light district. Yet another officer wanted to see Alice before his regiment marched. They walked together in the hospital garden, but Alice believed that he was 'weak' and did not have 'the back of a fish'. Frank Smith remained a focus of her attention, but still uncertainty plagued her. There was something about him that she wasn't sure of.

Nonetheless, they spent an afternoon driving around Cairo, followed by dinner at Shepheard's Hotel. 'Got home in time for 10 minutes canoodle before I must come on duty.'[17] Dinners and moonlight rides continued, but time was running out, for Frank was about to leave for the Dardanelles. Outings became more precious, and Alice began to like Frank more. 'He is a dear thing really and so jolly—I'm going to miss him horribly when he goes.'[18] Alice began to compare other men with Frank, among them Captain A.B. 'Banjo' Paterson, a writer turned Army stable manager, who had just returned from Cyprus after buying mules for transport work. Alice found him 'an interesting bombastic little chap'.[19]

In the three months since the nurses' arrival, their introduction to war had encompassed both an active social life and the sight of awful suffering and death. Alice lamented the loss of a 'fine lad of 24' to pneumonia. 'He told me in the morning that when he left Sydney he did not know that his people were coming over here—but that they came by a quick mail boat and were here to meet him when he arrived. He told me this so seriously and evidently believed himself that I did not realise until today that it must have been only delirium. He died very happy believing that his mother was beside him all the time.'[20] Experiences such as this would soon become all too frequent.

# 4

# THE PRELUDE

The Australian and New Zealand troops were restless and ready for action. But they had to wait, each in their own way anticipating what lay ahead. The nurses sensed their keenness to get on with it. In late February, when the AIF 3rd Brigade left Mena Camp, the nurses joined in the cheering and excitement. Elsie Cook, at church later with her husband Syd, noted 'the khakied boys and their keen, splendid earnest faces there'. Sensing the inevitability of Syd's departure, Elsie was determined to celebrate their 'semi-anniversary' on 19 March, donning her 'travelling dress hat, shoes and even gloves that I had worn after my wedding'. They strolled about the gardens and had tea on an island as a band played. On return to Mena, Syd was required for night operations. 'After dinner, I wrote letters home. So endeth the 19th. I wonder as I write where we shall be next 19th September, our real and first anniversary day? In Australia I hope.'[1]

The impatience of waiting was too much for other 'khakied boys' in Cairo. Not far from the terrace of Shepheard's Hotel, with its wicker chairs and tables so favoured by the officers and the nurses they entertained, was Haret el Wasser Street, where Australian and New Zealand soldiers went for entertainment on their days off. 'The Wazzir', or 'The Wozzer', as it was known, was infamous for its gut-tearing alcohol. It was also Cairo's red-light district. By the early months of 1915 the ranks of local and foreign prostitutes in the Egyptian capital had swelled to accommodate the leave-time needs of the Anzacs. Albert Facey, of the 11th Battalion, described the scene after his arrival in Cairo in February 1915, aged just twenty. While he did not find Cairo very interesting, 'a lot of lads' from his unit used to visit the city every chance they got. He had little doubt what was on their minds.

> I was shy where women were concerned and we had been lectured several times about the bad women who had come to Cairo when it was known that the AIF was there. One lecturer told us that it was estimated that there were some thirty thousand women doing a roaring trade as prostitutes, and the authorities were trying to make them submit themselves for examination for venereal disease. Many soldiers had contracted this dreadful disease. The lecturers didn't pull their punches when describing what could happen if you got a dose of venereal disease. So I completely refused to have anything to do with these women.[2]

Within a fortnight of their arrival 'a startling outburst' of venereal disease occurred among the troops. Over the next four months more than 2000 Australian soldiers were infected. One medical officer noted that No. 2 Australian Stationary Hospital, consisting of tents and marquees, soon had under treatment about 800 cases. Official medical historian Colonel A.G. Butler wrote that it was soon obvious that the problem required strong measures. 'The moral and patriotic aspects were forcefully put before the troops in a manly and straightforward letter by the Corps Commander, and with his approval, incoming transports were met by the registrar of No. 1 General Hospital for personal instruction.'[3]

In a letter to General Sir William Bridges at the end of December 1914, General Sir William Birdwood focused on drunkenness and venereal disease among the troops. 'I still hear of many cases of drunkenness, and this the men must stop,' he demanded. It would have been more in hope than expectation. 'Cairo is full of temptations, and a few of the men seem to think they have come here for a huge picnic; they have money and wish to get rid of it. The worst of it is that Cairo is full of some, probably, of the most unscrupulous people in the world, who are only too anxious to do all they can to entice our boys into the worst of places, and possibly drug them there, only to turn them out again in a short time to bring disgrace on the rest of us.'[4]

Birdwood said there was little time left for the two AIF contingents to make themselves efficient. 'But there is no possibility whatever of our doing ourselves full justice unless we are every one of us absolutely physically fit, and this no man can possibly be if he allows his body to become sodden with drink or rotten from women, and unless he is doing his best to keep himself efficient he is swindling the Government which has sent him to represent it and for it. From perhaps a selfish point of view, too, but in the interests of our children and children's children, it is as necessary to keep a "clean Australia" as a "White Australia".' At the end of January 1915, pay was stopped to men with venereal disease while they were absent from duty.

The affected men were sent to the 500-bed Contagious Diseases Hospital at Abassia, near Cairo. When many of the patients escaped for a night on the town, a barbed-wire fence was erected around the hospital, and sentries were posted outside. Even this failed to keep all of the men in. Nursing the infected men was made more difficult because of the lack of beds and mattresses and, in some tents, no covering for the sandy floor. When the wind blew, dust got into wounds. With hospital accommodation in such short supply, it was decided to send some of the venereal patients back to Australia.

The Australians and New Zealanders quickly gained a reputation for poor discipline, womanising and excessive drinking, but the nurses understood the temptations they faced. 'The Music halls are crowded and look most forbidding, poor boys, they have had some horrible experiences, but I should not like to put them on paper,' Elsie Eglinton observed discreetly.[5]

The situation did not change much over the next year, as Sister Evelyn 'Tev' Davies discovered in April 1916. She was a realist about their behaviour, commenting, 'You can't altogether blame the boys. I couldn't give you any idea of the wickedness that is rife in the city.'[6]

Not all the nurses were as tolerant, however, as Alice Ross King found with Sister Hilda Samsing. Alice noted that a 'nice clean boy' was in a tent alongside another soldier who had caught venereal disease from the Wazzir. The 'clean boy' soon contracted a gonorrheal infection of his eyes, and it seemed certain he would lose his sight. 'The sad part of it was that the nurse [Samsing] objected to nurse him for fear her own eyes became infected. I'm really longing to nurse that man and perhaps save his eyesight. This wretched woman made a fuss and would not go in the boy's tent—I could slay her.'[7] A few days later she noted that Major James Barrett had gone to 'meet the 3rd Contingent at Suez and lecture them well on venereal diseases. I hope to goodness he does some good. The first Contingent fell in terribly.'[8] And they continued to do so.

Emotions ran high, and the Wazzir became more unruly. On Good Friday 1915, as they awaited orders for Gallipoli, some 5000 Anzac troops were in the red-light district looking for a good time when a riot erupted. It ran for three days. There are various accounts of the cause, but it was commonly ascribed to grievances over the spread of venereal disease and higher charges by prostitutes due to increased demand as more soldiers arrived in Egypt. And the bad alcohol didn't help. Daisy Richmond heard of the riot, and that Australian and New Zealand troops were heavily involved. 'The real cause lay between a Maori and native woman so New Zealanders and our men joined in.'[9] Looting broke out, British military police—the hated 'Red Caps'—were called out, and more than fifty Australians and New Zealanders were arrested. News of the riot was quickly censored, but word soon spread among the sisters.

For Alice Ross King, Good Friday was not marked by hot cross buns 'or anything like that . . . There are terrible doings in Cairo. 20,000 troops are on leave—it being Easter. They have got into the lowest part of the town and are rioting.'[10] The scene was chaotic, with fire carts and military police everywhere. Hilda Samsing and her friend Sister Alice Kitchen were taking tea at Shepheard's when they heard shots fired. The next day, Easter Saturday, Olive Haynes reported that the sisters had been told it was not safe for them to go out alone or in uniform. Alice Ross King lamented that everyone was having a sad Easter. Rumours were rife.

It seems that some men who had contracted disease at one of these houses went back for revenge. About 150 others joined them. They threw all the furniture out of the windows into the streets and made big bonfires of it. They did not burn any houses in fact they put out the fire when it started in one house, but they wrecked several shops and gave the quarter a bad time. A company of Lancaster Rifles were called out and they fired on the mob. About 3 people were killed and a few dozen injured—the police were driven back, heavy missiles such as tables and big logs of wood thrown. One officer who went down to try to quell the disturbance got very badly injured.[11]

Alice was concerned that the men were 'getting terribly out of hand . . . Last night there was a row at Heliopolis and amongst other things the boys broke into the big Hotel across the way and stole all the ice cream and pastry they had prepared for Sunday's dinner—after all one can't blame them, they know they are going away and I suppose at least 30 per cent will never return.'[12]

In Australia, the poet C.J. Dennis, author of *The Sentimental Bloke*, heard of the riot. He wrote a poem called 'The Battle of the Wazzir', which tells how 'Bill from up the Billabong, 'oo's dearest love wus cow' fell to Eastern sin and his mates decided 'to clean the Wazzir out'. Within only three weeks the troubles in Cairo would seem like child's play.

With the fires in the Wazzir doused, the fractious mood subsided as the troops prepared to leave for Gallipoli. Walking to the camp with three other sisters, Elsie Cook found the scene abuzz. All the tents were down and the troops packing up and burning rubbish. They had tea and watched the 1st Battalion march away along with half of the 2nd Battalion as the band played the national anthem. After dinner, they sat for a long time talking over coffee. Elsie looked around the mess at the familiar faces and 'wondered how many would soon be missing from a future reunion'. After saying her farewells, she walked with Syd to the hill overlooking Mena to take a last look at the camp with its huge fires. They said goodbye at Mena.

Feeling miserable, Elsie sat with friends in her room and heard the 2nd Battalion marching past. They rushed out, hailed a taxi and went down the road, stopping ahead of the troops and waiting for them to pass by. Colonel George Braund, riding ahead, rode up and asked them to move. 'But on seeing who we were, the frown melted to smiles and he stayed with us. Meanwhile, I was staring eagerly into the faces passing looking for Syd, when he suddenly saw me and dashed out, gave me a parting hug and kiss and was gone again, so surprised to see me there. I feel so glad to have said goodbye actually en route.'[13] All next day could be heard the marching of departing soldiers. Things became 'horribly lonely and dull'. Syd wrote from Alexandria that he was on board a troop transport.

With convoys of men leaving daily, those still in Cairo sought out the sisters' company. After Frank Smith sailed, a Captain 'X' asked Alice Ross King to meet him on the hospital's flat roof. They met 'and flirted a little . . . He is a clever man and has well learnt the gentle art. But my real thoughts are still with dear old F.S. Still no word from him yet.'[14] Alice decided they would be 'playmates', but she was 'not quite sure if I like the man'. Captain X and Alice were creative in arranging their meetings. 'A note from X under the carpet this a.m. We have a little post office. It's the 3rd step under the carpet on the stairs. It's a great way of communication.'[15] Nonetheless, Alice confided to her journal that he was 'going a little bit too fast' in his amorous pursuit of her.

In Cairo, 25 April was a hot, windy and dusty day. It was the season when the oppressive *khamsin* blew. After dinner Elsie and another six sisters rode horses across the desert to the 4000-year-old New Tomb, which had just been discovered and opened up. She enjoyed the ride, under a brilliant moonlit sky. On their return, they sat in the garden and drank iced lemonade. She wrote a letter to Syd, now at a location unknown to her. Elsie went to sleep that night, unaware of the significance of the day.

That same day, Alice Ross King and six of her colleagues accepted an invitation from some 2nd Light Horse officers to drive the thirty kilometres from Heliopolis to Heliwan for tea in the Palace Hotel. She was introduced to a soldier she found interesting. A Boer War veteran, he had been a pearl-shell diver in Queensland. 'He hung on to me rather—is going to take me out riding. Brought us into town and to the amusement of others asked me to go to the picture show in front of them all.'[16]

The sisters' fun was short-lived. The next day, 26 April, Alice wrote that nothing much was happening. There was no mail for her, except a copy of the Melbourne *Argus*. She met Captain X on the rooftop. 'Kissed him but did not mean to do it. Won't let him do it again.' And then all leave was cancelled. Alice did not know it, but in the past forty-eight hours, the world that she, Elsie Cook and Kath King knew had changed dramatically. Just a few hundred kilometres away, the full fury of war had been unleashed.

# 5

# GALLIPOLI

The day that was to resonate down the decades in Australia and New Zealand, was one Kath King never forgot. From the vantage point of the evacuation hospital ship *Sicilia*, she witnessed the battle for Gallipoli. In front of her, just half a mile away, advancing men were shot down as they ran from cover to cover. 'Our men,' as she put it. Dead and wounded strewed the beach. The unimaginable was happening. The terrain, with its steep cliffs, narrow beaches, ravines and gullies, was as much the enemy as the Turks it hid. No one had dared think this would be the outcome when the Australian and New Zealand troops had set out for the Dardanelles.

The *Sicilia* had sailed from Alexandria on 12 April for the Greek island of Lemnos, in the eastern Aegean, arriving at the port of Mudros three days later. Hundreds of British and French ships, old and modern, had gathered in the harbour for war. From the *Sicilia's* deck, Kath watched crowds of townspeople line the port. Overhead, Allied reconnaissance seaplanes droned incessantly. The tents of the French gleamed white on the hillside below ancient windmills, and across the water floated the sound of trumpets calling the 18,000 French Territorials and Senegalese to battle practice. Troopships continued to arrive. As each ship passed the anchored British troopship *Ionian*, the men on board would shout a soon familiar cry: 'Are we downhearted?' The response from the *Ionian* was instantaneous, a mighty 'NO-O-O'.

The planned assault called for 75,000 troops, including the 30,638 Australians and New Zealanders who now comprised the newly named Anzac Corps under the command of British General Birdwood. The highest ranking Australian officer, General Bridges, and his New Zealand counterpart, General Sir Alexander Godley, were each in command of a division of troops under Birdwood. The overall attack was under the command of another British general, Sir Ian Hamilton. From the ships in Mudros harbour, the troops went ashore daily for drills, and Kath King noted that Australians seemed to be everywhere. Kath and her colleagues accepted an invitation to tea on the battleship *Agamemnon*, and were shown the sailors' quarters and numerous shell holes. She returned to the *Sicilia* 'just in time for dinner to find Gordon had been to see me but left a letter'.

On the eve of the assault, 24 April, Kath looked out of her porthole at 7 a.m. to find ships sailing away to the Dardanelles. 'It is a wonderful sight, shall never forget it.' One of the ships she saw was the troopship *Minnewaska*; unknown to her, Gordon Carter was on board. The harbour was soon almost deserted. 'We have orders to sail 7 a.m. tomorrow,' Kath noted. Casting a retrospective eye over the officers from the previous evening, she judged 'Major Willcox the N.M.O.B. [nicest man on board].' Among the officers she talked to was George Mackay, Third Engineer on the troopship *Ionian*, who would soon strike up an enduring relationship with her colleague Elsie Eglinton.

The date of the landing was fixed for Sunday, 25 April, and the part of the attack allotted to the Anzacs was at Gaba Tepe, on the left flank of the landing operations. The landing at Cape Helles, at the entrance to the Dardanelles, was to be carried out by British troops, while French troops were to carry out a mock attack to distract the enemy at Kum Kale, on the Asiatic side of the Dardanelles. In the attack at Gaba Tepe, the 3rd Infantry Brigade was first ashore at 4:30 a.m. But the unpredictable sea currents had carried the men three kilometres north of the planned landing beach. Instead, they found themselves at the foot of a 100-metre-high cliff rising straight up from the beach, in what would become known as Anzac Cove. An hour later, the 2nd Brigade began its shore assault. The 1st Brigade followed at 7:30 a.m., and the four battalions of the New Zealand Brigade landed between 9 a.m. and 2 p.m. The war correspondent Ellis Ashmead-Bartlett would later describe the landing.

> The Australians rose to the occasion. They did not wait for orders, or for the boats to reach the beach, but sprang into the sea, formed a sort of rough line, and rushed at the enemy's trenches. Their magazines were not charged, so they just went in with the cold steel, and it was over in a minute for the Turks in the first trench had been either bayoneted or had run away, and the Maxim guns were captured.[1]

For Lieutenant Gordon Carter, 25 April was his first day in action and 'a day never to be forgotten'. He described how the destroyers came alongside the troopships at 6 a.m. 'We had about 400 men in the destroyers and came close in, then discharged into boats and pulled ashore. I was thoroughly scared at first, but managed to rally the men. The shrapnel was very bad.'[2] Kath King also woke on the *Sicilia* at 6 a.m. on 25 April, just in time to see the hospital ship *Gascon* sailing towards the Dardanelles. It was, she noted, 'a most glorious Sunday'. An hour later the *Sicilia* sailed in a convoy of twenty-three ships on a perfectly clear day, the water as smooth as glass. 'From 8 a.m. we could hear the sound of distant heavy gunfire; as we approached the scene of the conflict the noise grew much more intense and more frequent and long before we could see the ships in action we knew that a very heavy bombardment was in progress.'[3]

The *Sicilia* anchored off the island of Tenedos, close to the entrance to the Dardanelles. Kath watched shell after shell burst. Observation planes flew low as they passed to and from their scouting work. The ship's armoured

French transport was steadily shelling enemy earthworks as it and other ships carrying French troops steamed towards the shore. Under cover of darkness, the troops landed. Soon after, Kath King began tending men who had been wounded in minesweeping operations. As she and the other nurses worked into the night, the *Sicilia* entered the firing line off Cape Helles. Kath now saw the full horror of war for the first time.

> Steadily throughout the warships kept up a heavy fire but it was impossible to see how things were going although one knew the fighting was terrific, we quickly got to work for a fleet sweeper was alongside as soon as we anchored with many wounded and dead from the beach. The former we dealt with at once.
>
> At 1:30 a.m. received forty-six wounded, mostly badly. Dreadful wounds. And nearly all were soaking wet, their clothes sticking into their wounds. It was just dreadful. We got them undressed, their wounds attended to, made them warm and gave them hot drinks, then all they wanted was sleep.[4]

Daisy Richmond, on the hospital ship *Guildford Castle*, arrived at the Dardanelles on the morning of the 26th as British, French and Russian battleships bombarded Turkish forts. The first casualties—eighteen men—arrived alongside in a barge at 2 p.m. Six hours later, *HMS Amethyst* came alongside with another 150 wounded. The workload was heavy, and shells and shrapnel from Turkish positions fell close to the hospital ship. In later years, Daisy would recall, 'It was terrible. Badly wounded men kept crawling in from the barges. At times we worked for thirty-six hours without stopping.'[5]

The engineer on the *Ionian*, George Mackay, witnessed the landing at Gallipoli and was stunned by what he saw.

> It was a heart rending sight to see men being shot even before they left the boats, some wounded in the water, but others flinging aside their

packs and fixing their bayonets jumped into the water and charged the Turks who broke and fled, closely pursued by the men of the 9th, 10th and 11th Battalions all mixed together. So terrible was the slaughter that by the afternoon, although there were several hospital ships to receive the wounded they were unable to cope with the vast numbers and it was necessary to convert several of the troopships into hospital ships to take on wounded.[6]

By 6 p.m. the *Ionian* had 700 wounded on board. The situation was distressing. Underlining the woefully inadequate preparation of medical and nursing services, there were only two doctors and no nurses on Mackay's ship to attend to the wounded.

But fortunately we had three stewardesses. These women worked unceasingly amongst those poor wounded men, doing all in their power to alleviate pain never ceasing until we reached Alexandria, a matter of two days and nights. I saw one doctor who had amputated a man's arm asking another patient where he was wounded and still having the amputated arm under his own arm. One soldier, when the doctor asked him where he was wounded replied, 'Just a wee bit off me dome' at the same time lifting his scalp, showing a gaping wound.

The heavy casualty count far exceeded expectations, and with no nursing staff on the ground at Gallipoli, the hospital ships effectively became casualty clearing stations for first-line medical treatment. By 2 p.m. on the day of the landing there were 500 wounded waiting for clearance to leave the beach. By mid-afternoon the number of serious cases—distinguished by a red tab tied to a tunic button—had greatly increased. The first evacuation began at 5:30 p.m. and continued under high pressure for the next six hours.

Evacuating the casualties was difficult because there were no piers or causeways. The men were brought down the steep cliff faces on stretchers or on the backs of mules. The shallow water meant barges had to be used to ferry the wounded from a makeshift pier out to the evacuation ships, where a crane lifted them on board.

As the second day dawned, Turkish defences in the village of Seddulbahir, on the tip of the Gallipoli Peninsula, were silenced and in flames, and Kath King had the satisfaction of 'seeing our men march in later in the morning'. The enemy were now in the valley behind the brow of the cliffs, and Allied guns were being dragged up. Several batteries were in action before nightfall. 'All day long we were kept busy, ships, boats, lighters, launches and trawlers bringing over wounded just as they had fallen on the field,' Kath continued. 'That night there was a sharp attack on our shore positions, as soon as the moon went down and we heard the bugles sound the charge and then all was quiet for the remainder of night except for the boom of the warships guns.'[7]

Sleep became a memory, with 27 April 'just as busy a day for us and those on shore as the day before'. The workload was constant, with as many wounded brought in during the night as during the day. If the sisters managed four hours' sleep it was as much as they could expect. On shore, the troops were engaged in seemingly endless actions. Enemy sniping in country intersected by trenches made life doubly hazardous.

It was not as if the sisters themselves were safe from the shelling. Warships around the *Sicilia* continued to shell enemy gun positions on the furthest hills and 'occasionally shells from their positions fell very near the [cruiser] *Euryalus* not 100 yards from us', Kath noted. 'Three fell into water, one barely missing a launch which was, curiously enough, bringing off with others a wounded Turk; one whizzed right over us and fell 100 yards the other side.'[8]

Kath began to understand just what was happening around her, and how different that was from the picture that would be painted for Australians half a world away. 'All the reports at home persuade people to believe that it is a very simple affair, this forcing of the Dardanelles; that they will eventually be forced it would be un-British to doubt, but it will be at enormous loss of life limb and ships.'[9] Kath was frantically tired, and the 'weird' way the *Sicilia* quivered to the vibration of cannon fire from the nearby English and French warships did nothing for her peace of mind. But the grind of attending to the avalanche of wounded was relentless. Two hundred of the less serious cases were sent to a transport ship to provide room for more.

The conditions the wounded men endured on these ships taking them to Lemnos and Egypt were dreadful. They lay crowded on bare decks in their torn and bloodstained clothes. The food was sorely inadequate, just 'ship biscuits and bully beef for men with shattered jaws!'[10] The doctors had no skilled assistance, as the orderlies on board were untrained, and, at that stage on the transports, there were no nurses.

Once beachheads had been secured at Cape Helles and Anzac Cove, the aim of Commander-in-Chief Hamilton was to open the peninsula land campaign. This would involve the main Allied force at Cape Helles breaking through the Turkish defensive lines, capturing the village of Krithia and its prominent hill feature Achi Baba, and so linking up with the Allies at Anzac Cove. Once Krithia was in Allied hands Hamilton intended to continue pushing northwards, removing Turks from the heights defending the Dardanelles as a crucial step towards the ultimate goal of capturing both the straits and Constantinople. The aim was to open up a crucial supply route to the Allies' Russian partners.

The first of three battles of Krithia began on 28 April with a moderate bombardment. The Allied attacks were finally repulsed that day, and the troops returned to the trenches. Towards sunset, Kath King on the *Sicilia* witnessed heavy enemy fire from the village. Ship cannon sought out Krithia, and by nightfall she saw a 'burning mass'. Kath thought the shelling was a wonderful sight: 'As each shell struck crowds of burning debris flew high in the air and in the dusk the scene was most weird and awe inspiring.' The challenge for the men, she decided, was exciting and fascinating—if they were 'fortunate enough to pull through'.

But one loses sight of all the honour and glory in work such as we are dealing with. We have nought but the horrors, the primary results of the war. Nothing will induce any of our staff to tell of the horrors they have seen and dealt with and no one who has not seen it in its awful reality could imagine a portion of this saddest part of the war. The fighting men push on and leave such sights behind.[11]

Kath now knew what 'honour and glory' really meant. Allied casualties during the first battle were heavy, with approximately 3000 losses from the original British and French force of 14,000 men. Such a toll only added to the already intolerable burden on medical capabilities. Australian surgeon Captain John Deakin recounted what it was like in the hold of the hospital ship where he was attending to the wounded.

Picture to yourselves the hold of a ship, the portholes open, a few electric fans revolving, scattered electric lights overhead, the mess tables and benches previously used by the troops still in position; the floors, benches and tables covered with wounded, some on blankets, others on the bare boards, a few specially bad ones on mattresses, an occasional delirious soldier strapped to a stretcher, and all the time a stream of wounded coming down the steps or being lowered down the gangway on slings. Such were the conditions under which we worked after the landing at Anzac.[12]

In one corner a mess table was set apart for operations. At one end of it sat a battered primus stove, which needed constant attention to keep it burning, sterilised instruments, and cotton wool used for swabs. At the head of the same table a wounded soldier in dirty and bloodstained clothes was anaesthetised 'by a man who in civil life was a commercial traveller, his whole experience in anaesthetics consisting in having once been anaesthetised himself'.[13] Standing between bench and table, the gowned and gloved surgeon was faced by his assistant, 'who until the war was a school boy about to commence his medical studies'. Chloroform was the only anaesthetic used. There were no deaths under anaesthetic, according to Deakin, 'but the strain of working under such conditions was considerable'.

Mostly, the wounded were strangely quiet. They bore their pain resolutely, the only moans being from unconscious men. One man had lost an eye and suffered severe damage to the other after being sprayed with shrapnel and dirt three days earlier. Although blind, he had stuck to the trench, digging shelter holes for his mates for two days before he would leave them. 'He had worked until his horny hands were a mass of raw blisters. He apologised for being a coward when he groaned as I examined his eyes!'[14] They did not touch the hopeless cases and, Deakin noted, 'undoubtedly many whose lives would have been saved in civil practice had to perish because we did not have the time to attend to them'.

With their cargoes of human suffering, the hospital and transport ships sailed for Alexandria. The mortality rate among the Australians was already frightening and still huge numbers of wounded were pouring into the hospitals. The first few days showed just how inadequate the military and medical preparations for the campaign had been. The reality made a powerful case for more nurses to be stationed closer to the front.

# 6

# BLOODED

———

In the urgency of the moment, the *Sicilia* delayed its departure from the Dardanelles to take on the rapidly increasing number of desperate cases. But the postponement was costly. By the time the ship reached Egypt, hospitals in Alexandria were overflowing with casualties. There were no beds to spare, and the *Sicilia* was diverted to Malta after offloading only its three most seriously wounded men. The voyage gave Kath King time to collect her thoughts and to reflect on the extraordinary experiences of the previous few days. What she had seen dismayed her. There was no glory in war, only suffering and grief. The social whirl of the past few months took on a new perspective, and life a new meaning.

Shall never forget the awful feeling of hopelessness. On night duty it was dreadful. I had two wards downstairs, each over a hundred patients and then I had small wards upstairs and some officers, altogether about 250 patients to look after with one orderly and one Indian sweeper; had two Turks and a Frenchman, both taken ashore at Alexandria. Shall not describe the wounds they were two [*sic*] awful, had one poor little boy who had a fractured femur, developed tetanus and died but I had to keep watching him all the time and every now and then I would hear a groan.[1]

In Egypt the authorities struggled frantically to cope with the sudden and unforeseen influx of wounded. Every available school or hotel in Alexandria had been turned into a makeshift hospital. On 29 April, Elsie Eglinton and seven of her colleagues were sent from Cairo to one of the hurriedly established hospitals in Alexandria to help receive the wounded. One of Elsie's group later recalled that they arrived at the hospital in the morning, met the matron, and were immediately given beds to make up.

It seems the orderly staff had been working very hard, but there were such numbers to be got ready, that we had plenty to do. Apparently the building was undergoing a lot of alterations, as I believe it had before been a College, consequently, there were numerous workmen about, and much hammering and inconvenience generally. The idea of bringing wounded men into a place of such unpreparedness, seemed almost impossible, however, in the midst of things the patients arrived. Some hundreds were admitted in a very short time.[2]

At first, Elsie proudly asserted that 'our boys are bricks' and that 'they have made a name for Australia'. But she quickly saw that their newly won reputation came at an awful cost, with 'hundreds of our poor boys arriving all the night on stretchers from various ships'. Some were dying, others were in a terrible state. No one could say enough 'about the noble way they all behaved'. A couple of hours into her shift, someone shouted that there was no sister in the upstairs ward.

So I simply flew upstairs and found hundreds of poor fellows in every condition. There were a few doctors and orderlies working steadily on trying to attend the worst cases as they came in. I helped the doctors

all night and did my best to instruct the orderlies, but as they were
mostly inexperienced it was hard work. But they did their very best.
We only had cold water for the wounded to drink but they were
thankful to get that. If there had been a few hundred sisters there we
would have been able to cope with the work but we were terribly
shorthanded.[3]

Some of the doctors and orderlies had been on duty for days and nights
without sleep. Among Elsie's patients was one young soldier aged just
twenty-one, who had been shot in the face and lost both eyes when the
8th Battalion landed at Gallipoli. 'He sits up in bed and sings or jokes to
keep the others cheerful. He calls himself "my little blind boy", his name is
Elmer Glew. He is a true hero. As soon as he hears my footstep at night
he calls out "Saceda" which means in Arabic a salute or blessing. I'm just
trying to work on and on and not think of the awful things which are happening around me.'

Elsie's friend Olive Haynes was at No. 2 Australian General Hospital at
Mena House, about eighteen kilometres from Cairo, when the first trainload
of more than 100 wounded troops were admitted on the 30th. A week later
the hospital would be relocated to the larger Ghezireh Palace Hotel, about
three kilometres from the centre of Cairo, with Mena becoming a convalescent depot. In a letter to her mother Olive recounted how splendidly the
Anzacs had fought, but said it was dreadful to think of how many were not
coming back: the 9th and 11th Battalions 'have just about been wiped out'.
It was terrible, but 'we are proud of Australia . . . Nobody can rest,'[4] she said,
noting that there were beds everywhere in the hall and on the verandahs.

Sister Emma Cuthbert was working at No. 1 Australian General Hospital
at Heliopolis when the first evacuees arrived in the foyer of the former hotel.
They were given hot cocoa and biscuits while their name and Army number
were taken and the nature of their wound recorded. They were then allotted
to the various wards, where they had a bath and were given a change of

clothes. These were mostly the less serious cases, and they feared for their more badly wounded comrades. 'We know they are badly wounded Sister, we saw them lying there in the field waiting for help, when we were just able to walk or crawl away.'[5] As Emma Cuthbert described it, the impact on the nurses was overwhelming.

> The strain and rush of work and keeping up supplies of dressings was terrific, and many a badly wounded boy would arrive only half clad, and the whole situation was so new to us, that many a Sister, when the badly wounded first arrived, had to at times suddenly disappear into the pantry to control her feelings for these poor suffering boys, and their wonderful patience and endurance, and kindly sympathy and care for each other, really seemed to make it harder for the women to bear.[6]

Alice Kitchen was also at No. 1 Australian General Hospital when the first batches of the wounded were admitted. 'One dreads to hear who next has gone.'[7] Two days later, on 3 May, she observed that many men had limb injuries.

> One poor lad had to have his leg amputated, gangrene from injury to main artery, I fancy. Most of them think the casualties were heavier than anticipated but it is very difficult to really know. Many think 6000 about the number, but one man told me 8000 would be nearer the mark. There will be grief and sorrow in many a home and I am afraid few of the 1st AIF will return except as cripples. It is all too dreadful and every day we hear of someone we knew being killed or wounded.

Keeping professional detachment was a struggle. 'Everyone has felt the awful strain of the last week,' Alice confessed. 'If we had been nursing strange troops we may have felt it less, but among our own people the horrors of war are brought home to one more intensely. Almost everyone on the staff has some relation or friend at the front and so you are constantly dreading to hear the latest news.'[8]

Daisy Richmond reached Alexandria on the *Guildford Castle* on the morning of 4 May, and spent the rest of the day disembarking the wounded. The lighter cases went to Cairo. 'Such a muddle as there appears to be amongst the medical authorities. There have been so many places opened and there seem to be no staff to run them.'[9] Because of this, some wounded had to be sent to Port Said, and this distressed Daisy. 'Dear fellows, how I hate them leaving under such conditions to be looked after mostly by untrained people, I just wish I could remain with them.'[10] A day later, she was headed back to the Dardanelles.

———————

Alice Ross King finally found time to open her diary again on 8 May. 'It is 10 days since I touched this book. What days!' On 28 April—three days after the Gallipoli landing—200 'very sick' troops had arrived from Lemnos and been taken to the Australian Auxiliary Hospital at Luna Park, a former Cairo amusement park where Alice had helped set up a convalescent depot. She arrived at Luna Park to find the skating rink filled with 500 cheap split-bamboo beds. Crammed onto the rink, and in a pavilion that had previously housed such sideshows as the skeleton house and scenic railway, they looked like chicken coops. In this bizarre environment, the operating theatre was set up in a former ticket office, less than twelve square metres in area. The medical staff lined the walls with mosquito netting to keep out the dust and flies. The equipment included a primus stove and two stools.

Within two hours of their arrival, Alice and her colleagues had 300 patients, all convalescents from the general hospital at Heliopolis Palace Hotel. The sisters worked frantically to make up beds, assign the patients and prepare diet sheets. That workload alone was 'almost overpowering', according to Alice. But it was a mere prelude. An hour later, the wounded began to arrive in droves. 'I shall never forget the shock when we saw the men arrive covered in blood most of them with half their uniform shot or torn away. We found then that 700 badly wounded had arrived.' With one sister still to come on duty, Alice and her two colleagues and two orderlies were responsible for more than 500 patients by nightfall. 'The meals had to be got and the wounded were clamouring to be dressed.' This had not been done for four days. When it was time for tea, the men rushed the barriers 'and those who were strongest got the most tea. It was a wild beast show.'

There was no pause in the admissions, with men coming in several at a time. There was no storage room, so they had to put their kits, stiff with blood and crawling with lice, under the beds. The atmosphere was heavy with the stench of wounded soldiers who had not had proper baths for many days. Basic equipment was nonexistent. The nurses found an onion at the bottom of a large jug of water that they had thought was sterile. Servants who had no idea of such concepts had brought it in from the cookhouse. There were no antiseptics, and kerosene tins had to be converted into arm and foot baths, and even dressing trays.

By the 30th, Luna Park was in turmoil. 'They had rushed the food at breakfast time and the temper of the ward was very ugly,' Alice noted. 'The men were hanging out on the street buying from the natives.' The staff worked to restore order, discharging 300 patients to a convalescent camp. That left 780 'pretty sick' patients in what had become a badly ventilated, stuffy and foul-smelling overflow hospital instead of a convalescent depot. Alice was worked off her feet. 'I must have done 400 dressings that day, no pause for refreshments.' That night troops who had been at Gallipoli since the first landings began arriving, including some from Frank Smith's 13th Battalion. No news, however, of Frank. 'I'm longing and longing to know about him,' Alice wrote in her diary, adding that everyone was shocked by the terrible wounds. 'The boys are such bricks about it too.'

The next day five regimental doctors from the Light Horse arrived. Alice established four dressing stations, with a doctor and two bandagers placed at each station, while she worked at another. They completed 800 dressings, extracting bullets where necessary. Most of the wounds were flyblown, and some were so severe that it was clear that amputation would be necessary. Some of the men were beyond nursing. Alice went to bed heartbroken by their suffering. 'They were lying there in misery and some so weak and miserable the tears were flowing. The flies swarmed over them and the heat was suffocating and we could not get enough food for them.'

Next day, twenty-three Australian sisters who had been en route to England were intercepted at Suez and brought to Luna Park to help out. Alice and her colleagues returned to Heliopolis Palace Hotel. In four days they had treated more than 1000 patients. 'It was chaos but that we were able to do it at all was wonderful,' she wrote with some satisfaction. 'The administration, after the first two days, was good. Everybody got a certain amount of food. All had their dressings done and their beds made and a wash.' Luna Park now had 1200 decently equipped beds. More had to be added soon after, filling the caves and scenic railways that had once held shrieking fun-seekers.

Back at No. 1 General Hospital, Alice was immediately assigned to a surgical ward. The cases were terrible. 'Legs and arms off. One man in [ward] 10 with his jaw and part of his neck blown away—they have to nasal feed him. Many amputations, great big sloughing wounds.' She concluded that three head cases were going to die, while there were two spinal cases 'without a hope'. While the troops were 'bonny boys', Alice was far less impressed by the behaviour of three men in a designated officers' ward. 'These officers are disgusting. They will not attempt to do a thing for themselves although only slightly injured. In the general officers wards the boys are bricks—but these three are behaving very badly. One is a New Zealander.'

More auxiliary convalescent depots were quickly established. No. 2 auxiliary was in the Atelier, in a building previously used as a furniture factory, where machinery and the overhead apparatus for removing sawdust were still in position. The asbestos roof was high, ventilation was poor, and low-quality beds were jammed twenty abreast on the rough tile floor. Problems common to all the hospitals were overcrowding, poor ventilation and shoddy beds that either broke or had to be destroyed because of vermin. Recovery for the Australian and New Zealand convalescents was at best uncomfortable. But of the sisters they had no complaints.

The gruelling workload and appalling injuries tested the ability of the nurses to remain professionally detached. After one of the theatre nurses broke down under the stress, Alice took her place. Already 'nearly knocked out' from the demands of work on the wards and long hours, she too was soon near breaking point. 'I could not look or speak to anybody without crying,' she wrote. During one shift, the theatre matron realised she needed a rest and told her to go off duty for six hours. The four sisters running the theatre toiled in fifteen-hour shifts, with Alice working from 3 p.m. to 6 a.m. Operations were mostly performed in the afternoon and at night, with three operating tables going at once. Mistakes occurred. A young surgeon 'made an awful mess' of a couple of cases. Two of the patients died.

The Light Horsemen were being dismounted and sent as infantry to the Dardanelles. Alice knew one of them, and he came around to say goodbye. 'He is funking it badly.' Another also visited, wanting her to go out with him, but 'I have no time for affairs of that sort just now.' That night, Alice assisted with operations until 1 a.m., but at least the next day brought news from Frank that he was all right. Alice was realistic enough to know that since he wrote the note, on 19 April, 'anything might have happened'.[11] That was the universal fear among the sisters. They all seemed to know someone, either a relative, a friend from Australia or someone they had met in Egypt, whose fate was unknown. Rumour and speculation about the well-being of many of the troops swirled through the hospital wards.

The nurses shared this aching void while trying to get through the long hours and tend ghastly injuries for which no training could have prepared them. Thanks to the manifestly inadequate preparation of facilities by the Army hierarchy, the sisters had been thrown in at the deep end, but they had

responded with courage and intelligence, whatever their personal reactions
might have been. The nurses, like the men, had been blooded. Thus began
the mutual respect between the Anzacs and the sisters who would care
for them over the next four years.

# 7

# NOT MUCH COMFORT
# TO A MOTHER

Gordon Carter couldn't understand it. Somehow he had survived Gallipoli. A bullet had passed through the back of his uniform, and shrapnel had torn another hole in his sleeve. He thought himself lucky. In a letter to his parents on 30 April, he could find no explanation that he was alive 'except the mercies of providence'. He and his troops were now resting after four days and three nights of incessant pressure, practically no sleep and very little food. 'The strain is the worst for we were absolutely fighting for our lives,' he wrote. He had come ashore on the day of the landing at 7 a.m, three hours after the first troops captured the beaches. He had landed under no enemy fire, but had been called on to reinforce the line a few minutes afterwards.

I never hope to have to go through such a fire as we were subjected to all day. The worst of it was coming direct from the flank—enfilading us. The shellfire was the worst but their machine guns did a lot. I was thoroughly scared and wondered how on earth any one was to go through a campaign at this rate for I had no idea as to whether the conditions were normal for war or not.[1]

In a letter on 5 May, Gordon thought the situation in the trenches a bit milder, 'but nevertheless the war game is not what it's cracked up to be. It's pretty nasty to hear of a lot of one's friends getting knocked.' His parents could not have been reassured by his letter. Before long he would be the sole survivor of a group of friends who'd been photographed together a few weeks earlier.'

That same day, the *Sicilia* sailed into Malta before dawn, disembarking the wounded after daylight. The condition of most of the troops had improved on the voyage. But Kath King was appalled when she heard about the squalor endured by the 850 wounded on the troopship *Clan McGillivray*. Just two doctors and thirty orderlies 'who didn't know much' attended the patients. 'They say the men were never washed and some didn't even have their wounds dressed,' Kath wrote in her diary, adding that by comparison the *Sicilia*'s patients must have felt they were in heaven. She thought the situation was completely unsatisfactory 'when Australia is paying so much for hospitals and everyone is helping such a lot'. The Maltese authorities were 'delighted at the way our patients were landed and congratulated the OC [Officer Commanding]'. Kath had no doubt what this meant: 'I certainly think there should be women on every ship.'[2]

Back in Cairo, Elsie Cook had no word about how Syd was faring at Gallipoli, but the huge casualties gave her reason to worry as she went about her duties. On 29 April, as hundreds of wounded Australians headed for Alexandria, she was one of eight sisters from No. 2 Australian General Hospital detailed for duty in the new British military hospitals in the port. 'Feeling anxious about Syd, can hear nothing,' she wrote in her diary.[3]

At Alexandria, an officer met Elsie and her colleagues and drove them to the Beau Rivage Hotel, where, after dinner, she met a colleague from Sydney, Sister Nellie Morrice, whose pet dog, Tip, brought some sense of normality. Elsie started work the next morning at the British 17th General Hospital, a former boys' college, just as word came that the ambulances were on their way 'and my first experience with wounded began'. Within minutes her wards were full of badly injured men.

In this blur of activity, reality hit. One of the wounded had news of Syd. 'My first patient was a 2nd Battalion boy who told me that Syd had been wounded and was in Alexandria—shot through thigh.'[4] But the soldier had no information about where Syd was, or his condition. Elsie didn't have time to dwell on the shock, for she was 'frightfully busy, getting off their bandages and dirty blood stained clothes, washing them—the wounds to be dressed, some had not been touched for days'. The 'poor old things' were simply starving. 'Then we were busy at dressings 'til night. When I eventually got back to the hotel, tried to ring up to find Syd, but without success.' At 11:30 p.m. Elsie was called out of bed to return to the hospital because another batch of wounded had arrived. Thoughts of Syd again had to be put aside.

The wards were in chaos, littered with 'boots, packs, bandages [and] blood stained tunics'. The men were miserable and dirty and had not slept. There were 'shocking cases' among them, and the operating theatre was going all night. Elsie finished duty at 2 a.m. She noted next day that they were terribly short-staffed in the hospital. 'We have got 700 badly wounded men and six sisters and matron!'[5] Tents were erected in the grounds to provide extra beds. The nurses worked non-stop, dressing wounds from early morning until late at night. There was no time amid the frenzy to search for Syd. She had to trust that he was alive.

Elsie feared Syd had been sent to Cairo, but a wire came confirming that he was in Alexandria, at the Deaconesses Hospital. With great relief, she made up her mind 'to go to him when I got finished, even if it was 2 a.m'.[6] She reached the hospital at 10 p.m. and surprised Syd by switching on the light. 'Poor old thing, it seems so queer to see him lying there wounded, a patient, in hospital attire.' Elsie could not stay long, but Syd was delighted to learn that she was working in Alexandria.

———

After the failure of the first Allied attempt to capture Krithia and Achi Baba on 28 April, a second attempt was made on 6 May. The forces for the renewed attack had been boosted by two Anzac brigades and now totalled 25,000 men. Nevertheless, there was an ammunition shortage, and the Turks had also been reinforced. Gains from the attack were negligible. Yet another attack on 8 May resulted in a further loss of 6000 men for the gain of just a kilometre, and Achi Baba remained in Turkish hands. The net result was more feverish work to evacuate the wounded from Gallipoli to Lemnos and then to Egypt.

Arriving in Alexandria, the wounded often went straight to the operating theatre 'just as they arrived, dirt, blood, boots and clothes', Elsie Cook noted. 'Pathetic old things they do look coming in—crushed, crumpled dirty uniforms, wearing a ticket with the nature and severity of their wound, pinned or tied on to the front of them, smelling strongly of "Gallipoli" as the other boys say—and how happy and contented they look when they get bathed and nice clean pyjamas on and get into a comfortable bed with sheets on. They haven't slept between sheets or in a bed for months.'[7]

Elsie was responsible for several wards, looking after about 200 patients. She was 'simply running all day, dressing, washing and feeding them and yet the awful feeling that they were not getting the right attention—simply impossible'. By the second night the death rate was high. The lack of sisters meant the surgeons had to operate without assistance. Working from 4:30 a.m. to 11:30 p.m. daily, Elsie had no time to see Syd. Nevertheless, he was soon well enough to visit her at work, tottering along with the aid of a walking stick and 'wearing a very battered cap'.

Elsie was thrilled when Syd came to see her at the Beau Rivage Hotel. 'We had dinner in the summer house—Syd the sole man with ever so many Sisters. He had to be in by 10 p.m. I felt amused to think of Syd in hospital clutches and feeling the pinch of hospital discipline and rules re "time off"—shall appreciate my feelings of past days now.'[8] Within days, Syd was discharged from hospital and allowed to convalesce with Elsie at the Beau Rivage for a week. 'Wound healed, but he still limps a good deal and can't run as quickly as I can yet,' she noted playfully.[9]

Meanwhile, at the hospital disorder reigned, the situation reminding Elsie 'more of what a clearing hospital or dressing station at the Front must be like'. Her goal was to get the wards and patients into something approaching a normal hospital. 'Only time to do their dressings and give them food. Except for the very ill ones, no one has been washed or their bed made, unless they could wash themselves since they arrived.'[10] To ease the congestion it was decided to send some patients to England, and 'a great stir' ensued to find those who would sail on the first hospital ship.

On 9 May Kath King was on the *Sicilia* as it steamed out of Mudros harbour at Lemnos for the Dardanelles to take on more casualties. Moored off Cape Helles, Kath soon had a ward with 112 patients, and could hear battle raging all day. Shells were bursting around the ships. A 'no lights' order was issued, and Kath sensed danger ahead. When she next opened her diary, she noted that her 'diagnosis [was] correct'. Around 1 a.m. on 13 May a Turkish torpedo boat eluded two British destroyers and fired three torpedoes, striking the old battleship HMS *Goliath*. The ship capsized almost immediately, taking 570 of the 700 crew to their deaths. The tragedy was harrowing for Kath: 'The *Goliath* was only a few hundred yards from us and the screams could be heard quite distinctly as the poor men were being carried down stream.'[11] She and her fellow sisters were being exposed to experiences far more ghastly than they could have imagined or their training prepared them for. Daisy Richmond, on the *Guildford Castle*, looked after some of the luckier *Goliath* survivors, who were suffering from shock and the effects of immersion. In their distress, men had been dragging one another under, they told her. Gallipoli was already a nightmare, and the nurses on the ships knew it.

Soldiers began showing a delayed reaction to the shock and trauma. When Daisy reached Alexandria, she went out in a party of officers and nurses. She didn't like what she saw. 'All the cafes are filled with our men and New Zealanders, many of them drunk.'[12] Alcohol numbed the senses.

Back at the Dardanelles, there was no let-up in the pressure to evacuate the wounded. But getting them off the beach did not end the danger they faced. Some men died when Turk shells hit barges taking them out to the ships. One ship, the *Ajax*, crowded with wounded Indian troops, was shelled. Less than a kilometre away, Kath King watched from the *Sicilia*. 'Hear quite a number were wounded but they managed to quell the fire and get away.'[13] Along with the Turkish fire, German aircraft flying overhead added to Kath's sense of danger. The *Sicilia* shifted anchor to a slightly safer position. 'We are now allowed to have lights again, which is a blessing,' Kath wrote.[14]

On 18 May, fifty more patients came aboard. Her friend Gordon Carter had also been injured, but he was not among those taken to the *Sicilia*. Gordon, who had shell shock, was transported to hospital on Lemnos. His injury was not serious, but he was out of action for the next eleven days.

Three days later, the *Sicilia* anchored off Anzac Cove and near Australian troops. 'Another busy day but it is just great being with our own again,' Kath noted.[15] 'The Turks attacked them last night; they had a lot of re-inforcements but our men gained two trenches only and gave them a bad time at the point of the bayonet.' Enemy wounded were taken aboard. 'I have two wounded Turks in my ward. They are very dirty and smelly.' The *Sicilia* was ordered to sail immediately for Lemnos when a submarine was sighted. German submarines were now a constant danger. At Mudros, the ship offloaded thirty-four patients in eight minutes and took more on board. 'It is rumoured there are five German submarines knocking around,' Kath wrote, adding that she had stayed on duty until after 11 p.m. 'going like lightning'.[16] The ship sailed for Alexandria the next day, 24 May, where Kath spent more than five hours unloading her 142 patients.

Daisy Richmond arrived on the hospital ship *Neuralia* just as Kath was leaving Lemnos. Her news from Gallipoli was depressing. 'We hear our men are driven back almost to the shore and that the waters of the Dardanelles are so unsafe that only trawlers take the troops up and the wounded back here for no big craft are safe.'[17] The *Neuralia* took more than 700 wounded on board, Daisy working feverishly as they sailed to Malta.

The return to Alexandria gave Kath a day off duty. She caught up with two Australian soldiers who were recuperating from their injuries. They were on crutches; one had been thrown from his horse and the other shot through the knee, and both looked 'pretty pale'. They took Kath to see a friend who had been shot and lost the use of his left arm. Kath thought he seemed 'a little queer, quite upset me', but she believed he would recover.

The wounded men cared for by nurses on hospital ships were the fortunate ones. The writer Ion Idriess, a member of the 5th Light Horse, himself wounded, watched as doctors and male orderlies dressed wounds all day aboard the auxiliary hospital ship *Franconia*. Without the advantage of nursing training, many of the orderlies appeared 'quite incapable of doing up a simple bandage'. Idriess was unimpressed by what he saw. 'An assistant took the bandage off my leg and then started to pick hairs and fluff from the inflamed wound with a squat thumb-nail under which the dirt was thick.'[18]

While Kath King was trying to make the best of worrying news about wounded friends, the news for other nurses was even worse. Sister Hilda Samsing was told that one of her and Alice Kitchen's friends, Colonel Robert Gartside, had been killed, along with General Bridges, the Australian Army's most senior soldier. One by one their 'soldier friends' were dying. Alice Ross King also heard that General Bridges had died. 'He was shot through the femoral artery and they were going to amputate the leg but he begged to be left until morning. In the night he haemorrhaged and died at Alexandria.'[19]

The death of soldiers in hospital was now all too common. Some cases touched the nurses more than others, as Elsie Eglinton found at her Alexandria hospital. 'I lost one dear boy last week who had been shot through the lung,' she wrote in her diary of Reginald Kavanaugh, aged twenty-four, a private in the 6th Infantry Battalion.[20] He was from the Shepparton area in northern Victoria, and Elsie knew a good many of his friends, 'so he used to cling to me and being the only Australian nurse in the ward too made him depend on me more'.

> This poor boy knew at 2 o'clock that he was dying so he got the doctor to help him make his will, then he said, 'Now I must live 'til 8 o'clock to say goodbye to the night sister.' Doctor told me that the poor boy fought very hard to keep alive till I came on duty. Doctor said that he would have sent for me had he known just where to find me. When I went on duty the sister in charge hurried me to his bed. I shall always remember his dear bright face as he clasped my hand and said 'Goodbye,' he only lived about ¼ hour after and I stayed beside him. The English sisters waited in the ward to give me any orders for the night. That is the sort of thing that wears us out, not the hard work.[21]

Elsie wrote to the boy's mother to tell her about his illness and death, lamenting that while it would be best if the 'office people' wrote, 'they don't know all particulars and that's not much comfort to a poor mother'.

———◆———

In theatre at the Heliopolis Palace hospital in Cairo, Alice Ross King was critical of many aspects of the treatment of the wounded. She thought some surgeons were incompetent, including one who let 'the patients haemorrhage far too much and has already lost a few cases that should have been saved'. And conditions in the theatre were frightful. The heat was getting worse, making life more difficult. Conditions were oppressive and 'almost unbearable' during operations. 'One leg and one arm amputated and 15 other operations. The leg and arm were both very offensive and the heat overpowering,' Alice wrote.[22]

The stories coming back to the hospital wards painted scenes of hell. 'One boy was wounded on Sunday and lay on the battlefield until Wednesday among the dead before being picked up. They saw Turks come round and kill wounded.' One story that Alice heard concerned an officer who 'went mad with the horrors of it all' in the trenches. 'He jumped up shouting and immediately was killed by the Turks.'[23]

Alice got word from an officer that Frank Smith was alive, but that seventeen out of thirty-two officers of the battalion were dead, wounded or missing. Perhaps she was yearning for Frank, but he was not the sole focus of her attention. Helping to keep her sane amid the mad turmoil and the heat were her 'little minutes with X at the end of the day . . . We sit on the roof under the great big stars in the lovely cool night. He is a dear restful middle aged thing and I think I can trust him.'[24]

X was not her only rooftop friend. Captain Arthur Logan, a New Zealand dental surgeon, was another. Alice met him when he extracted a tooth stump that was giving her a dreadful time. 'It hurt me very much and I felt very sick. Capt. L. seems a nice boy. I have promised to see him on the roof tomorrow.'[25] Despite no sleep and a busy day in theatre, the meeting went ahead, allowing Alice to form some impressions even though she was 'too sick to notice him much'. The captain was thirty but looked much younger and was 'not bad looking—with rather a sensitive face'. He had 'peculiar' eyes and a slight limp. 'Anyhow I feel drawn to him and I think we shall be good chums. He looks a clean man.'[26]

Despite lingering pain in her throat, mouth and jaw, Alice met the captain in the moonlight on a little balcony off the dentistry rooms. A cool breeze was blowing, and they spent time looking at photos. They 'came to a pretty fair understanding'. 'He pretends to be really in love and talks of forever and all that. But we are only to be chums and if he worries me or gets too loving I'm going to *imshi*.'[27] In the Anzac vernacular, picked up from the Egyptians, Alice was saying she would leave very quickly. A letter from Frank Smith arrived. He had been slightly wounded in action, but it was his tone that worried Alice. 'It is a peculiar letter and I can't quite catch the spirit of it. He is evidently not trusting me. But he was always changeable and a bit suspicious.'[28]

If Alice was worried, so too was Elsie Cook. Her time with Syd was coming to an end. He had spent several days recuperating at the Beau

Rivage, enjoying the beachfront, the open-air dining room and manicured gardens. Elsie was given a rare day off, and they 'donned swimming suits and went in for a surf' in the Mediterranean. In a reminder of days gone by in Sydney, they relaxed on the beach. 'Simply delicious to laze out in the sun on the sands and dreamily gaze at the beautiful blueness of sky and sea. So utterly luminous and restful after the last few stressful weeks.'[29] Then came the 19th, a day Elsie always remembered, as it was the day on which she and Syd had married. 'As it is the 19th, we knew something would happen. A telephone message came for Syd to return to the Dardanelles tomorrow.'[30] His departure left Elsie feeling 'miserable, dull and desolate'. It would be another three months before she saw him again—and in very different circumstances.

# 8

# HEARTILY SICK OF IT

By mid-May some medical officers at Gallipoli had seen enough of the slaughter to conclude that the Anzacs were in a fight they could not win. This was not the message wanted by the public in Australia or New Zealand, even after the first Gallipoli casualty lists were published in May 1915. People were stunned. No one wanted to believe the numbers of dead and wounded were so high. No one had expected that the fight against the Turks would go so disastrously, nor last so long that it could not be won. But at Gallipoli, Lieutenant-Colonel Dr Percival Fenwick of the New Zealand Medical Corps saw the disaster at first hand. He expressed his anger and frustration in his diary.

> Practically we are like a rat in a trap. The rat cannot get out and the owner of the trap does not like putting his hand in, and can only annoy the rat by pushing things through the bars. Unquestionably we are held up. What good we are doing I can't say; perhaps the War Office can, but N.Z. is losing good men for some reason or other. A friend put it tersely, 'It's a bally failure but we can't chuck it.' This is the true solution.[1]

Fenwick would soon regard the continuing conflict as 'murder and nothing else' as it lapsed into stalemate. The sound of gunfire and exploding shells never seemed to let up as casualties escalated. Anchored off Gaba Tepe, the flow of wounded to the *Sicilia* seemed a mere prelude to more deaths. To Kath King, the scale of the casualties was almost overwhelming. She took 'crowds of wounded' Australians on board after they won, and then lost, two Turkish trenches. Many of the men were seriously wounded. The tide of wounded did not lessen for several days.

Among the endless convoys of the wounded coming on board, some stood out for her. 'I got such a nice boy in haemorrhaging and was taken to theatre, operated on, returned to ward with my hat pin through his neck,' Kath wrote, adding that he 'died suddenly in about half an hour after returning to ward'. (It could be speculated that the hat pin was used to staunch bleeding.) The ward was frightful, with patients 'dying almost as quickly as they are admitted'.[2] The high death rate took an emotional and physical toll on Kath. 'Have about six patients dying in my ward, it is dreadful, I get very tired and am very worried about them,' she wrote just a week later as the *Sicilia* prepared to take the wounded to Malta.[3]

Whether on a hospital ship or at a hospital in Egypt, the numbers and plight of the injured were depressing. In Alexandria, Elsie Cook's ward at the British 17th General Hospital was in pandemonium when she returned to duty after a horse ride along the beach. 'Several new and very badly wounded men in while I was away—one, a New Zealander, with shocking abdominal wound, already looks like death.'[4] Despite the wretchedness she had to contend with, Elsie soon developed a proprietorial liking for her ward. It was her territory.

Her rides provided a brief release from the awful sadness. She often rode with the hospital's senior surgeon, Captain Bourne, galloping along the wet sandy foreshore of the Mediterranean 'with pebbles flying and water splashing', exploring inlets and sightseeing 'around those beautiful blue bays with a brown, heather and gorse covered sloping shore'. On occasion, they

struck out into the desert, finding beautiful palm gardens replete with
camels and buffalo. Riding across the desert and through the groves, she
found 'the desert wonderfully soft in the white moonlight'. The rides were
not without incident, however. On a hot day in mid-June, Elsie and Captain
Bourne took the usual route, passing through the estate of the ex-Khedive,
the former ruler of Egypt. But this time they ran into 'an antagonistic reception'. Egyptian keepers and gardeners shrieked curses at them, chasing and
hunting them wildly along the garden paths.

> We rode helter skelter into a stable, thought it a means of exit and this
> caused a great stampede amongst the Arab horses and stable bays. On
> we went, galloping along, they tried to catch our bridles, one threw his
> fez into Mr Bourne's face, another levelled an antiquated rusty
> looking gun at us, which gave me an uncomfortable cold shiver down
> my spine—dogs barking, children yelling—awful din and panic. At
> last we escaped out a side gate and didn't stop 'til we got far away, then
> laughed heartily over our wild escapade.[5]

Meanwhile, a letter arrived from Syd to say he had been promoted in
charge of D Company. He was now 'Captain Cook', his wife noted wryly. But
Elsie's sojourn on the shores of the Mediterranean was coming to an end.
'Matron rang up to say that all Australian Sisters at No. 17 were recalled and
had to return to Cairo on Monday—horribly sorry, [Ruth] Earl and I very
miserable and dejected indeed—dear old No. 17, how we love it!'[6] Elsie
could not bear the thought of her 'dear old ward' passing into other hands.
'It has been so much mine, from those awful first days after its creation, it
has slowly merged from chaos and muddle into its present orderly and
cheerful state and now I have to go and leave it. I shall never like any ward
so much as this.'[7]

But there was time for one last ride. 'By a lucky accident, the old gate
leading to our old route round the Sultan's forbidden garden and those

delectable bays, was left open. Rode on past the iron fence and thro the shallow surf to Aboukir. Feeling very sad on the way home, to think I should probably never ride along that seashore and home by the desert again!'[8] Changing into an evening dress, she went to a dinner at the Summer Palace. It brought a final memory before leaving: 'Had a nice little table out on the piazza, with a red shaded electric light, such a beautiful light, all the small tables dotted about with these red lights, the orchestra playing, overhead the moon shining.'[9] The next day it was back to the stern realities of No. 2 Australian General Hospital in Cairo.

---

At No. 1 General Hospital at the Heliopolis Palace Hotel, Alice Ross King mixed frenetically busy nursing with interludes with her male admirers. Arthur Logan was persistent in his ardour. She was beginning to like him, but although she thought he was 'a delightful boy', she did not understand him. 'He talks of marriage etc but I can't think that he is really in love though he imagines so himself. Anyhow he is a dear boy and wonderfully well behaved.'[10] Despite developing a bad throat infection and being restricted to her room, Alice still 'nicked up on to the balcony and had an hour' with Arthur. 'He is very lonely tonight and thinks I'm tired of him because I wanted to come back early.'[11] Alice's health deteriorated further. Three days later she complained to her diary: 'I simply wept this a.m. when they would not let me go on duty. All the same I am pretty sick—got a rotten bronchitis.'[12]

Two days after the start of the Third Battle of Krithia on 4 June there were 2000 wounded Australians lying in a hospital transport off Alexandria. Alice, still too ill to work, was given permission to go to the port city, where she recovered at the Beau Rivage Hotel. The sea breeze that had enchanted Elsie Cook, was 'just glorious . . . Alexandria is full of soldiers of all descriptions,' Alice noted. 'Frenchmen with their brilliant blue trousers and red tunics and yellow trimmings, Indians in [their] various uniforms and Australian and English soldiers.'[13] Many were wounded. Still more were fresh reinforcements waiting to go to the front. Every hotel was full, every tram crowded with soldiers.

On her return to Cairo, Alice was confined to bed, frustrated at not being able to nurse the 'great rush of wounded'. Arthur Logan sent her a box of sweets and a letter seeking a tryst on the balcony, where he professed his love. 'He swears that he really and truly loves me. I don't know what to make of him. It is only the thought of Frank [Smith] that keeps me from liking him too,' a confused Alice wrote. There is little doubt that Arthur was affected by the deaths of many of his comrades. Alice was moved to comment that 'such a number of Arthur's New Zealand friends have been killed'. He was a generous suitor, giving her 'a beautiful piece of Turkish work which a Turkish lady whose tooth he pulled gave him'.[14]

There was another side to relations between the Anzacs and the Turks, as Alice noted after talking to Captain Atkins, who had just returned from a casualty clearing station at Gallipoli. He had worked with shells bursting all around as they operated. 'He says that no one has actually seen any cruelty of the Turks and that they have found our Australians who had to be left wounded in a trench all night had been dressed and given a drink in the night by the Turkish doctors. He also says that our men have gone just mad and needlessly kill the Turks. Cutting their throats. He tells one story of two stretcher bearers who came in and gleefully recounted how they had met a Turk and had taken his rifle from him and one stretcher bearer sat on his chest while the other cut his throat.'[15] Good and bad were often difficult to distinguish in war.

A letter came from Frank Smith in Alexandria, saying he had been badly wounded in the chest. Alice realised he 'must be pretty bad' because the medical staff was drawing off fluid and the bullet had not been found. Her heart went out to him. 'My Dear Boy. It's terrible. Yet I do thank God that he is out of the firing line and how now thankful I am for my own sickness which gives me a chance to go to Alexandria again.'[16] Alice managed to get a week's leave and caught the overnight train to the port.

Frank looked bad and had 'lost a tremendous lot of flesh', but he was better than Alice expected. She thought he would be all right, and professed 'how I love him'.

Frank had been wounded during mine-laying operations. The Australians had been in the trenches for some days when they heard the sounds of Turks digging a mine towards the Australian trench line. They immediately counter-mined and blew up the Turks. A few days later the Turks repeated the exercise and this time succeeded before ultimately being driven back by bayonet-wielding Australians. Frank was off duty asleep when the explosion occurred, but jumped up and ran to the scene, where he was shot through the ribs.

As Frank recuperated, Alice fended off the attentions of other officers. She recorded her irritation in her diary. 'The men over here are simply the limit, the moment they meet one they invite one to dinner or driving or riding or something. This captain, I don't know his name, wants me for dinner on Tuesday night,' she wrote.[17] It seemed to Alice that she was 'the only Australian girl they have talked to for a long, long time'. But she had been forewarned. On the train to Alexandria, on her way to see Frank, she had shared a cabin with an acquaintance, Mr St Clair, a wealthy forty-year-old English bachelor working in the Egyptian railways who often entertained the sisters in his flat. During the journey he alluded to a perception that had already developed of the close relations between Anzac troops and Australian nurses. 'He inferred that people are talking scandal of the Australian nurses and the soldiers and I was very cross about it.'[18] Yet the perception would persist.

A few days later, Alice was selected to accompany badly injured troops back to Australia. She was given little notice, but had the chance to say goodbye to Frank before boarding the troopship *Ballarat*. Already another captain was trying to take liberties with her, driving her to the wharf at Alexandria and insisting on a farewell kiss in front of another nurse. Alice dismissed him as 'more touched than I thought'. All around her, men were seeking reassurance and solace from the sisters. When the wounded began to arrive, the reason became clearer. Even Alice was stunned. 'It was terrible. Such a lot of arms and legs missing. Blind boys and deaf boys and chest cases and spine cases. It was just heart breaking.'[19]

———

At No. 2 Australian General Hospital at Ghezireh Palace Hotel in Cairo, Olive Haynes was dealing with two typhus cases following an outbreak of the disease in the Dardanelles trenches. But the men in her ward had other things on their minds—they wanted to escape to the Wazzir at night. Olive was exasperated. 'The wretched men coming in at all hours—it's no use reporting them. The [Officer Commanding] is too soft.'[20] The officer in turn blamed the sisters for not being strict enough. Meanwhile, the wounded were a constant stream of sorrow. Fifty came in during one night, 180 another. By mid-June, Olive was 'feeling tired as 60 cats'.

When Elsie Eglinton finished night shift on 4 June, she was given two hours' notice that she was to sail to the Dardanelles to help bring back wounded to Alexandria. She boarded the *Dunluce Castle*—'a beautiful ship, but only a transport, not a painted Hospital Ship as she sometimes carries troops'. Fortune smiled on them during the voyage to Lemnos. 'A big troop-ship coming along behind us was torpedoed. We did not go to her assistance as it is against the rules,' Elsie noted in her diary.[21] In the months ahead, other nurses would not be so lucky.

Among the wounded were men suffering from dysentery and typhoid, their guts turned to water, running high temperatures and screaming for a drink. After three weeks on Lemnos, Elsie returned to Alexandria with 100 typhus patients. Because the *Dunluce Castle* was not a hospital ship, she worked in semi-darkness at night. The experience was awful. 'It is impossible to keep them all in bed, they are delirious and crawl around the deck the moment you turn your back.'[22] Elsie became preoccupied with the condition of one of her delirious and raving patients. To calm him down, she went to give him opium pills.

The ward was half dark and I knelt down by his mattress which was on the floor and tried to get him to take them but he refused and said I was going to poison him. I went to another patient to stop him from getting up and when I was coming back he sprang out at me and gave me such a blow on the right arm which knocked me right across the deck. He said, 'You won't poison me now.' It appears that he is a great pugilist and I was lucky to escape with a black arm but, poor boy, it brought him to himself and he was quite upset. He kept saying, 'I hit poor sister,' whenever I go through his ward he says, 'There is the poor sister which [*sic*] I nearly killed.'[23]

Around the same time in Cairo, Olive Haynes recounted another worrying incident. The Royal Field Ambulance was moving into a nearby camp, and a drunken member of the Army Medical Corps 'knocked a nurse down' who 'was nearly killed in consequence'. Such incidents involving soldiers were accidental so far as the sisters were concerned. But nerves were fraying.

There was a poignant moment for Olive when 400 wounded were brought to the hospital. 'One of the men asked if Sister [Lily] Campbell were here because he wanted to tell her about her brother being killed, and it was poor old Campbell herself he asked. It was such a shock, but she went on working just the same,' Olive observed.[24] Lily's brother was Trooper John Campbell of the 7th Light Horse, a farmer from the Richmond River area of northern New South Wales. He was killed in action on 28 June 1915 during an operation to prevent the Turks from reinforcing their position at Krithia. According to his army record, he 'carried wounded men from [the] firing line under heavy fire until he himself was killed'. Another sister, May Tilton, recounted how Lily, after receiving the news, 'bravely buried her sorrow and carried on smiling among the sick'.[25]

Daisy Richmond, on the *Neuralia*, was at the Dardanelles as June drew to a close. The ship anchored off Cape Helles, very near where the fighting raged.

She watched as the Turks tried to destroy the Allied guns and was appalled by what she witnessed. 'One can see where the trenches are and the movements of the troops, and one poor fellow after one big gun fire was seen to fall, rise, and fall again.'[26] Injured men came aboard the next day, their wounds 'very foul and dirty' from the heat and filth. The *Neuralia*'s wards were soon full, and it left for Lemnos.

On board the *Sicilia* as it sailed back to Malta, with yet more badly wounded and the inevitable deaths, Kath King was in despair: 'Have about six patients dying in my ward, it is dreadful, I get very tired and am very worried about them.'[27] Arriving at Valletta four days later, Kath was reluctant to leave a dying patient. 'I have such a nice boy too sick to be moved. I stayed with my patient and instead of dining relieved my feelings in my room. My patient died 10:10 p.m.,' she recorded simply, adding: 'I have had nineteen deaths in a fortnight and such bonser boys. Am heartily sick of the whole war.'[28] She was not alone. Some of the sisters took to drink. When the *Sicilia* headed back to Lemnos, 'one of our English Sisters was put off in Malta as she imbibed too freely'.

Around this time, nurse Evelyn 'Tev' Davies, was aboard the *SS Mooltan* in the Mediterranean. Hailing from Healesville, outside Melbourne, the thirty-one-year-old thought some of the young Australian troops on board, aged about eighteen, looked 'such children, but they seem to enjoy life alright [*sic*]'.[29] They had to endure a lecture by the ship's doctor on 'the Ideal Nurse'. Amused, Tev noted in her diary, 'He spoke of a nurse's duty to herself and said each nurse needed a sleep in the afternoon if she could possibly manage it. Matron was sleeping just at his side and several nurses were also asleep. I could hardly help laughing.'[30] Such humour was all too scarce.

# 9

# THE KIWIS ARRIVE

Hordes of people jammed verandahs and shop doorways, clapping and cheering, as nurses in full uniform marched through the streets of Wellington in a farewell parade. They were leaving for Egypt on the New Zealand hospital ship *Maheno*, and among them on that July day in 1915 was Auckland nurse Charlotte 'Lottie' Le Gallais. Her brother Leddra, known as Leddie, had left for the Dardanelles a few weeks earlier, and Lottie prayed she would see him again over there. As she waited, she wrote to him on 8 July: 'Dear Leddie, ship leaves tomorrow. I wrote yesterday and sent you my address. It has now been altered so will send correct on.'[1]

Lottie was one of eleven nurses staffing the *Maheno*. With them were seventy passenger nurses, and together they made up the third contingent of New Zealand nurses to head to the Middle East. The women were keen to play their part. But unlike the country's soldiers, who went abroad with their Australian counterparts shortly after the outbreak of war, the New Zealand Army Nursing Service had to overcome political and bureaucratic obstacles. The idea of women serving their country in war was one the government of the time found distasteful. Its position could be justified by the fact that New Zealand was not supplying a full division, for which it would be necessary under Army regulations to provide a fully equipped hospital. So there was no necessity to send nurses. It was further argued that there would be enough nurses available in England. Many nurses refused to accept this. By the end of 1914, with casualties in Europe soaring, the government's opposition crumbled.

In December 1914, at the urging of the New Zealand Trained Nurses Association, the government agreed to contact the British War Office. A cable was sent to the Secretary of State for the Colonies on 7 January 1915, informing him that New Zealand nurses were anxious to serve, and that the government was prepared to send fifty. A telegram was also sent to the Australian Prime Minister asking that New Zealand nurses be considered for inclusion among Australian nursing reinforcements being sent to the front.[2] The reply reflected complacency and a tragic underestimation of the need for nurses: 'Not anticipated any nurses as reinforcements will be required for some months. If reliefs sent will endeavour to include some New Zealand nurses.'[3]

Britain, however, accepted the offer. The nurses were required to have completed a full three years of training in a general hospital, and were to be treated as officers. In reality, they would have to fight for recognition of their rank. Hester Maclean, as the first New Zealand matron-in-chief, made up the quota of fifty nurses from as many different hospitals as she could. With most people still believing the war would be short, Maclean was given six months' leave to accompany the nurses to England or, as she put it, to take them 'Home'.

As the party was being selected, on 25 March the Australian government suddenly cabled Maclean asking for two sisters and ten nurses to join a contingent of Australian nurses travelling to Egypt. Hurriedly selected from the reserve and volunteer lists, they left Melbourne on the *Kyarra* on 13 April. The England-bound group of fifty left shortly afterwards aboard the SS *Rotorua*. The two groups were the forerunners of more than 500 New Zealand nurses, about a quarter of the nation's nursing workforce, who served overseas during the war.

When the second party embarked, the Red Cross provided them with deck chairs, torches and books, and crowds of friends and relatives saw them off. A representative of the Patriotic Society handed Hester Maclean a basket of flowers as a band 'played cheerful airs'.[4] Another seven nurses went to England on their own account; they later had their fares reimbursed by the New Zealand government. Several more, who had been in England when war broke out, had already joined the Imperial Military Nursing Service, the Red Cross, or the French Flag Corps.

The *Rotorua* reached Plymouth on 19 May 1915, and the contingent travelled by train to London, where they were reassigned to Egypt. The decision to send it eastward via the longer Cape Horn and the Atlantic Ocean route rather than west via the Suez Canal, had been costly. The delay in sending the New Zealand nurses to Egypt meant they were not there to care for their compatriots wounded in the Gallipoli landings. As Hester explained, the commander of the New Zealand forces 'cabled to have us sent direct to Egypt, but too late, for we were on the high seas in another direction . . . So much time lost, so much more expense!' She and her colleagues felt the wasted time keenly: 'Had we gone direct to Suez, we should have arrived just when the rush of sick and wounded was most acute.'[5]

When the nurses arrived in Egypt, some stayed in Alexandria at the British 15th and 19th General Hospitals. The rest went to Cairo's Citadel Hospital or the 250-bed Egyptian Army Hospital at Pont de Koubbeh, in the desert between Cairo and Heliopolis. A month later, this hospital became No. 2 New Zealand Army Stationary Hospital. As Pont de Koubbeh was already set up as a hospital, the New Zealanders started on a far better footing than the Australians had done.

But they still had to contend with prejudice from the Imperial male hierarchy. Hester later recalled a visit from a War Office inspector.

He thought that the sisters should supervise only, and that the actual work of nursing should be done by male orderlies, as was the custom in the regular military hospitals. I argued that men, especially the untrained men retained for orderly service at that time, could not possibly nurse the patients as they should be nursed, and I held to my point that we needed every one of the sisters. I remember saying to him, 'New Zealand sent the nurses to care for the men themselves, to work, not to simply supervise.' I am glad to say our nurses were not taken from us.[6]

When Lottie Le Gallais and her colleagues arrived two months later on the *Maheno*, Matron Maclean met the commanding officer and was 'surprised to be asked regarding the status of the nursing service'. She 'informed him that the Minister of Defence had announced that the nurses were to rank as officers'.[7] This seemed to greatly annoy the officer and his adjutant, and 'they actually refused to believe me . . . I had nothing with me to confirm my statement and it was only later that I found out the cause of their incredulity. Much to my indignation, I found that the passenger nurses had been treated with the greatest lack of consideration and courtesy, so much so, that they were expected to wait entirely upon themselves, even to getting their meals from the galley, cleaning their bathrooms, etc.'

One of the nurses, Ida Willis, who was in charge of the passenger nurses, had refused to continue under these conditions. She threatened to land at Adelaide and report to headquarters until the colonel on board allocated stewards to the party.

Soon after arriving and settling down, Ida went to Heliopolis to visit Hester. She found her with Australian matron Jane Bell, and joined the pair for a journey to the Pyramids. 'The two Matrons-in-Chief had taken with them tea and cakes, sandwiches and fruit and we sat and had supper in the never-to-be-forgotten place—our eyes drawn to the moonlight-drenched Sphinx with the pyramids in the background against the blue sky. We were so captivated by the scene that we missed a tram and had to wait an hour for the next.'[8]

There was little organised entertainment at Pont de Koubbeh, except for occasional visits from British music-hall-style concert parties. One evening the New Zealand nurses were invited to a French silent-film screening. A New Zealand doctor, Sir Fred Bowerbank, who was also there, recounted how Matron Bertha Nurse abruptly 'rose to her feet, made animated gestures to the sisters to follow her, and walked out of the marquee, the picture of outraged dignity'.[9] Bowerbank thought the film harmless, but the incident underlined the strict mores matrons were expected to observe.

When New Zealand No. 1 Stationary Hospital arrived at Port Said on the *Maheno*, a former mission school was requisitioned for its use. With just one large room that could be used as a ward, the majority of patients had to be housed in tents on the sand. No sooner were things in working order than a shipload of sick and wounded arrived from Gallipoli. Stretchers and mattresses were everywhere, and the tents were soon filled. For the next few days the staff worked night and day. In the various hospitals where they were assigned, the New Zealanders were soon working the back-breaking hours to which their Australian colleagues had become accustomed. Sister Fanny Speedy noted that there was no such thing as time off duty, with nurses working 'from 7 a.m. till 11, 12, 1 and perhaps 2 a.m'.[10] The hard floors of the former school buildings made their feet ache, the heat was oppressive, and bugs infested the beds and got into the women's long hair.[11]

For Waimate nurse Mary Gorman, her introduction to Alexandria's No. 17 British General Hospital was easier. 'We have been taken out a good deal for rows on the Harbour and drives to all the interesting places, and am having the best time I have ever had although the work is hard,' she wrote home. And hard it was. 'The heat is so great and the perspiration just flows off you while you are doing the work. The Australian and NZ sisters will work here but the English were regular shirkers and are just out for a good time. The men say unless they are officers they won't do anything for them,' she added on 1 August.

The nurses struggled with military hospital red tape and the necessity of working alongside male orderlies. British Army officers, not matrons, organised hospital routine, and relations with New Zealand doctors failed to improve. Hester Maclean was caustic in her assessment of them. 'More than one of the New Zealand medicos, when dressed up as soldiers, ignored the claims of the nurses, and refused to associate with them on the terms of equality to which their professional, as well as social status, entitled them. It seemed a case of being afraid to lower their great dignity.'[12]

---

Lottie did not stay at Port Said, but remained on the *Maheno*, bound for Gallipoli. In the Canal on the way to Port Said there had been French warships and troopships from India, Australia, Ceylon and Canada. Everyone they passed wanted to know where they were from. 'New Zealand!' they shouted in unison from the deck. The Canal was flanked with sandbags and barbed wire, and bands played as men marched on the shore. They saw some Australians, who sang *Tipperary*. 'The doctors and padre are tying bundles of papers and books up,' Lottie wrote. 'As we pass they throw them in and the boys jump in after them.'[13] But there was something more important on her mind: she wanted to contact her brother, Leddie. She heard that the 5th Reinforcements, of which he was a member, had been under fire at Gallipoli, but there was no news of him. In Port Said she sent a cable to Alexandria 'to see if I can hear anything of Leddie'.

Lottie wrote home that 'the whole place seems full of wounded', with ships arriving daily. 'We hope to be at [the] Dardanelles now in [a] few days and are all busy with our final work. We can't find out much New Zealand news, so have not heard of Leddie at all yet. May hear more from Alexandria.'[14] All Lottie knew was that the casualties were dreadful and 'to see the wounded, well, it's awful!' The brother of a New Zealand doctor had lost both eyes, while a nurse's brother had lost one leg and was likely to lose the other. 'Fifth Reinforcements, they say, have suffered horribly.'[15] All Lottie could do was hope.

# 10

# NONE OF THE OLD
# SMALLNESS IN IT

For Alice Ross King, the *Ballarat* was a ship of sadness. Many of the invalided troops returning to Australia had had arms or legs amputated or were blind or deaf. Isolated in the front of the ship were 150 men with venereal disease who had come aboard at Suez. Of the total of 633 patients, just 160 were in cabins; the rest slept in hammocks.

When the ship left Alexandria on 29 June, Alice thought the wounded officers were 'all very nice' and were 'prepared to make a fuss of us'. Her colleague Alice Martin 'flirted with the officers most of the day and I had the work to do'. Another four nurses had joined the *Ballarat* at Suez. This had pleased the men, Alice Ross King noted, because they thought 'something might happen interesting enough to pass the time'. But 'the four were the most uninteresting and elderly girls one could strike in a bunch'. Alice was relieved, 'because the nursing now will take first place instead of the flirting'. Nonetheless, she noted that she and Martin were 'the popular favourites still with the officers', a situation she clearly liked.

The ship's company set out to buoy the spirits of the wounded, trying as best they could to help them forget their battlefield ordeals. A sports committee was formed and concerts were held. The first one made a deep impression on Alice, for it featured the 'hearty singing of "Are we down hearted? No!" by the boys. It was touching to see them—blind and legless and armless ones all shouting "No!"'[1]

Alice Martin was one of the sisters at her mess table. 'Vulgar but clever with a loud voice which talks everybody down but she is always entertaining,' was Alice Ross King's assessment. She was a keen observer of the people around her, among whom—also at her table—was the ship's master, Captain F.W. Hanson, 'a clean faced, great big man with beautiful honest brown eyes'. He was 'steady and thoughtful, gentle mannered and manly' with 'no suspicion of flirtation'. He thought the world of his 'dear wife and two children'. He was shy and was 'the kind of man I would like to marry'.

Others at her table included several wounded officers, whose injuries were not always visible. The former commander of the 8th Battalion and, briefly, the 2nd Infantry Brigade at Krithia, Colonel William Kinsey Bolton, had had a nervous breakdown. At Krithia he had seen the 2nd Brigade lose almost a third of its men. Alice recorded what she heard about it: 'He wept on the battlefield and was quite useless. He is an old campaigner but his nerve is completely gone.' What made it worse for Bolton—described by Australia's official war historian, C.E.W. Bean, as 'a soft-hearted commander very solicitous for his men'—was that he had raised the battalion from rural Victoria. A hill and ridge on Gallipoli were named after him, yet just a few weeks earlier on 18 May, he had written a letter from Gaba Tepe to the commander of the AIF 1st Division:

> I respectfully apply to be relieved of command and to be transferred to Intermediate Base Depot or Australia: I feel this would be in the best interests of the Service as the strenuous work of the last three weeks has been too much for a man of my years [he was fifty-three] and I am broken down in body and mind: the horrors and strain of

8th to 12th inst. at Aitchi Baba were more than I could stand, my
nerve is completely gone, I have no confidence in myself and I shall
never be able to take troops into action again, and I earnestly ask that
this application be favourably considered.[2]

While the military hierarchy was yet to acknowledge or fully understand
combat trauma such as this, Alice saw its effects at close range. Lieutenant
Arthur Priestley was 'a neurotic Englishman' from Western Australia whose
first child had been born just four days after he left Australia for the front.
'On the way out—they say he was one of the jolliest. Now he is <u>really</u> a
nervous miserable wreck with no buck up in him. His horse rolled on him.
He will probably develop into a chronic mental invalid.'[3]

Another at her table was Captain Mervyn Herbert, a South Australian,
who had been wounded in the left shoulder and had two fingers shot off.

Easily the most interesting man on the boat. He is running a newspaper on board which is full of clever things. He is very dark with
peculiarly white teeth and brown sharp eyes that always make me
think of a snake, they are so steady and glistening. He is an attractive
man. On the surface he appears quick-witted, cutting and very smart.
But underneath I feel that he is very, very lonely and hungry and
very sensitive. A man with a lot of ambition and force but very little
self content.[4]

Lieutenant Joe Sparks from Queensland was twenty. His left forearm had
been amputated, shrapnel had badly lacerated his feet and legs, and he was
now permanently incapacitated. Alice clearly liked him, and saw him as
'a brave little kid'.

Just promoted, he was throwing hand grenades on 19 May at Gaba
Tepe when one exploded in his hand and another at his feet and blew

him out. He was one of the first in bayonet charge and for two weeks was grenade throwing within 5 yards of Turk trenches. He is a very advanced kid, drinks his whiskey neat and is trying to drink himself to death.[5]

Alice gave 'the kid' her special attention during the voyage and believed she had helped him deal with his trauma.

Captain Eric Sexton, who sat beside Alice in the mess, had been shot in the left arm and right shoulder at Gallipoli. From South Australia, he was a 'beautiful manly boy of 21'. He would blush healthily. 'Evidently brought up in a home with a good mother. Does not drink or smoke and is thoroughly clean I believe.'[6] As the voyage progressed, he became her 'dear friend', and Alice was teased constantly about their liaison. But, she assured her diary, she 'never flirted with him'. Indeed, her 'special pal' turned out to be the married Captain Hanson, who pretended to be in love with her. 'Anyhow we have sworn eternal friendship—exchanged photographs, locks of hair etc.'[7] Nobody on board suspected.

When the *Ballarat* anchored at Albany, its first Australian port of call, things started to go awry. While she might have regarded her flirtations as innocent, it seems that Captains Hanson and Sexton saw things differently: 'It was a beautiful moonlight [*sic*] night and the boronia was fragrant but most of it was spoilt for me by H. being jealous of Sexton during the first part and by Sexton being bad tempered over H. the latter part of the night.'[8]

All through the voyage, the men on board had been 'very restless' and 'hard to keep in hand'. Word reached them (falsely, as it turned out) that the people of Albany had prepared a banquet for them. Although no leave was granted while the *Ballarat* was in port, a group of about forty men succeeded in launching a lifeboat. They rowed ashore, where they 'painted the town red . . . The others sat on a coal lighter beside the ship and cursed and swore and raised Hell generally,' Alice wrote.

At 4 a.m. one lot came back in the lifeboat bringing drink with them. Just as the ship was starting in the morning another lot arrived in a boat they had 'borrowed'. This they left tied to one of the buoys. Two sergeants got themselves locked into a cabin and nearly fought each other to death. 7 orderlies got so drunk that they were unable to work for a few days. One orderly who had been a bit strict with the men was knocked down and given two black eyes and had 7 pounds stolen from him. From Albany on, the troops forward (VD) gave a great deal of trouble. They have broken all the electric light bulbs just for the fun of hearing them pop. Now when they have no lights they collected a bit of paper and wooden boxes and made a bonfire on the [wooden] deck.[9]

When the ship left Albany, leaving stragglers behind, the men on board broke into the hold and stole forty-eight dozen bottles of beer. As soon as the theft was discovered a search was made, but the troops poured out most of the beer through the portholes.

In Adelaide, all leave from the ship was stopped. Anyone who went ashore would have to stay there. Alice saw 'a strong guard around the wharf with fixed bayonets but the troops went mad'. The disembarkation of those choosing to leave the ship was the signal for other patients to try and escape.

They resisted the guard. Two or three of them were roughly bayoneted. Then commenced a real rough up. They got hold of several bags of potatoes and made war upon the officers and guard with well-aimed potatoes. The visiting Lieut. Colonel got a potato fair in the back of the neck. By midday it was found to be impossible to hold them, so they were put on their honour for good behaviour and to return to the boat before 6 a.m.[10]

Eric Sexton's family met him, and he immediately asked his brother to go and get some flowers for Alice. That afternoon Eric took her sightseeing. Driving through the Adelaide Hills with the wattle just blooming and the waters in the distance shining as the sun's rays broke through the clouds, Alice was entranced. She spent a happy evening with Eric and his family before heading back to the ship.

The men had gone out on the town, and the train Alice boarded for the return journey was crowded 'with our boys all more or less merry . . . Poor little Sparks was a bit gone too, but he promised me to go straight to bed and he did.'[11] Next morning they had to wait for 'the boat load of boys' who had been left behind at Albany.

> They were brought on as prisoners. The sea was very choppy and they were transferred in a small tug. There was great difficulty in landing them on to our ship at all. They came on quite pleased with themselves but our boys were annoyed with them for keeping the *Ballarat* waiting and they were met with hoots instead of the reception they expected.[12]

According to Alice, the new guard from Adelaide 'came on intoxicated, so we had a merry picnic. From Adelaide round to Victoria we had it very rough and the men were in a very nasty mood by the time they got to Port Melbourne.'

On the wharf in Melbourne, the mood was restive. Friends and relatives waited behind a line of cars on the dock. The troops, fed up with their cramped quarters, wanted to disembark. Alice observed that it was almost impossible to hold them in check. 'They were ready for anything. A drunken man on the pier commenced to hand up bottled beer and the guard stopped him. That made the men wild. They started to throw mouldy cigarettes down to the bystanders and to complain of the food.'[13]

Eventually the disembarkation was completed without incident. The forty remaining venereal patients were transhipped to the Mornington

Peninsula, south of Melbourne, where a special tent hospital for soldiers with venereal disease had been established. Herded behind barbed wire and guarded by 200 militia men, the infected troops were regarded as untouchables. If the troops had been farewelled as heroes, the return of those on the *Ballarat* opened the eyes of many Australians to the wildness war could unleash.

Alice's duty of care did not end when the last soldier left the *Ballarat*. She booked into a hotel where some of the troops were also staying. Two of them bought tickets to the theatre and invited Alice, who was happy to go, 'as I wanted to keep them off the whisky'. Next day, while she dined at the hotel with her mother, the two men returned after having 'met the mob from the boat and had all come home feeling very merry. Fortunately I did not see them.' Also at the hotel was the 'brave kid' Sparks, who had evidently joined in the mob's drunken exploits. Alice was unimpressed by their behaviour. Later that week she got a group together to attend a reception at the Melbourne Town Hall for the returned wounded. Alice Martin came, along with one of the two men who had gone to the theatre with her. 'It was great to see our lambs on their best behaviour all looking very self conscious and drinking ginger beer and sandwiches. We who knew how those sandwiches would disappear if the boys were not on their best behaviour. It was very funny.'[14]

Eric Sexton wrote to Alice. Captain Hanson also came to see her, and a platonic friendship was consolidated. Her time in Melbourne was over all too soon. Less than three weeks after her return, Alice boarded another troop transport, the *Anchises*, for the long journey back to Cairo. There were 1400 men on board, and Alice was saddened as she watched 'the pain in the faces of the women left behind on the pier'. She knew that for many there would be more pain to come.

At sea, new friendships were soon struck up. Alice loved a chat, and the stories she heard were often poignant, and redolent of young love.

Yarning to one this afternoon who was married 8 days before leaving. She is a sweet-faced girl. Their wedding photographs are taken on postcards, the boy is in uniform. He is only a lad of 22. Another is an orderly who proposed by letter to a girl after leaving Sydney. He got her wire of acceptance at Fremantle today.[15]

A few days into the voyage Alice vaccinated 100 men. She also surveyed them for romantic potential. 'Nobody is standing out of the crowd very clearly yet except a tall fair man with glasses—Lieut. Moffitt. I think he has the common touch but he seems more interested in Martin than in myself.'[16] Blue-eyed Harry Lowry Moffitt was a thirty-two-year-old accountant from the Victorian town of Gisborne. Alice was also interested in Lieutenant Samuel Montgomery, a Briton who had been 'getting colonial experience' in Australia for the previous six years. He was thirty-three, of medium build and also blue-eyed. Alice thought him 'the most beautiful man I have met'. But Harry Moffitt was 'making a fuss' of her. 'I think he is only out for "fun" though and does not understand things properly yet. I am terrified that he will spoil my friendship with Montgomery.'[17]

Moffitt and Montgomery were soon in competition for Alice's company. When the ship anchored at Fremantle, she went for an evening stroll with Montgomery and some others. 'On the way down at 9 p.m. Moffitt managed to cut me away from the mob and I had to fence very much to avoid getting too friendly. Moffitt is one of those men who believe in [Arab poet-philosopher] Omar Kyam [sic] and think there is nothing after death. He is such a contrast to Monty who is full of idealism.'[18] Alice and Harry were soon friends, however.

Two evenings later Alice was with Harry on the deck, leaning over the rails looking at the phosphorescent water. 'A little officer came up. He did not see us but he threw himself down on the dark deck and rolled in agony of mental pain. It hit Moffitt up badly because in his cabin they have been holding a gambling school and already a great deal of money has been lost and a good deal of bad influence going [on] generally.'[19] Alice was spending time with both Moffitt and Montgomery. She thought Harry was pretending to be serious, but she did not know whether she could trust him. 'Just now he appeals to me as a clever man with a keen sense of the beautiful only in material things. I mean he would admire the artist who did the thing well more than he would admire the beauty of the picture.'[20] By the next evening, Alice had decided that Harry was 'really serious' but 'not the kind of man that I would like to love really and truly'.

That began to change when she heard from Alice Martin, who was also returning to Cairo, that Montgomery had been 'talking to her in exactly the way that he talks to me'. The next evening Montgomery asked her not to spend any more time with Harry, sparking a dilemma for Alice. 'I have fallen in properly this time and stand to lose a good friend on either hand. However I have gone too far with [Harry] to turn him down—besides I like him too much. Still I am in a nice pickle altogether.'[21] Alice did not touch her diary for a few days, but when she opened it again she wrote that 'wonderful things' had happened.

I am really and truly in love. I have never felt like this before for anybody. It is such a great pure love with none of the old smallness in it. I am very happy because I believe [Moffitt] loves me as much. He wants me to marry him after the war but I feel I cannot look away ahead to then but I am so happy in the present. I do not know the man or his character and I do not care, I only know that I love him wonderfully and that I am no longer interested in other men. I wonder if this is going to last. It is great. He is the only man in the world for me.[22]

Memories of Frank Smith and Arthur Logan in Cairo evaporated, and Eric Sexton too faded from the scene. Even her lingering feelings for Samuel Montgomery paled into insignificance. She saw him now as 'a bit of an old woman I'm afraid'. There was just Harry, and Harry alone. She was in the grip of love.

But she watched her fellow officers closely in the mess. The colonel, she thought, was an old man with a small voice and 'I should think no driving power'. She suspected a married captain was a 'man who would play a fast game if allowed, he is clever but conceited'. The ship's doctor was a Scot, aged about thirty-six, who was clever and a gentleman 'but subject to periodic attacks of drunkenness'. The ship's other medical officer had a 'face like a cup of weak tea', while the padre was a 'gentle old chap with an insinuating smile and a real parson voice and a weak drooping moustache'. The ship's chief engineer always reminded her 'of a rabbit the way he sits with his head hunched up'. There was a lieutenant whom she saw as a 'small-faced and small-souled little pig', another was 'vulgarity itself and utterly impossible'. Next to him at the table sat Harry Moffitt, 'my loved one . . . Tall and good looking—with fair sunny short hair. A large head and remarkably small face, a short fair moustache and sweet merry blue eyes and a slightly prominent chin. To look lightly at him I would say—clever, cynical and a little bit conceited—but a good sport and every inch a man.'[23]

By the time they reached Egypt, Alice was confiding to her diary that she was 'falling deeper and deeper in love till it is taking up all my thoughts and heart'. Harry was posted to Gallipoli, but before he left Cairo their romance flourished. They climbed a Pyramid and had tea on top before venturing inside. They explored the tombs of the Caliphs and dined together as often as they could. On the evening before Harry sailed, they went to Shepheard's Hotel. 'The parting was terrible for me. I knew so well what he had to go to, while he had a great glamour over it. All the time he was away my love developed more and more.' For Alice, everything centred round Harry now. 'I know that this is the great big love at last.'[24] She also knew enough about the Dardanelles to be worried for Harry.

After two weeks on Gallipoli Harry, like thousands of his comrades, fell sick and was transported to hospital in Alexandria with mild dysentery and typhoid. Alice went to see him and found him looking thin but well. 'Dear old beautiful Boy! I don't think he is a very strong character. Still he has every bit of my heart.'[25] Alice had found the love of her life, but the juggernaut of war moved on.

# 11

# BROKEN BODIES

After weeks of wearying work among the injured on the *Sicilia*, Kath King had a surprise in store when she arrived in Egypt. Granted two days' precious leave, she caught a hospital train from Alexandria to Cairo. There to greet her was her younger sister Wynne, a nurse at No. 1 Australian General Hospital, who had arrived a few weeks earlier with a group of nurse reinforcements from Australia. They had not seen each other since Kath left Sydney the previous November. It was an emotional meeting after seven eventful months. Kath booked into Shepheard's Hotel and enjoyed the luxury of breakfast in bed. She shopped and had dinner with friends. Among them was Captain Gordon Carter's sister Ursula.

The break was all too short. Three days later, Kath sailed with the *Sicilia* for Mudros and then Gallipoli, where there was no let-up in the stream of wounded. However, time was made for dinner with General Birdwood. It was very much Birdie's style to include the sisters, and they, like the men, considered him a decent person. Not all the generals were so well regarded. After nine days at the Dardanelles, the *Sicilia* returned to Mudros, taking with them as a patient another British general, Aylmer Hunter-Weston, the commander of VIII Corps. Kath was responsible for his care.

Known as the Butcher of Helles, Hunter-Weston had been in command of Allied forces for the disastrous attacks on Krithia and was thought to care little for the welfare of his troops. Many of the wounded on the hospital ships owed their damaged bodies to Hunter-Weston's recklessness. After the British 156th Brigade had been decimated at the Battle of Gully Ravine at the end of June, he reportedly said he had been 'blooding the pups' when he ordered an attack without artillery support. More than one man in three had been killed.[1] After the bloody and abortive battle at Achi Baba on 12 July, he was invalided for nervous exhaustion. In the view of Gallipoli commander Sir Ian Hamilton, Hunter-Weston was 'suffering very much from his head', and had had a 'breakdown'.[2] Kath found him thoroughly dislikeable. 'I have the pleasure of looking after General Hunter-Weston who is a crotchety old man,' she wrote.[3]

Among those brought out from Gallipoli on the *Gascon* just a few days earlier was Gordon Carter's younger brother, Sapper Edward Carter. He had joined the 1st Field Company Engineers, which arrived at Gallipoli in early June. Gordon was 'glad to see the lad', but their time together was to be short, as Edward was shot in the left leg and foot on 12 July. In a letter two days later to his parents, Gordon assured them that the injuries were 'nothing very serious', but Edward's condition worsened and he was sent to Malta. He had become dangerously ill with tetanus, and died on 23 July. When Kath arrived in Malta five days later, Edward had already been buried. Death was commonplace now, but this death, unbeknown to Kath, would have a personal connection for her.

Kath returned to Mudros and Anzac Cove in preparation for the August offensive that was set to begin on the 6th with assaults by the Australians at Lone Pine and the New Zealanders at the heights of Chunuk Bair. From there it was hoped a break through the Turkish lines towards the Dardanelles would end the stalemated campaign. But casualties were horrific. When it was all over four days later, the Australians had lost eighty officers and 2197 men, the New Zealanders had lost 852 men and the Turks around 6000.

Thousands more were wounded. Seven Australians and one New Zealander were awarded the Victoria Cross.

On the first day of the offensive, the *Sicilia* began taking on the wounded at 1:30 p.m., and within fourteen hours the ship's cranes had lifted more than 1000 men on board. At the nearby island of Imbros, 400 were transferred to another ship for the voyage to Mudros. Later that day, the *Sicilia* returned to Anzac Cove and took on yet more wounded, keeping Kath 'frightfully busy'. The firing was continuous, extending into the next day and night, when the *Sicilia* took its cargo of wounded to Mudros. Kath returned to Alexandria and joined the *Grantully Castle* to care for wounded troops heading for England.

The evacuation of the wounded from this offensive, although more carefully planned than that of the Anzac landings, ran into major problems. Of the twenty-eight hospital ships now doing service in the Mediterranean, three were always anchored off Gallipoli. But barges were slow to remove men waiting on the beaches at night. Each dawn revealed large numbers of wounded still lying half exposed among the sand hills. The congestion worsened. By the third day, about 2000 wounded lay in extreme heat, awaiting nightfall.

Among those evacuated was Gordon Carter, who was suffering from severe exhaustion after Lone Pine. As the SS *Canada* carried his group to Alexandria on 10 August, he relived the assault. 'Passed a restless night fighting Turks all the time. Had a good clean up, shave etc. I am very weak and seem to have hardly any flesh on me—no wonder the bullets miss me. I shall try to get a good holiday so as to be properly built up before I return again. The strain of this last action has been worse than I expected.'[4] Gordon may have been worn out, but he hadn't lost his dry humour and inner strength. He would need it.

Gordon was admitted to No. 1 Australian General Hospital in Cairo, where he was reunited with his sister Ursula. Neither yet knew that Edward was dead. When the news reached Ursula on 15 August, she immediately told Gordon. 'It came as a great shock to both of us,' Gordon wrote.[5] Debilitated himself, he took the news hard, writing in his diary that, 'being among so many deaths etc. makes it perhaps harder . . . It is very noticeable to me the small amount of feeling of sentiment I have for anything—nothing astonishes me—and I don't feel glad or sorry about anything—it seems like being a sort of human machine. It appears to be a mental deafness—so to speak—my brain seems dull to all sentiment i.e. does not reflect any feelings.'[6]

A medical board decided that Gordon needed two months' rest and recuperation. Kath King, having returned from her voyage to England, met up with him again. They had dinner and 'a bonser drive', and Gordon presented her with a huge box of sweets. While it felt just like old times, their experiences and the death of Gordon's brother had touched them in ways that neither could have imagined in their first days together just a few months earlier.

The brief interlude lifted their spirits, giving both something to hold on to. But next day Kath left for Lemnos and the sobering reality of the war. 'About 11 a.m. a German submarine followed us and we are now going full steam ahead.'[7] The Mediterranean and the Aegean were alive with enemy subs.

In mid-July Elsie Eglinton joined the *Galeka*, which, swathed in brilliant bands of green electric lamps and with a blazing lamp in the centre, stood out at night as a 'painted hospital ship'. The men ashore thought it looked like a Venetian fete. Elsie felt safer on the *Galeka* because it could travel with all lights on. But after only ten days on board she was transferred to the transport *Ionian*—which had to travel in semi-darkness.

With so many ships sailing the Mediterranean at night with their lights out, the risk of collision was high. Sailing from Lemnos after a night when several patients died, the *Ionian* came close to grief. Elsie learned that 'our ship was nearly put down at 2 a.m.' The *Ionian* was headed straight for a blacked-out troop transport, 'and as we got almost face to face, the other ship saw us and put full lights on and just managed to glide past the side of us'.[8] As the voyage continued, Elsie was in for another shock, which she described in a letter to her mother.

> The *Ionian* is infested with rats just now and the flies are dreadful, it's quite difficult to eat a meal. I'm sure we must get an occasional one in our mouth at times, I mean a fly, not a rat, it's horrible to think you are digesting flies, isn't it? Last night I was lying quietly reading in my berth, my life belt hangs above my bed, a large rat sprang off it right on to my book and its tail swept across my face, it's a wonder you didn't hear my scream. We are used to meeting them in the corridors.[9]

As she waited at Lemnos for the troopships to take the men to the Dardanelles for the battle of Lone Pine, Elsie reflected on the war.

> It's fine to hear the cheerful way the boys go off to the Peninsula. A big boat load starts off and one of them calls out 'Coo-ee, are we down-hearted?' and the rest all shout 'No.' The same boat comes back next day loaded with sick and wounded. Some of the boys are splendid, the manly way they treat each other, it's quite a common sight when we are taking wounded on board to see a boy with a wounded arm pig-a-back another with a wounded leg or foot onto the ship.[10]

On the first day, several hundred sick and wounded were taken on board. Elsie was aft with 300 patients, while another sister was forward with 400, 'so our time is fairly taken up during the night'. The decks were covered with mattresses. 'We have to do all our dressings etc, on our knees and they are so close together that we can scarcely kneel between two mattresses [and] as most of the poor fellows have body lice on them, the blankets are crawling, [and] we get covered ourselves before morning.'[11] Elsie sailed for Alexandria, noting two burials at sea on the way.

Daisy Richmond was also on ship duty in the wake of Lone Pine, sailing between Lemnos and the Dardanelles on the *Neuralia*. Returning from the fighting packed with wounded men, the ship came under fire. The nurses hardly had time to notice, such was the workload.

The girls on day duty are working till 1 and 2 a.m. as they did the night before. We were well under fire, many bullets coming on the decks. I was speaking to one boy, moved away to another patient when a bullet hit him and lodged in the thigh. I just missed it. We have to move a little further away to get patients as the present position is too dangerous for the transport of such.[12]

The sea travel was made increasingly hazardous by prowling German submarines. Returning to Alexandria, the *Neuralia* passed through wreckage from the troopship *Royal Edward*, which was torpedoed on 13 August, killing more than 1000 men. Daisy could not help but notice the shattered wooden cabin doors and overturned lifeboats.

At times nurses faced pressures from unexpected quarters. On the *Ionian*, Elsie Eglinton was concerned about the behaviour of one of the pursers, 'a most objectionable fellow. I was sitting in a corner quietly reading just now and Sister Kearns was sleeping in her deck chair. He came along and thought she was all alone and tried to kiss her, she jumped up and so soundly smacked his face that I guess it will be some time before he tries it on again.'[13]

Elsie had no such problems. The staff, in particular the ship's third engineer, George Mackay, a Scot from Glasgow, were willing to give her 'great assistance', she wrote. Elsie had several New Zealand patients. 'One boy who was delirious pulled off his pyjama suit and laid under a water tap on the deck with the water full on, he was in a very high fever and he was a great deal better afterwards. When they are delirious they often imagine that they are in a battle or else German prisoners and it's rather dangerous work trying to manage them.'[14]

As she nursed in Alexandria, Mary Gorman was shocked to hear of the death at Gallipoli of a New Zealand soldier, Willie Tavandale. Willie had been a friend at home and Mary feared that his mother would be 'in an awful state'. Besides a gaping abdominal wound, both his legs and arms had been blown off. Willie only lived 90 minutes. Mary had quickly learned that such shocking injuries were not isolated. 'Another boy about 20 has had both eyes shot out and as for arms and legs blown off you can't count them,' she wrote home in mid-August.

It was not just the dreadful wounds and broken bodies that troubled the sisters, but also the sheer physical toll that the fighting took on the men. They tried to cheer them up with treats like condensed milk, and gifts of shirts and socks sent by the Red Cross. 'We go around with a notebook and make a list of the very worst shirts, ones dropping to pieces, filthy or covered with dried blood and then if we find we haven't enough shirts to go round we have to still further condense our list. It's pathetic to see the poor boys looking with such eager eyes to see if they are going to get a clean shirt.'[15]

Pathetic it may have been, but it was nonetheless preferable to what was happening on Lone Pine—as Lieutenant Syd Cook, husband of Elsie Eglinton's colleague Elsie Cook, could attest.

# 12

# TEARS IN THE DARK

When the whistles blew at Lone Pine, the Anzac 1st Brigade rose as one in the trenches and went over the top. Lieutenant Syd Cook's 2nd Battalion led the attack. Seconds later, bullets from Turkish rifles and machine guns flew like hail into the charging Australians. Those who reached the Turkish front line were faced with an unforeseen problem: aerial reconnaissance had failed to show that the trenches were roofed with pine logs. The Turks had left just one pine tree standing.

Some men fired down through gaps in the lumber, while others lifted logs and dropped into the enemy dugouts, or ran past the front line into the communication trenches in the rear and advanced from there. Men fought with bayonets, bombs and fists as they sought to take one of the Turks' strongest positions. The Australians took the main trench within twenty minutes. But the Turks counterattacked. Syd Cook was shot in the head and evacuated to Alexandria.

It was a week before Elsie Cook, in Cairo, heard the news via a message advising her 'to go to Alexandria at once'. Syd was there 'dangerously wounded!' Worried and upset, she phoned No. 19 Hospital, where he had been admitted, and urgently sought information before asking permission to go. Her friend, Ruth Earl, volunteered to work her night shift. A colonel took her to Cairo railway station, where she caught the 11:30 p.m. train. Elsie had 'a wretched night' on a slow train that did not arrive in the port city until 6 a.m. 'All manner of conclusions fill my mind,' she wrote grimly in her diary.[1]

At the hospital, no one seemed to know where Syd was. He was just one soldier among a big convoy of wounded that had come in the previous day. Records were in a mess. Pushing through the confusion, Elsie searched the hospital herself and found him 'lying out on a verandah bed, head swathed in bandages, thin and pale and weary looking'. He 'just gave a wan faint smile of recognition' and closed his eyes again. Syd was 'unable to speak' and 'could only make queer sounds' and signs. Elsie was shocked by his condition and very anxious. Syd had been wounded before, in May, but this time his injuries were far more serious: the bullet had fractured his skull.

At Elsie's insistence, Syd was given special attention. Two doctors she knew approached the eminent English neurologist Sir Victor Horsley, director of surgery with the British Army Medical Service in Egypt. He gave no definite opinion, deciding to wait for an X-ray, but the medical staff were soon 'very hopeful' about Syd's chances of recovery. Years later, the *Lithgow Mercury* published a letter from a Londoner who had fought with the Australians at Gallipoli and been wounded at Lone Pine. He had been in the same ward as Syd.

One day I heard that young Lieut. Cook was rather an important patient. He had been hit in the head up on the Peninsula. Sir Victor Horsley came to see him, and as he stood between our cots, Sir Victor put his hand on my head, asking, 'And what's wrong with this boy?' They took the lid off my arm-bath for him to see, and I heard a surgeon say it was 'coming off tomorrow'. 'Don't do that,' said Sir Victor. 'Let him go home to England first. You never know what the

voyage will do for him.' So I kept my arm. I have it still—thanks
entirely to the fact that young Mr Cook, of Australia, was in the bed
next to me. His father was the Commonwealth Prime Minister who
later came to London as Sir Joseph Cook, to be High Commissioner.
Young Mrs Cook was a wonderful nurse. I shall always be grateful to
this daughter of Australia.[2]

Elsie was determined to stay with her husband. She immediately sought,
and received, permission to transfer to nurse him. She spent the first day by
his bedside. By the second day, she thought Syd looked better, having 'lost
some of that weary worn out expression'. Elsie cabled Syd's family in Sydney
to tell them how he was. As the son of a prominent politician and former
prime minister, his brush with death was noted by the Secretary of Defence,
who wrote to Sir Joseph Cook on 16 August. Five days later he wrote again
to tell Sir Joseph that the head wound was serious.

With many 'very sick' soldiers arriving, the workload at the hospital was
heavy. Elsie was run off her feet, but she knew she was lucky to be able to
care for her husband. 'Seems so funny to have Syd for a patient and so nice.
I can't realise my great good fortune in being able to be here on the spot.'[3]
But her presence caused a stir among the English nurses staffing the
hospital, not least because of her uniform. 'Went down to the dining room
tonight—a strange, bewildering sea [of] new, enquiring faces. My scarlet
cape causes comment as only Imperial Regular Sisters are allowed to wear
them in the English hospitals.'[4] For the rest of the war Australian nurses
continued to ignore British objections to their red capes.

Elsie was faced with competing pressures. Her immediate inclination was
to nurse only Syd and the few other patients on his verandah. But the ward
was so busy and the staff so shorthanded that she felt she simply must
help more. Besides, she reasoned, Syd slept all day so he did not require
that much attention. In normal circumstances, Syd would have qualified
for what the nurses called 'specialling', or one-to-one care. But this was

war, and nothing was normal. Elsie worried about the other patients and wondered, 'if we are doing the sufficient amount of treatment their condition requires'.

Syd's condition fluctuated. 'Poor old Syd has bad headaches continually, sleeps in a heavy drowsy way nearly all day,' Elsie noted on 15 August.

Feeling very worried about him indeed, don't like the look of him at all and I fancy the other sisters think he is worse, although they do not say anything to me. Sat up with him after I finished my work in the ward tonight and couldn't help shedding some tears in the darkness, it all seems so terrible. Went downstairs and wrote a few lines to Mrs Cook to let her know how Syd is, and am going to bed, very tired and very miserable.[5]

Syd did improve in time, and began taking nourishment more willingly. It seemed strange to Elsie to be feeding him and coaxing him to eat just a little more. Eight days after Syd was shot, his doctor showed Elsie his wound for the first time. It was much bigger than she had imagined, and was 'very dirty, discharging pus very freely'. He was having warm foments applied every four hours to keep the wound clean. It was agreed that Elsie would put on his dressings in future.

While he began to look better and brighter, Syd complained of a constant headache and had trouble speaking. But Elsie's presence was paying off. Eleven months after they had been married, Syd croaked out his first words since being shot. Elsie was thrilled that the anniversary of sorts had spurred him to speak again. 'This morning Syd remembered the date, the 19th, and in a funny old cracked voice for the first time spoke and reminded me of the fact! Started to talk in a broken, uneven and disjointed way to Mr Jenkins in the next bed! Great sign of improvement, seems funny to hear him speak after such a silence, a week for me, and nearly a fortnight since being wounded.'[6] It would be another week before Syd began to speak normally,

although he would still 'get tangled up now and again'. After three weeks he
was allowed to move onto a couch, but he felt giddy and light-headed if he
sat up. He was still very weak, and found it difficult to walk without shaking.

Syd went before a medical board, which ruled that he should go to
England to recuperate. Elsie resolved to 'beard the lioness' and lay out her
case for joining him. 'Called at [Matron] Oram's office and put my petition
before her—"might I go on duty on the hospital ship that should convey my
husband to England, please?" Got rather a cool reception, and all sorts of
obstacles raised. Miss Oram said I must have Australian permission from my
own hospital, as well as "Imperial" permission.'[7] Elsie wrote to Matron Nellie
Gould in Cairo to ask for 'Australian' permission. She was granted six weeks'
leave of absence. 'Simply mad with excitement all day, so much so that I
forgot to dress poor Syd's head all day.'

While waiting for a ship, Syd and Elsie returned to Cairo, visiting
Groppi's, the fashionable Cairo café, for tea.

> Most interesting and in some ways amusing to see the poor old con-
> valescent wounded soldiers come in. Some with arms in a sling, some
> on crutches, hands bandaged, heads bandaged. I used to feel so
> mightily proud of Syd's bandaged head, quite the most conspicuous
> there, until one day another head similar to Syd's walked in, but I
> quickly noticed with great inward pride that Syd's bandaging was far
> superior. There the fashion is in style and cut of bandages—effect of
> war on fashions.[8]

They left for England on 18 September on the *Tagus*. The next day, Elsie
reflected: 'Little did we think last 19th September that we should be leaving
Egypt for England on a hospital ship with Syd as a patient! Strange that we
should leave on our anniversary too!' Syd would forever retain a groove in
his scalp from the bullet wound.

That same month, Daisy Richmond was at Lemnos on the ship *Neuralia* when a wireless message came through that the troopship *Southland* had been torpedoed about thirty kilometres away. The *Neuralia* went to her aid immediately, but the ship was already listing and its lifeboats were full. Daisy began preparing the wards for the Australian, New Zealand and English survivors. When the ship drew near, those on the *Southland* and its boats 'gave us a terrific cheer when then saw us coming at 14½ knots an hour . . . We went down to greet them and shook hands with them all. We were glad to see them and to hear how pluckily they had behaved.'[9]

In Malta, Auckland nurse Lottie Le Gallais prepared herself for the next trip to the Dardanelles on the *Maheno*. It was not easy. To her dying day, Lottie said, she would never forget the weeks going back and forth to the Dardanelles. Each time a lighter left the shore with casualties the bugle sounded. For the next thirty-six hours the nurses would help load the patients on board, filling the ship's cabins and decks.

We anchor about half a mile from [the] firing line—guns going off all round us, shaking the ship and startling the life out of me each time they begin. It's a dreadful place Gallipoli, dreadful and awful. Don't think I regret coming, the work is terrible but we are needed badly. The Australians and New Zealanders have made a glorious name for themselves everywhere. They bear their wounds, they have never been known to even flinch. I suppose the nurses in the hospitals have to work hard, but they get the men from the ships after we have washed and cleaned them. You probably don't know what clean means—no-one could—what with flies and other creepers. The poor men![10]

She was still trying to find news of her brother Leddie. No one seemed to know his whereabouts. 'I have not been able so far to find anyone who saw Leddie. I have met several who knew him, but they never hear what becomes of their chums.'[11] Gallipoli frightened her. 'I have a horror of that place, which I can't get over; the shells I am used to and the noise and firing,'[12] Everyone said the peninsula was 'hell and death'. And that was where her brother was.

At Alexandria, Mary Gorman had some good news. Her friend Catherine (Kitty) Fox, who was also from Waimate, had sent a postcard from Port Said where she was attached to No. 1 New Zealand Stationary Hospital. They would catch up, but now, like Lottie Le Gallais, Mary was about to board the *Maheno* to sail to the Dardanelles. Aware of the danger now involved in sailing the Mediterranean, Mary wrote on 11 September, 'I hope we won't be torpedoed by the Germans.' She wasn't, and a month later Mary was back in Alexandria, nursing scores of bad typhoid cases. She had never worked so hard as that week. 'Nothing all day long but wash patients—I will soon turn into an automatic washing machine,' she wrote with grim humour on 10 October. Adding to the desperate mood was the death of a British volunteer aid nurse from dysentery. 'There was a military funeral . . . The last post was played and the whole thing was very sad.'

The night before, however, diminutive brown-haired Mary had had an all-too-brief interlude away from the hospital gloom. 'I was taken out to dinner last night by a Captain Burke and wore my evening dress although we are not supposed to go out in anything but uniform. It is the last time I will be able to wear my dress as the silk has simply gone to pieces.' She remembered that she had had 'some very pleasant times' in that dress. And there was the splendid news that she had been attached to No.1 New Zealand Stationary Hospital. Not only would she and Kitty Fox be re-united, but the hospital would be leaving Port Said for an unknown destination. 'I am really excited about it as we don't know where we may be sent,' Mary wrote. She would have to buy a camp kit, at a cost of six pounds. She might be refunded, but Mary knew that nothing in life was certain, particularly here.

# 13

# THE SHABBY SISTERS

On the barren and windswept Aegean island of Lemnos, the guns at Gallipoli could be heard rumbling just sixty kilometres away as a large group of Australian nurses came ashore in August 1915, cheered by men on ships anchored in Mudros harbour. In their grey ankle-length uniforms, they made their way cautiously over a stony field while a bagpiper played them into camp. Aside from hospital ships, Lemnos was the closest location to Gallipoli where nurses could serve. The proximity fired their emotions. Staff Nurse Nell Pike, from Sydney, 'could imagine no greater joy than to be working under the canvas so close to the gallant men of Anzac'.[1]

Just five hours away by sea, Lemnos was the perfect location for the Allies' advance naval and' military base. The huge, deepwater Mudros harbour was alive with action as hundreds of battleships, destroyers, troop transports and hospital ships came and went. Elsie Eglinton, on the transport *Ionian*, captured the sight as the sun rose over the port.

The water was very dark green and the shadows of all these huge battleships was thrown right across the harbour, the reflection of the sky in the water as it kept changing colour was beyond description—

one minute it was crimson and the next like a sheet of gold, such vivid colours, quite different to the soft Egyptian skies.[2]

The reality of working on Lemnos was far from enchanting, however. The conditions there were probably the worst experienced by any nurses during the war. Originally Lemnos was planned as a forward medical base to receive and treat slightly wounded troops so they could be sent back to the fighting after a few days. The plan broke down under the weight of casualties. Instead, the slightly wounded were sent to Egypt, while the more seriously wounded stayed on Lemnos. During July, four stationary hospitals had been established on the island, one of which was Australian. The War Office decided to upgrade facilities to cope with more serious cases and No. 3 Australian General Hospital, under Colonel Thomas Fiaschi, was sent to Lemnos.

For Matron Grace Wilson, the war was already closer than for most. Three months before, a Turkish sniper had killed her brother, Lance Corporal Graeme Wilson of the 2nd Australian Light Horse, at Quinn's Post at Gallipoli. Shot in the thigh, he had bled to death, aged just twenty-five. Grace heard the news at Alexandria on 1 August, just before she left for Lemnos. She wrote to her sister Minnie: 'Tell mother from me to be thankful if he fell in action—I am, after what I have seen. All I can hope is that he was killed at once.'[3]

The process of establishing No. 3 General Hospital was chaotic. The hospital's male staff arrived on Lemnos on 29 July, only a week before the August offensive was to be launched. The hospital's equipment did not arrive for another three weeks. On 5 August, Grace Wilson arrived a day ahead of nearly 100 nurses who would staff the hospital. She found the situation 'just too awful for words', with no tents and only bits and pieces of equipment.

We are the first women to come so far, except for the sisters on the hospital ships. This waiting exhausts our spirits and roughing it will be beyond description. If you can imagine at present a bare piece of ground, covered with stones, from the size of pebbles to boulders, the men in their clothes lying on it, waiting, and we sisters imprisoned on a ship opposite, also waiting and doing nothing, and you have [No. 3 General Hospital] after touring for eleven or twelve weeks.[4]

While they waited for their equipment, the sisters had to rely on the barest essentials, mostly from their own kits, such as small methylated spirit stoves, cotton wool and a few instruments. They tore up their own clothes for dressings. They tended hundreds of patients on the open ground, where the nurses also slept. As one plaintively wrote, 'How we longed for a hole for our hips!'[5] Finally the tents arrived, and two rows extending to the water's edge were pitched as the sisters' quarters.

To cope with the casualties, two vast tent cities had sprung up around the harbour. The main Australian camp was at Mudros West, high above the harbour on the bare and roadless promontory known as Turk's Head. It was here that No. 3 General Hospital and No. 2 Australian Stationary Hospital were set up, along with two Canadian stationary hospitals and one British. The pressure on them was heavy. By mid-October, just under 4000 cases passed through No. 3—thirty per cent Australian, thirteen per cent New Zealand and fifty-seven per cent British and Indian.[6]

In the two months to October, 57,000 sick and 37,000 wounded men were evacuated from the beaches at Gallipoli.[7] Hospital accommodation at Mudros was increased to 9000 beds, about half of them Australian. But the flood of injured troops had become a crisis. So-called 'black ships'— ordinary armed transports—were kept busy plying from Lemnos to Egypt, Malta and England. In the three months from August, more than 100,000 sick and wounded left Mudros.

A water shortage on Lemnos made it difficult to treat the wounded—or even to give them drinks, as Olive Haynes soon discovered. She had been keen to go to the island, to work at No. 2 Stationary Hospital, but soon found she could not wash the men coming off the hospital ship *Assaye*, anchored in the harbour with 700 badly wounded on board. It was virtually impossible for the nurses to take a bath, and many cut their hair short to keep it clean. Until a distiller was installed, water had to come from the warships. Even then, the nurses were left just two buckets of water outside their tents for washing in enamel bowls. If they were lucky, they occasionally got hot water from the cookhouse.

Sanitary arrangements on the island were primitive. Wells were not protected and contained 'a large number of germs with some pathogenic organisms'.[8] Amoebic dysentery was rampant, and a Canadian matron and two orderlies died of it. Already beset with lumbago and neuralgia, Olive Haynes fell ill with dysentery—Lemnitis, as it was known—along with another six Australian and five Canadian sisters. Olive could not go on duty, and 'felt pretty bad all day'. Nell Pike noted that doing the laundry for the dysentery cases was an enormous problem. Soiled linen had to be put aside for long periods to be washed when water became available. When the laundry went putrid, it was destroyed in bonfires.

Snakes, scorpions and centipedes were rife. Moles were also an issue. As she recuperated, Olive searched her bed every night and generally managed to catch something. Every time she woke up, 'I clasp the Insectiban and sprinkle it over me and the bed.'[9] After her bed broke, she had to sleep on the floor. Tev Davies wrote to her family about the moles. 'I have never seen one but on my tent floor there is a fresh bulge each morning where they have been burrowing. I am quite expecting to be lifted heavenward some night, a patient told me they are a little larger than rats.'[10] The work was tiring and, Tev added tongue in cheek, 'we get plenty of air'.

We are all still swatting flies Mum, they are fearful nothing can be left uncovered it is quite common to see each sister with her left hand over her tea cup, we do not indulge in saucers, if flies do get in the tea we fish them out and swallow the tea to get in first, fancy doing that at home we'd feel sick for a day but I'll not be fussy after this.[11]

Tev explained that sleeping out became impossible as summer gave way to the chill of autumn. The wind was blowing solidly. 'Tent life is very airy for me, a wonder they do not blow down some days or nights. I often have to crawl out and fix the flaps, then it is I long for "my little gray [*sic*] home in the West" I can tell you. Still it is all in the game and everyone seems happy.' Nell Pike was. When Colonel Fiaschi asked how she liked serving on Lemnos, she replied that it was 'fun'. This surprised him. 'But I meant it. We Australian nurses were very patriotic and anything we were doing we were doing for England. We were all glad to be taking part in the "great adventure".'[12]

Others, however, soon became less sanguine as winter neared and the weather turned bitterly cold. Dust and flies, mud and wind tested the sisters' sense of humour. When it rained the clayey soil became a quagmire. They were issued with heavy Tommy boots. Hospital tents blew down in high winds as the pegs failed to keep them anchored. There was no kerosene for heating. Some of the nurses, Olive observed, 'are fed up already with this place'.

Tev felt much the same, writing to her mother that 'any old place will do me after this . . . We are being supplied with riding pants, tunics and gum boots. Golly! Won't we look tragic? I can see our photos in *Table Talk*, "Australian nurses at Lemnos". You wouldn't recognise me. I have become so fat, really my rotundity is quite embarrassing, nearly all the girls are the same.'[13] In October, the Red Cross delivered some tinned rabbit, but mostly Tev and her colleagues ate bully beef, biscuits and tinned carrots. The taste was vile.

Then there's some chewed up looking stuff called concentrated vegetables, it's a little of everything and highly seasoned, the smell gives one indigestion. The people who can foods etc must be making money out of this war, for it's the greatest rubbish, we existed on bully beef and biscuits for a while, the latter were like plaster of Paris, honestly you have to bang them on the table to break them and then they don't always break, you gnaw small pieces off the corners, girls

were breaking their teeth wholesale. On the Peninsula the boys grind
them with stones and make porridge of them. I'm as fat as an ox and
yet I can do nothing but discuss food in my letters.[14]

Because of the lack of fresh vegetables, the sisters had to drink lime juice
to prevent scurvy. With eggs, meat and potatoes in short supply, Nell Pike
was surprised one day when her senior orderly beckoned her outside the
tent and cautiously passed her a soiled parcel of sacking with blood seeping
from it. Inside was a large cut of steak, which the orderly had 'taken' from
the British ship SS *Aragon*, anchored in the bay where, to the disgust of soldiers on shore, supercilious English officers lived in indecent luxury in a
virtual floating hotel that was reputedly costing £15,000 a month.[15] Troops
would later joke that the *Aragon* was stranded on its own bottles in Mudros
harbour. Thirty-nine-year-old Anne Donnell, at No. 3 hospital, was under
no illusions about life on the neglected island.

To-day in the lines I passed a dear little dog, stopped to make a great
fuss of him, then it suddenly dawned on me what a changed life we
are living, and growing accustomed to. No little children to love, no
trees, no flowers, no pets, no shops, nothing dainty or nice, practically
no fruit or vegetable, butter and eggs once in a month, twice at most.
Please don't infer from this that I am complaining, far from it, and we
have so much to be thankful for, but how we wish that we could give
our serious cases the very best of food and delicacies. Of course it's
only natural that we should wish, for our health's sake, to have some
nourishing food. I do have it though in my dreams at night when I
visit the most beautiful fruit gardens and pick the sweetest flowers
while little children play around; don't smile, for it's quite true. It
reminds me of these words:
I slept and dreamt that life was beauty
I woke and found that life was duty.[16]

The Australian sisters were the most poorly paid of the nurses on Lemnos, and this made it more difficult for them to supplement their food from canteens and hawkers. Olive Haynes fantasised about what she would most like when she returned home. 'I want a nice soft bed with sheets, a hot bath, hot buttered toast, tea with not condensed milk. You must have plenty of strawberry jam and cake ready.' If any of the men grumbled about their food or conditions, she noted, their comrades would chafe them by suggesting they would be 'wanting flowers on your grave next'.[17]

If the conditions were harsh on Lemnos, the chauvinism of military officers did nothing to lighten them. The presence of women within sound of the guns at the Dardanelles was an affront to some officers, who argued that male orderlies would do just as well as the nurses this close to the front. Such attitudes, said Sister Nellie Morrice, made the nurses' work an uphill battle.

> I have known the officers in charge of the ward to come in and fire an order direct to the orderly in front of a sister. At times our presence was ignored by the officer, with the result that we had very little control over the orderlies, the officer seemed to want the orderly to know that they were quite satisfied with the work the orderlies were doing and that sisters were quite unnecessary.[18]

The patients, she noted, 'thought otherwise'.

Colonel Fiaschi in particular was seen as antagonistic towards the presence of women. Grace Wilson was no fan of Fiaschi. 'The colonel is a very hard man—declares the sisters are all too soft, and to my astonishment, announced that he fully expected half of them and almost half of the Officers to die—he has no consideration whatever for his personnel.'[19] However, others, such as Anne Donnell, admired his 'strong personality' after he fell ill with beriberi, caused by vitamin deficiency. He sought no special favours, according to Anne, 'roughing it equally with the men, sleeping between coarse blankets, with no pillowslip on the hard pillow'. Ill as he was, he continued to take a cold dip in the sea at dawn each day until his condition deteriorated so badly he had to be stretchered on to a hospital ship.

Shortly afterwards, Lieutenant General R.H.J. 'Bertie' Fetherston, the Director-General of Australian Army Medical Services, made a tour of inspection on Lemnos. He did not like what he saw. Unlike Fiaschi, Fetherston thought that all sisters should be on an equal basis with the officers. In conversation with Anne Donnell, he said he was 'not too pleased with the accommodation and comfort of our nurses generally out here'. Married to a nurse in Melbourne, Bertie Fetherston was well placed to understand the needs of nurses.

Fetherston was unhappy with the hospital tents and marquees he saw on such a barren and windswept island. He said the nurses had endured especially tough conditions, living in tents, eating little more than service rations, with no baths or bathing facilities, and poor sanitary conditions. It had been a mistake in the first place, he added, 'that the camping ground used by the native Egyptian labourers on the Island should have been used as a hospital site'.[20]

Fetherston insisted that the nurses be provided with huts, warm clothing and better mess and bathing arrangements. He lauded Grace Wilson's work, control and leadership. 'The matron of this hospital deserves the highest praise and commendation, and under her the whole nursing staff have done wonderfully fine work,' he wrote. While not expecting elaborate food for active service or at the front, 'when hospitals are established and female nurses sent, it is expected that reasonable good food will be available'.[21] Fetherston was so appalled that he said no more Australian nurses should be employed on Lemnos until conditions there improved.[22]

But by 30 November the nurses were still housed in unlined bell tents and warm winter uniforms were still to arrive. They tried unsuccessfully to keep warm with their own clothes. 'We all suffered terribly with the cold, and with all our warm clothing we couldn't get warm day or night,' Anne

Donnell complained. 'Personally, I shivered for three nights without sleep; I have chilblains and my two small toes are frostbitten—agony.'[23] She empathised with the Anzacs on the Peninsula, hearing stories from her patients of men who had drowned because their feet were so paralysed with cold that they could not crawl away to safety in time. Sentries were found dead at their posts, frozen and still clutching their rifles. Many who managed to keep their blood circulating by moving about 'could only grin at the Turks because their fingers were too frozen to pull the trigger'. Some in the hospital were losing both feet, some both hands. 'It's all too sad for words, hopelessly sad.'[24]

Fetherston was also alarmed by the use of 'black ships' staffed by nurses to take invalid soldiers to Egypt, Malta or England. This was wrong, he said, given that submarines could attack them at any time. Fetherston concluded damningly that those in command at Lemnos had 'not risen to the occasion'. With the decision in December to evacuate all troops from the Dardanelles and admit that the Gallipoli campaign had been a failure, Fetherston's recommendations for reform came too late.

The sisters celebrated Christmas on Lemnos, with turkey and champagne, thanks to some visiting sailors. But Olive Haynes noted, 'We have lived so plainly for so long that we couldn't eat half as much as we thought we could—it was too much for us.' The Turks had an extra Christmas present for them too, an aeroplane dropping three bombs. A relieved Olive wrote, 'missed us'.

In mid-January 1916, the sisters boarded the hospital ship *Oxfordshire* for Egypt. The nurses were thankful they were not spending the rest of the winter on Lemnos. The night after they boarded the ship a gale blew, and by morning no tent was left standing. As they sailed to Cairo, Tev Davies was struck by the contrast with conditions on the island. Not only was the ship food good, but there was fine china, good cutlery and table linen. 'It will spoil us for rough living once more but we'll settle down I suppose if necessary, anyhow we can't have worse times than we had for first two months on Lemnos. Still I never regret going there.'[25]

Olive Haynes also had to pinch herself.

I have a cabin to myself and the stewardess brings us hot water and fills our bags and the meals are very fine, especially after Lemnos. We (the wild Australians) have all our meals together and the English in another saloon. We have to keep reminding each other that there are salt-spoons and we needn't use our knives for mustard, and that there are plenty of spoons, not to dip the soup spoon into the sugar, and above all not to over-eat.[26]

Anne Donnell was reflective.

We have just seen the last of Lemnos. Of course we are glad, yet there are many things we will miss; the unconventional freedom and the unique experiences we had there. Good-bye Lemnos. We take away many happy memories of you. I would not have liked to miss you, yet I have no desire to see you again.[27]

Over the previous five months, the Australians had treated thousands of patients, with a death rate of just two and a half per cent. In his official history of Australian medical services in the war, Colonel Arthur Butler dismissed any criticism of the nurses. He said that at No. 3 General Hospital, 'it was found that the trained female nurses brought order out of chaos in a way that would have been possible to male orderlies only after long training in "Regular" Army service.'

The Honorary Assistant Surgeon at Sydney's Royal Prince Alfred Hospital, Major John Morton, who was on Lemnos, paid tribute to the nurses' work. 'They did splendid service, and have established themselves as a necessary factor in military organisation. I feel sure that no one who had experienced what the nurses meant to the sick at Lemnos could again tolerate the system of nursing by orderlies.'[28]

The experience bred a strong camaraderie among the sisters, and their achievements were recognised by officers who had worked with them. Anne Donnell recounted a conversation with 'one top-notch' medical officer nursed on Lemnos who reputedly had told a fellow staff member that 'If No. 3 [hospital] sisters came within coo-ee of them, the No. 1 sisters would have to look to their laurels . . . We were envied, I think, for roughing it as we did. We have many smiles over our experiences now, and when we first came to Cairo we were known as "those shabby sisters with the bright colour".'[29]

Their work had been anything but 'shabby', and if there was one person most responsible for this, it was their Matron, Grace Wilson. As one sister put it, 'At times I think we could not have carried on without her. She was not only a capable Matron, but what is more a women of understanding. She saw and understood many things without having to be told—and she was very human too'.[30] Bertie Fetherston had no doubt about the role she had played. She was, he said, 'the best of all our Matrons'. But for the nurses led by her, the hospital would have collapsed. Like so much of the Gallipoli campaign, the planning at Lemnos had failed the very people who were needed to keep it going.

# THE MARQUETTE

# 14

# ALONE IN THE AEGEAN

⸻

Ammunition, mules and nurses make a strange mix, yet in October 1915 they were among the cargo and passengers of the tramp steamer *Marquette* as it lay at anchor in Alexandria harbour. Launched at the end of the 19th century, the *Marquette* had been hurriedly converted into a troopship when the war broke out. Her year-old coat of military paint did not disguise the fact that she had no claim to luxury or even to much comfort.

Labourers had worked for days to load the *Marquette*, which carried No. 1 New Zealand Stationary Hospital and its staff of twelve officers, nine non-commissioned officers and seventy-seven orderlies of the New Zealand Medical Corps. With them were thirty-six nurses of the New Zealand Army Nursing Service, some 500 officers and troops of the British 29th Divisional Ammunition Column, tons of munitions and equipment, and about 100 crewmen. The ship carried 741 people in all, along with 491 mules and fifty horses.

Most of the nurses came from the South Island and had left Wellington on 11 July aboard the *Maheno*. Thirty of them were attached to the stationary hospital; the other six had been called up from the 21st British General Hospital in Alexandria. They were under the leadership of Wagga

Wagga-born Matron Marie Cameron, who had worked in New Zealand for several years. In the words of Edith 'Poppy' Popplewell, No. 1 Stationary was a 'grand hospital' that would leave Egypt 'wonderfully equipped' with 'X Ray plants and dynamos for electric lighting the whole camp, and one hundred European pattern tents, etc'.[1] Another sister from the hospital, Isabel Clark, could not have been happier when she was told in early October that she was to leave Port Said, where she had spent the previous three months. In a letter to one of her sisters back home, the thirty-year-old from Oamaru, near Dunedin, described Port Said as 'the rottenest place on the face of the earth'.[2]

The nursing staff left Port Said on the moonlit night of 18 October, arriving at Alexandria about 3 a.m., when they were directed to their bunks on the Marquette. Ina Coster remembered that tea had been made for them. 'So in the moonlight we climbed the steep, steep gangway to our new abode, the Marquette,' she wrote later.[3] The unknown question was their destination. 'We haven't the least idea where we are going. Places have been mentioned from Jerusalem to Salonika—Imbros, Lemnos—Asia Minor, Persian Gulf etc. We think it might be Lemnos,' Isabel Clark wrote.[4]

With waterside workers on strike, New Zealand troops, including Private Vic Nicholson, 'helped to dismantle the hospital, pack it up, and load it on ship' for the voyage to No. 1 Stationary Hospital's new destination.[5] Among the equipment they loaded were eighteen-pound guns, which struck Nicholson as 'a funny sort of business, because it's only a short hop to Mudros', where he and others believed the ship was most likely heading. He was not impressed with the 149-metre-long, and 7000-ton Marquette. 'It was a dirty old tramper. That's why they took it, for the accommodation for the horses.'[6]

Just a few hours before departure, Isabel Clark contemplated the adventure ahead. This was, after all, what she had longed for. Now that she was in a position to use her skill and experience in the theatre of war, she was not about to let any qualms about personal safety override her sense of duty.

We don't know where we are going. Another transport is going out as
well. Went ashore for a couple of hours this morning. Alex. is a much
nicer place than Port Said . . . we are supposed to sail this evening. It
will be rather exciting crossing the Mediterranean. I suppose we will
run the risk of being torpedoed.[7]

The ship was under the command of Captain John Bell Findlay, a hardy
Scots seafarer who had served on it for four years. As Vic Nicholson would
recall, 'the skipper opened his sealed orders eight hours out and found he
was not going to Mudros, he was going to Salonika'. Bulgaria had entered the
war on the side of Germany. It had pushed into neighbouring Serbia, cutting
it off from the Allies and prompting Greece to break its treaty with Serbia.
To prevent the northern Greek port of Salonika from falling into enemy
hands, the Allied command decided to establish a stronghold there, with
France and Britain agreeing to send a division each from the Dardanelles.
Isabel Clark captured the prevailing thinking in a letter home. 'We have just
heard that Bulgaria has joined in against us. It is to be hoped that Greece
won't follow suit.'[8] Ina Coster probably spoke for all the nurses when she
said that No. 1 Stationary Hospital 'very much felt the honour that had been
conferred it by being sent to so important a field'.

If there was concern over the strategic situation, Edith Wilkin had a private
worry about the ship. 'Such a beautiful big boat, Mother,' she wrote home later,
'only its number was B.13 so of course it couldn't be lucky.'[9] As it pulled away
from the dock, the nurses lined the deck rails, and sailors on nearby British
and French warships broke into loud cheers and rounds of *La Marseillaise* and
*God Save the King*. But the rousing send-off quickly gave way to trepidation.
The ship was just about to clear the protective harbour boom when the
steering failed. The *Marquette* swung around, narrowly missing the minefield
at the entrance. An urgent investigation revealed a cotton rag twisted around
a piston rod in one of the engines. Hilda Hooker, from Napier, later recalled:
'We wondered if it was sabotage.'

After a two-hour delay, the *Marquette* had barely cleared the heads when Hilda and her colleagues again had cause for alarm. Someone on deck noticed smoke coming from a large case that had been carried on board at the last moment by men wearing Red Cross uniforms. Crew members quickly threw it overboard. 'It was just fortunate that it had arrived too late to be placed in the hold—as all the hatches had been closed, it had been left on deck,' Hilda noted.[10] Rumour spread that the case had almost certainly contained a time bomb.

That night Commander General for Egypt Sir John Maxwell cabled the War Office in London that the *Marquette* had sailed for Salonika. In the document, marked 'secret', he noted that the 29th Divisional Ammunition Column and the New Zealand Stationary Hospital were on board.[11] The presence of the ammunition column would make the *Marquette* an attractive target.

With all portholes closed and in complete blackout, the *Marquette* sailed into the night. A destroyer escort joined her, and they began to zigzag through an area infested with mines. Submarines were also now a constant threat. Despite the ominous departure and the treacherous seas, Hilda Hooker remembered that the 'atmosphere was free and easy, we had no thought of mines or submarines'. Ballarat-trained Poppy Popplewell, who had worked in New Zealand for some years, also recalled no great sense of apprehension. Though she was still grieving the death of her brother, Private Cecil Popplewell, at Lone Pine, she thought the next three days were among the 'happiest and most peaceful' she had ever known at sea.

It was calm and sunny and everyone was so well. No one even tried to be seasick. The Imperial officers were so good to us. It was all very nice and very comfortable. There were rumours of torpedoes, of course, and we had lifebelt drills for two days, but we really hardly took it seriously I am afraid.[12]

During the day they played the usual deck games, wrote letters and read. Sailing into the Aegean Sea, they passed a series of Greek islands. On the fourth evening the escort, the French destroyer *Tirailleur*, obeying instructions, left the convoy. The instructions later proved to be false, the enemy apparently having 'discovered the code'.[13] At breakfast the next morning, 23 October, with the *Marquette* now in the Gulf of Salonika, it was announced that the ship would enter the port by midday. Danger, it seemed, had passed. The weather, though, had abruptly turned cold and grey, in sharp contrast to the heat and flies of Egypt. Several nurses went for a stroll on the promenade deck, chatting among themselves and searching in the mist for glimpses of the coastline.

The Medical Corps quartermaster, Captain Dave Isaacs, was on the top deck with two or three nurses when, at 9:15 a.m., he suddenly said, 'I wonder what that is coming towards us?' What he saw was a 'straight thin green line about 50 yards away streaking through the water towards the ship', with a periscope cutting the surface. Jeannie Sinclair was on the upper deck when she also saw 'a green line coming through the water'. Mary Grigor remarked, 'I wonder if it's a torpedo?'[14] The Officer of the Watch saw the torpedo about fifteen metres from the ship, 'and at first took it to be a fish'.[15] Its ominous swishing sound could be heard distinctly as they watched, mesmerised. Seconds later, the missile struck the forward starboard side. Some on board recalled 'a dull thud, which shook the whole ship'.[16] The German submarine U-35, the most successful U-boat of the Great War, had doomed the *Marquette*.

Mary Beswick was walking around the deck with another nurse when the torpedo hit. 'Away we flew for our lifebelts, and to the places we had been told to go if anything happened,' she wrote later.[17] In the smoking room, Edith Wilkin and Susan Nicoll 'felt a jar' and instinctively knew what had happened. 'The steamer quivered and then started to list,' Edith recalled.[18] In the mess room, in the bow of the ship, Vic Nicholson had just sat down to a plate of steak, onions and fried potatoes. 'I picked up the knife and fork and bang! The torpedo hit on the starboard quarter of the ship, right on number 2 hold, and it threw all the whole company in the air,' he recalled.[19] The hatch on No. 1 hold blew up instantly, sending a column of water spurting high in the air.[20] Several of the crew, of whom at least seven were standing round No. 1 hatch at the time, were probably killed or injured. All available deck hands had just been sent down into No. 2 hold to get some rope. There was soon doubt about how many of them escaped.

The torpedo ripped through the hull and smashed a second gaping hole in the port side. As water rushed into the ship, it listed to port, then righted itself and began to sink by the bow. The siren and bugle giving the alarm sounded almost simultaneously, but the ship's death throes made it difficult to put on the cork life jackets and make for the lifeboats. The companionway leading down to the mess room had been blown away and the men were forming a human ladder. A rope was found for the last man up. By then the men had been ordered to remove their heavy boots, and with the ship so far down in the water it was possible to swim off from the deck.[21] Victor Peters, of Christchurch, and another member of the medical unit were seen throwing rafts overboard, helping the wounded and concussed. They helped several men into life jackets before getting them overboard and then jumping from the deck themselves.

Trying to swim away from the suction was hard going. It was pathetic to see scores of men, mostly from the 29th Divisional British Ammunition Column, who had crowded to the stern. The stern looked so high from the water. Some of the men jumped and struck the rudder or the propeller. This deterred others, who appeared to go under with the ship. It was not a pleasant sight. As the propeller came out of the water I was quite close to four men on a raft who were sucked into the propeller. The raft was smashed to matchwood but by a miracle the men were not killed. I saw one man's hair literally stand up on end; he had red hair. I don't think I imagined seeing this. Until then I had thought that such an event was only an old wives' tale.[22]

In the mayhem, Vic Nicholson and a mate, George Cook, knew immediately from their rural upbringing that the panicked horses and mules could cause havoc if they got among people. They picked up a couple of rifles and prepared 'to shoot any horse or mule that came into sight'. They also saw the periscope of the sub, almost a metre out of the water and not more than 150 metres away, and 'were tempted to blow the lights out of his periscope'. They decided not to, wrongly thinking the sub would surface and pick up survivors.[23]

The nurses assembled at their stations, eighteen on each side of the ship, with Lieutenant Colonel Donald McGavin and three officers in charge. Poppy Popplewell recalled that everyone was calm, 'and although men and girls alike were as white as sheets, no one cried out or spoke even, except to give orders'.[24] The boat drills they had practised during the voyage paid off, but the task was made hazardous by the sharp list to port, reducing the number of boats that could be lowered from the starboard side. An open iron door on the mule deck below, which projected just underneath the davits, compounded the difficulty.

On the port side of the deck, the nurses were going about things quietly. Jeannie Sinclair later recalled that there was no noise—not even a single scream—as they prepared to get into the lifeboats. 'I cannot think how it was that we were so cool and collected.'[25] About ten of the sisters stationed on the port side had clambered into the first forward boat and were being lowered into the water when it was realised that the ropes could not be unhooked. The boat dropped astern, broadside.

The remaining nurses on port stations swarmed down a rope to reach the second boat which, still attached by ropes, appeared to be resting on the water, hanging far out from the ship's side. It was lowered with the first boat directly underneath. As it hung about two metres above the water, the officer in charge immediately stopped lowering it, but when the ship rose by the stern it swung forward. The ropes broke under the strain and fell heavily on the first boat and its shrieking occupants, tossing nurses out, Catherine Fox among them. Marie Cameron and Hilda Hooker were severely injured. Amid the panic, Mary Gorman, a strong swimmer, jumped into the water and gave her lifejacket to her friend Catherine Fox, a non-swimmer, but they were pushed under the lifeboat and drowned. Two of the four port boats were now unseaworthy. Jeannie Sinclair was in the first boat, but it was soon full of water. 'The men in the top boat pulled two of the nurses in and I was pulled in as well, but the boat was hopelessly overloaded,' she recounted.

It was a dangerous situation for the ropes had not been cut free and the *Marquette* was slowly coming over. One girl ahead of me had decided to swim for it, so I followed her example though I cannot swim much. However, one of the crew was swimming clear, and I asked him to give me a tow, which he did. It was awful going past the ship and seeing a large, gaping hole, and all the mules there, and wondering if the vessel would fall on top of us and I would be killed. At last we got past her propeller, to which some men were clinging. Ultimately, we cleared the ship altogether.[26]

Fanny Abbott and Poppy Popplewell were also fortunate. Fanny had been bathing when the torpedo struck and had only a pair of slippers on her feet. She was in the boat that crashed on top of her colleagues and immediately 'sprang into the water . . . I always thought I could not swim but somehow or other I got away from the ship, although the suction of the ship was so great I thought the propeller would hit me. The great big thing seemed to lift right out of the water and go straight down.'[27] She surfaced and grabbed a life belt floating nearby before finally grabbing hold of a raft. Poppy, 'floundering in the sea', feared that the listing *Marquette* would roll on top of her. But 'an absolute miracle happened'. In what seemed barely a second, a wave carried her and those nearby past the end of the stricken ship.

But not all the women on the port side had been put into lifeboats. One survivor, believed to be Mabel Wright, later recounted that she owed her life to the *Marquette's* chief officer, who picked her up and put her in a boat. She then described the fate of Marion Brown and Isabel Clark, who 'got a few steps down the gangway and jumped into the sea'. They were not seen again. Many of the men also jumped. Captain Isaacs later wrote that the scene was awful. 'Men jumping from great heights, some striking the side with sickening thuds, others, with arms and legs stretched out, landing on the propeller and being cut to pieces, whilst others reached the water safely.'[28] Before long the port deck was at water level; then it slid underwater.

On the starboard side, when a lifeboat was lowered to the promenade deck level, New Zealand Medical Corps Captain J.L. Frazerhurst found it contained soldiers who thought the sisters had already gone. He ordered them out of the lifeboat. Eighteen nurses clambered over the deck rail and got in. Because the boat was lower at the bow than the stern, Captain Frazerhurst ordered a soldier to release the stern rope. The stern end of the boat dropped suddenly, throwing it into an almost perpendicular position. Five sisters fell into the sea. Captain Frazerhurst helped release the bow end of the boat, jammed against an open door on the mule deck. The door stove in the side of the lifeboat.

Mary Beswick was one of the nurses still in the boat, which was finally lowered into the water. They pushed off from the ship, but because of the hole it quickly began to fill. They began baling, Mary using her shoes while another nurse used a man's cap. Someone was using a small bowl, but they could not keep the boat clear of water. Four of the sisters thrown into the water clambered into other boats or grabbed onto rafts that troops had thrown overboard. The fifth nurse picked up, Margaret Rogers, was close to death.

Fanny Abbott had seen Lorna Rattray on board after the torpedo hit. Clearly terrified, Lorna had managed to put on just one sleeve of her dress as she struggled to fasten her life belt while coming up the stairs to the deck. She managed to get off the ship. 'The poor girl was very frightened and absolutely demented before she was five minutes in the water,' Fanny remembered.[29] As the lifeboat filled with water and rolled from side to side, Mary Beswick soon realised she had to swim for it. 'This I did, and swam for a raft on which were perched about 12 men. They willingly gave me a corner.'[30] The boat that she left capsized. When righted, it held just six nurses—Edith Wilkin, Nona Hildyard, Violet McCosh-Smith, Mary Rae, Bessie Young and Mary Christmas. Two of these women would not survive. Another nurse, Emily Hodges, would later recall falling off the side of the *Marquette* as it was sinking, and being amazed that she was still alive when she came to the surface.

After helping a patient from the ship's hospital into a life belt, Private William Tennant, of Christchurch, slid down the sharply listing deck and into the water. He swam away as quickly as he could, but he thought he was going too slowly.

> The steamer continued to list over and the mast was right above me and it looked as if it was going to 'clout' me, but swim as I would I couldn't get out of its way when suddenly the boilers burst, and everything came flying round about, but nothing struck me except the soot, which got me on the back of the head and neck.[31]

People, wreckage, rafts and boats littered the sea. Everyone who could looked towards the sinking vessel. As they watched, the stern rose about thirty metres into the air and pitched forward and down. The *Marquette* slid through the grey water. William Tennant thought it was 'truly a magnificent sight'. There was a dreadful, unforgettable sound as hundreds of terrified mules squealed and wagons, heavy machinery and cargo rolled around, crashing and grinding, inside the ship. To Captain Isaacs, it seemed 'as if the engines had slipped out and were tearing their own way down the bow'.[32] As the *Marquette* made her final plunge in a cloud of smoke and steam, sliding down almost perpendicularly, it was accompanied by a strange keening moan from the survivors. It rose from 'an aloneness feeling', said one of the men, remembering it long afterwards.[33] And they were alone, adrift with land twenty-five kilometres away to the west and nearly sixty kilometres to the east, at the mercy of the sea.

# 15

# 'WE THOUGHT THEY
# WOULD LET US DIE!'

From the moment the torpedo struck to when the *Marquette* sank, only eight to fifteen minutes passed, according to the survivors. Loose and buoyant fittings shot to the surface, striking and damaging some of the lifeboats that had floated free. However, two of these boats were serviceable, and survivors clambered into them. Several nurses were pulled aboard.[1] People scrambled or were helped onto many of the *Marquette*'s thirty-six rafts, as well as several metre-square copper tanks. Medical Corps Staff Sergeant Len Wilson recalled that 'We had four on our raft, one with a broken arm and the other three fairly solid chaps.'[2] They were soon thirty centimetres under water.

Within a short time people began to be pulled away by the current or to tire in the cold water. Many drowned because of their shock and injuries, or because they simply could not hang on to whatever they were using for flotation. They slipped from the sides of boats or rafts and disappeared. Some gave up their places aboard to others who were in greater difficulty.[3] Survival became a question of endurance. But amid the shock of the tragedy there was a surprising calmness among some of the survivors, one of whom would later remark, 'It might really have been a bathing party except that we had our clothes on.'[4] When Captain Findlay drifted past some nurses on a raft, he hailed one and asked how she felt. 'She laughed and replied in a very cheery manner, "I'm all right, how are you?"'[5]

Someone called, 'Shark!' The panic abated when another survivor shouted back that there were no sharks in the Aegean, and a sister declared that it was not a fin but the ear of a mule—one of several that had been seen swimming away from the ship. One mule even had a nurse clinging to its neck. Sucked under when the ship went down, she caught hold of the animal and rose with it to the surface.[6] The many mules and horses swimming about were 'one of the biggest dangers', Len Wilson said. A mule kicked Matron Marie Cameron in the water, adding to the injuries she had already suffered.[7] She was pulled into a lifeboat and collapsed.

When the ship disappeared, Chief Officer H.L. Saunders was in the water nearby, somehow not sucked under in the final plunge. He heard a cry and looked around to see a nurse about twenty metres away. He swam towards her, adjusted her life belt and fetched her a lifebuoy that was floating nearby. He then looked around and saw a boat with one soldier standing up in it, about 100 metres away.

I told the nurse that I would go and fetch the boat to her. She asked me not to leave her, but I took no notice of this and swam to the boat. On reaching the boat I saw a soldier holding on to the lifeline, and with the assistance of the soldier in the boat helped him in. He immediately collapsed in the bottom. I then scrambled in myself and got the other soldier to take an oar. We went back to the nurse I had just left and got her on board safely. About fifty yards away I saw a great quantity of wreckage, with more nurses and a number of soldiers clinging to it, and calling out, 'Here we are, Chief, this way, there are nurses among us.' I proceeded towards them, and as I approached some of the soldiers left the wreckage and swam towards

the boat. I kept calling to them, 'Not yet, not yet, the nurses first.'
I then noticed two nurses more or less detached from the rest, whom I
safely got on board. I think the matron was one of these. Hearing a
voice calling out at the side of the boat, I looked over and saw the
adjutant supporting another nurse, whom we took on board.[8]

Saunders pulled another two nurses on board, making six in all along with
twenty-three men, in a boat that was about one-third full of water. The
Court of Inquiry into the disaster would later report there was unanimous
praise of the conduct of the nursing sisters.

From the first moment when they fell in quietly at their stations,
whether clinging to wreckage, sitting in a water-logged boat or on a
raft, they exhibited a calmness and cheerfulness wonderful to see.
Survivors say that many men on the point of giving in to exhaustion
and letting go their hold were encouraged and cheered to fresh efforts
by these brave women, who called out such things as 'Come on boys;
are we downhearted?' and in other ways infused new courage and
endurance into them.[9]

The starboard boat, laden with nurses and a few soldiers, became completely waterlogged and capsized, rolling over and over. Those aboard held
on to the boat and succeeded several times in righting it. As exhaustion
overtook them each time the boat rolled over, some of the survivors would
disappear. Some succeeded in reaching floating wreckage and rafts, but
others drowned. Swimmers who came from wreckage nearby and held on to
the boat also frequently upset it. After three hours, those aboard found it
possible to keep the boat upright in the water provided there were no more
than fifteen people in it, ensuring that the gunwale stayed a few inches above
the surface. 'It thus acted as a support for the women and several men, while
a few swimmers held onto the gunwale and so kept the boat steady.'[10]

A month later, an unknown nurse gave an account to the *Auckland Weekly News* in which she described how the sea was full of soldiers struggling and clinging to pieces of rafts and other wreckage. The lifeboat in which she was a passenger had been holed.

> We were swamped again and again until we were exhausted. It was pitiful to see the nurses and soldiers gradually becoming tired in their frantic struggles and finally releasing their grasp upon the gunwale, floating for a few seconds and then slowly sinking without a murmur. Dr Harrison was swimming near our boat, supporting a nursing sister whom he assisted onto the raft to which many others were clinging. I last saw that sister some time afterwards, floating near a raft, while I was almost dead beat holding on to an upturned boat. She was my greatest pal. She nodded feebly but I was powerless to help her. That was the last I saw of her, but I was told she had been assisted back to the raft and afterwards placed in a boat which, like ours, was constantly overturning. Like many others, she collapsed after a time and died of exhaustion.[11]

In a letter to relatives in New Zealand, Jeannie Sinclair recounted how the survivors floated with boards, lifebuoys and anything they could catch hold of in the frigid water.

> When I was getting tired, [Seaman] Joseph sat on a board and rested me across his knees. Then he would put his arm across a board and let me rest my chin on his arm. He helped others in this way as well. It was dreadful to see some of the other men going whitey-yellow and then blue around the nose, mouth and eyes and, a little later, passing out. One man, who died early in the morning, floated with us all day. I only saw one sister in the water the whole time.[12]

Poppy Popplewell had the fearful experience of what seemed to her like 'touching the bottom of the sea' before she found herself, her 'little chum' Lorna Rattray and a Tommy clinging to a bit of wreckage, near death from cold. They floated for a while with other survivors. Eventually they were separated from the others and joined by another sister, Mary Walker. 'We four just managed to hold on by our hands to our life-saving board.'[13] Mary Grigor would later recall that although her arm had been crushed between a lifeboat and the *Marquette* and she was feeling sick and sore, she managed to swim for hours before a crew member saw her and came to her assistance.

> I really did not much mind what happened to me. After I was able to take stock of what was going on, I saw some men hanging on to wreckage, and called to them to ask if I might also hang on, and they said it was no good—there were already too many there. Then one of the crew saw me and swam to me with a piece of board, to which I clung for some time.[14]

Shortly after, they made for a submerged boat in the distance. There were several men already there.

> We got into this and immediately turned turtle, and continued to do so every five minutes of the remaining number of hours we were in the water. My rescuer died soon after this from cramp and exhaustion. I was sorry I could do nothing for him. Sister Rae came up afterwards, hanging to the lifebuoy of one of our New Zealand boys. She asked me if she could come into the boat. I said, 'Yes, sister, but you had better be hanging on to something else, as this boat keeps turning turtle, and it is such hard work clambering over and into it again.' She held out for a while, but soon after showed signs of exhaustion and died. I wondered if I should be next. Men died on all sides. Some lost their reason and went away from us all.[15]

On Mary Beswick's raft three of the twelve men aboard decided to swim for another raft, making it slightly less crowded. But the raft was below the surface of the water, and the remaining passengers became cold and cramped. 'I suggested paddling with our hands on both sides in order to give them something to do. After a few turns and twists, and nearly bobbing off the sides or back and front, we managed to adjust ourselves, and got on fairly well with our paddling, hoping to reach shore before night.'[16]

By now it was around 2 p.m., and as the day wore on, more and more of the men and women succumbed to the cold, exhaustion and injuries. According to Fanny Abbott, several men 'dropped off about an hour before help arrived'. An unnamed nurse, quoted in *Kai Tiaki* in January 1916, described how 'it was dreadful to watch these strong men fall off and die, one after the other. Some of them went raving mad.' Mary Christmas managed to get hold of the rudder and clung to it all day until she was rescued. Despite being injured in the failed attempt to launch the starboard lifeboat, Nona Hildyard did her best to keep spirits up, singing *Tipperary*, before she suffered heart failure and died in the water. Survival was made more difficult by the nurses' uniform of pantaloons, two petticoats, starched grey dress, long sleeves and stiff collars and cuffs. Soon waterlogged, the clothes were a dead weight. Vic Nicholson and Mary Gould were together all afternoon in the water. Vic recalled how he took off his life jacket and put it under her 'so she came up to the top of the water'. Thanks to this, Mary survived.

The last two boats to get away from the port side, heavily laden, found it necessary to keep their stern to the wind and sea to avoid being swamped. They reached the western shore of the Gulf of Salonika about 4 p.m. Leaving the majority behind, a party of about seventeen walked six kilometres to a railway station, where the authorities offered help. A small party, carrying stretchers for two injured men left on the beach, then returned with a guide and found that all but four had been picked up by boats from two French destroyers, *Tirailleur* and *Mortier*.

The survivors still in the water continued to drift with the current, which seemed to be carrying them towards steamers in the distance. They could see ships passing, but evidently no one on board saw or heard them. Vic Peters thought they might deliberately not have stopped for fear of becoming a submarine target. Mary Beswick watched in frustration as smoke from four steamers appeared in the distance and then one by one the ships sailed away from the sloshing lifeboat in which she, five other nurses and twenty-one men huddled. In the same boat, Chief Officer Saunders described the heartbreak as one ship passed oblivious. 'We did everything possible to attract her attention, waving handkerchiefs, shouting, whistling on mouth whistles, sticking up an oar.' Mary Grigor shared the frustration. '[We] thought that because they were neutral they would let us die!' she said later.[17] Finally, however, a ship took notice.

Late in the afternoon one stopped and seemed to look at us, turned back, and steamed away, then stopped again and lowered a boat, then picked it up and steamed away. Luckily for us our own English patrol boat saw her movements and became suspicious, journeyed over to see, and caught sight of one of our boats in the distance. She then informed two French destroyers, [and] all three came to our rescue.[18]

These were hours that the survivors would never forget, bobbing in the chill waters of the Aegean, many hovering between life and death, just hoping and praying.

# 16

# NO TIME FOR
# MOCK MODESTY

———◦◦◦———

The message was barely discernible. 'S.O.S., S.S.S. off Salonika.' When the *Marquette* was torpedoed just after 9 a.m., the chief wireless operator found that the main radio equipment had been damaged by the shock of the explosion. Resorting to the emergency set, he managed to transmit several weak signals that would alert rescuers to the ship's distress. The second message was more urgent: 'S.O.S., S.O.S, S.O.S., S.S.S., S.S.S., S.S.S., struck 36 miles south of Salonika.' Shortly after, the operator corrected this to 'struck 36 miles south of Dangerus Point'.[1] Not only were the messages faint, but the interference was bad. The Court of Inquiry found that although the alarm was detected, no ship had heard the *Marquette*'s position.[2]

The senior wireless operator on the hospital ship *Grantully Castle*, anchored in Salonika, picked up one of the poor signals. The command of the battleship *Albion* gave orders for the *Grantully Castle* to proceed from Salonika to search. But she was overtaken by British and French destroyers and ordered to return to port. The French destroyers *Tirailleur* and *Mortier* and the British destroyer *Lynn* began to sweep the Aegean at full speed in widening circles. Around 3:30 p.m. the *Tirailleur*, with HMS *Lynn* not far behind, reached the scene of the sinking. The two ships lowered all their lifeboats and picked up all the survivors, who were found in an area about five kilometres by one kilometre.[3]

Alex Prentice would later assert that a lifeboat flare he held aloft was the sign that attracted the *Tirailleur*. The flare handle became a valued memento. The destroyer changed direction, the nearby *Mortier* and *Lynn* were informed, and the engines were rung down. Officers looking through their binoculars soon realised that what looked like bits of wreckage were human beings. 'It was just getting dark when a French destroyer spotted us and pulled us with the steam winches and put us down into the engine room to thaw out, as we were all stiff with cold,' Len Wilson recalled.[4] The *Tirailleur* rescued 290 people in all, the *Lynn* 170 and the *Mortier* ninety.

For many, the rescue vessels had arrived just in time. Along with other nurses, Hilda Hooker had floated for about seven hours in the intense cold, clinging onto buoys, boards or anything that could be grasped. Nearing the limit of her endurance, she had been pulled into a boat that an engineer managed to right. Later, she remembered saying, 'I can't keep going any longer . . . I was just going under when a boy . . . grabbed me feet first, and hauled me into the boat.'[5] Marie Cameron, the seriously injured matron, and Mabel Wright were also in the boat. The engineer asked for a hand-kerchief or rag to tie on to the end of an oar, but no one could help until Ina Coster, one of two sisters who had drifted alongside, produced a red handkerchief. Hilda Hooker believed this had saved their lives. Poppy Popplewell fought hard to survive and to help Lorna Rattray. The pair had become close friends on the voyage over on the *Maheno*. After the *Marquette* went down, they were together in the Aegean.

We kept together the day of our disaster and hung on to the same piece of wreckage, but Lorna was not as strong as I am and simply couldn't do it. I held her on for a long long time and then she died of utter exhaustion not long before we were picked up—it was so dreadful. I was just able to hold up her face while she died and then so soon I had to let her go I couldn't hold her any longer but it was the most awful thing having to let her go and seeing her little grey body float right away from me—another Sister and I then climbed up on the boards we had and lay front down and didn't care a bit what the sea did to us. However it carried us up to a lifeboat sent off from a British mine sweeper—and so we were alright [sic].[6]

On the *Tirailleur*, Vic Nicholson watched as the French slashed bootlaces and uniforms from men and women alike.

It didn't matter whether that was nurse or soldier or who it was, that was the way it went. Half a pannikin of hot wine poured over you and a couple of rough towels and away you went, wrapped in a hot blanket heated on the engine room vents. Wrapped in a blanket and onto a table which ran down into a boardroom and then up and heaved into a hammock. Whether you landed right way up or not, that's where you stayed the night.[7]

Among those picked up by one of the French destroyers was Emily Hodges. Though she couldn't speak French nor the captain English, she recalled his friendliness. 'He just patted me on the shoulder two or three times during the night and that was all.'[8] On the *Lynn*, a sister described how an officer picked her up in his arms and carried her to his cabin. 'He put me on his bunk and stripped off my wet clothes, saying: 'This is no time for mock modesty, you're done.' Indeed I didn't even think of such a thing—and oh the comfort of the warm, dry pyjamas; and the hot coffee and brandy his steward brought me was delicious.'[9]

Reaching Salonika and moved to the French hospital ship *Canada*, the survivors were given clothing, hairpins and toothbrushes by the nurses on board. Jeannie Sinclair was handed an overcoat and slippers before she was transferred to the *Grantully Castle* nearby. The ship's matron was English and the sisters Australian. Edith Wilkin remembered that they 'simply robbed their wardrobes on our account, and did everything they could to cheer us. They were a splendid band of women.'[10]

In a letter she wrote shortly after being taken onto the *Grantully Castle*, Fanny Abbott recounted, 'I have on baksheesh [Arabic for nothing] under-clothes with the exception of slip and slippers from the Red Cross Society. Like a silly, my leg strap I had taken off with stockings now reposes at the bottom of the Gulf of Salonika with many other treasures. Oh it just makes one's heart break when one thinks of it all. Never mind I suppose I ought to be thankful to be here and alive.'[11] For Fanny, there was also the knowledge that the war had claimed the lives of two of her three brothers in the previous six months.

Salonika was in a state of political upheaval. The survivors were not allowed onto the streets but, according to Ina Coster, 'some of the doctors took one or two of the girls to a couple of shops, and they got such neces-sities as hairpins and handkerchiefs'. She added, 'You keep forgetting that everything is gone, and get many shocks when you realise what it means.'[12] Emily Hodges was among those who went shopping. The first thing she did with the money that was raised for the sisters was to buy a pot of face cream and some face powder. 'After I had been floating in the sea for eight and a half hours, my face was the colour of mahogany. And I had no hair pins.'[13]

Kath King was one of the Australian sisters on board the *Grantully Castle*, and she did what she could for the women. 'We took on all survivors, at present there are 99 missing out of which are ten sisters, which seems a very large percentage; quite a number are very ill but most are suffering from shock. The Matron [Sister Cameron] is seriously ill, they think pneumonia.'[14] The next morning the sad business of a roll call was made, revealing that 167 people from the *Marquette* had lost their lives, including ten sisters of the New Zealand Army Nursing Service and twenty-two other ranks of the Medical Corps. The nurses who died were Marion Brown, Isabel Clark,

Catherine Fox, Mary Gorman, Nona Hildyard, Helena Isdell, Mabel Jamieson, Mary Rae, Lorna Rattray and Margaret Rogers.

Around 27 October a boat was seen floating upside down at the Greek coastal town of Zagora. Towed ashore, it was found to contain the bodies of four men and two women, the only bodies of missing nurses to be recovered. All six wore life belts and were tied to a boat thwart. A British naval commander reported that no identity discs were found, nor papers on the bodies. But one of the women wore a gold watch with 'Margaret Rodgers [sic]' engraved on it. An Army Nursing Service badge was also recovered. When the commander saw them, the bodies were 'in a very bad state and were lying in coffins'.[15] The second body was believed to be Helena Isdell. The one presumed to be Margaret Rogers was buried in the Mikra British Cemetery at Salonika with full naval honours. Helena Isdell is remembered along with the eight other nurses lost to the Aegean on the Mikra Memorial within the same cemetery. The memorial commemorates 'the nurses, officers and men of the forces of the Empire who lost their lives in the Mediterranean and whose only grave is the sea'.

The surviving nurses left on the *Grantully Castle* for Alexandria on 29 October. The journey back was distressing, Poppy Popplewell noted: 'It's a sad and sorry feeling to be going back; nothing would matter if all were here; that is the awful part.' Clad in borrowed Red Cross singlets and khaki woollen golf coats, they managed to laugh and joke about their destitute state, Poppy acknowledging that 'that part of it matters least after all'. She remembered the precious belongings and personal mementos that lay on the seabed but she realised that 'grieving over sunken treasures' made her feel ashamed. Edith Wilkin wrote to her mother of her regret at the loss of her collection of curios, 'but above all your ring and the wee chain with my tiki'. These were the 'little things one can never replace'. But they were alive.

On 2 November, New Zealand nurse Fanny Speedy was on duty at the 19th British General Hospital in Alexandria when the badly injured and pneumonia-stricken Marie Cameron and three other survivors were admitted. Mabel Wright had concussion from a fracture to the base of her skull, Susan Nicoll had thrombosis of one leg, and Elizabeth Wilson had dysentery. Fanny noted that they all seemed 'rather nerve shattered, which is not surprising'.[16] Edith Wilkin and Poppy Popplewell spent time convalescing at a hospital at Luxor, while Mary Christmas and five other survivors were sent to the nurses' rest home at Aboukir, near Alexandria. As she recovered, Mary wrote to Mary Gorman's sister. She expressed her own and Jeannie Sinclair's sorrow, and described how hard the Waimate nurse had worked before she left Alexandria. Sister Sinclair, she said, would never forget her help in the wards.

Marie Cameron was desperately ill. Several of her ribs were broken and one had pierced her lung. She not only had concussion but was paralysed down her right side. She had been taken onto the *Grantully Castle* at Salonika in an invalid's chair, 'nursing a teddy bear from which she would not be parted. She did not know any of her friends', one sister wrote.[17] Among the nurses who met and cared for her in Alexandria was her sister Annie, who was on the nursing staff of No. 1 Australian General Hospital in Cairo. Later awarded the Royal Red Cross, Marie Cameron lived the rest of her life at private hospitals in Sydney and Wagga Wagga, where her family lived. She had to learn to speak again, and to use her left hand. Her nursing career was over, and her fragile health would not recover.

Lottie Le Gallais heard about the disaster when the hospital ship *Maheno* left Southhampton in early November to return to Egypt. There was little detail, and she feared for her friends. When she reached Alexandria, the picture became clearer. Ten of the rescued sisters were waiting for the ship when it berthed. In a letter home, she wrote that Marie Cameron 'went grey in one night'.[18] New Zealand nurses collected clothing and £100 for the survivors' immediate needs. A further shock lay in store for Lottie: her friend Sister Ada Hawken, who had asked her to bring some things back from London, had died of typhoid in Alexandria three weeks earlier. 'That is 11 of the girls of the *Maheno* gone,' Lottie wrote in shocked disbelief.[19] A headstone that had just been placed on Ada's grave stated that she had 'died for her country's service'.

In his report on the tragedy, New Zealand Surgeon-Major D.S. Wylie was full of praise for the conduct of the nurses. 'At no time did I see any signs of panic or any signs of fear on the part of anyone, and I cannot find words adequately to express my appreciation of the magnificent way in which the nurses behaved, not only on the vessel but afterwards in the water. Their behaviour had to be seen to be believed possible.'[20] He attributed the deaths of some of the nurses to the incident in which one lifeboat crashed onto another in the escape from the sinking vessel. Their injuries were such that 'their subsequent existence in the water [was] impossible'.[21] But how the tragedy had come about remained a mystery.

# 17

# THE PRICE OF SACRIFICE

New Zealanders seethed with indignation when they learned that a German U-boat had torpedoed a ship carrying nurses. Their nurses. Ida Willis, stationed at No. 2 Stationary Hospital at Pont de Koubbeh near Cairo, wrote that the 'tragic news cast a deep gloom' over all New Zealand personnel. Olive Haynes, on the nearby island of Lemnos, was shocked when she heard of the deaths. 'Very bad news from all around. Transport torpedoed not far from here and 12 [sic] Sisters out of 40 missing.'[1]

To New Zealanders and Australians, the deaths of the ten nurses were linked in heroic sacrifice with the execution of the English nurse Edith Cavell just eleven days earlier. In the propaganda battle, Cavell, who had also tended wounded German soldiers with devoted care, represented all that was good and noble in nursing, while Germany was portrayed as an enemy without morality. Her execution was one of the great German blunders of the war. From November 1914 to July 1915, wounded and derelict English and French soldiers were hidden from the Germans by a French prince at his château near Mons, and then conveyed to the house Cavell and others occupied in Brussels, where they were given money to reach the Dutch border with the help of guides.

On 5 August 1915 the Germans arrested and imprisoned Cavell. She admitted having sheltered and helped to convey to the border about 200 English, French and Belgians. Court-martialled, she and a Frenchman were sentenced to death. The two were shot on 12 October 1915. She faced the firing squad with a dignity that moved the world. To the chaplain who administered the last sacraments, she remarked, 'Patriotism is not enough.' The phrase reverberated in the lands of the Allies, not least in Australia and New Zealand.

Soon after a memorial service for Cavell in Melbourne, the *Argus* printed a letter from a New Zealand nurse who had been aboard the *Marquette* when it was torpedoed. It related how the passengers had struggled for life, hanging onto pieces of raft, and said the 'nurses behaved with grand courage ... It will be a comfort to the relatives of the nurses in N.Z. to know that they were so splendidly brave and self-sacrificing in the face of death.'[2] In New Zealand, the Christchurch *Star* editorialised on the disaster:

Amid the horrors of war women play a truly heroic part. To their gentle care is confided the wounded soldier, and not thousands but tens of thousands of men have been nursed back to health and strength by the willing hand that serves under the Red Cross. It comes as a great shock, comes in fact with a poignancy nothing can equal, to learn of women who were devoting their skill to the alleviation of pain, and working for the welfare of humanity, being among the victims of war. Against a background of carnage their work, for friend and foe alike, stands noble and inspiring. While men fight one another, women tend the wounded, and there can be no doubt at all but that their's [sic] is the nobler part. Naturally enough the eyes of the world are on the firing line and sometimes the work of the nurses, from the very firing line to the hospitals is overlooked. It was ever thus. Those who scar the tree of life, a great thinker once said, are remembered by the scars, but those who water its roots have nothing by which they may be known. But their's [sic] is the tree.[3]

Some days after the sinking, a letter from one of the nurses on the *Marquette* reached a friend in New Zealand. The *Otago Witness* published part of it on 10 November 1915: 'There is no romance about war. It spells suffering, hunger, and filth, and how thankful I am every day that I came to do what I could to help relieve our brave boys.' The author of the letter was Margaret Rogers, who had been found dead in the capsized lifeboat. It was the last letter she ever wrote.

In Egypt, many of the surviving nurses volunteered to return to Salonika to help establish the replacement hospital, but they were turned down and sent either home or to the New Zealand Hospital in London. It was thought they had been through enough. Edith Wilkin and Poppy Popplewell were sent to work light duties at a hospital at Luxor, 600 kilometres south of Cairo until they had fully recovered. But Edith Wilkin was disappointed that they could not 'go on with the No. 1 Stationary Hospital to make a new start'.[4] In a letter home, she wrote of how she would love to return to New Zealand for 'just a little while', cautioning, however, 'you must promise not to keep me home because I must come back—you see we are needed here so badly'.[5] In the next five months the new hospital would treat nearly 7000 patients in Salonika.

Australian Army Nursing Service Sister May Tilton met the survivors, having been transferred to the Egyptian Government Hospital at Suez in October.

Several of the sisters were in the water seven hours before they were rescued. These were the girls we met. They had all volunteered to go on, but the [officer commanding] said the day for such heroines was past, and he insisted that all of them must return home after such a dreadful experience. He said they were the most wonderfully brave and plucky women he had ever met. One only had to look at them to realise they had suffered a ghastly experience. The expression in their eyes haunted me for days.[6]

Ida Willis pointed the finger at the decision by British Naval Command to send the nurses on a ship such as the *Marquette*. 'It seemed a dreadful mistake to send a complete hospital unit on a transport carrying soldiers and munitions of war. Hospital ships were respected and safe.'[7] New Zealand Matron-in-Chief Hester Maclean had not long returned to Wellington when she heard of the sinking. While she mourned the nurses' loss, she was 'proud to remember that they were New Zealanders, and that they gave their lives for their King and their Country'.[8] The calamity, she continued, 'inspires us with awe'. Years later in her autobiography, there was less imperial hyperbole. While praising the nurses, Matron Maclean sharply criticised the British military command's decision to send the New Zealand contingent on the *Marquette*. Like Ida Willis, she believed the reason that the ship was torpedoed was 'most probably' that she was carrying a 'big British ammunition column'.

It appeared a strange thing that the valuable hospital equipment, as well as the more valuable lives should have been risked on an ordinary transport, which was conveying soldiers and munitions of war, when constantly hospital ships were coming and going from Alexandria. The torpedoing of the *Marquette*, being a transport was quite within the rights of the enemy, and at that time hospital ships were not being attacked. This loss of our sisters and hospital orderlies was the first and possibly the most disastrous of the many at sea, which afterwards occurred.[9]

And that was the issue—the *Marquette* had been carrying munitions. A survivor, New Zealander Arthur Judge, agreed. 'We shouldn't have been put on it although we had to do what we were told of course. But the point is that this was an ammunition ship.'[10] To this day mystery surrounds the circumstances that led to the sinking. At the very least, it was a dreadful blunder by the British Eastern Mediterranean Command. Press reports published in later years claimed that the nurses were ordered aboard the

*Marquette* 'despite a German warning that it would be sunk'.[11] A Court of
Inquiry, hastily convened on board HMS *Talbot* in Salonika three days after
the sinking, did not help matters. Many witnesses were still in shock or
exhausted and probably confused. A key witness, Lieutenant Colonel D.J.
McGavin, the hospital's commanding officer, who had lost ten of his nurses,
was not even in Salonika. Stranded on a beach, he did not arrive for another
two days—by which time the inquiry had concluded.

Two nurses appeared before the inquiry, Edith Wilkin and Poppy
Popplewell, but their evidence was brief, dealing mostly with their recollection of events and personal experiences. The affair had been 'very trying', but
Poppy recalled that the inquiry officers were 'so good and kind, and made us
laugh and petted and flattered us as though we were queens instead of two
very draggled looking nurses in shrunken dresses and no hats and black
eyes … When they couldn't show their sympathy and kindness any more
and we were just leaving, the commander called for cheers for New Zealand
nurses from the bluejackets, and I wish you could have heard those three
British cheers. It made one thrill.'[12]

The court concentrated almost exclusively on the way the ship was
handled after the torpedoing: whether she was following the instructions in
her sailing orders; the launching of the boats; the transmissions of the SOS
messages; and the discipline of the soldiers and crew. In its findings, the
court said of the nurses: 'On all sides nothing but praise and admiration is
expressed for their discipline, courage and unselfishness; their fine example,
combined with their cheery encouragement, undoubtedly prevented many
men from giving in.'[13]

The reason why a major hospital unit might have been transported on an
ammunition ship has been the subject of considerable speculation. It has
been asserted in various books and published articles that No. 1 New
Zealand Stationary Hospital and its staff should have sailed from Alexandria
on the British hospital ship *Grantully Castle*, as that ship had been ready to
leave from another berth in the port.

Kath King's diary, however, makes it clear that the *Grantully Castle* was not in Alexandria at the time.[14] She had been on board the ship since it left Alexandria on 29 September 1915. It then sailed for the islands of Lemnos, Imbros and Malta, where it arrived on 5 October. Five days later it arrived back in Mudros harbour and on the 12th sailed for Salonika, arriving the next day. It remained there for the next sixteen days, during which time Kath wrote of receiving seventeen patients on board, going ashore, and rowing around the harbour. The *Grantully Castle* was still moored in Salonika harbour when the *Marquette* was torpedoed on the 23rd. Indeed, when the *Marquette* survivors arrived in Salonika they were taken to the *Grantully Castle*—an event that Kath had both photographed and recorded in her diary.

The myth that the stationary hospital should have been transported on the *Grantully Castle* rather than the *Marquette* was fanned by John Meredith Smith's otherwise comprehensive account of the tragedy, *Cloud Over Marquette*. However, despite there being no evidence to substantiate that claim, it has since been perpetuated by other historians. That, of course, does not excuse the British Eastern Mediterranean Command for sending the nurses on the *Marquette*. The decision itself was not discussed at the Court of Inquiry, prompting the suspicion that it was deliberately avoided. The court also failed to request a report from the transport officer who had been responsible for placing the hospital unit on the *Marquette*.

It is evident from Kath King's diary that the nurses on the *Grantully Castle* had little work to occupy them. This raises the further question of whether the ship could have been sent back to Alexandria to pick up the New Zealand nurses, medical staff and equipment.

The Salonika destination, Smith points out, had been a secret kept very close by the Naval Command. Although a New Zealand hospital was the subject of the move, New Zealand military and medical leaders were treated contemptuously. The Command did not keep New Zealand informed. Several requests by Major General Alexander Godley, Commander of the

New Zealand Expeditionary Force, early in October to have the No. 1
Stationary Hospital sent to Lemnos where they could treat Anzac troops
were simply ignored.[15] Colonel Heaton Rhodes, the New Zealand Red Cross
Commissioner, had also asked that the hospital be established on Lemnos.
The reply was that its destination had yet to be decided.[16]

It is certainly true that for strategic reasons, the Allies had resolved
to establish a troop presence at Salonika. But the haste to transport the
hospital unit to the Greek port on the *Marquette* was a reckless and counter-
productive decision that put the nurses, medical officers, orderlies and
equipment at risk. While No. 1 Stationary Hospital did open when it took
over the site and tents occupied by the 25th Casualty Clearing Station at
Lembet, near Salonika, on 12 November, the hospital was a shadow of what
it was intended to be. It had to wait for new equipment and, as the survivors
had returned to Egypt, it had no nurses.

The loss of the nurses, medical personnel and their equipment had
been entirely avoidable. Two other troopships, the *Royal Edward* and
the *Southland*, had been torpedoed in the Aegean in the weeks before the
*Marquette*, highlighting the extreme risk from German submarines.
At the time, the Germans were not attacking hospital ships with Red Cross
markings. Without the Red Cross painted on its sides, the New Zealand
nurses were deprived of the protection of the Geneva Conventions. The
U-boat had been within its rights to target the *Marquette*.

In a statement to the court, Lieutenant Colonel F.J.S. Cleeve, who com-
manded the 29th Divisional Ammunition Column, described how he was
ordered at Alexandria to embark the *Marquette* and found that New Zealand
Medical Corps personnel and stores for a hospital, as well as officers and
nursing sisters, had been allotted to the same ship. He initially planned to
house the Medical Corps on the fore troop deck, but he was told this could
not be done, as that deck 'was required for stores'. The Corps subsequently
joined the ammunition column on the aft troop decks. This perhaps shows
how the New Zealanders were rated in order of importance.

Before sailing, on the evening of the 19th, Cleeve said he received 'a confidential memorandum as to action against submarines', which in effect required him to use rifles in the hope of smashing or splashing the periscope mirror.[17] This clearly shows that a submarine attack was regarded as a serious possibility, and further underlines the irresponsibility of the naval command.

Colonel Cleeve said he regretted the deaths of two Divisional Ammunition Column officers, but expressed no regret for the dead sisters and medical staff, or indeed for those who had survived. Instead, he noted, 'Many of these ladies appeared next day as if nothing unusual had occurred on the preceding one.'[18] It was as if their traumatic experience, and sacrifice of their colleagues, was trivial compared with that of his own officers.

The New Zealand government reacted quickly to prevent such a tragedy occurring again. The Governor, Lord Liverpool, wrote to the War Office on 8 November 1915 politely but firmly demanding procedural change. 'In view of loss of *Marquette* my Government would be glad if arrangements could be made whereby medical units, such as stationary hospitals etc. should when possible be transferred by sea in a hospital ship.'[19] While not directly allocating blame, this quick response left no doubt about the New Zealand government's conclusion as to the cause of the tragedy. Notice was taken: after the *Marquette*'s sinking, No. 1 Stationary Hospital travelled on hospital ships.

A sidelight to the scandal was a series of claims and counter-claims about the treatment afforded the nurses as the *Marquette* was sinking. On 15 April 1916 the *Evening Post* carried a story in which Colonel McGavin denied any implication that the men had neglected the nurses. Many men were imperilled, he told the newspaper, 'and some possibly actually lost their lives in gallant attempt to save the nurses'. He added that he himself 'saw that all the nurses were clear of the ship' and gave an assurance that they were all off the *Marquette* 'some little while before it sank'.[20]

Hester Maclean noted, in relation to the nurses on the port side of the *Marquette*, that the medical officer responsible for them thought they had all got into lifeboats. However, a letter to her from fellow survivor Mabel Wright described how, while standing on the deck, she had seen 'a boat load of men in uniform getting away'. Mabel continued: 'I wondered why we nurses were left on deck, without a chance of getting into a boat . . . Perhaps on the starboard side the nurses may have all got into boats; but not on the port side. Sisters Brown and Clark [who both died] got a few feet down the gangway, took each other's hand, then jumped into the water. Sister Coster and myself did not get off the deck—we both helped two sick orderlies on to the gangway, and in doing so lost our chance of going down. One of our own NZ doctors came up to me in a few mins [sic] and asked me if I could swim. I told him, "No." He just looked at me and said, "not much hope for you".'[21]

Mabel and the doctor did not see each other again for some time, and when they did, he was astonished to see her alive, saying he'd been telling everyone that she had gone down with the ship. She was upset about this, and made more so by Colonel McGavin's comments. 'When one is treated like that, and to read statements in the paper as in last night's, then I think, Miss Maclean, it is our duty to speak out and let the truth be known.'[22]

Hester Maclean informed Defence Minister James Allen but realised there was little point in pressing the matter to a public stoush. There had already been enough trouble and doubt generated, she reasoned. Instead, she focused on the professional attitude of the sisters involved. 'It is amazing to think that after this sad experience, not one of the sisters wished to give up their work and all continued to serve for the remainder of the war.' But they carried the memories of that day for the rest of their lives.

Lottie Le Gallais also had her memories. Not long after the *Marquette* tragedy, a letter she had written to her brother Leddie in July was returned to her. The envelope was stamped, 'Reported killed. Return to sender'. Leddie had been killed at Shrapnel Valley at Gallipoli on 23 July, shot in the head, just days after she sailed from New Zealand. Now he lay hastily buried in the Shrapnel Valley cemetery. Lottie returned to Auckland Hospital, grieving for the brother she had so wanted to meet on the other side of the world. She kept Leddie's last letter to her, written in April, as he prepared amid the rousing departure celebrations to sail for Gallipoli. 'Dear Lottie—Am quite well. Goodbye. Goodbye again Leddra.'[23] The letter was simple but precious. In the bottom right-hand corner, Leddie had scrawled a large 'X' for a kiss. In the other corner, Lottie pasted his death notice.

# THE
# WESTERN FRONT

# 18

# THE FIRST ANZAC SERVICE

———◆———

A bonfire in the distance, at an Australian Army camp, lit up the night sky over Cairo. It was New Year's Eve 1915, but revelry was muted. Suffering from dysentery and jaundice, Lieutenant Harry Moffitt had been admitted to No. 1 Australian General Hospital, where Alice Ross King was based. He was weak but slowly recovering. Alice and Harry had declared their love for each other and become engaged. 'I sat with him on the piazza until nearly ten, listening to the music and watching the big bonfire in the distance.'[1] It was a moment to treasure.

The next morning was the first time Alice had slept the New Year in since her sixteenth birthday. The first line of her diary entry for 1916— 'Hold Thou my hand, the way is dark before me'—was from a popular hymn. Reflecting a sense of foreboding, Alice added: 'I did not have my usual good omen for the New Year last night.' Nonetheless, she and Harry were determined to make the most of their time together as he recovered. They were, Alice reassured herself, 'still as much in love as ever'. Over the next few days they would take drives together and spend the nights after dinner on the piazza. The days together were 'glorious', she wrote. 'Every day my love grows deeper.'[2]

Elsewhere in Cairo, Elsie Cook's festive season had not started well. The matron at No. 2 Australian General Hospital had informed her that because she was married she would not be promoted to the rank of Sister. Though disappointed, Elsie wanted to celebrate Christmas and New Year even if Syd was still convalescing in England. But the Australian military authorities had other ideas for New Year's Eve. It was rumoured that the Australians were threatening to burn down Shepheard's Hotel and a few other places. With the so-called Battle of the Wazzir still fresh in everyone's memory, the commanders banned leave for the Australians.

As the Cairo Citadel gun boomed, Elsie saw in the New Year praying in the Ghezireh Palace gardens, remembering the tragedy of 1915. She was reminded that on the previous New Year's Eve she had watched the dawn from the deck of the *Kyarra*. 'This is the old grotto in the gardens of Ghezireh Palace, where will the next year dawn, I wonder? On peace and Australia and St Moritz, I hope fervently. Here endeth poor old 1915.' As she knelt in the stone grotto, she was certain that 'everyone's silent prayer for 1916 is the same, I'm sure'. Despite the no-leave order, Elsie was determined to attend a New Year's Day party and dinner. 'Well, we waylaid the colonel and got him to cancel the ultimatum as regards the Sisters and to tell [Matron] Gould so, and he did!'[3] Elsie knew how to be persuasive.

That same New Year's Day, Elsie Eglinton was sailing back to Egypt, newly promoted to Sister. She had been on transport duty to Australia with wounded soldiers. Among them had been 'a poor blind boy', Private Bertie Prentice, who was to disembark at Fremantle. 'He is a dear boy and we all are very fond of him. He often has three afternoon teas given him in one day by different people, it amuses him very much. We are getting up a collection for him and are going to put it in the bank for him in WA as he does not want to accept it.'[4]

With the Gallipoli campaign now over, Anzac nurses in Egypt prepared for relocation. Some, including Kath King and Elsie Cook, also sailed to Australia with wounded men. Others waited to follow the troops to France.

The New Year was just two days old when Kath King said goodbye to Gordon Carter at Cairo's main railway station and, with her sister Wynne, also a nurse, boarded the SS *Ulysses* for Australia. Arriving in Sydney on 8 February 1916, they were met with 'great cheering from all the ships, they all saluted us and blew their whistles'.

The two nurses were stunned to be greeted as heroines when they got home to Orange. 'Father met us. Great excitement, crowds of visitors all day,' Kath wrote in her diary.[5] Visitors continued for the next four days, 'all making a great fuss of us. Terrible bore.' That was just the start. Then there was 'a blessed reception for us in Town Hall . . . It was packed and decorated, even the stairs, great speeches, poor Wynne and I felt most uncomfortable. We then had tea and were surrounded by people of all kinds and description.'[6]

It was a grand event, with flags and bunting decorating the hall, dignitaries everywhere, and crowds of local people. It made the Orange *Leader*'s front page, under the headline 'OUR BRAVE NURSES'. In his official welcome the mayor said the two sisters had been 'doing such noble work for our soldiers and our Empire' and had 'toiled in the interests of you and me, and the good boys at the front . . . These nurses are as much wanted to assist the Empire as the boys in the trenches are to-day. With their assistance we have been able to send back to the front thousands and thousands, fit and well, after receiving their careful nursing.'[7] The mayor added that when the troops landed at Gallipoli 'our brave nurses were there to assist them', and after the first assault, when thousands were taken to the hospital ships, 'our good nurses were there to meet them'.

For Kath, being on a hospital ship at the Dardanelles was her duty. She and Wynne knew there was no glory in war, only death and pain far removed from the frivolity of this reception in their honour. They found the event difficult, but the people of the Orange district seemed to be in awe of their work. The visitors—including, as Kath put it, 'half Manildra, I think'—did not let up over the next five days. A crowd turned out at 10 p.m. to see them depart for Sydney, where the entertainment continued at the swank Hotel

Australia in Martin Place. Six weeks later, on 2 April, the sisters boarded the troopship *Euripides* and set sail for Egypt—no doubt relieved to put all the fuss behind them.

Somewhere in the Indian Ocean they passed Elsie Cook, on the way back to Australia on board the *Demosthenes* with thirteen 'mental cases' and 200 'undesirable' troops. Elsie's husband, Syd, was following on another ship to continue his convalescence. She was 'wildly excited' and did not sleep for two nights as her ship made its way up the Australian east coast for Sydney. She awoke at dawn on 22 April, looked out her porthole and 'saw the sun rising on Sydney Heads!' Her father-in-law, former Prime Minister Joseph Cook, came aboard at Woolloomooloo docks and gave her the news that Syd would arrive in ten days. Family members gathered at Elsie's family home, Kassala, at Burwood for lunch. 'Tongues wagging and questions asked etc. How very good it is to be home again!'[8] But because she was married, the Australian Army Nursing Service would not let her go back to Egypt. While Syd recovered from his gunshot wound, an unhappy Elsie was placed on home service at No. 4 Australian General Hospital at Randwick. She knew that her nursing career in the Australian Army was over. But, as with Syd, nothing would stop her from returning to the war.

Meanwhile, in Cairo, No. 1 Australian General Hospital was preparing to close and move to France. Alice Ross King and Harry Moffitt tried at every opportunity to meet up in Cairo before they each left Egypt with their units. All through January they were inseparable as they travelled back and forth between Cairo and the Helouan Convalescent Depot, where he was now staying. They took the ferry to Sakara, where they hired donkeys to visit ancient tombs and lunched on boiled eggs and sardines.

The glow on the desert was glorious and we came across beautiful patches of desert wildflowers. Discharged the guide and the donkeys near the sphinx. It was moonlight. Had a love and a kiss and then dinner at a wee restaurant out there and motored in to Cairo in time to catch Harry's 9 o'clock train to Helouan. A glorious day indeed.[9]

They would wander the bazaars of Cairo, drink coffee at old stalls, or sit on the piazza at Shepheard's Hotel, 'watching the crowd'. Although Harry was improving, some days he overdid things and tired quickly. Alice thought he still looked weak and sometimes shaky. A former suitor met her, with love on his mind. Alice wasn't interested. 'He asked me not to become engaged until Xmas time, as he will then know his own position. Felt thoroughly disgusted with him.'[10]

Once Harry had to come to Cairo on duty and Alice managed to spend the day with him, accompanying him in a horse-drawn gharry. Later they sat on the balcony at Shepheard's Hotel, away from the hustle of the streets. They talked of their future, spellbound by a wondrous apricot-hued sunset. 'When we're married I'll give you a dress that colour,' Harry told Alice.[11] That night, he caught the 8 p.m. train to the Suez Canal and his unit. Alice noted that there was 'much talk of the [hospital] Unit moving to France'.

———◦●◦———

For the Anzacs, the focus of the war shifted in late 1915, when the German High Command decided to push for victory on the Western Front, in France. Already, the Germans had staged a sustained attack on the fortress town of Verdun. After Gallipoli, with the help of recruiting at home, the AIF was reorganised and expanded from two to five infantry divisions, all of which were progressively transferred to France from March 1916. There would soon be 90,000 AIF troops stationed in France and another 90,000 training in England, leaving 25,000 in the Middle East. New Zealand troops, after returning from Gallipoli, were also reorganised and reinforced into four brigades that comprised the New Zealand Division. They sailed for France in April 1916. Before the war ended, more than 46,000 Australians and 12,500 New Zealanders would die on the Western Front.

To better use limited resources, the Allies decided to integrate their armies more closely. This meant that the operations of the Anzac hospitals and casualty clearing stations ostensibly came under the direct control of

British General Headquarters. However, as they were still regarded as 'imperial', a degree of difference from British establishments was accepted. The new policy saw the sisters of the Australian and New Zealand Army Nursing Services working at times in various British and Canadian medical units. Three Australian general hospitals, three Australian casualty clearing stations, and No. 1 New Zealand Stationary Hospital were also established on the Western Front.

The question of whether nurses should be attached to casualty clearing stations was hotly debated in military and medical circles. Colonel George Barber, the Deputy Director of Medical Services, and Colonel Wilfred Giblin, a surgeon, strongly opposed the idea. Working at such stations was the closest nurses got to the front line. It was argued that the risk of death or injury to nurses was too great, and that they might be made prisoners of war. The nurses themselves were not of one mind. Some thought the services of a highly trained nurse were wasted at a casualty clearing station, while others strongly believed the contrary. Medical staff working with Australian Army nurses in other theatres of war were generally in favour.

According to the official Australian military medical historian, Colonel A.G. Butler, the presence of trained female nurses on the Western Front changed the military status of casualty clearing stations from clearing houses to forward centres for 'scientific treatment' of the wounded. They were generally located in pairs on or near railway lines, as close to the front as was safe and practicable, with encampments and cemeteries close by. Troops were taken to the clearing stations if medical officers at dressing stations on the battlefield decided they needed emergency surgery and evacuation. The stations enabled the wounded to get lifesaving treatment far earlier than if they had had to wait to be taken to hospital. The sisters staffed resuscitation wards, where, Butler wrote, men were sent 'whose spark of life flickered—often to extinction. But if [the system's] tragedies were many and poignant, its triumphs were often dramatic, and success was surprisingly frequent, even among seemingly moribund men.'[12] Over the next two and a half years the sisters were integral members of the stations' surgical teams.

On 24 March 1916 Alice Ross King received her orders to sail to France. She and her fellow nurses from No. 1 Australian General Hospital waited on the pier at Alexandria, weighed down with the booty from a final shopping spree. One nurse had a canary in a cage. A captain was told to make sure all the nurses were on board the hospital ship *Braemar Castle*. 'Not knowing the AANS he told us to form a double row to "number off",' Alice recounted. 'He wanted 120. Each time he got a different number. He was terribly worried. Finally our big [commanding officer] Col De Crespigny came down the gangway to see what was the matter. In his tired voice he called out, "Sisters! Form a fairly straight line. Left turn! Get on board." "Oh! Sir," said Matron, "they are not all here." "Then they'll be left behind," said our CO. Our first hard lesson! We had always been fussed over [and] spoilt before,' Alice wrote, with a shade of overstatement.[13]

The *Braemar Castle* reached Marseilles in early April, but planning was in a shambles, and the sisters spent three days on board awaiting orders. Finally news came through that some would go to Le Havre and some to Rouen. Alice Ross King was detailed to Rouen, while another No. 1 Australian General Hospital nurse, Pearl Corkhill, was among those going to Le Havre. Sisters from the No. 2 hospital, including Olive Haynes, stayed at Moussot, near Marseilles, to re-establish the hospital there. It was to serve as a quarantine station to prevent infectious diseases being carried to the Western Front by soldiers transferred from the Middle East.

When the nurses from No. 1 hospital boarded the troop train heading north, they soon found there were neither compartments nor a toilet. Quickly assessing the lack of amenities, they decided that if they were to get through the journey ahead there was only one thing to do. As Pearl Corkhill explained, 'Then we all scooted down to a little wine shop and bought drinks for the journey. The orderlies could not come so we bought stuff for them.

It was rather funny to see us coming back loaded with bottles.'[14] It was spring, and the scenery in the Rhône Valley was glorious. But the journey was uncomfortable, disjointed and long.

Large numbers of Australian troops, including most of the 1st Division going up the line, passed them, 'cheering when they saw the Aussie sisters hanging out the windows'. One of the shuntings left them at Dijon for six hours, enabling the nurses to wash at the railway station. 'There was no water on board, so you can imagine how we got on,' Pearl Corkhill remembered. 'We used to wash ourselves with some eau-de-cologne or water out of a bottle poured on the end of a handkerchief. Of course we never got our clothes off.'

Reaching Rouen, normally an eight- to ten-hour journey, took three and a half days. Fifty of the nurses were then transferred to various hospitals; Alice Ross King and two others to a stationary hospital on the edge of the Forêt Verte. Accommodation was a tent, and to keep warm they were given two dirty brown blankets. 'The matron was very imperial,' Alice noted. 'Always talking about "you Australians" or "you colonials".'[15] It was a sign of things to come.

Staff Nurse Annie Shadforth was among a group of twenty nurses who went to Etaples and Boulogne. The trip to Etaples, on two troop trains, was disorganised. They were shunted off to a siding and left for several hours. Food was at a premium. As they finally headed towards Etaples, still hungry, a British Tommy 'took pity on us and crawled along to one carriage with some bully beef and bread'.[16] The sisters greatly appreciated this act of kindness. Arriving at No. 20 British General Hospital at Etaples, Annie felt homesick, but 'when we got to one ward to find all Australian boys as patients we immediately felt at home.'

Further south, at the port of Le Havre, Pearl Corkhill was sent to No. 2 British General Hospital. There was nothing much to see but ships coming and going, and the weather was always rough and windy. Like Alice Ross King and Annie Shadforth, she could not wait to get back to 'our own hospital and amongst our boys'.

Some of them came in here about a week ago, also some New Zealanders which [sic] are the same as the Australians to us and they look on us in the same way as the Australian lads do. When I saw our boys coming in I went and spoke to each one, as soon as they saw I was an Australian they were delighted, said in their wildest imaginations they never expected to be greeted by an Australian sister in this hospital. There are no boys like our boys. Even the Canadians are pleased to see us and look upon us as more like friends than the English, and the South Africans always give us a big broad smile.[17]

At Marseilles, Olive Haynes made her home in an army bell tent with 'Pete' Peters. Elsie Eglinton was in a tent nearby. Working alongside English sisters and Indian orderlies, they staffed a temporary hospital in a large château, but none of No. 2 Australian General Hospital's staff was happy to be staying in the Mediterranean port. Olive and Pete's first day's rations consisted of a tin of bully beef and a loaf of bread. Without plates, they did as best they could. 'We managed, too, I can tell you, as we were pretty hungry.'[18] They considered themselves lucky to have a tin of raspberry jam. They soon found food 'frightfully dear . . . I suppose it is on account of the war and they see us coming'. It made Olive homesick. 'I haven't seen a place anywhere, so far, that is a quarter as nice as Australia. I am not a bit keen on getting to England. It couldn't be as nice. The boys all say the same— "Australia'll do me."'[19]

The boys also loved Olive's gramophone. She had to promise it days ahead to the different huts and tents. 'They start it going the minute they awake and never stop until they have to. I am going to try and get some more records when I next go into Marseilles.'[20] The gramophone and her primus, on which she occasionally cooked an Irish stew, were Olive's two most valued possessions. Olive and Pete grew accustomed to their tents and were initially unhappy about being ordered to move to a hut. But they soon realised they would be more comfortable, and began by pinning postcards and photos to the wall and making red curtains. A Tommy made them a table out of a box, and they covered it with an oilcloth. As well as the primus, they had plates and cups, and paid an Indian a rupee twice a week to scrub the floor. Olive went into town, bought some food, and invited four colleagues to a Good Friday supper. 'We had cold ham and new potatoes and asparagus and cherry jam and bread and tea. It was a fine party (a pay-day one).'[21]

Good Friday and Easter passed quietly, but the first anniversary of the Anzac landing at Gallipoli was approaching. Australians and New Zealanders everywhere were focused on the date that marked the birth of the Anzac legend. Memories were still fresh. The first official Anzac Day brought ceremonies and services around Australia. In Sydney, wounded soldiers from Gallipoli, attended by nurses, were driven through the streets in a convoy of cars. In London, more than 2000 Australian and New Zealand troops marched through the streets to the cheers of tens of thousands of people. The crowds answered sustained cries of 'coo-ee' from the Anzacs with a reciprocal 'Ay!' according to *Kai Tiaki*.[22] A London newspaper head-line dubbed them 'THE KNIGHTS OF GALLIPOLI'. A sister from Wellington noted that the New Zealand High Commissioner in London arranged for ten of the country's Army nurses to attend the Anzac Memorial Service at Westminster Abbey, at which the King and Queen were present. 'It was a day never to be forgotten. The Londoners gave the boys a splendid welcome.'[23]

En route back to Egypt, Kath King noted, 'Fancy Anzac Day, one whole year, what a lot has happened. We kept it up fairly. Had an Anzac menu for dinner.'[24] At the Australian camp in Cairo, a sports day was held, followed by a concert at night. Sister Anne Donnell did not approve of the celebra-tions and instead went with several others to a memorial service in the Anzac Hostel in Cairo, conducted by the Bishop of Jerusalem. The large auditorium was packed, and the walls were a mass of flowers grouped in wreaths and crosses, with Allied flags hanging from the walls. An orchestra played the Dead March and the Last Post. Chaplains spoke, and Kipling's

Recessional was sung, its final line destined to live down the ages in Australia and New Zealand:

> God of our fathers, known of old,
> Lord of our far-flung battle-line,
> Beneath whose awful Hand we hold
> Dominion over palm and pine—
> Lord God of Hosts, be with us yet,
> Lest we forget—lest we forget!

Anne glanced up at the gallery and 'saw one young laddie in khaki quite overcome . . . Yet, sad as it all was, one came away with the feeling of being drawn much nearer to those who had given their lives twelve months ago, and that they were the richer by far, and that their deeds will live and be a lesson for all time.'[25] Sister May Tilton attended the same service. She found it 'inexpressibly moving . . . Some of the men near me were sobbing. The landing of 1915 had been a much easier thing for them than this first service in commemoration of it. Most of them, broken in health, remembered only too vividly. During that short but touching address was one of life's terrible moments when no man dared look into another man's eyes.'[26] A sombre procession of a thousand Australian soldiers behind ambulances full of flowers marched to the Cairo Cemetery, where wreaths were placed on the graves of 500 Australian sons.

At Le Havre, Pearl Corkhill and two of her colleagues were determined to commemorate the occasion.

So we bought cigarettes and matches and made up little parcels and tied them with red white and blue ribbon and wrote on the outside, 'Anzac Day April 25th. From 3 Aust. Sisters' and gave one to each of our boys (and the NZ we consider them ours also). They were pleased, they could scarcely thank us. Luckily we each had a green

Australian gum leaf with Dardanelles 1915 on it, and we wore them on our capes. Of course they caused some comments from the other sisters here who hardly knew what Anzac day was. We knew and our boys knew so that was all we cared.[27]

Pearl Corkhill understood the poignancy of the moment, and the deep impact that the events at Gallipoli a year earlier had had on the psyche of Australians and New Zealanders. A tradition had begun.

# 19

# WAITING FOR HARRY

Major Gordon Carter marked 11 June 1916 in his diary with two crosses. Still in Cairo awaiting transfer to France, he clearly thought it an auspicious day. Over the past month he had resumed his courtship of Kath King now that she and her sister Wynne were back in Cairo. On her arrival, he picked her up in a taxi and they drove to Shepheard's, where they had a 'glorious' dinner. They drank champagne and later went out for a little 'sphinxing'. These were heady days, and over the next few weeks their romance flourished. By early June they were inseparable, strolling among the flame-coloured poinciana trees at the zoo, or dining at Shepheard's and taking moonlight drives to the Pyramids. Gordon was building up to a proposal of marriage. But before he could make it, there was a problem—his teeth were giving him trouble. How could he propose with a toothache?

His teeth fixed, a relieved Gordon 'called for Sister King and took her to lunch at Shepheard's'.[1] In the previous fifteen months they had shared the Gallipoli experience. It had been harrowing for both, but it had become part of the bond between them. 'And then he proposed to me,' an excited Kath wrote in her diary. 'Accepted.' As if to reassure herself that it was true, she added: 'Became engaged to Gordon.'[2]

They filled in 'a very nice afternoon' collecting photos before returning to Shepheard's for afternoon tea. Later, Gordon caught the train back to camp at Ismailia and reflected on the day in his own diary. 'Became engaged to Sister King during the afternoon but can't say that I felt myself any violently different person as a result (such as one might expect). Things seemed to go on quite normally. I don't think either Kathleen or myself quite realise what we are in for but we decided to leave things in abeyance 'till European affairs got more settled. Then we would think of ours.'[3] Gordon was ever the realist. He was also proper; only now did he begin referring to Kath by her Christian name.

Eight days later, Gordon left Alexandria for France and the Western Front, no doubt hoping that 'European affairs' would be settled quickly so he and Kath could get on with their lives. Shortly after, Kath and Wynne were among fifty reserve sisters who set sail for England to work at the 2000-bed Netley military hospital in Hampshire. Not until October would Gordon, on leave from France, be able to present Kath with a 'bonzer engagement ring'.

Alice Ross King, too, had her fiancé on her mind. Because of the secrecy surrounding troop movements she had not seen Harry Moffitt since 14 February. Now she was one of seventy Australian nurses in Rouen, and the workload should have given her little time to think of anything else. But she did, alternating between yearning for Harry and worrying about him. She waited anxiously for his letters, not even knowing whether he was still in Egypt. Harry's May 3 birthday came and went. Still no news.

As the large convoys of wounded rolled in and the days became busier in the tents and Nissen huts that covered the Rouen racecourse, there were touches of humanity that uplifted her heart. 'A wonderful packet of old linen from Penzance Red Cross. Beautiful fine linen sheets cut to large hand-kerchief size. Scented with lavender. Such a boon! Poor old gas gangrene patients can have their sweating faces wiped.'[4] This was the smallest mercy for men with flesh-rotting infections for which there was no effective antiserum until 1918. Gas gangrene bloated the tissues around a wound with gas and, if the limb was not amputated, led to shock, kidney failure and death. Hundreds of thousands of soldiers died of gas gangrene during the war.

One day the British Director-General of Medical Services arrived for a ward inspection. Alice's tents were the first on his itinerary. She was disgruntled: the officer 'tried to give me the "glad eye" . . . So marked was it that even the [officer commanding] and the patients spoke of it afterwards.'[5] She found English doctors, matrons and nurses difficult. 'I hate the English. Loathe them. They are treating our men disgustingly.'[6] Shortly afterwards, the epileptic Princess Victoria visited. The staff made no special preparations but learned later that they had been expected to do so. 'The princess gave out penny boxes of cigarettes, the English boys were very disgusted but the Australians were only disappointed because she did not take a fit.'[7] Black humour and irreverence had not deserted them.

Alice decided to give her patients a treat, taking four of them by taxi for a picnic in the forest, eight kilometres from the hospital. It was the first time they had been out for two months. She bought a strawberry tart, cakes and ox tongue, as well as two bottles of light wine. When she got back there was a letter from Harry. She could hardly contain her excitement and relief. 'Such joy. Only two weeks old it is. He is adjutant of the 53rd Battalion and will shortly be over in France. My love for him is enormous.'[8] But letters from Harry were rare; Alice feared they often went astray. As May ended, she noted in her diary, 'No letters. It's very few I've had from Harry although I know that he has often written. How I love that boy!'[9]

The plight of the wounded, and their struggle to survive, touched Alice. A Tommy was admitted with a fractured spine, the bullet still embedded. He was only twenty-five and had married two days before returning from England on his last leave. He was now a paraplegic. Among the many letters she was writing to families, Alice wrote to his wife to give her the news. Then there was the seventeen-year-old who had been wounded in seven places.

'The little Irish boy with his leg off is a fowl plucker in private life and is delighted that his foot is gone because now he won't have to return to the trenches and he may not be inconvenienced in his work by a missing limb.'[10] A soldier with gas gangrene had to be operated on immediately. 'His leg is in a fearful mess, he is also shot through the lung and in the head . . . I'm afraid he is dying.'[11] He had a photograph of his wife and 'wee baby girl'. Alice was struck by his sweet eyes. He died that night. And then there was Harry. She couldn't get him out of her mind. Alice hoped he was on his way to France. Her love for him helped her cope with the enormity of the suffering and death around her. He represented hope.

The pace of events was quickening. On 7 June she heard that the Allies' war supremo, Lord Kitchener, had drowned two days earlier when the HMS *Hampshire* was torpedoed. No one wanted to believe it, so overwhelming was the news. A rumour began the same day that the Germans had broken through the line at Ypres, 200 kilometres to the north. Alice was unsure. 'Certainly the guns were much nearer and clearer last night. But they may be our own guns.' Nonetheless, orders were given to evacuate patients as fast as possible. 'How terrible it all is. I comforted myself tonight by developing some prints of Harry. How I long to know that he is safe.'[12] Two days later she heard that Harry's brigade was in England. 'My heart is very sorrowful when I think of him.' The Germans, she noted, had apparently had some successes at Ypres. She wrote to Harry that night, only to hear the next day that his brigade was not in England after all.

Another case touched her. A seventeen-year-old American had run away to join up in England and was now badly wounded. The pain was worsened by his circumstances.

His father and mother divorced. He said they would not miss him. A kitten from the Q store wandered into the ward. He asked if he could have it. I let him have it on his bed. He has lost both feet and one leg has gas gangrene. I don't think he will recover. I asked him if he liked cats and he said, 'YES! They used to call me "Tom" when I was little because I always brought home stray cats.'[13]

Her 'little American boy' died four nights later.

Alice heard that Harry had been in France for two weeks. Then a cable came saying that he was still in Egypt, at Ismailia. It read simply, '53rd Battn. Greatest love.' Her relief was palpable. 'How different I am tonight. My heart is overflowing with joy and love. This man has all my inmost soul. Thank God for his great goodness to me. Harry is just all I admire in a man. I adore all his shortcomings.'[14] But deep down something still troubled her. Perhaps it was an unconscious self-protective instinct reminding her that in war nothing was certain, and that love alone might not be enough. 'I wonder if I shall have him with me. I don't know if I want to marry him—but there is no doubt about my love.'[15] The cable kept her feeling warm for another day, and she kept it close by all the time. Despite her hesitations about marriage, she was increasingly certain she wanted to be with Harry. But that didn't stop her from looking at others. A certain captain came to say goodbye and waxed sentimental. 'I like him, but my good old times are past. Bother Harry! 'Tis strange how one changes. All men have to stand beside my beloved and they are not worth talking to then.'[16]

The sisters and their patients could hear the guns in the distance every night now. As the injured continued to arrive by convoy, and friends were farewelled to the front line, it was announced that the hospital would expand to 2000 beds. A new sitting-room tent was opened, complete with furniture hand made out of boxes and other odds and ends. The nurses went to some trouble to give their utilitarian living quarters a touch of home. 'The girls all brought home plants in full bloom and so we startled the community by suddenly having a beautiful garden blooming where only grass was to be seen the day before,' Alice wrote proudly.[17] They tried to live as normally as circumstances would allow by picnicking at Forêt Etienne, a beautiful old orchard filled with wild foxgloves. Incongruously, as they drank tea and ate tarts, the cavalry drilled among the trees.

Towards the end of June, a letter from Harry arrived. It was nearly four weeks old, and full of reaffirmation of their relationship. Alice was overjoyed. 'It is full of love and I'm so happy.'[18] As June ended, a wire came saying he was coming through Rouen with the 5th Division. Harry's 53rd Battalion had left Alexandria on the same day as Gordon Carter, who some weeks earlier had transferred from the 53rd to the 5th Pioneer Battalion. Harry had finally arrived in Marseilles from Alexandria on 28 June. Alice was elated. 'He is coming through and I want to see him,' she wrote excitedly.[19] They had not seen each other since that day in Cairo, all those months ago, when they had sat on the piazza at Shepheard's Hotel and Harry had promised to buy her an apricot dress. She rang her friend Major John Prior, who did all in his power to find out when the train was due.

On 1 July Alice went to the railway station and stood there for hours, waiting. Just a glimpse was all she asked for. But there was no sign of Harry. 'All the afternoon I spent on the railway station hoping against hope that I might see Harry come through. But no luck. Major Prior and Capt. Ford were with me and were most good to me.'[20] The disappointment was dreadful, and the strain was beginning to tell. Alice confessed that she was feeling 'fearfully tired out'.

On that day the war took a turn for the worse, for it was the start of the Allied offensive against the Germans aimed at destroying Germany's manpower reserves, and diverting German forces from Verdun. The Battle of the Somme took place in a landscape of rolling downs, woods and meadows, among peaceful streams, canals and picturesque villages. These days, the country is again a picture of bucolic charm, with little trace of the bloodbath that the Somme offensive became when men laden with more than twenty-five kilograms of equipment went 'over the top' of the trenches. One Australian nurse working for the British Red Cross in a casualty clearing station was later moved to describe the sounds from the

Somme this way: 'We could see the Somme River—or, rather, one little bit of it. I was greeted by the sound of the guns—one continuous rumbling, like Coogee, Manly, and all the surfs in a heavy storm rolled into one.'[21] On the first day of the Somme alone, the British Army suffered 57,470 casualties, including 19,240 killed, representing Britain's worst-ever twenty-four hours in battle. Over the next four months, the armies of Britain and its dominions would suffer some 420,000 casualties, including 131,000 dead.

The cost of that first day soon became clear. On Day 2, 20,000 casualties came through Rouen, and hospitals at Boulogne and Le Havre took in thousands more. Because of the appalling numbers, it was only possible to keep and care for the worst of the wounded. The rest went straight to England on hospital ships. English war correspondent Philip Gibbs visited the hospital at Corbie, near Amiens, christened the 'Butcher's Shop' by a colonel of the Royal Army Medical Corps who invited Gibbs to have a look. The correspondent found himself 'trembling in a queer way'. What he saw sickened him.

In one long, narrow room there were about thirty beds, and in each bed lay a young British soldier or part of a young British soldier. There was not much left of one of them. Both his legs had been amputated to the thigh and both his arms to the shoulder-blades . . . another case of the same kind; one leg gone and the other going, and one arm . . . I spoke to that man. He was quite conscious, with bright eyes. His right leg was uncovered, and supported on a board hung from the ceiling. Its flesh was like that of a chicken badly carved—white, flabby, and in tatters. In bed after bed I saw men of ours, very young men, who had been lopped of limbs a few hours ago or a few minutes, some of them unconscious, some of them strangely and terribly conscious, with a look in their eyes as though staring at the death which sat near to them, and edged nearer.[22]

Trains were commandeered and the wounded were brought in by any means possible. One of the sisters doing train duty was Annie Shadforth, who had 'heard the great barrage' that announced the opening of the battle. Annie had a busy time collecting patients from various casualty clearing stations and unloading them at the different base hospitals, on each trip carrying between 500 and 600 patients. This went on for a fortnight. At the Gazencourt clearing station, she found the grounds, as well as the tents, packed 'and ambulance cars and a small train almost like a toy train bringing in more'.

A guard had to be placed all around the train as the poor boys were so anxious to get away from it all back to the base and perhaps further on to Blighty. But the ones there were wounded badly [and] had to have the first attention and these patients were put on the trains before less severe wounds. We had a good many deaths during that time on the train although if we noticed a patient not [doing] very well the [commanding officer] had the train pull up at a station at the nearest point to a hospital and the patient taken off there.[23]

On one shift alone, Alice Ross King reported 500 admissions to her ward. 'I have one man who is quite mad. He got into the 4th line of German trenches and went to take some prisoners. They cried mercy and while he hesitated one threw a bomb right into his face. The fire enveloped him and he says he lay there grovelling in the earth. For two days he was not picked up and today when we took his dressings down his eyesight was not gone. He wept for joy.'[24]

The sight and sounds of the wounded were heartbreaking. 'Nearly all the boys are a bit mad and they all talk nonsense,' Alice observed. 'One beautiful fair haired boy who had his leg off yesterday was crying wildly, "Bulldog breed sister. Boys of the Bulldog breed. We mustn't let them beat us sister." It's very pathetic.'[25] Going to church, Alice was distracted. She found she 'could not get into sympathy' with the organ. Emerging, she ran into four 5th Division artillery officers, whose train had arrived at 8 a.m. and was not leaving until 4 p.m. 'To think that Harry had not had that luck!' she lamented. 'All day long my thoughts have been with him but I have had no letter. I cannot think that he would so neglect writing to me if he really cared for me. Still it is a blow.'[26] Try as she might, she could not hide her disappointment and frustration at not seeing Harry.

Alice's mood had changed from those early carefree days in Cairo where she was free to play the field and flirt. Now she had a man she dearly loved and feared losing. Two days later a letter finally arrived from Harry. 'It has taken 10 days to come, but it is one full of love and all my confidence is renewed.'[27] That same day a convoy of badly wounded soldiers arrived. The men were infested with lice. All had been lying out in the open for between six and eight days, in places where stretcher bearers could not get to them. One soldier had stretched out his hand for a water bottle and his wrist had been immediately cut to pieces by a bullet. 'One man says the Germans played the machine guns over the wounded. This man was out for five days without food or water. He was at last rescued when the Scottish regiments took the Germans' front trenches. One man is shot through the bladder and half the perineum shot away. He was rescued by the padre who went out and hauled and pushed and pulled him in.'[28]

Another heavy convoy followed early the next day. One soldier had been shot through both legs and was left lying on the battlefield for three days. Then, while his legs were being bandaged, a shell exploded near him, killing the dresser and wounding the soldier in the chest. He was only eighteen, and 'such a sweet kid', Alice wrote. 'The patients are not only very sick, they are mental and nervous. They were most depressed this afternoon so I got in the gramophone which was much enjoyed.'[29]

People did not yet understand the causes of what is now termed post-traumatic stress disorder, or how caring for these cases of so-called shell shock affected the nurses themselves. By 16 July the wards were full. Alice worked all day as hard as she could. The next day it was the same. The mood in the wards was grim. She was stunned when a patient punched her. 'I was doing a dressing. He was very nervous. When I pulled off some wool that was stuck to the hairs of his leg he screamed and turned on me like a rat and with his hard knuckles gave me a terrific punch.'[30] The war had raged now for two years and physical and emotional reserves among the troops were exhausted. Alice understood this, but she was now struggling to maintain her own equilibrium.

Olive Haynes, a picture of Edwardian innocence, at her 'coming out' pre-1914. Little could she have known the horrors of war she would see just a few years later. (Photo courtesy of Margaret Young)

Elsie Cook sent this photo to her mother to mark her departure on the hospital ship *Kyarra* in December 1914. Years later, Elsie was the first nursing sister to join the RSL. (Photo courtesy of Hartley Cook)

Kath King (left) and her sister, Wynne King, in Orange before the outbreak of war. They both started their training at Orange Hospital. (Photo courtesy of John Carter)

Elsie Cook was one of the first nurses to leave Australia for war service when she sailed from Sydney in December 1914 on the *Kyarra*. These nurses are waiting to board the *Kyarra*, nearly three years later in 1917. (Photo courtesy of the Australian War Memorial PB0518)

With Gallipoli beckoning, Lieutenant Gordon Carter (left) stands on the deck of the troop ship *Minewasaka*. Alongside him are Major William Davidson, Lieutenant William Duchesne and Captain Albert McGuire. By 19 August 1915, he was the only one of the group alive. (Photo courtesy of John Carter)

Australian nursing sisters had to prepare for all eventualities. Here a group of nurses are seen wearing life jackets during a drill on board the hospital ship *Karoola*. (Photo courtesy of the Australian War Memorial PO5382.014)

Time on board ship allowed some moments of normal life for these New Zealand nursing sisters on HMHS *Egypt*. (Photo courtesy of the GT Nevill Collection, Alexander Turnbull Library, Wellington, NZ)

Alice Ross King, wearing her Associate of the Royal Red Cross medal and the Military Medal, arrived in Cairo in 1915 with expectations of a great adventure. (Photo courtesy of Marion Sanders)

The narrow streets of Cairo with their shops selling exotic goods fascinated Alice Ross King, who took this photo. (Photo courtesy of Marion Sanders)

Groppi's was a favoured Cairo restaurant for officers to take nurses to afternoon tea and dinner. (Photo Kath King, courtesy of John King)

Australian nurses enjoyed being tourists while they could. Here a group are on an excursion to ancient Luxor. (Photo Kath King, courtesy of Royal Prince Alfred Hospital Museum)

'The Minx by Spoonlight'. The Sphinx was a favoured attraction for officers to visit with nurses. (Photo courtesy of Margaret Young)

The Minx by Spoonlight.

Officers and nurses socialised whenever opportunity allowed. (Photo Kath King, courtesy of Royal Prince Alfred Hospital Museum)

LEFT: Alice Ross King and Harry Moffitt at the Sphinx. (Courtesy of Marion Sanders)
RIGHT: Alice Ross King photographed her handsome lieutenant, Harry Moffitt, standing astride the Colossus of Ramesses. (Photo courtesy of Marion Sanders)

Alice Ross King was a keen photographer. She took this photo of Australian troops on a route march in the lead-up to the Gallipoli landing. (Photo courtesy of Marion Sanders)

Another photograph from Alice Ross King, this time of a group of Australian soldiers having a breather in the desert near Mena. The officer in the middle is probably Harry Moffitt. (Photo courtesy of Marion Sanders)

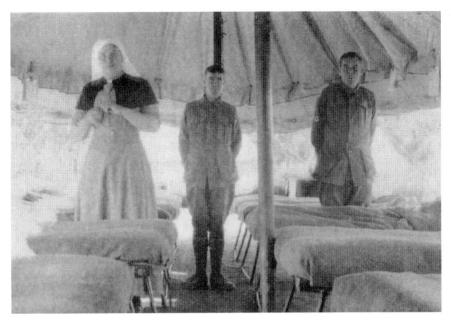

Erected on sand, the hospital tents in Mena were open to the elements. (Photo Kath King, courtesy of the Royal Prince Alfred Hospital Museum)

Kath King (second from left) with doctors and fellow nurses on board the *Sicilia*. It was from here that she watched the battle for Gallipoli. (Photo courtesy of John Carter)

Wounded soldiers were moved by flat-bottomed barges from Gallipoli to hospital ships waiting off Anzac Cove. (Photo courtesy of the Australian War Memorial A02740)

They were then hoisted on board in a specially made wooden cradle. (Photo courtesy of the Australian War Memorial C02277)

Wounded soldiers were then either transported to Army hospitals on Lemnos or in Egypt. Here a nurse supervises the unloading of wounded soldiers from a hospital ship docked at Alexandria. (Photo courtesy of the Australian War Memorial H00828)

Australian hospitals in Egypt weren't prepared for the rush of wounded from Gallipoli. Here, at No. 2 Australian General Hospital at Mena House, Olive Haynes photographed the wounded sleeping on the roof on 1 May 1915. (Photo courtesy of Margaret Young)

Olive Haynes (right) enjoying a moment off-duty with fellow nurses. (Photo courtesy of Margaret Young)

Wounded Australian troops recover in an ornately decorated makeshift ward at No.1 Australian General Hospital in the Heliopolis Palace Hotel. (Photo courtesy of the Australian War Memorial H18486)

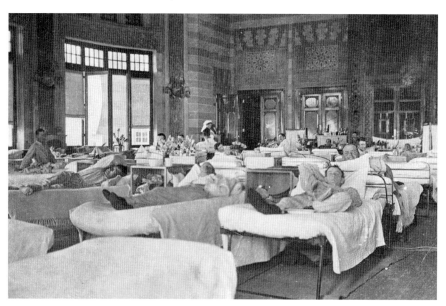

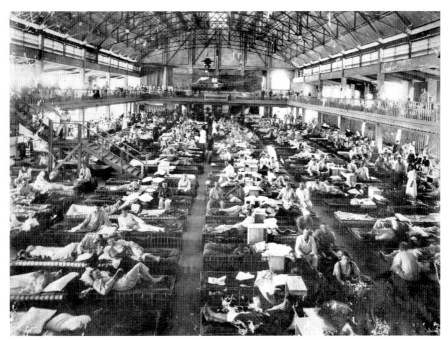

The skating rink at Luna Park was used by No. 1 Australian Auxiliary Hospital to help cope with the overflow of wounded. Here they lie on beds made of palm wood. The crowded wards were a challenge for the nursing sisters. However, conditions would only get more difficult as the war progressed. (Photo courtesy of the Australian War Memorial P01350.013)

A group of unidentified spectators at a sports meeting held by No. 3 Australian Auxiliary Hospital in the grounds of the Heliopolis Sporting Club. As an indication of how the sisters became avid photographers, three of them hold cameras. (Photo courtesy of the Australian War Memorial C00360)

Nurses of No. 2 Australian General Hospital, Ghezireh Palace, waiting for another group photograph. On one such occasion Alice Ross King was so annoyed at being ordered out of bed after night duty, and kept standing for ninety minutes, that she sat down with her back to the camera. (Photo courtesy of the Australian War Memorial J06857)

The nursing sisters liked to keep active when off duty. Here, sisters at No. 3 Australian General Hospital at Abbassia, near Cairo, line up for a donkey race at a sports meeting. (Photo courtesy of the Australian War Memorial J01748)

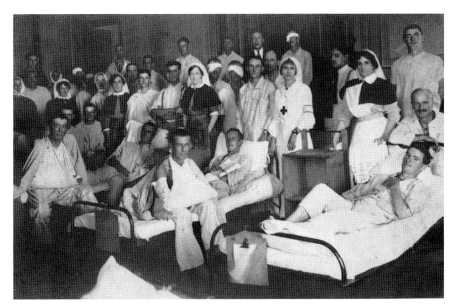

A ward at No. 2 Australian General Hospital at Ghezireh Palace. Soldiers returned from Gallipoli with horrific injuries. Gangrene and amputations were common, leaving men crippled and challenging the professional detachment of the sisters. (Photo courtesy of the Australian War Memorial P00152.009)

The eyes of the soldier on the right, recovering from a head wound at No. 1 Australian General Hospital at Heliopolis, reflect the horror of Gallipoli. (Photo courtesy of the Australian War Memorial P00229.010)

Picnics were a popular escape. Here, at Spinney Wood, Ismailia, Australian officers and nurses enjoy time away from the wards and the battlefields. (Photo courtesy of the Australian War Memorial J05885)

On the first Anzac Day in Cairo, Australian soldiers and nurses visited graves of fallen comrades to lay wreaths and bouquets after attending a memorial service and marching through the city streets. In the foreground is the grave of Sister Norma Violet Mowbray of the Australian Army Nursing Service, who died of pneumonia on 21 January 1916. (Photo courtesy of the Australian War Memorial C01794)

Time away from the demands of the wards was precious. Here, Sister Ada Smith of No.2 Australian General Hospital relaxes in a housecoat on a balcony at Mena House, where the hospital was located. (Photo courtesy of the Australian War Memorial P00156.025)

It was common for Australian units to use animals as mascots. Here, a sister at No.3 Australian General Hospital, Abbassia, holds a koala as she stands outside with patients. (Photo courtesy of the Australian War Memorial J01714)

With the number of casualties outstripping expectations, the entertainment venue Luna Park was secured for the expansion of No.1 General Hospital. This group of Australian nurses enjoy some respite away from the pandemonium of the overcrowded wards inside. (Photo courtesy of the Australian War Memorial C05290)

Despite the circumstances, nursing sisters in Egypt tried to make Christmas Day 1915 special by decorating the mess room. (Photo courtesy of Iain McInnes)

Sister Nell Pike (right) with Sister Ruby Dickinson, who later died of Spanish flu in England. (Photo courtesy of Patricia Williams and Daphne Tongue)

Sister Nell Pike (back row, right) enjoying a dip at Alexandria, 1916. (Photo courtesy of Patricia Williams and Daphne Tongue)

Nurses endured primitive conditions, as shown by this photo of a group hand washing clothes in tubs outside their tent quarters at the 60th General Hospital, Hortiach, near Salonika. (Photo courtesy of the Australian War Memorial C04337)

Lottie Le Gallais and her ship-board orderlies. In the face of daily despair, they managed smiles on this occasion. (Photo courtesy of Auckland War Memorial Museum, PH95-2)

Sister May Tilton served in Egypt and then in France. Her experiences on the Western Front left her physically and emotionally battered. (Photo courtesy of Judy Dyer)

Lieutenant Harry Moffitt returned from Gallipoli like many of his fellow Anzacs suffering from dysentery and jaundice. Alice Ross King watched over his recuperation, the couple taking day trips from Cairo as they waited to be sent to France. (Photo courtesy of Marion Sanders)

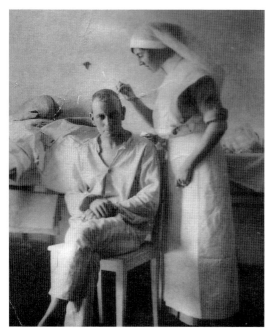

Elsie Cook tends the head wound her husband Syd received at Gallipoli. (Photo courtesy of Hartley Cook)

Elsie and Syd Cook, his head still bandaged from the gunshot wound that would leave a permanent groove on his scalp. (Photo courtesy of Hartley Cook)

Kath King (right) and her sister Wynne (centre) aboard the troop ship *Euripidies* returning to Egypt in May 1916. The inscription on the back reads: 'This will remind you of your two daughters. It is so nice to be together. Only hope we will continue. Sister Brown is the other sister with us. Love Wynne 15.5.16. Have not heard from Tom yet'. (Photo courtesy of John Carter)

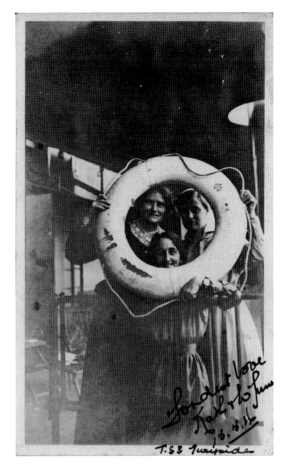

Nurses of the Australian Army Nursing Service share a meal with wounded Australian soldiers aboard the Australian hospital ship *Karoola* while returning to Australia. Nearly all of the men have eye or faciomaxillary injuries. Sister Elsie Eglinton made one such trip on the *Karoola* before returning to the war. (Photo courtesy of the Australian War Memorial P01667.002)

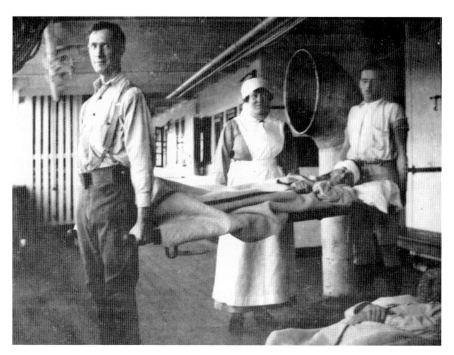

The demands of nursing the wounded did not end once soldiers were evacuated back to Australia. Here a patient is being carried to the operating theatre aboard the Australian hospital ship *Karoola*. (Courtesy of the Australian War Memorial H15309)

Nurses from No. 2 Australian General Hospital at the Cairo railway station waiting to leave for Alexandria on their way to France. They travelled with very little luggage. (Photo courtesy of the Australian War Memorial P00156.043)

Nurses of No. 3 Australian General Hospital behind their matron, Grace Wilson, and second in command of the hospital, Lieutenant Colonel J.A. Dick, ready to follow a piper into their camp at Mudros West, Lemnos. (Photo courtesy of the Australian War Memorial A04118)

Inside the laboratory on Lemnos, the Aegean island just five hours by sea from Gallipoli, where conditions were among the worst endured by nurses during the war. (Photo courtesy of Margaret Young)

Life on Lemnos was one of weather extremes. Here, Sister Evelyn (Tev) Davies looks 'tragic' in winter clothing. (Photo courtesy of the Australian War Memorial A05374)

While the weather was warm, sisters from No. 3 Australian General Hospital would take early morning dips in Mudros Harbour. (Photo courtesy of the Australian War Memorial P01480.002)

There were also moments for socialising. Sisters from No. 3 Australian General Hospital with naval officers on the deck of a destroyer in Mudros Harbour. The privations experienced by nurses ashore weren't shared by the British naval officers aboard ship. (Photo courtesy of the Australian War Memorial P01480.001)

And there was time for romance on Lemnos. Sister Clarice Daley walks through an arch of drawn bayonets after her marriage to 1st Light Horse Sergeant Ernest Lawrence in 1915. (Photo courtesy of the Australian War Memorial P01360.001)

Sisters from the 3rd Australian General Hospital on Lemnos with their patients. In summer, conditions were dusty and dry. (Photo courtesy of the Australian War Memorial J01438)

The tent wards on Lemnos, which were impossible to keep warm in winter and sand- and dirt-free in summer, made for very difficult nursing. (Photo courtesy of the Australian War Memorial J01446)

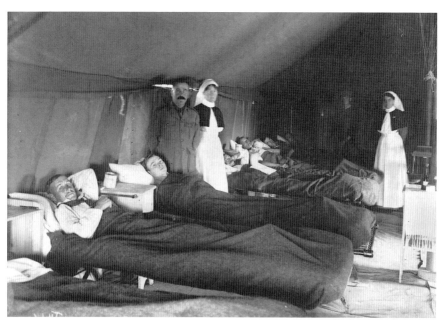

Sick Australian sisters convalescing along the tent lines of No. 3 Australian General Hospital at Mudros. Painted rocks mark the edge of the tent surrounds and hospital paths. (Photo courtesy of the Australian War Memorial J01455)

Huddled against the elements, nurses from No. 3 Australian General Hospital, Lemnos, wait on a barge for their transfer to Egypt. (Photo courtesy of the Australian War Memorial J01510)

LEFT: New Zealand Matron Marie Cameron survived the *Marquette* disaster, but was an invalid for the rest of her life. (Photo courtesy of Judy Bailey) RIGHT: New Zealand Sister Edith (Poppy) Popplewell, at the Walton-on-Thames Hospital, the No.2 New Zealand General Hospital. A survivor of the *Marquette* sinking, she clung to wreckage for several hours before being rescued. (Photo courtesy of Sherayl McNabb)

New Zealand nurses who survived the *Marquette* tragedy aboard the hospital ship *Grantully Castle* in Salonika. (Photo courtesy of Kippenberger Military Archive and Research Library)

The New Zealand nurses who died when the *Marquette* was torpedoed (from top left to right): Mary Gorman, Nora Hildyard, Mabel Jamieson, Mary Rae, Lorna Rattray, Margaret Rogers, Marion Brown, Helena Isdell, Catherine Fox, Isabel Clark. (Photos courtesy of Sheryl McNabb)

On their way to work in French
hospitals, and accompanied
by their French teacher, the
twenty Australian Red Cross
nurses known as the Bluebirds
aboard No. 2 Australian hospital
ship *Kanowna*. Included in the
group were Elsie Cook (third
row, third from the left), Hilda
Loxton (third row, far right),
Fraser Thompson (second row,
second from the left) and Nellie
Crommelin (front row left).
(Photo courtesy of the Australian
War Memorial P02628.001)

Sister Ada Smith of No.2
Australian Casualty Clearing
Station stands at the entrance of
the tent that was her home for
some months at Trois Arbres,
near Steenwerck. (Photo courtesy
of the Australian War Memorial
P00156.058)

The Anzac Angel at work.

To many of the wounded soldiers, the nurses represented a role beyond that of just physical care. That sentiment is captured here in a pencil sketch from the wartime autograph book Sister Ida Moore kept in France. (Courtesy of Iain McInnis)

Sister Olive Haynes was stationed at No. 13 Stationary Hospital at Boulogne caring for wounded troops such as this man. 'Both his arms are wounded, his chest and head, and he is all slung up, and a man came and took this photo one day. He thought he looked so cute smoking with all that,' she wrote to her mother. (Photo courtesy of Margaret Young)

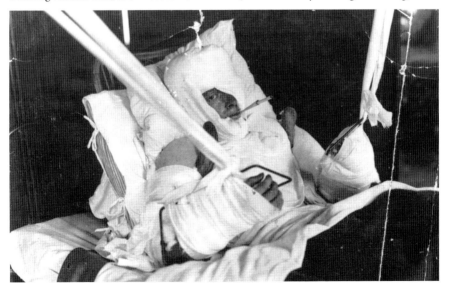

Sister Olive Haynes (left) and her friend, Sister 'Pete' Peters, about to go on leave at Boulogne. (Photo courtesy of Margaret Young)

Sister Kath King (third from right) on her wedding on 31 January 1917. Regulations required her to resign from the Australian Army Nursing Service because she was to be married. Gordon Carter (second from right) had just been promoted to Lieutenant Colonel. (Photo courtesy of John Carter)

New Zealand nurses and medical officers at the New Zealand Stationary Hospital, Wisques, France. The camp was entered through an elaborately carved traditional Maori gateway. (Photo courtesy of the Royal New Zealand Returned and Services' Association Collection, the Alexander Turnbull Library, Wellington, NZ, G-13478-1/2)

Four New Zealand nurses look out of the windows of their hut, 'The PoppInn', at the New Zealand Stationary Hospital at Wisques. New Zealand nurses, like their Australian colleagues, tried valiantly to make their accommodation as homely as possible. (Photo courtesy of the Royal New Zealand Returned and Services' Association Collection, the Alexander Turnbull Library, Wellington, NZ, G-013482-1/2)

Inside the nurses' mess hut at the New Zealand Stationary Hospital, Wisques. (Photo courtesy of the Royal New Zealand Returned and Services' Association Collection, the Alexander Turnbull Library, Wellington, NZ, G-013472-1/2)

Inside the sisters' lounge at the New Zealand Stationary Hospital, Wisques. (Photo courtesy of the Royal New Zealand Returned and Services' Association Collection, the Alexander Turnbull Library, Wellington, NZ, G-013483-1/2)

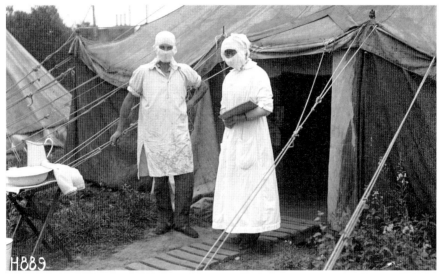

A New Zealand nurse and orderly outside the diphtheria ward, New Zealand Stationary Hospital, Wisques. So contagious was diphtheria that it was a problem throughout the war. (Photo courtesy of the Royal New Zealand Returned and Services' Association Collection, the Alexander Turnbull Library, Wellington, NZ, G-013466-1/2)

Bluebirds helped staff a mobile hospital established by a rich American woman, Mrs Bordern Turner, to operate behind the lines on the Western Front. Here, Sisters Hilda Loxton (back left), Lynette Crozier (front, second right), Helen Wallace (front, third right) and Minnie Hough (far right) stand outside one of the hospital buildings in 1917. (Photo courtesy of the Australian War Memorial P01908.007)

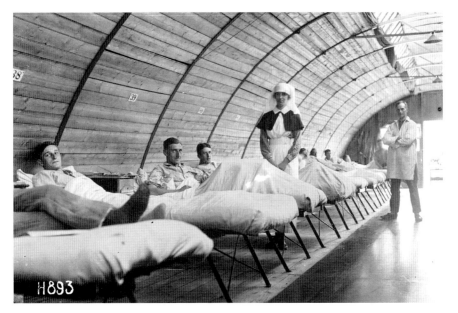

Nurses and patients at the New Zealand Stationary Hospital, Wisques. Once they reached a stationary hospital, the wounded troops received more permanent care than was available in advanced or casualty clearing stations. (Courtesy of the Royal New Zealand Returned and Services' Association Collection, the Alexander Turnbull Library, Wellington, NZ, G-13470-1/2)

With the Battle of Fromelles imminent, Lieutenant Harry Moffitt hurriedly wrote this letter to his sweetheart, Sister Alice Ross King. (Courtesy of Marion Sanders)

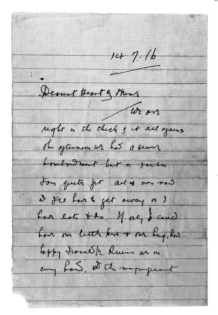

An advanced dressing station, the Ypres Salient, the Western Front, 19 October 1917.
A wounded soldier lies on a stretcher on the muddy ground, while his compatriots gather
around an ambulance. The wounded were treated here straight from the battlefield,
before going on to casualty clearing stations. (Photo courtesy of the Royal New Zealand
Returned and Services' Association Collection, the Alexander Turnbull Library,
Wellington, NZ, G-012928-1/2)

A graphic example of the horrific wounds troops suffered and that doctors and nurses had
to deal with. Here, a French surgeon and an English nurse working with the Australian
Bluebirds study the sutured leg of a wounded French soldier. (Photo courtesy of the
Australian War Memorial P01908.026)

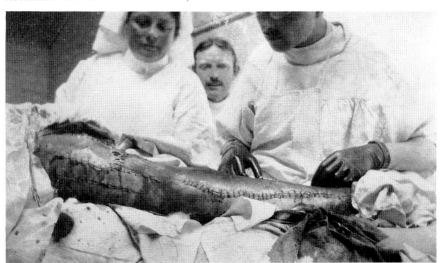

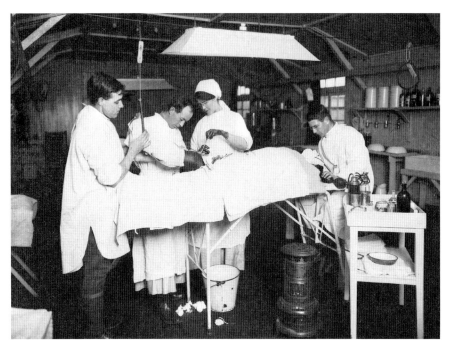

An operating theatre of the 1st Australian Casualty Clearing Station. Surgeons and nurses made do with what they had. Note the bucket for waste underneath the operating bed and the heater to its side. (Photo courtesy of the Australian War Memorial E01304)

Bluebird sister, Dorothy Duffy, is seen here acting as an anaesthetist while a surgeon and his assistant operate at French Hospital No. 46 at Beziers on 20 March 1918. (Photo courtesy of the Australian War Memorial P02298.008)

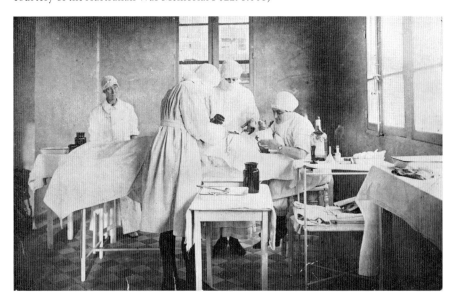

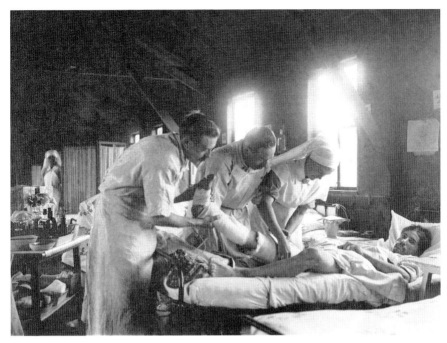

Sister Lynette Crozier and a medical orderly apply a dressing to the leg of a wounded French soldier at a mobile hospital established by Mrs Borden Turner south-west of Amiens. (Photo courtesy of the Australian War Memorial P01790.001)

Sisters Annie Shadforth (left) and Margaret Nisbet (centre) standing in the acute surgical ward at the 1st Australian General Hospital, Rouen, France. The tall beds on the right were for the elevation of limbs. (Photo courtesy of Des Ryan)

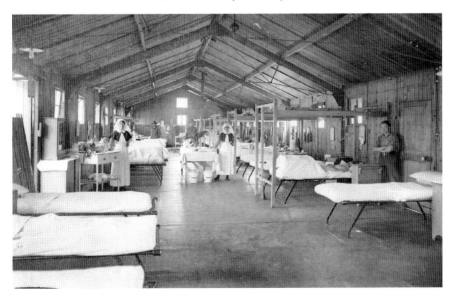

Bluebird, Sister Minnie Hough, poses wearing a gas mask — an apparatus that became all too common for nurses in France. (Photo courtesy of the Australian War Memorial P01908.017)

Matron Ida O'Dwyer, wearing her service medals. After enlisting on 21 November 1914, she served in Egypt, in England where she was in charge of the Nurses' Hospital in London, and in France where she was the Head Sister of No.3 Australian Casualty Clearing Station. One of her duties was to write letters to the mothers of men who had died. (Photo courtesy of the Australian War Memorial P00848.002.)

Bluebird, Sister Hilda Loxton (third from left), familiarises herself with a slit trench in the grounds of a French military hospital during a visit to Essay in 1917. (Photo courtesy of the Australian War Memorial P01790.002)

Two nurses from No. 2 Australian General Hospital at Wimeraux, France, stand at the entrance to the nurses' dugout. The hospital experienced many air raids. (Photo courtesy of the Australian War Memorial H04152)

Just how close nurses often were to bombing raids is underlined by the devastation shown here of a Red Cross hospital at Etaples, which was destroyed by German bombs. The raid killed several patients and nurses. (Photo courtesy of the Australian War Memorial H09726)

LEFT: Pearl Corkhill was awarded the Military Medal for her bravery during a German bombing raid on a British casualty clearing station at Longvillers in the Somme on 19 July 1918. (Photo courtesy of the Australian War Memorial, A04728) RIGHT: Sister Rachel Pratt, wearing the Military Medal awarded to her for bravery during a German air raid on No. 1 Australian Casualty Clearing Station at Bailleul on the night of 3–4 July 1917. Injured by an exploding bomb, she continued to nurse a patient. (Photo courtesy of the Australian War Memorial, P05664.001)

July 12 was a big day for Elsie Cook, Fraser Thompson, Frida Warner and Fanny Harris for it was the occasion when they were presented to King George V at a sports day at Henencourt. Elsie is probably the nurse on the left. (Photo courtesy of the Australian War Memorial EZ0153)

On 9 July 1917, Queen Mary visited the No. 1 Australian General Hospital at Rouen. She was accompanied through a guard of honour of Australian Army nurses by the hospital's commanding officer, Colonel Trent Champion de Crespigny. (Photo courtesy of the Australian War Memorial K00019)

Sister Nell Pike of the Australian Army Nursing Service nursed at Abbassia in Egypt, on the island of Lemnos, in France and finally in England where she married Lieutenant Charles Laffin on 28 September 1917. (Photo courtesy of Patricia Williams and Daphne Tongue)

An intercessional service commemorating the fourth anniversary of World War I, Etaples, France, 4 August 1918. A large contingent of nurses attended the service, standing with the troops among the graves of the fallen. (Photo courtesy of the Royal New Zealand Returned and Services' Association Collection, the Alexander Turnbull Library, Wellington, NZ,G-013757-1/2)

A wounded New Zealand soldier talks to a New Zealand nurse at a garden party in the grounds of the New Zealand Stationary Hospital probably at Hazebrouck, 24 June 1917. The bonds between the nurses and wounded soldiers in their care extended beyond the wards, the sisters buoying spirits of men physically and psychologically battered by the war. (Photo courtesy of the Royal New Zealand Returned and Services' Association Collection, the Alexander Turnbull Library, Wellington, NZ, G-012800-1/2)

Former Prime Minister Joseph Cook visited the Australian Comforts Fund in London during 1918. Here, he is photographed at the entrance to the Fund's headquarters with his son, Major Syd Cook (furthest right) and his daughter-in-law, Sister Elsie Cook (second left). (Photo courtesy of Hartley Cook)

With the war won, sisters and patients prepared to celebrate Christmas 1918 in one of the wards at No. 3 Australian Army Auxiliary Hospital at Dartford, England. (Photo courtesy of the Australian War Memorial H03905)

Time for some fun. Australian Army nurses and wounded Australian Army soldiers take part in a snowball fight in the grounds of No 1 Australian Auxiliary Hospital, Harefield Park, England. (Photo courtesy of the Australian War Memorial H16672)

# 20

# HARRY'S LETTER

Eighty kilometres north of the Somme River, Harry Moffitt and his comrades settled into camp in peaceful farming country near Fromelles. The village was in German hands and close to the front. Notable for a slight rise to the west known as Aubers Ridge, the area was unusual, as the water table and destroyed irrigation had forced both sides to build up their trenches rather than dig down. The thick sandbag walls had the appearance of medieval battlements facing off on either side of no man's land. A feature of the line was a bulge known as the Sugarloaf salient. In mid-1916 the Sugarloaf was a strategically important German stronghold, an elevated concrete fortress bristling with machine guns.

Today, the Sugarloaf seems barely a blip on the horizon as you trudge towards it along the edges of freshly ploughed fields. But this bucolic scene is deceptive. Nearby is the cemetery of VC Corner. There are no individual headstones here, just one mass grave containing the unidentifiable remains of 410 Diggers. At the back of the cemetery, on a perimeter wall, are the names of a further 1298 men of the 5th Division who died in the area and have no known grave. And not far away, in a field known as Pheasant Wood, it is now suspected that around 170 more Diggers were buried by the Germans in a mass grave.

Harry Moffitt's 53rd Battalion was part of the 14th Brigade. Along with battalions making up the 8th and 15th Brigades, it formed the AIF 5th Division, established only a few months earlier from a nucleus of Gallipoli troops. The 5th Division was the last AIF division to sail from Egypt in June 1916. The Australians thought they were going to a 'nursery' area on the Flanders front, where the fighting was light. They would have time to adjust and acclimatise to vastly different conditions. Instead, they found themselves preparing for immediate action on the Western Front.

The British Commander-in-Chief, Field Marshal Sir Douglas Haig, feared that the Germans might move troops from Flanders to reinforce their Somme forces. He wanted to keep the Germans in place. All he needed was to show his forces and keep the Germans guessing about his intention. They would not move men south if they feared an attack. For days the Allied generals bickered about the best plan. Some were in favour of trying to fool the Germans with a feint attack; others wanted a pure artillery barrage; infantry operations were proposed, planned, cancelled and reinstated. The object was to take the Sugarloaf, and about a kilometre of German reserve line that was presumed to run parallel to the front.

The 15th Brigade leader, Brigadier General H.E. 'Pompey' Elliott, was profoundly concerned. As his biographer Ross McMullin has noted, Elliott thought the operation inadvisable for a host of reasons: preparations would be rushed, the artillery was inexperienced, and parts of no man's land were too wide—up to 400 yards in places. The distance was crucial: for troops carrying a full twenty-five-kilogram pack, the maximum for an infantry charge to be effective was half that distance. Elliott's men would also have to advance opposite the formidable German strongpoint at the Sugarloaf.

With Elliott's misgivings growing, he met Major H.C.L. Howard, a visiting staff officer from Haig's headquarters. As McMullin describes it, Elliott took Howard forward not just to the front line but beyond, to a post in no man's land that afforded a good view of the Sugarloaf. Elliott showed Howard his plans and draft orders and asked for his frank assessment.

'Visibly moved, Howard predicted the attack would prove "a bloody holo-
caust". Elliott urged him to go back to Sir Douglas Haig and say so. Howard
promised he would. Whatever Howard may have said to Haig, the attack was
delayed but not cancelled. The attack was fixed for 19 July.'[1]

Despite the clear shortcomings in planning and preparation, an AIF
artillery bombardment in preparation for the attack went ahead on the
morning of the 19th. Because of inadequate equipment, training and insuf-
ficient time for the artillery to become familiar with the battlefield, the
bombardment failed to cut the barbed wire or destroy the machine-gun
emplacements at the Sugarloaf. The 5th Division, under the command of
Irish-born Australian Major-General James Whiteside McCay, was given the
task of taking the German trenches. The division was to link up with a
depleted British territorial division, the 61st, which, although short of manpower and training, was responsible for the Sugarloaf. This was some task,
as there was no cover across no man's land and the bulge was protected by a
host of German machine-gun nests capable of enfilading, or firing, on the
British and Australian troops from the side.

At 5:45 p.m. on 19 July, in the first AIF action in France, the infantry
climbed over the sandbagged parapets and attacked across the shell-holed
and featureless meadow, notable only for a muddy, metre-deep stream, the
Laies, that ran through no man's land and impeded progress. The broad
daylight of midsummer meant the Germans could see the troops coming.
Having observed the build-up from balloons and from the higher ground at
Aubers Ridge, they were well prepared for the assault. There have also been
suggestions that there were spies and collaborators at work: the clock in
the town tower moved faster during relief changeovers, white horses were
moved into certain paddocks, different-coloured washing was hung out.
According to one story, the Germans held up a sign saying, 'Aussies come on,
you were meant to be here yesterday.'

As the infantry attacked across a narrow section of no man's land, the
Germans unleashed a deadly machine-gun barrage. The AIF 15th Brigade

and the British 184th Brigade were decimated. The 15th had the widest section to cover, about 400 yards. Compounding the difficulty was the uncut barbed wire. The German machine guns were aimed between the men's waists and knees to ensure their upper bodies were hit as they fell. As the German guns rattled away, the men fell in their hundreds, the atmosphere alive with the lethal sound of bullets *zip, zip zipping* into their bodies. As one survivor later described the scene, 'the air was thick with bullets, swishing in a flat, crisscrossed lattice of death. Hundreds were mown down in the flicker of an eyelid, like great rows of teeth knocked from a comb . . . Men were cut in two by streams of bullets [that] swept like whirling knives . . . It was the charge of the Light Brigade once more, but more terrible, more hopeless.'[2] The 15th Brigade lost eighty per cent of its men and the battlefield was awash with blood.

The goal of Harry Moffitt's 14th Brigade was to reach the German line, about 250 yards away. Despite the Sugarloaf machine guns, somehow men from the brigade managed to storm the German front line within thirty minutes, and to hold the gains overnight. But the gains came at a dreadful cost in officers as well as men, which meant they soon needed not just more troops but someone to give orders. After eleven hours these remnants of the brigade were all that was left of the disastrous plan. They were still in the German trenches when a counterattack began, leaving them in a desperate position. Orders were given to retreat. The commander of the 14th, Colonel Harold Pope, boasted later that his was the only brigade that had to be ordered back.

By 8 a.m. on 20 July 1916, the battle—also known as the Battle of Fleurbaix—was over. A 59th Battalion corporal, Hugh Knyvett, wrote, 'If you had gathered the stock of a thousand butcher-shops, cut it into small pieces and strewn it about, it would give you a faint conception of the shambles those trenches were.'[3] According to the official Australian war historian, Charles Bean, the sight of the Australian trenches that morning, 'packed with wounded and dying, was unexampled in the history of the AIF'.

The four trenches which had been dug into no man's land in the sectors of the several brigades were full of helpless men. Especially in front of the 15th Brigade, around the Laies, the wounded could be seen everywhere raising their limbs in pain or turning hopelessly, hour after hour, from one side to the other.[4]

The wounded lay in no man's land, 'tortured and helpless' among the dead, 'within a stone's throw of safety but apparently without hope of it'.

In his book *Don't Forget Me, Cobber*, Robin Corfield wrote:

At this time on no-man's land there were probably in the vicinity of 1000 men so disabled by their wounds that they had no alternative but shelter in shell-holes or ditches, or in some cases, in the water of the river Laies. They would call out for help or in pain. Their hand would be seen above the edges of the hole in which they sheltered, waving to gain attention. Others silently bled to death in the grass or the river. Those alive were of course in great need of water as well as bandages.[5]

By midnight on the night of the 19th, it was clear that a major medical tragedy was unfolding. There were so many wounded to clear from the battlefield that the stretcher bearers became exhausted by the grim task of carrying them to the regimental aid posts and then to the advanced dressing stations. From there, the wounded were taken to the two main dressing stations, where they were evacuated at a rate of two a minute. Ambulances took them to No. 2 Australian Casualty Clearing Station at Trois Arbres. At 10 o'clock on the evening of the assault, the first ambulance convoys began to arrive. They kept on coming until the next morning, when the station was ordered to close until it could be cleared of the wounded. A nearby British casualty clearing station at Bailleul opened its wards to cope with the overflow.

No. 2 clearing station had more than 800 patients, some in the theatre but most in the care of the sisters, who were all flat out doing dressings and giving anti-tetanus inoculations. At 5 a.m. on the 20th, the duty nurses were given four hours off. They slept, then went back on duty to clear patients out to the base hospitals on two ambulance trains. The men were gone by nine that night. Next day came another ambulance convoy. The operating theatre just kept going.

The scene was worse at the British casualty clearing station. Nurses there described the situation as 'a butcher's shop' as they dealt with joints and limbs mutilated by shellfire. Many men had not been evacuated quickly enough. Sometimes, nurses found the wounds crawling with maggots where flies had settled on an undressed wound in the field. Helpfully, the maggots ate up the putrefying tissue and helped keep the wound clean. There were no miracle drugs to combat infection in 1916, just disinfectant to keep the wound clean and, with luck, keep sepsis at bay so the wound could heal. Sometimes, if a wound was stitched up too early, there would be a 'flare' of infection later. Gangrene could set in and kill a patient within twenty-four hours.

The wards were like battlefields, with wrecks of men in every bed and stretcher. Those with abdominal wounds were the worst. Fewer than two in 100 survived. A huge number had bullet wounds, and if the projectile had gone straight through them without hitting bone, they were mostly all right. The soldiers with head wounds were almost all hopeless cases. There was little the nurses could do for them but keep them comfortable and help them die decently. Mercifully, there was plenty of morphine.

The 5th Australian Division suffered 5533 casualties, including 1917 killed in action. It was the most costly and tragic twenty-four-hour period in Australian history. The casualty list represented an extraordinary fifty per cent of all troops engaged. Normally in the AIF the ratio of 'wounded' and 'died of wounds' to 'killed in action' was approximately four to one. In the 15th Brigade at Fromelles, it was less than three to two. The increase was a consequence of men being shot to death as they lay wounded in no man's land, or dying there for want of assistance. The casualties decimated the 5th Division for months to come.

Historians have ascribed the main responsibility for the defeat to the British Corps commander, Lieutenant General Sir Richard Haking, who argued for the feint attack. Someone who knew him was Lieutenant Colonel Phillip Game, who served in a division under Haking and was later to become famous as the New South Wales Governor who sacked Premier Jack Lang. To Game, Haking was a 'vindictive bully' and a 'bad man' who could not be trusted 'halfway across the road'.[6]

The Australian commander, General McCay, was also far from blameless. It was his decision to stop an armistice arranged with the Germans to collect the dead and wounded from the battlefield with the claim that it was illegal. A history of the 5th Division published four years after the event suggested that the armistice was called off because orders from General Headquarters forbade negotiations with the enemy. However, the Manual of Military Law did allow for a cessation of arms for the burial of the dead. McCay's reputation never recovered. He was ever after known as 'Butcher' McCay.

In his report, Haking patronised the Australians and ignored his own culpability. Indeed, he portrayed the disaster as a success, saying 'officers and men displayed a fine spirit throughout the attack and drove back the enemy with true British vigour'.

I think the attack of the Australian Division which was new to fighting out here, was carried out in an exceptionally gallant manner. There is no doubt that the men advanced with the greatest determination. Their difficulties on the right flank were caused by the failure of the 61st Division to carry the SUGARLOAF. On their left flank the Australian Division was unable to consolidate sufficiently during the night and consequently when that flank gave way the remainder of the line was compelled to withdraw.

I am quite sure that on the next occasion when the Division is ordered to attack it will distinguish itself even more than on this occasion. I have nothing but admiration for the fine fighting spirit displayed by Commanders and all ranks in the Division.

The artillery work turned out even better than I expected though many of the batteries had had very little experience.[7]

On 21 July McCay published a special divisional order in which, with 'great pleasure', he passed on complimentary remarks from Haig and the Commander of the 2nd Army, General Sir Herbert Plumer. McCay congratulated 'all ranks in the Division who have so gallantly maintained the ANZAC tradition'. Haig wanted the men to 'realise that their enterprise has not been by any means in vain and that the gallantry with which they carried out the attack is fully recognised'. Those who survived knew the emptiness of these words. The Diggers barely contained their anger at the debacle. They also now understood what they were dealing with in Haig, who, just a month earlier, had told Britain that it 'must be taught to bear losses'. Victories, he added, could not be won 'without the sacrifice of men's lives'.[8]

A communique on the battle issued to the press by British General Headquarters on 20 July raised divisions between the Australians and the British: 'Yesterday evening, south of Armentieres, we carried out some important raids on a front of two miles in which Australian troops took part. About 140 German prisoners were captured.'[9] The British generals were already covering up and rewriting the history of the disaster. It was all too much for Elliott, who had learned in horror of the decimation of his 15th Brigade, from which a third of the Australian casualties came. Fromelles was, he said, a 'tactical abortion'. He wept for the 5th Division's dead.

Harry Moffitt was among them—one of thirty officers of the division who did not survive the battle. He was among the first killed on the evening of the 19th. He went over the top as adjutant to Lieutenant Colonel Ignatius

Bertram Norris, who was leading the battalion. According to Robin Corfield, the first wave vanished in the smoke and dust and then Norris, Harry and other staff followed. As they reached the German line a well-sited machine gun killed them all.

There were eyewitnesses to the deaths of the two men, which happened at around 6 p.m.—within minutes of the attack's start. But, understandably given the confusion of battle, the accounts differ on some details. According to Corfield, one of the men who witnessed Norris's death remembered him shouting to his men: 'Come on, lads! Only another trench to take!' as he moved over the German line. Then he was hit and fell, and his last words were: 'Here, I'm done, will somebody take my papers!'[10]

It was Harry Moffitt who answered Norris's call. The official battalion report of his death says he was killed on the evening of 19–20 July, 'while attempting [to] assist' Colonel Norris, who was hit while attacking the enemy line. Harry was 'hit by machine gun fire and death was instantaneous'. According to Sergeant Patrick Lonergan, Norris 'was killed by a shell . . . Mr Moffitt called out for 4 men to bring the Colonel in. He had no sooner done so than he himself was shot in the back of the head and fell dead across the Colonel's body. I was quite close by and saw this myself.'[11] Another member of the battalion, Private John Morlock, said Harry 'was calling for volunteers to take back the colonel's body and stood up in the trench. His head was blown off.'[12] Yet another witness said Harry was 'killed by a bullet, probably by sniper—was shot a few seconds after his colonel'. What is beyond doubt is that Harry was going to Colonel Norris's aid and was killed immediately after him. Because the Germans recaptured the territory the next morning, neither body was ever recovered.

Two days after the battle, Major John Prior at No. 1 Australian General Hospital, Rouen, heard the news about Harry and told Alice Ross King. Words could not convey her grief. Her Harry was dead, and the news struck her senseless. She did not touch her diary for ten days. When she did, her diary entry simply stated:

Harry Killed in Action
Fleurbaix
19th July


Her heart was broken, her hopes for the future shattered by a futile and wasteful military misadventure. Harry's life had been taken, and Alice was numb. As she struggled to find the strength to keep going, a letter from Harry arrived in the post. The kaleidoscope of emotions Alice would have felt can only be imagined, as can her heartbreak on realising that his last letter had taken longer to arrive than the news of his death. Inside, she read an avowal of love from someone very much alive as he waited for the battle.


14.7.16

Dearest Heart of Mine

We are right in the thick of it all again. This afternoon we had a severe bombardment but as you see I am quite fit. All is over now and I'll have to get away as I have lots to do. If only I could have one little kiss & one hug, how happy I would be. Ruins are on every hand & the magnificent growth of poppies & cornflowers make a wonderful contrast to the surrounding scene of desolation. The trenches are a great improvement to those at Gallipoli, but the work darling is long. I seem to be going day & night. I get down for a moment and then I am called up. I love you long & dearly love of mine. So think longingly of me, & dream that I am as you know I am in your waking moments.

Ever yr Sweetheart

Harry[13]


When she resumed her diary on 29 July, urged on by her colleagues, Alice was gutted. 'Well, my world has ended. Harry is dead. God, what shall I do!'

She agonised over how to carry on. 'Nothing on earth matters to me now. The future is an absolute blank. I have kept on duty but God only knows how I have done so. Everyone has been most kind to me. Oh my dear, dear love what am I to do? I can't believe he is dead. My beautiful boy. I'm hoping each day that the news will be contradicted.'

She did not know how to face 'the lifeless future . . . I feel Harry's presence constantly with me and my love is growing stronger and deeper even since his death. I cannot really believe the news yet and each day I long for a letter telling me he is only wounded. How am I to bear life?'[14] She wrote to Harry's mother, at Gisborne in Victoria, trying to soften the blow for her. Work was a struggle, but she tried to show 'a frivolous face . . . Oh God my heart is breaking, and tears are mine that I never thought I should shed.'[15]

Then there was the question of what had happened to Harry's body. Five weeks after his death Alice heard that there was 'no hope of getting Harry's grave fixed up'. It had not been possible to bring in the wounded and they were 'still lying there unburied'. Alice pointed no finger, but clearly knew of the fiasco surrounding the failed truce. 'For days one could see occasional signs of life, an arm would wave or there would be slight movement but it was quite impossible to collect the wounded beyond a certain distance. Thank God I am almost certain that death was instantaneous.'[16] She had seen too much suffering among the badly wounded for whom there was no hope. Her only comfort was the thought that Harry had died quickly.

# 21

# GRASPING FOR HOPE

The days dragged by in 'awful weariness', and Alice's nights were full of longing for Harry. The pain of his death grew daily, though in time she became 'calm of eye' as she learned to control her visible emotions. But the condolences from family, friends and colleagues only reminded her of her loss. 'The worst of it is people speak of my trouble in the past tense. I go out a good deal when off duty for I hate my room and yet I hate talking to people too.'[1] Major Prior kept a watchful eye on her, taking her out on her days off for picnics in the nearby woods, where she was 'able to read or write or sleep'. He would organise afternoon tea and talk about his wife and children and his home. He was her 'good pal', and would remain so in the years ahead.

But these interludes aside, Alice believed her heart was 'too dead for anything', even for keeping her diary. She took solace in a new poem by American Ellen Gates:

> I shall not cry Return Return
> Nor weep my years away.
> But just as long as Sunsets burn
> And dawns make no delay
> I shall be lonesome. I shall miss
> Your hand, your voice, your smile, your kiss.[2]

The poem spoke of a tempest sweeping a garden bare, 'And then you passed, and in your place Stood Silence with her lifted face.' In hope, Alice looked to eternity, and the day when she might 'find the way you go' to join her lost love. She would do her 'task and wait the opening of the outer gate'.

There was never a shortage of wounded to provide distraction for her. A new form of treatment was being tried whereby wounds were not dressed but allowed to heal under their own pus. 'The patients are very discontented about it and the wards stink to high heaven,' Alice observed, unconvinced by the results.[3] In her view, further doubt was cast over the treatment when an amputation patient whose leg was being treated with a pus poultice had a severe haemorrhage. The patient blamed the lack of dressing. 'The surgeons are discontented about this treatment but the D.G. [director-general of medical services] says it must be given three months trial.'[4] It would not last long. But something had to be done to improve existing treatments, for men were dying like flies from dreadful festering wounds.

The Allied hospitals tried another new treatment named after its developers, the American Dr Henry Dakin and the Frenchman Dr Alexis Carrel. It involved cleaning suppurating wounds but not dressing them; instead they were irrigated with bactericidal fluids. It was considered effective, but Alice disliked it because it immobilised the patient. 'If he does move, the drip pan tips up into the bed. It will be awful when the cold weather comes.'[5]

As a hospital in a war zone, No. 1 Australian General Hospital at Rouen was hardly the place to help Alice come to terms with Harry's death. An influx of New Zealand troops from the Somme stirred her to bitter despair. 'The New Zealanders have been in it badly and we are getting a lot of them in. They are being applauded in the papers, which means of course that they are practically wiped out—like the Fifth Division. One never hears of it now. It is finished. It was someone's terrible blunder and it took my beloved one from me.'[6]

The death of another New Zealander also touched Alice deeply. He had been admitted with a compound fracture of the femur after the battle for

High Wood at the Somme. Gas gangrene suddenly developed. 'He made up his mind to live and he made a brave effort,' Alice wrote. 'He ate his food well and battled even when he had no pulse at all. At dinner time I was feeding him with chicken gravy when he said, "Can't hang on any longer." He was dead at 3:30 p.m. He sent a message to his girl saying "I'm sorry I'm going out but I'm not whipping the cat." '[7]

The same day a soldier was admitted who had been shot in the back, neck, arms and legs. He was paralysed and incontinent. Another had fractures in both legs and bullet wounds in both arms, while a third had his left foot amputated and a compound fracture of his left arm. After cleaning up these 'frightfully dirty' patients, Alice gave them egg flip and brandy. They cheered up. ''Twas then about 6 p.m. and I turned on the gramophone. It was delightful to see them join in the singing.'[8] Even as these broken men lay in their hospital beds there was time for humour. A soldier who had lost his lower jaw when it was shot away somehow remained full of fun, even as saliva dripped out over his dressing. 'I was doing his dressing when I sneezed twice (twice for a kiss). He wrote, "Sneeze again Sister. There's nothing doing." '[9] Another patient told Alice he was a 'seeder' in civilian life. She asked what that was. He told her that he worked the machine that made the seeds to put in raspberry jam. Most of the jam was made from pumpkin, then coloured, a few raspberries added and then the seeds put in.

The overwhelming sadness of it all took its toll on Alice. The matron noticed, and gave her twenty-four hours' leave. Alice was relieved, but when the matron increased this to three days she became scared. That meant more time to think of Harry. 'The thought of time ahead with nothing to do but think frightened all sleep from me. I was relieved by tears at 10 o'clock.'[10] She took the highly unusual step of taking some morphine. It had little effect except to make her feel 'deadly sick'. The day went by in a dream.

The matron gave Alice's friend Clarrie Green two days off to spend time with her. Alice saw her as 'surely a good counter irritant'. Clarrie dragged her around Rouen on uninteresting errands during the afternoon before taking her for a forest drive. On their return, they saw Major Prior, who had just come back from England. Catching up again with her friend and mentor had a sobering effect on Alice. 'Seeing him makes me realise how much I have gone off in the last week and makes me wonder if I am for a break up [breakdown]. I don't want a dementia break. Anything that would pass me out would be welcome indeed, but to be useless for some months is no good to me.'[11]

Heartbreak in the ward was common, and death frequent. An eighteen-year-old had a fractured skull from which shrapnel had been removed. 'He ate rice pudding for dinner,' Alice noted. 'I was in the middle of writing a letter to his mother when he began to sob, great tears running down his face. About 10 minutes later he stopped breathing. Pulse remained good for about 20 minutes. After respiration ceased I did artificial respiration but it was of no avail.'[12] Yet another soldier with a compound fracture of the sacrum and pneumonia was trying to tell Alice his fiancée's address for her to write. But he died before he could make himself clear.

She managed to cheer up another eighteen-year-old, who had lost both legs and one hand, by buying him a watch. 'He was thrilled when I fastened it on his wrist. We have had such a fight to save him.'[13] His parents were cane growers. The irony was that they made walking sticks. She wanted to 'special' a young Canadian who had a perforated intestine and was in great pain. She made him comfortable and hated leaving him for time off, but knew that in a military hospital she had no choice. 'Rules have to be obeyed and the girls would feel hurt if I stayed thinking I distrusted them.'[14] He did improve. Alice was held in high regard. She heard that Major John Tait, a surgeon, had said of her that she knew her 'work from A to Z and never lost my head'. Despite her anguish, she managed to retain her focus, which became even more important when she transferred to a casualty clearing station a few months later.

Life at one of these stations close to the front lines was a far cry from caring for the wounded at base hospitals, as Sister Ida O'Dwyer discovered. From Bendigo, she had sailed on the *Kyarra* with Alice, and served with her in Cairo before being posted to No. 3 Australian Casualty Clearing Station at Gezaincourt in the Somme. Here the wounded men arrived straight from the battlefield. In the base hospital's operating theatre, the men had at least been washed. At the clearing station, if a soldier 'should have a fractured thigh the patient is still left with one leg clothed in khaki boot and mud of the trench with a splint over all that was supplied at the Dressing Station'. Every act here was urgent: time was of the essence.

The first thing Ida saw on arrival were the 'rows of duckboards everywhere' connecting all the wards and the quarters as far as the road. 'This seems very strange after the well regulated lines and hard paths of the base hospital,' she observed.[15] The clearing station's nursing staff varied in number according to the work. When a battle was imminent, the staff would be brought up to strength the day before. More often than not the station had just moved to its new location and had only tents for shelter, no flooring and scant equipment when the fighting began.

A key issue was always lighting in the theatre. Ida recounted how in one case, carbide flares had to be held over each operating table for a day and a night before a generator and electric lights could be installed. 'This class of work was all very new to the sisters having come straight from the base hospital where everything is at hand before they start work, and yet they carried on in the usual calm way as if nothing were out of order.' Within a few hours hundreds of wounded would be admitted, for treatment or swift evacuation to a general hospital. Work was unending, and 'the first thing a sister realises is not what is to be done but what must be done first'.

Two roads enabled admission and evacuation to be carried out simultaneously. The admissions tent was where wounded soldiers were received and classified for either evacuation or on-the-spot surgery.

There is one continuous rush between cases, the sister clearing her tables and re-sterilising her instruments and dishes while the orderly is dispatching the patient and receiving the next. While the surgeon attends to the Field Card everyone has his or her set duty, perhaps not a word spoken for hours except may be to call for a special instrument or dressing. During a rush of work they have to be reminded that there are meals to be partaken of. Work will stop for about an hour, which to the surgeon does not mean a rest, he is urgently required to see special cases for perhaps more urgent operation. As for the sister, she makes the most of the short time after a hurried meal to readjust her table to get stock ready to continue endless operations. This pressure continues for some days to a week during a battle, everyone working a period of sixteen hours a day. After twelve hours assisting at operations, the sister overlooks the preparation of sutures, gloves and splints for endless operations of the next day.[16]

The most distressing part of a casualty clearing station was the resuscitation ward, which held those too gravely ill to undergo surgery. 'This is really the biggest test to the sister as she has never experienced anything like it before in her career,' Ida observed. The patients here required immediate attention. Some died before they received it.

Every man is just as he was carried out of the trenches in his wet khaki and stone cold. All these men have to be undressed, a very difficult matter when collapsed with several wounds and broken limbs and the majority being extremely restless, yet not one complaint.

You can see death written in most of their faces, they realise to the full the great pressure you are working at, yet the thirst is so intense they gasp with apology for a drink. Yet with it all every man's face wears a look of content or resignation. He waits his turn and never asks. That's when a wounded soldier commands the respect and admiration of anyone in this world. The biggest percent of this ward die.

Sister has her trials, it is not as if she has a trained staff of stretcher bearers to help her, they are mostly volunteers from the infantry camps nearby waiting their turn in the trenches and often don't know a wounded man's head from his foot so invariably picks him up by the wounded limb.[17]

The acute surgical ward accommodated those returned from theatre. During the busiest time these men were evacuated as soon as practicable. 'The ward is one constant for sister to get a drink here, move a limb there or ease a pain somewhere else,' Ida explained. 'She steadily goes on receiving patients, all the time transferring the better ones to less acute wards to make room for the constant incoming of collapsed operative cases—never stopping except for meals. A sister's whole time is spent in relieving pain, giving nourishment and making them comfortable.'[18]

In the evacuation area there were wards full of men waiting for the train. 'Every man lies quietly on his stretcher and hardly murmurs. Sister goes round seeing each is warm with socks and comforter, the orderly following giving drinks and nourished where it is allowed. Sister's work here is just as hard as all her cases lie on stretchers on the ground, packed closely together to make more room. She does not realise how the day has flown, except that her back is aching having put in some very trying hours.'

Ida described how the walking wounded were 'mostly coiled up on their stretchers fast asleep, as nothing matters now, or they are seated about in little groups, friends having each other telling of experiences of the last 12 hours or so . . . As the work slackens the sister starts to get her ward into working order having carried on through that terrible rush usually on half equipment. By the time the next rush arrives she is ready to carry on her usual quiet way.'[19]

Olive Haynes moved from Boulogne to No. 2 Australian Casualty Clearing Station at Trois Arbres just a month after the Battle of Fromelles. Olive was close to the front line, close enough to find bits of shell and shrapnel outside her tent one morning. Disturbingly, bullets even fell beside one of her patients. 'The aeroplanes are always flying around here above us and, as soon as the Germans spot them, they open fire and we do the same when theirs appear,' she wrote to her mother, who could hardly have been reassured.[20] There was a huge fourteen-inch gun hidden nearby, which Olive went to inspect. 'When it fires the windows smash in the houses around and everything shakes.' She and her colleagues struck up a friendship with the engineers who looked after the gun, sharing tea with them. The sisters were fascinated by the immense size of the Allied guns, to which the troops gave names like Little Elsie, Cranky Cissie and Funny Fanny Flanders.

The bombing seemed incessant, but the sisters rapidly grew accustomed to the sound. Olive had a chance to go on a transport wagon to a nearby town, but the colonel would not allow it because the place was being shelled. 'I would love to have gone in spite of the shells. He won't let us go anywhere, though, nearer than we are.' He had good reason. A few days later some German aeroplanes flew over, drawing fire from the Allied guns. Shells flew everywhere. 'We heard a whizz, and you should have seen everyone duck. A shell landed just near us and made a hole 4 ft. deep. The boys dug it up and gave it to matron "pour un souvenir".'[21] They were finally issued with steel helmets and gas masks to wear during German attacks.

For the patients who poured in, the task of mere survival was uppermost. In the argot of the day, they sometimes asked Olive, 'Sister, am I going west?' When they died the nurses wrote to the soldiers' mothers. Among the Scots troops were 'baby Jocks', as the sisters called them. They were just sixteen or seventeen, and it was so sad to see them die. 'They are plucky little boys. You'd give anything or do anything to save them.'[22] The letters to bereaved mothers only became more frequent.

Humour helped the sisters through it. 'It is funny to hear the yarns our boys tell the Tommies,' Olive wrote to her mother. 'They believe most of them, too. We tell them about the kangaroo feathers and how we live in humpies and how we ride buck-jumpers.' They also tried to fool the Scots, one of whom was told a 'very tall yarn . . . Yes, I know the Anzacs swallow battleships and you only know they've swallowed one when the funnel is sticking out of their mouths,' he responded. 'The Jocks are canny—you don't pull their legs much,' Olive wrote, 'but the British Tommy is as gullible as anyone. We bluff them we have never heard of the Thames and ask them do people in England live in houses or out in the open like we do.'[23] Olive liked the Canadians, but not the English. To her, they worried too much about appearances, were scared of what other people would think, and were subservient to authority.

The Australian sisters always knew when Australian boys arrived, for they called out, 'Hello, Australia.' And they recognised the Australian sisters' uniforms. The compatriots were drawn to each other. They felt forgotten when, longing for letters, they saw the frequency with which the English nurses received mail from just across the Channel. To assuage her homesickness, Olive Haynes went into an English bookshop in Boulogne and asked for author Henry Fletcher's *The Waybacks*, a series of books chronicling the fortunes of the unsophisticated Wayback family in rural Australia. She was astonished at the sales staff's reaction. 'Do you know they had never heard of them! I told them we [had] had no idea of the frightful ignorance over here.'[24]

Further north, at Amiens, the 700-bed No. 1 New Zealand Stationary Hospital occupied a girls' school and part of a convent. A convoy of 350 wounded men arrived one day in mid-September. Three operating tables were occupied night and day. For most of that time an orderly sat almost continuously sharpening scalpels. Another orderly packed and sterilised drums of dressings, towels and bowls, while a third continually removed splints and instruments for re-sterilising and padding. A sterile-clad corporal passed everything required with forceps, no one else being allowed to touch the tables. The surgeons, working superhuman shifts, carried on until they could no longer handle a scalpel.

New Zealand Sister Ida Willis was on duty at the hospital when a German prisoner was admitted with gas gangrene. His arm was grossly swollen from shoulder to wrist, a hopeless case, or so it appeared. 'The surgeon slashed the arm in deep gashes, swiftly put on large dressings, shaking his head, while the patient was removed into isolation,' she related.[25] Astonishingly, he made a complete recovery.

Just as had occurred at Gallipoli, the sisters were faced with the strange dilemma of caring for enemy wounded. Often, it was not easy to reconcile their humanitarian obligation with their feelings. 'You did your work without a vestige of sentiment, just for duty's sake,' as one Australian matron put it. 'Fritz made a good patient, but I am sure he had not the fine sensibilities of our own British boy.'[26]

Like the surgeons, assistants and orderlies, the sisters worked for twenty-four to thirty-six hours at a stretch, pausing only for meals and coffee. Sitting in a chair and dozing for an hour during the night, or lying on a rug with a pillow on the floor, was often their only rest.

Sometimes, because of the pressure of work, theatre staff wore the same garments in six or more operations.[27] Soiled instruments and dressings were dropped into special containers and quickly removed from the theatre. So were amputated limbs. The wounds were ghastly. Heads of shells eight centimetres across were found embedded in men's backs, arms and legs. A sister at No. 1 New Zealand Stationary Hospital, who wrote to *Kai Tiaki* in New Zealand, had endured more than she ever wanted to. 'We are losing a lot of our New Zealand boys, at present we have numbers in here,' she wrote. 'The convoys the last three days have been most terrible—gas gangrene cases are too awful for words, and the trouble is so advanced before we get them. I never want to see another amputation while I live.'[28] That day, the operating theatre did not stop until 3 a.m.

Meanwhile, at No. 1 Australian General Hospital in Rouen, Major Prior sent Alice Ross King a note saying he had some information about Harry. Her hopes rose. The major had a list of the names of 5th Division troops who'd been taken prisoner at Fromelles. Alice was grasping for any evidence that might promise to bring Harry back. His name was not on the list, but she still wanted to believe there was a chance.

# 22

# THE CHILL OF WAR

So many men dead, and so many missing, presumed dead. If there was no
report of a man's burial, there was always a chance he might still be alive,
perhaps a prisoner of war. To such faint hopes the bereaved would cling,
Alice Ross King among them. But at least there was someone she
could turn to for help—Vera Deakin, daughter of the former Australian
Prime Minister Alfred Deakin. She had been in London when the war
began. On returning to Australia, she joined the Red Cross and began
studying nursing. Impatient to play a bigger role, she went to Cairo and,
in October 1915, founded the Australian Wounded and Missing Enquiry
Bureau.

The bureau was devoted to finding information on behalf of the
relatives of Australian soldiers lost at Gallipoli. In 1916 it shifted operations to London. The Army did not view Vera's work favourably because
grieving relatives, unsatisfied with military explanations, came to regard
the bureau as more helpful. In her anguish over Harry, Alice wrote to Vera,
hoping she could shed some light on his fate. On 28 October 1916,
Vera replied.

Dear Madam,

With reference to your inquiry for Lt. Harry L. Moffitt, Adjutant 53rd Battalion, AIF, we beg to inform you that we have received the following unofficial report from a man in the battalion. Informant states that on July 19th about 6 p.m. he was killed by a shell in No Man's Land, about 100 yards from the trenches, while leading an attack. The same shell killed Colonel Norris and Major Sampson. Colonel Norris' body was recovered, but he does not know if Lieut. Moffitt's was also recovered and if so where it was buried.

We are still making further inquiries and shall let you know if we hear anything further.

Yours faithfully,

V.D.[1]

Vera was as good as her word, writing to Alice again just six days later to inform her of a further report on Harry. A member of the 53rd Battalion had told one of the bureau's researchers that Harry had been killed when he went out to bring in Colonel Norris. Vera assured Alice 'of our deepest sympathy'. A fortnight later, she wrote again with another eyewitness account of Harry's death. At Alice's request her friend Major Prior wrote to Vera, pointing out that there was no record of a burial or of Harry's body being found.

There is just the remotest possibility that Lt Moffitt was taken prisoner after having been wounded as it is definitely stated by an eyewitness that he was struck in the head by a Machine Gun Bullet, but as the Battalion had to retire very shortly afterwards, nothing further was seen of him.

The abovementioned Sister who was Lt Moffitt's fiancee, will be very glad if you can add his name to your list of enquiries and so verify (or otherwise) this last hope concerning him.[2]

Crossing this note in the mail, a letter from Vera arrived two days before Christmas. Inside was the information Alice did not want to hear: Harry Moffitt's name was on an official German death list, dated 4 November 1916.

Dear Madam,

We regret to inform you that the name of Lt. HARRY L. MOFFITT 53rd Batt A.I.F. has appeared on a German death list under date Nov 4th. This does not necessarily mean that he died a Prisoner.

On the contrary, we think that the Germans found his paybook and identification disc, or even his dead body, and have in this way let us know that he is dead.

Should any further reports be received, we shall at once communicate with you.

Yours faithfully,

V.D.[3]

The letter played on Alice's mind over Christmas. For five months she had been on an emotional rollercoaster. Christmas could not have been sadder. Her patients, though, were looking forward to Christmas Day, and the sisters made sure the occasion was festive. The Red Cross gave every patient a present and provided turkey, ham, plum pudding and fruit. Best of all, each patient had a bottle of beer or stout and an after-dinner smoke. In Alice's ward, chestnuts roasted and popped on a fire. 'The long hut was a picture at 2.30, empty bottles on each locker, nut shells and the evidence of feasting everywhere, while the men exhausted by the slight excitement had all gone off to sleep,' she recorded.[4]

Later, Alice had the duty of censoring their letters, noting the wistful pathos of the oft-repeated remark to mothers or wives about the dinner, 'I wish I could have saved some for you.' Many wrote quite truthfully, she decided, that it was the best meal they had ever eaten. On Boxing Day, Alice replied to Vera Deakin.

Dear Miss Deakin,

I cannot tell you how grateful I am for the trouble you have taken in sending the news gathered about Lieut. Harry Moffitt. The last news convinces me that what I suspected was true. I heard from one man that he was wounded and not killed.

I think he might have been picked up by the German Red Cross, altho', as you say, they may have taken the name from paybook etc.

I know you will let me know if any more news turns up—which is unlikely I'm afraid.

Again thanking you with all my heart.

Yours very sincerely

Alice Ross King

Sister[5]


On New Year's Eve, Alice saw the old year out remembering her last New Year's Eve with Harry when they sat on the piazza in Cairo, watching the flames of a bonfire in the night sky. The past year had been tragic, and she hoped that 1917 would be different. She wanted a ray of hope as she watched the first day of the year dawn. 'The end of the New Year showed a brightening in the sky but it was very distant.'[6]

In the first week of January 1917, Vera Deakin wrote again to say that a sergeant in the 53rd Battalion 'says that Lt. Moffitt was killed by a bullet— probably a sniper's, a few seconds after Colonel Norris'. Vera sent the same information to Major Prior. A week later he wrote back to thank her. 'This information concerning the late Lieut. Harry L. Moffitt, whilst not very cheering, will most certainly allay the fears of Sister Ross King that he was a prisoner in Germany. It is indeed consoling to know that he died a true hero for King and Country.'[7]

In early January Alice was promoted to night superintendent, but the work was uninteresting, 'chiefly going round in the cold and wind and rain collecting reports'. Emergency operations for haemorrhages and leg amputations often saw her in the rudimentary theatre at night. She went out seldom, feeling tired and seedy, but 'chiefly sick at heart'. Watching other sisters when their sweethearts visited was difficult. 'If I had not lost Harry how different things would be. Still I must go dumbly on, but the pain is awful.'[8]

Alice was no longer the carefree spirit she had been in her first eighteen months at the war. She had seen too much. And now her future seemed bleak. It was the pluck of the patients that buoyed her. 'One old boy with two eyes blown out and face badly cut' was having his wounds dressed. Managing a grin, he said to her, 'Will you give me a drop of Cheer-up fluid after this is done?' Alice thought they were all 'very brave', but she was nonetheless bitter at the personal toll the war was taking on men like him and on her, too.

In her work she tried to keep standards high. She spoke to a nurse who had been hard on the patients. 'I heard a man moaning pitifully and went to the ward to find her half asleep. When I asked about the patient in pain she said she did not believe the man had pain. He is an operation who I took the other night and he is on the D. I. [dangerously ill] list. I looked at the man and he most evidently had pain.'[9]

To help mend her fraying nerves, Alice was given a pass to England for a fortnight. In London, she saw the musical *Chu Chin Chow*. Written by Australian Oscar Asche, it had opened a year earlier and was regarded as a must-see by all the Anzac sisters. The play would run in London's West End until 1921, setting a record that would last nearly forty years. The break was welcome, but as soon as she was back in France thoughts of Harry returned. She had been hoping for a letter from his mother but was disappointed to find none waiting. 'Feeling Harry's loss more than I have ever done before, I do not know how I can continue.'[10] But she did not have time to dwell, for the war was getting closer to the hospitals. Despite retreating, the Germans were mounting air raids, and their bombs fell close to No. 1 General Hospital, shaking the building.

Sister Laura James knew what the air raids were like. Having joined the Imperial Military Nursing Service in August 1914, she was now in charge at No. 37 Field Ambulance, twelve kilometres from Arras. In February 1917, it was in ruins from the German onslaught. The Field Ambulance was based at an old chateau, where a small operating theatre and hospital had been set up. There were only two or three such hospitals, each with a small staff of sisters, and they were much closer to the firing line than the casualty clearing stations. 'The one of which I am in charge, is for severe abdominals, chest wounds, or head injuries only. Our ward linen has been frozen in the tubs at the laundry for a month, indeed, some for six weeks!' As she wrote, the guns were busy. All day the shelling nearby continued. 'Whilst I have been writing this, the force of the explosions has shaken this chateau considerably. At night the sky is lit up by each flash, and when an explosion sounds more than usually near, it gives one a horrid little quaking feeling.'[11]

There were few comforts. Because sugar was in short supply, the nurses had to do without cake two days a week. That was the least of their troubles. The winter of 1916–17 was the coldest recorded in France for a century. Water in shell holes froze into ice blocks a metre deep, and the frozen ground made digging trenches all but impossible. But at least it did away with the mud, and in places the roads even became dusty. The weather had been changeable all the previous summer and 'people began to mutter darkly that the fearsome bombardments on the Western Front were causing vibrations in the atmosphere and affecting the climate'.[12]

Pearl Corkhill's first sighting of snow at No. 1 General Hospital in Rouen entranced her. There was a great cry of 'Oh, it's snowing,' she wrote. 'So as soon as there was enough snow to make into balls they started snow balling. The boys started to snow ball every sister they saw. They used to wait for us round tent corners.'[13] By January–February 1917, however, the temperature was often from twelve to eighteen degrees Celsius below freezing, and moats around the chateaux were frozen solid.

At Rouen, blocks of ice floated in the River Seine, while inside the hospital fountain pens burst as the ink froze and expanded. Letters home had to be written in pencil. 'We are having a water famine because all the water is frozen in the main pipes,' Alice observed late in January. The sisters could not wash the patients in the morning and they were forced to use the solid ice out of the fire buckets to make cocoa for them. A coal shortage made Alice 'nearly mad with the cold'. Her head hurt and her back ached, 'so intense that I did not know what to do. It sometimes seems impossible to carry on.'[14] For six days there was no water. Finally the hospital was connected to Rouen's main supply.

At No. 2 Australian General Hospital, in Wimereaux, Elsie Eglinton lamented, 'We have to melt the ice over our spirit lamp before we can get a wash. The floors freeze directly they are washed and we slip on the ice. I spilt a cup of coffee down my apron last night and it was soon frozen stiff, sometimes it's almost unbearable. Now we are getting floods of rain and strong winds which nearly blow our tents down.'[15]

Sister Ida Willis, at No. 1 New Zealand Stationary Hospital in Amiens, saw water flowing from the houses into the street gutters freeze hard; it had to be cut daily. Those like her who had transferred just a few months earlier from Egypt 'felt the change of climate keenly'. The town's old men and women scraped with pitchforks through the household refuse piled in the snow in front of the houses in the hope of finding tiny lumps of coal, coke or anything that would burn. The sisters took pity on them and gave them their left-over rolls for breakfast.

During January 1917, it was so cold many of the stretcher cases came in almost frozen. 'They do enjoy a big mug of cocoa and hot water bottles in their beds,' Elsie Eglinton wrote. 'Some of the patients who can walk are given a hot bath and they have a short distance to walk and before we can get them into their bed, their hair is frozen stiff.'[16] The night sisters tried to stay warm by wearing balaclavas and looked 'like a lot of teddy bears getting around in all our woollies'. The hospital was 'so short of water now that we have to melt the snow to wash our patients in'.

We couldn't even get a cup of tea for breakfast this morning. The water pipes are all frozen. Some of the boys walked over to the frozen pond and broke the ice with an axe and brought some back in lumps. We then made a cup of tea in our ward. We get a few falls going to our tents in old post holes etc but owing to the quantity of clothes we wear we only bounce and don't get much hurt.[17]

The spring on Elsie's gramophone snapped twice because of the cold, but ingenuity and repairs kept it serviceable. Her friend Olive Haynes had been posted back to No. 2 General Hospital at the start of 1917, and she was pleased that the gramophone had been mended. 'We have to keep it in a blanket and hot water bag at night—it feels the cold so terribly,' she noted whimsically.[18] To save water, Elsie re-boiled water emptied from hot water bottles and used it to make coffee for her boys in the ward. 'My poor orderly complains that his boots are frozen still when he puts them on at night and they make his feet sore.'[19] She had to stand a bottle of ink on the stove before she could write a letter. A doctor later recalled the scene in the tent wards with the wind howling through and only snow water to drink:

I can see the sisters now—their noses blue and nipped with cold—their fingers like bulky sausages in thick woollen gloves, cap comforters peaking up over their hair and strapped round their ears—warm bed socks tied on over their shoes—a sight to laugh at, chaff at, yet to love and reverence. We would make our rounds sharing a hot water bottle, cuddling it alternately to thaw our hands: then, after a round, often perfunctory, in spite of repeated resolves to stick it out, off I'd go to a delicious 'Fugg' in our mess, lying torpid in front of a roasting stove, sucking a most comforting pipe, chivalrously leaving sister and the boys to stick out the arctic wards as best they might.[20]

As the sisters shivered in France, across the Channel another of the first *Kyarra* contingent, Kath King, married Major Gordon Carter in Southall, England. They had planned to marry in March, but the wedding appears to have been brought forward to 31 January when, in November 1916, AIF Matron-in-Chief Evelyn Conyers told Kath she would be sending her and her sister Wynne to France 'very shortly'. Wynne was one of Kath's bridesmaids, and she showered the couple with confetti when they left by train on their honeymoon. For Gordon, it was '18 days of the most glorious holiday I ever expect to have'.[21] Kath agreed, writing in her diary that their time on the Devon coast was 'most delightful'.

With the rules requiring her now to resign from Australian Army Nursing Service, Kath ended her work as an Army nurse. She started work at Harefield Park hospital in London as an assistant house sister, while Gordon went back and forth to the battlefield.

# 23

# NO PLACE TO HIDE

---

In earth torn up by shells, bombs and tank tracks, it takes seasons for flowers to appear. In the spring of 1917, thousands upon thousands of white crosses stood where primroses and poppies had once bloomed. While men had died in legions, centuries-old villages and towns had been reduced to ruins. Ypres and Pozières were razed, Bapaume blown to pieces, Arras all but demolished. There was a ghostly quality to the landscape. Limbless oaks and beeches stood bleakly in what once were woods. Fields that had supported aeons of agriculture were reduced to a quagmire of craters. Troops came out of the trenches soaked to the skin and covered in a thick, glue-like mud. Some did not make it out but drowned in the pools of grey slop.

This was the countryside that the Anzac sisters on the Western Front came to know, especially those in the casualty clearing stations. They had no illusions about what they were confronting: the wastage of life, the pain and misery. They removed filthy, blood-encrusted uniforms, bathed the men, administered blood, gave injections, monitored vital signs, debrided, sutured and dressed wounds. In 1917, during the Ypres Offensive, they too felt the impact of long periods of monotony punctuated by frenetic action and extreme terror. The trauma of war was taking its toll.

Danger came in many forms and on different levels, from shelling and bombs to gas. The Germans first used poison gas in the Second Battle of Ypres just nine months after the war started, shocking the civilised world but heralding the dawn of a new era of warfare. Soon its use was widespread: first chlorine and phosgene, then mustard gas. After just two minutes breathing in as little as one part chlorine to 10,000 parts air, people developed lesions in their lungs. Phosgene was more powerful and could be distributed in an even lower concentration, one part to 50,000. Inhaling it for only one minute reduced men to helplessness. They went blue as they struggled for air. By the time the war ended, 185,000 troops had suffered its effects. Mustard gas caused terrible burns. While many gas victims returned to duty, the worst affected were permanently debilitated. Many suffered intensely for weeks or months before dying.

Sister Evaline Jones, a Victorian-trained nurse working at the British No. 1 Casualty Clearing Station, saw many gas victims. After one attack, more than 350 gassed men were brought in within twenty-four hours. 'Their eyes are all in a terrible condition and their skin often burnt, occasionally a blister, but mostly skin unbroken, but burnt a deep plum colour.'[1]

At Wimereaux, Elsie Eglinton was startled by an explosion. Five minutes after a troop train had gone past, the railway line was blown up. 'We thought that it was a bomb at first, dropped from an aeroplane but it was a time exploding bomb placed on the line. If the train had been a few minutes later there would have been a great loss of life.'[2] At Amiens, Ida Willis, who had survived several air raids, noted that 'occasionally pieces of metal or leaden balls found their way through the shutters of our bedrooms. On one occasion a piece of flying metal actually cut my shoe while I sheltered in a doorway during a raid which started when I was on my way home from the hospital.'[3] And the danger would soon be worse. Much worse.

This was the world that Elsie Tranter, a grey-eyed, twenty-nine-year-old petite nurse from Geelong, found herself in not long after she arrived from Australia. She was posted to British General Hospital No. 26, near Etaples.

The village had become a giant hospital city staffed by Australian, New Zealand, Canadian and British medical units. Row after row of tents and huts made up an enormous camp containing seven hospitals. Elsie had dreamed of going to the war since that first Sunday in August 1914 when she had heard the cry of the Melbourne *Herald* paper boys: '*Herald* Extra'ordinary! Special, here y'are.'[4] Now she was in the midst of it and learning fast.

The suffering of the boys sickened her, and she knew that the pounding of the guns in the distance meant more casualties would be filling the wards. She quickly became accustomed to the sight of horrific wounds—and filled with admiration for the soldiers' stoicism. 'The boys are absolute bricks and make no complaints when their dressings are being done. The wounds are ghastly—any one of the boys in "D" if in hospital at home would be considered in need of a day and night Special, but here is just one of the many.'[5]

Elsie was in a ward that was using the Carrel-Dakin method. There were hundreds of tubes to be syringed every two hours around the clock. 'I did dressings most of the morning. The boys are so frightfully mutilated it would not be possible for one person to dress them. Every minute is more than full.' She thought it just as well. 'If we did not have to work hard all the time we could not stand the strain of the awfulness of it all. Work and want of time to stop and think is a boon to us. With our boys it is not only their wounds but so many of the poor dears are so frightfully sick from a rotten gas infection. They are tired out when they come to us.'[6]

---

In April 1917, the Allies opened their long-planned spring offensive. Easter Monday, 9 April, brought the battle of Vimy Ridge, about eight kilometres north of Arras. The Germans had held the heights there since the trench lines settled in late 1914. The Canadian attack went well, securing the first unequivocal success gained by Allied forces since trench warfare began. Not only did the attack gain the commanding position on the heights but it also drew German reserves away from a planned French offensive on the Aisne

River a week later. Victorian Sister Valerie Woinarski was sent to a British casualty clearing station just before Vimy Ridge was taken:

The station consisted simply of a tin shed, with rows of wooden trestles on which the wounded men were laid as they were brought in from the trenches. We had no beds for them, and we simply tucked them up with blankets and hot water bottles while we dressed their wounds, and did all we could for them. Then if they were fit to travel they were put into the hospital train and sent down to the base. We had to work by the light of hurricane lamps, and when the air raids started, even these had to be put out.[7]

When Vimy Ridge fell, No. 1 New Zealand Stationary Hospital admitted 1000 stretcher cases to its grounds in a single morning. Here the patients were examined and labelled, and their dressings were replaced. They were then fed and sent to base hospitals, the moribund and urgent operation cases staying behind. A New Zealand medical team, including Ida Willis, was assigned to join one of eight British teams helping a British unit with the battle casualties. 'It was a great grief to the New Zealand team,' Ida Willis lamented, 'to see the poor nursing of the serious abdominal cases, and we tried when possible to slip into the wards to offer assistance.'[8] English sisters, Ida Willis, noted, were used only to supervising and 'made no attempt to nurse the patients themselves as we New Zealand Sisters did'. The war had shown that Australian and New Zealand nurses were better trained and more practical than their British counterparts.

As the spring offensive continued, Elsie Tranter was on theatre duty at No. 26 General Hospital, and worked most days from early morning until late at night, sometimes into the next day. She and another sister took it night about for frequent emergency calls, almost invariably for haemorrhages. It was not unusual for her to assist at ten amputations, one after another. 'It is frightfully nerve-racking work. I seem to hear that wretched saw at work whenever I try to sleep.'[9]

On the morning of 5 May Elsie noted that the hospital had 'quite a little excitement ... A German aeroplane passed over us. The anti aircraft guns (Archies) got busy. One bomb was dropped but no damage done. This is the first time I have seen shrapnel bursting in the air.'[10] A week later another German plane attacked, and shrapnel fell on the hospital. 'Six of our planes chased the intruder and brought it down the other side of the village.'[11]

She had care of several young boys—'baby soldiers'. There was Jock Brise, with his right arm gone and his chest badly lacerated. 'He looks such a wee boy and when I ask him what is keeping him awake he tells he me he is a "wee bit too tired to sleep".'[12] Baby No. 2 was 'a little scrap of a boy named Hancock' with a bad abdominal wound. He did not look a day over fourteen, and got the men to give him their cigarette cards.

Baby No. 3 was a Staffordshire lad named Dart with a tremendous wound in his back. When this had to be dressed, a corporal held him up in his arms. 'The poor little chap cries piteously when we go to do him.' One night in his sleep he called out, 'Come out of that dugout, you chaps—there ain't no souvenirs there.' Baby No. 4 was O'Donnell, nicknamed the Sparrow on account of his size—or lack of it. He had an abdominal wound and a ruptured bladder. 'When I am ready to syringe his wound in the night I have to wake him right up first so I flick his nose with my finger, then pop a lolly in his mouth. He is quite used to this now and as soon as I waken him he doesn't bother to open his eyes but opens his mouth instead.' The boys did not stay long at the hospital. As soon as they were fit they were evacuated to Blighty to make room for others. 'Poor boys, it must be just awful in the trenches in this cold weather. We find it trying enough and yet we live in luxury compared to the boys.'[13]

Anzacs were among the injured Elsie cared for. One of them was Private Edward Mullard, a twenty-one-year-old from Sydney, who was wounded in both hands and had some fingers amputated. He was also wounded in his buttocks and right foot; his left leg had gone. 'He is getting on well now but suffers a good deal and sometimes I find him biting hard into his blankets to keep him from calling out. Lots of them are minus an arm or a leg but after they have been in for a day or so and get a little rest from pain they are just full of fun and nonsense.'[14]

Where the earth remained untouched by war, spring was managing to provide 'a feast of beauty', with flowers blooming, restoring the spirit of the sisters and the wounded. Elsie was entranced. 'Never have I seen such gorgeous tulips [of] all shades, brown, gold, red and such perfect blooms.' Far out to sea, the brown sails of the fishing fleet were set against a clear blue sky. 'It is refreshingly beautiful. If only we could carry the calm of those few moments through the turmoil of the long days and wearying nights—if—but we don't.'[15]

Over one four-day period in May 1917, Elsie Tranter's workload was extraordinary: on the first day she assisted at twenty-three operations and went off duty at 1:30 a.m.; the next day she assisted at twenty-two operations and finished at 2 a.m.; on the third day she assisted at eighteen operations and finished at midnight; and on the fourth day she assisted at twenty operations and clocked off at 1 a.m. Such long hours inevitably brought tension and frayed tempers. Working with English doctors did not improve matters for Elsie. One English surgeon, a Captain Grieves, she disliked intensely.

> He hates the Aussie boys as much as I hate him. Last night I lost what little respect for him that I had. It was not much to lose. I had been on duty from early morning and this particular operation was the 24th I had assisted at for the day and the day before I had done 15 hours theatre duty. Capt. Grieves knocked down some forceps—muttered something at me. I didn't hear so he swore at me, swore at the unconscious patient and at the orderlies. Our Aussie boys whom he so despises may be able to hold the premier position anywhere for their extensive and illustrative vocabulary—but the roughest of them keep within reasonable limits when there are women about. But of course Capt. G. is not a rough digger but an educated English gentleman.[16]

Elsie's attitude towards British officers was common among the Anzacs, whether sisters or Diggers. Kath King's husband, Major Gordon Carter, rated English troops as 'OK', but had little time for their officers, whom he blamed for many of the Allies' problems. Behind it all were the 'social qualifications' which seemed to determine promotion in the British Army. 'The military qualifications seem to be left in the background. I have often been appalled at the ignorance of even senior officers in military matters and they seem rather to glory in it,' Carter wrote witheringly to his parents.[17] Years later, Matron Grace Wilson commented, 'It seemed at times to the Australian Sister that the Q.A. [Queen Alexandra's Imperial Military Nursing Service] Sister laid more stress on the care of equipment—the orderliness of her ward—and the filling in of Military Forms than the actual nursing of her patients.'[18]

Ada Smith, a thirty-one-year-old Sister from Warwick, Queensland, was posted to No. 2 Australian Casualty Clearing Station at Messines, south of Ypres and just twenty minutes' walk from the front. It was June 1917, and the Battle of Messines Ridge was imminent. To take the position, which the Germans had held since late 1914, the Allies dug 8000 metres of tunnel and laid twenty-one mines, nineteen of which were detonated early in the morning of 7 June. The explosions were heard in London and Dublin and killed some 10,000 Germans. In their wake, nine divisions of infantry advanced under protection of a creeping artillery barrage, tanks and gas attacks. Within three hours all initial objectives were taken in an action that greatly boosted morale, German casualties far exceeding those of the Allies.

But as Ada Smith soon found, that did not mean that only the Germans suffered. 'At 7 a.m. we heard the Ridge had been taken with "light casualties" and shortly afterwards the first wounded began to arrive. I couldn't see where the "light casualties" came in as all those healthy men came in dead, dying, unconscious or moaning,' Ada wrote.[19]

There was no time to think of the hundreds of casualties. We only knew that work was waiting to be done everywhere, and men were suffering—waiting to be dressed, or to have an injection of morphia, strychnine or other stimulant, and that many had not had food or drink for hours. Everybody worked many hours at a stretch. We had a day and night staff, but how could anyone go off duty with dying and wounded men all waiting for their turn to be next, and you know that it would be hours, before the night or day staff as it happened to be, could cope with the crowded wards?

Everybody tried to have enough sleep to keep them going, without interfering with the way they did their work, realising the best work could not be done without some sleep. But how could anyone sleep, with our big guns firing a short distance from us. Shells bursting overhead, anti-aircraft and machine guns going continually with the noise of the general bombardment and the screach [*sic*] of shells overhead on their way to Bailleul or Neuve Englise. Colonel received great praise, afterwards, for putting through 2,300 cases in 19 hours—the greater part of whom were operated on, and the foreign bodies removed.[20]

A week later, 14 June, the entire Messines salient was in Allied hands.

At No. 3 Australian General Hospital, Abbeville, Anne Donnell was depressed by the injuries she had to treat. 'In France we see the acutest work, and the havoc the war plays on our precious human lives,' she wrote. 'It's a very sad sight, and while we are doing our level best to restore life, there in the distance is the continual boom, boom, booming from the great guns, which only means more suffering and sadness.'[21] The blast from shell explosions could kill by concussion. In addition to the physical effects of shell fire there was the psychological damage. Men who had to endure a prolonged bombardment would often suffer debilitating shell shock, a condition that was not well understood at the time.

At first, affected soldiers were regarded as weak or cowardly. But as the war progressed, and the number of cases increased, shell shock was formally recognised as an illness. The sisters soon discovered that they too, were considered at risk. At No. 3 Australian Casualty Clearing Station, Gertrude Doherty found the work 'exciting', but the shelling dreadful. 'After we had been in Bapaume a week the Deputy Assistant Director Medical Services rang up to ask if any of the sisters were suffering from shell shock and if so they were to be sent away, and if any of us were frightened we could go back and that it would be no disgrace to us. When the [commanding officer] put it to us we just roared laughing.'[22] The shelling did not improve, and she felt especially sorry for the head cases 'because the shells distressed them so'.

At night in the blacked-out wards, men relived their battle experiences, grappling with unimaginable demons and screaming in terror. 'Some of the poor old boys seem in their delirium to live through all their awful experiences again,' Elsie Tranter recounted. 'They call out and seem quite relieved to find one of us near them when they open their eyes instead of the actual fray.'[23]

But the fray was never far away. The sisters could not escape the sound of shells exploding, the roar of planes overhead or the moans of the wounded. They daily saw young men with smashed faces and pulverised limbs, men with chest wounds spitting blood and gasping for breath, bodies riddled with shell fragments, and the stumps of torn-off limbs. In outbuildings the nurses would find rows of corpses and piles of freshly amputated arms and legs.

And then there were the rats. One of Elsie Tranter's colleagues set a trap in her tent one night and caught seven before sunrise. One morning, while Elsie and three other sisters were chatting, a boot against the wall began to squeak. The boot's owner went over to investigate. 'She put her hand down and there in the toe of one of them was a nest of young mice. Pleasant surprise, wasn't it.'[24]

# 24

# BOMBS AND BASINS

The first anniversary of Harry's death was approaching. For Alice, it had been a year from hell as she grieved and pined for him. On 19 July 1917, a desolate Alice wrote to Harry's mother in Gisborne to share her grief. All Harry's bereft parents now had to remember him was what the Army had shipped in a sealed trunk earlier in the year. Inside were his last personal effects—among them shirts, trousers, khaki shorts, his dressing gown, a bible and letters (Alice's likely among them). They also had his identity disc, which had come from Germany via London.

By now Alice was much closer to the front line. She had been sent forward to No. 2 Casualty Clearing Station at Messines. Among her colleagues there were two Australian Army nurses, Sisters Clare Deacon and Dorothy Cawood, who had sailed with Alice on the *Kyarra* and served at Mena House in Cairo during the Gallipoli campaign. Staff Nurse Mary-Jane Derrer, who had followed later and served at No. 2 Australian General Hospital in Cairo, was also there.

In the wake of the Battle of Messines Ridge, No. 2 was one of nineteen casualty clearing stations preparing for the Third Battle of Ypres, which over the next three months would result in an estimated 310,000 British and

Dominion casualties, with German losses slightly lower. The strategic aim of Third Ypres was the liberation of the Belgian Channel ports and their denial to U-boat operations. But the attacks in the summer and autumn of 1917 took place in the wettest weather in seventy-five years. The vital drainage channels of this low-lying area of Belgium were pounded out of existence by the British and German artillery. The water table of the region turned into a sea of mud and blood that became known as Passchendaele, after the village that crowns the horseshoe of ridges that lie to the east of Ypres. The village was only ten kilometres from the offensive's start line near Ypres, but it took the British, Canadian, Australian, New Zealand and South African troops four and a half months to reach that goal.

As the troops massed and hospitals and clearing stations were set up, the Germans launched preliminary raids ostensibly focused on military targets. But the medical units did not escape the bombing. Head Sister Ida O'Dwyer, who would soon be posted to No. 3 Australian Casualty Clearing Station, understood the dangers.

War of the present day brings the enemy near with aerial bombing and long range shelling—the hospital must be put in a spot convenient to ward and railway, which is usually a target for the enemy, and it is not necessarily the hospital that is aimed at though it very often suffers. This brings a big disadvantage as most of the work is done at night with practically no light and now-a-days the Gothas [German aircraft] do not always wait for the full moon. They come after night and drop bombs on all the areas round, looking for railway dumps and camps. This affects the condition of the patients very much as they feel so there is no protection and they are so helpless—the buzz of the enemy engines is familiar to all and everyone knows of his presence in the sky long before the searchlights appear in the sky from all corners. He is very soon picked out with the light and will even then keep touring round dropping bombs everywhere though full fire is turned on him.[1]

On the night of 22 July, three days after Alice wrote to Harry's mother, the Germans began a bombardment on her clearing station. She was summoned to attend a delirious pneumonia patient at 10:25 p.m. She was walking along the duckboards behind Private John Wilson, an orderly, on the way to the patient's tent, when a German aircraft was caught in the searchlight just above the hospital. Another orderly caught her arm, stopping her and motioning to her to look up. 'Doesn't he look pretty, Sister?' he said.[2] As Alice watched, Private Wilson walked on ahead, swinging a lantern. Then they heard the whirr of a bomb dropping. 'Get down, get down,' someone cried as they dived under a ward table. Alice ran on after Wilson, expecting the bomb to hit the railway line, but it fell ahead of her, at the rear of ward C5, the pneumonia ward, which consisted of four small marquees arranged in a square. The bomb blew a crater five metres in diameter and about two metres deep, completely destroying one tent and leaving the others unfit for use. A second bomb dropped outside the southern boundary of the camp, near the cemetery.

Although the camp had been targeted before, this was the first time that the clearing station itself had been hit. In the dark, Alice could see little around her, but she could hear. 'The noise was so terrific and the concussion so great that I was thrown to the ground and had no idea where the damage was. I flew through the chest and abdominal wards and called out, "Are you alright [sic] boys?" "Don't bother about us," was the general cry.' Alice raced along the duckboards towards the tent of the pneumonia patient. Although every light was out and there was a faint moon, the sky was bright from numerous searchlights. Fragments from the bursting anti-aircraft artillery dropped like rain, one landing immediately in front of Alice. She met the cook running along the duckboards, making for an adjacent paddock and swearing hard. When he saw her, he shouted, 'It's put out my bloody fire, Sister, it's put out me bloody fire.' A patient in pyjamas ran past her, yelling, 'I've got me paybook, Sister.' Alice raced on. 'The next thing I knew I went over into a bomb crater. I shall never forget the awful climb on hands and feet out of that hole about five feet deep, greasy clay and blood, though I did not know then that it was blood.'

The crater was immediately in front of the tent with the pneumonia patient. But the tent, which consisted of three marquees joined together, had collapsed. In all, there were forty-six stretcher cases inside. Alice shouted, but nobody answered, and she could hear nothing above the roar of the planes and the anti-aircraft guns. 'I seemed to be the only living thing about. I tore along to the theatre, the lights were out and the doors shut. I hammered on the door and called out, "Help, help, we've been hit," but no-one came.'

Sister Topsy Tyson was there. But every bottle of anaesthetic in the theatre had been broken. With so much chloroform and ether unleashed, they feared moving in the darkness because of the risk of fire. Running back to the tent, Alice saw the padre. She told him she didn't know what to do because she could not find help. The 'dear old pet', as she called him, replied, 'Just leave it to the Lord, Sister.' Alice thought him a 'very decent chap', but the raid had clearly shaken him badly. He added, 'I'll go and get some help, Sister, but you must get under cover.'

I tried to get into the tent again and got hold of a stretcher handle under the fly. There was a patient on it but he was dead, as I found afterwards. The stretcher handle must have been splintered and I fell backwards into the crater again.

She kept calling for Wilson to help. When he did not come, she thought he was 'funking'. Somebody got the tent up, and when Alice reached the delirious pneumonia patient, he was crouched on the ground at the back of his stretcher, at the far end of the tent.

He would not take any notice of me when I asked him to return to bed, so I leant across the stretcher and put one arm around him and tried to lift him in. I had my right arm under a leg which I thought was [the patient's], but when I lifted I found to my horror that it was a loose leg with a boot and puttee on it.

It was Wilson's leg, which had been blown off. Next day they found the torso up a tree about twenty metres away. 'I have no very distinct recollection of what followed but apparently I carried on with the job,' Alice wrote. The bombing destroyed the mortuary and, aside from Wilson, killed his fellow orderly Joseph Cox and two patients, one of whom was found still on his stretcher, embedded in the ground. Alice's next clear memory was of just before dawn, when the Germans flew over once more, prompting her to get 'a bad attack of trembling when I heard Fritz again'. Three bombs fell on the camp, causing more casualties. The commanding officer, Lieutenant Colonel J. Ramsay-Webb, believed that the Germans were attacking a kite balloon section of the Royal Flying Corps, which was close to the hospital.

Alice was not the only nurse who sped to the aid of the patients that night. Clare Deacon was off duty at the time, but ran into one of the shattered wards and removed patients to safety. Dorothy Cawood and Mary-Jane Derrer also ran back into the wards, doing what they could to protect the patients, placing basins over heads and tables over beds as they ignored the soldiers' cries for them to go to the dugouts for their own safety. Alice later noted that 'all the boys are very wild with Fritz and they went out last night on reprisals'.[3] She wrote to a friend in Melbourne, saying that had the attack arrived 'two minutes later it would have got me, too'.[4] The four nurses carried out their duties with conspicuous bravery, but thought little more about it.

The previous year, the Military Medal had been instituted as an award for bravery in the field for non-commissioned officers and privates, and had since been extended to nurses. The decision that nurses should be eligible for the Military Medal and not the Military Cross, which Army officers received, reflected their ambiguous position as honorary officers. A month after the German raid, on 17 August 1917, the commander of 1 Anzac Corps, Lieutenant General Sir William Birdwood, wrote to inform the four nurses that they would be awarded Military Medals. In his letter to Alice, Birdwood wrote: 'I well know the value on such occasions of the courage and coolness which you displayed, and which has fully earned you this decoration, upon which my heartiest congratulations.'[5] But no award could heal Alice's sorrow.

For Alice, bombing seemed to become a constant. Just a fortnight after the fatal raid, the Germans struck again. A piece of shell case fell through the theatre roof, destroying the metal operating table and the floor.

Captain Calson had been giving an anaesthetic and had lifted the patient's head while orderly lifted feet to place him on stretcher on the floor, otherwise it would have caught both anaesthetist and patient in the head. Captain Calson very shocked and had to go off duty. I wet my pants.[6]

A day later, Alice was having a bath when the Germans returned, again targeting the balloon. 'I could hear the whirr of a fragment. It fell six inches outside [the] washhouse. Never forget how it felt naked and shivering.' She spent a day off shortly afterwards at the nearby town of Hazebrouck, having hitched a ride with an ambulance. The town had been heavily shelled earlier in the morning in a barrage that ended just half an hour before she arrived. She noted later that people were hiding in cellars and shops were closed. 'I did not know anything was wrong and was walking round the square quite unconcernedly whilst all the soldiers stared in surprise.'[7] On the way home that afternoon, Alice returned via the route she believed 'my Harry' must have taken on the way to his burial in the Anzac Cemetery at Sailly-Sur-La-Lys. (But Harry's body was never recovered and there was no report of his burial. As his name was on an official German death list, it seems likely that he was buried by the Germans near the battlefield, possibly in the mass grave at Pheasant Wood, which was partially excavated in mid-2008. His name is among

1299 commemorated on a memorial wall at VC Corner Cemetery at Fromelles.)

As air raids continued without let-up during July and August 1917, more nurses were decorated for bravery. The *London Gazette* announced on 18 July that a New Zealand nurse, Sister Laura James of Queen Alexandra's Imperial Military Nursing Service, had also been awarded the Military Medal. While no date was given, the incident for which she was honoured must have occurred some weeks earlier, probably making her the first nurse from Australia or New Zealand to win the medal. The *Dominion* newspaper would later report that she had been the sister in charge of the operating theatre one night when shells were 'flying around', and it was for her fortitude during this raid that she had been awarded the Military Medal—the only one given to a New Zealand nurse during the war.

Another Australian nurse working with the Imperial Military Nursing Service, Sister Eileen King, also won the medal for her actions while serving at a British casualty clearing station. The *British Journal of Nursing* announced that the King had approved her medal in early February 1918, which means the action in question most likely occurred in the second half of 1917.[8] According to a newspaper report,

Eileen King was serving in a tented field hospital in France when it was struck by a stick of bombs. She had part of her left thigh broken away and received other serious wounds but broke no major blood vessel. She remained on duty and managed to get her wounded out of the burning tent. Soldiers who knew her described her as one of the bravest women they had ever met.[9]

In late June 1917, Ballarat nurse Rachael Pratt, who had been awarded the Royal Red Cross 2nd Class a year earlier, was working at No. 1 Australian Casualty Clearing Station, near Bailleul. On the night of 3–4 July, the Germans attacked the station. Bomb fragments from the raid burst through the top of her tent, tearing into her back and shoulder and puncturing her lung. The only nurse wounded in the raid, she carried on until she collapsed. She was evacuated to England to convalesce, promoted to Sister, and awarded the Military Medal for her bravery under fire.[10]

This was a trying time for nurses and patients alike. Two weeks after the Battle of Passchendaele began, Sister Alicia 'Rachel' Kelly, from Perth, was on duty at No. 3 Australian Casualty Clearing Station at Brandhoek. It had eight operating tables going night and day. Head Sister Ida O'Dwyer was also there at the time, and noted that the Germans dropped bombs and shells on August 16, 17, 18, 19 and 21. It seemed as if the unit was under continual attack. Ida recalled one raid, on a 'beautiful clear night', when the injured were arriving in convoys and doctors and nurses had all been ordered on duty to start operating.

In the theatre not a word was said, every table was busy—bombs, someone said. Surgeons stopped in the middle of tying a blood vessel to perhaps utter a word that had no relation to the wound. Sister, who was noted for her quickness, did not get the catgut through the needle so smartly. That was all the difference it made, yet each was wondering who might be hurt and where they fell. In the busy ward with the rush of work the staff hardly realised what had happened 'til someone made the familiar remark, "where did that one go".[11]

The attack on the 21st killed a Canadian sister in a nearby clearing station and left fifteen English nurses shell-shocked. May Tilton recalled how an agitated medical officer pushed his head into her tent. 'Come on, you girls. Put on your coats and slippers. The [commanding officer] says you have to get into a dugout at once. They are shelling us.'

May and her colleagues were incensed because he would not allow them time to dress. 'We wanted to go to the wards, not into a burrow in the ground.'[12] Running in her slippers, May heard a long-drawn-out crescendo following her. She thought she was gone. Men shouted at her to run, others to drop. 'My slipper tripped me, and I fell, just as the shell fell in the cemetery behind. I looked back to see a huge mass of black smoke and debris flying in all directions; felt myself lifted and dragged into a huge dugout where all the day staff had gathered. Every one of them was upset at the C.O.'s orders, and distressed to leave the patients.'[13]

Ida O'Dwyer decided to make the best of the situation, sitting on the sandbags with the mess book, calmly calling on the sisters to fix up their accounts before she lost sight of them. May had no money. 'Well, find it somewhere,' Ida replied. 'You will probably be scattered all over the country, and I won't see you again, and we must pay our bills.' The boys paid their debts.

In the meantime, Rachel Kelly had refused to leave her patients. She stayed in a hospital tent holding one man's hand and doing her best to calm him and others. Chaplain G.C. Munschamp recalled her actions with admiration:

We have been bombed continually. The noise of the guns, only a hundred yards from the camp, has been startling and deafening. One bomb fell close to the sisters' quarters, killing an officer and an orderly, and riddling the sisters' tents in which they were sleeping, fortunately on the ground.

Finally came the day when the Germans deliberately shelled the camp, and no one who has not seen it can realise what it means to have huge armour-piercing shells fall in your midst with a burst of [a] quarter of a mile all round.

We got all the sisters away to a trench at the back of the camp, but when all had gone we found Rachel alone in her ward, giving to each patient an enamel bowl to cover his head from flying pieces of shell— absolutely comforting all these poor frightened helpless creatures in her calm and sweet mothering ways, and we had literally to drag her to a place of safety.[14]

The Chaplain said Rachel did not know that 'she had been perfectly heroic . . . She was only troubled that she couldn't obey the order to seek shelter, because her poor boys looked so frightened, and all the orderlies had run out of the ward.'[15] According to May Tilton, when the first shell fell, Rachel 'rushed for the enamel wash basins and covered the patients' heads to protect them from bits of flying shrapnel, then stood in the middle of the ward, encouraging and cheering her helpless patients'.

Rachel was transferred to No. 3 Australian General Hospital and awarded the Military Medal. In the space of a few months, seven Military Medals had been awarded to Australian nurses and one to a New Zealander for their courage under fire. This extraordinary achievement has not been equalled in any campaign involving the Australian Army Nursing Service since the Great War. But those were not the last Military Medals to be awarded to Anzac nurses during the conflict.

# 25

# DESOLATION

———◦►◄◦———

Alice Ross King could not get away from the bombing. It seemed every night during August 1917 at Messines was spent in a dugout as the Third Battle of Ypres raged. After General Birdwood presented her and her three colleagues with their medals, they were feted with a dinner at Anzac headquarters at Hazebrouck. The town was bombed while they were there. They left in an ambulance, bombs falling all the way. One landed immediately in front of the vehicle. 'Very narrow escapes,' Alice noted succinctly.[1] Such experiences were now almost a normal part of life. She knew that No. 3 Clearing Station had been destroyed by shelling, and that No. 1 near Bailleul had been targeted but the bombs had not exploded: 'We are taking their cases.' She was working from 7 a.m. to 2 a.m. The Germans were still shelling Bailleul, 'and each day the shells go whining over our heads to the back areas.'[2]

When the Germans started using gas shells, the dangers intensified. Wind carried gas along a shallow valley to No. 2 Australian Casualty Clearing Station. One morning Alice was woken by a clamour of alarm bells. She thought it was a signal that the Germans had broken through, but the bells were warning of the gas. The deadly fumes quickly engulfed the hospital, and Alice felt the effects before she understood what was happening.

'My throat and eyes were smarting and I felt awfully sick.'[3] Topsy Tyson told her it was gas and they quickly donned their gas masks. But something else worried Alice—her new kitten was missing.

The kitten had lived in the trenches, somehow surviving on the scraps of food the men left, and had not yet seen milk when Alice took it in during July 1917. It arched its back and spat at her on their first meeting. But they grew on each other, and the kitten settled in, running up soldiers' legs and playing with their rank badges. When General Birdwood visited, the kitten befriended him. He didn't seem to mind, putting it on his shoulder and stroking it as he stood talking to Alice and the matron. Now her pet was in danger from the gas. Alice dashed outside, but the kitten did not recognise her in the gas mask and ran under the hut. Next day it returned, none the worse for wear.

The same could not be said for German prisoners. One day, as Alice was about to go off duty, she heard feeble, anguished moans coming from a tent that had been neglected for three and a half days. Inside were fifty-three badly wounded German prisoners who had no water or food. The medical staff were too 'dead beat' to come and attend to them. She searched until she found a doctor who would. Together, they treated forty men in forty-five minutes. Thirteen had already died. There was no waiting for chloroform for amputations. Somehow they got all the men onto a train ninety minutes after Alice had found them.

The doctors and sisters worked tirelessly, but the sheer volume of casualties and the severity of the wounds taxed them to their limits. And the threat of aerial attack was always there. An order went out: 'All Sisters to go to Dugout when Fritz is overhead.' Alice thought it silly. 'I expect they want to get rid of the lot of us if there is a direct hit,' she wrote, her black humour irrepressible. Even so, they were spending more and more nights in the dugouts, under orders from General Birdwood to leave the patients during raids. He had warned that he would withdraw the sisters if he learned they had been exposed to fire. As Fritz flew overhead 'doing his stuff', Alice tried to use the time to keep up her diary, with the gramophone playing in the background. A bottle of brandy was sometimes taken down, and the sisters had a drink to calm their nerves.

Alice did not take kindly to the warning to stay in the dugout and leave her patients. She was a nurse first, and in the Army second. During one raid, she 'nicked down to the wards to see if the orderlies were there or hiding in the soap drain . . . A Fritz flew along the duckboards as I was running back—seemed to be right on top of me.' Luckily, the aircraft was a fighter and not a bomber.

The battle to save the wounded often seemed futile. 'The last post is being played nearly all day at the cemetery next door to the hospital. So many deaths,' Alice lamented. With so much carnage from the Ypres Offensive, her faith began to falter. The padre was always praying that 'Right will prevail', but Alice was beginning to wonder. 'I can't believe there is a God. It is too awful for words.'4

Those around Alice, especially her friend Topsy Tyson, realised that she was feeling the strain. A 'nasty near miss with a bit of H.E. [high-explosive shrapnel]' did not help. She stayed on duty but now 'wet my pants whenever Fritz came over'. This was shell shock. For her own good, Topsy informed Evelyn Conyers, the Army Nursing Service Matron-in-Chief, that Alice showed signs of having been at the station for too long. 'So I had,' Alice reluctantly agreed. She was sent back to No. 1 General Hospital at Rouen, further from the front line. As 1917 drew to a close, Alice learned that besides the award of the Military Medal she also had been Mentioned in Despatches twice—another commendation for gallantry or otherwise meritorious service.5

———————

Across the Channel, at Queen Mary's Hospital in Lancashire, Elsie Eglinton read a letter from her orderly. Ernest Hewish had gone into battle with the Australian Army Medical Corps' 6th Field Ambulance as a stretcher bearer. He was a pharmacy student and, like Elsie, from Adelaide. They had worked

together before—first at the Ghezireh Palace in Cairo in 1915, and then at
No. 2 Australian General Hospital at Wimereaux. Elsie thought he was 'a
bonza boy' from the start.

At the hospital, they had a bit of fun with Matron Nellie Gould one
night.

> There was an empty bed in the corridor so I told him to get in and
> have a sleep and I would call him if he was required. He had just got
> in and made himself comfortable when who should come along but
> Miss Gould. She mistook him for a patient and bending over him
> said, 'Why are you not sleeping, are you sure you are quite comfort-
> able?' Little did she know that he was fully dressed and should have
> been walking around. Poor boy said that he was terribly scared, but he
> really must tell her the joke when the war is over.[6]

A little more than a year later, they had been together again at Wimereaux.
'My dear old orderly from Ghezireh Palace is in my ward,' Elsie wrote. 'I like
him better the more I see of him. He would work his fingers to the bone for
the boys. He is so gentle and kind. He is longing to get into the line but I tell
him he is too young to go up there. We call him "Hughie" but his name is
Hewish.'[7] Aged just nineteen, Hughie called Elsie 'Aunt'. Now, in June 1917,
he was up the line, along with his friend and fellow South Australian Ronald
John 'Joe' Rowett, a private in the 43rd Battalion.

> Dear Aunt,
> Just a few lines to let you know that I am still alive and in the best of
> health and so far have not received any injuries. The nearest shell
> landed about 20 yards away and a piece went through my coat sleeve.
> I do not want it any nearer than that. We are living in a tiny dugout,
> just room for two, but it's fairly safe against anything but a direct hit
> from a shell. We have just about completed our time and hope to be

relieved soon. We cannot complain because we have had quite an easy time this trip.

Isn't it glorious weather and doesn't it make you glad to see all the grass shooting up and to hear the birds whistling.

. . . I cannot tell you much about our camp life as we are always on the move and very seldom settle down in any place for more than a few days. I like this life a great deal better than the hospital and I am sorry I did not get out of it sooner than I did, but we could hardly help that.

Sincerely yours

E. Hewish, No. 8282.

P.S. Since writing this we were moved to another spot and it proved to be a very hot spot, it is where we are making advances but I cannot mention the name of the place. We had to carry across country continually being swept by the enemy shellfire. Joe was unfortunate enough to get hit in the head by a piece of shell and I think it just about bad enough for a 'Blightie'. I only saw him for a few minutes after he was hit. He seemed to be pretty right then. I think he is one of the luckiest men alive, for had it not been for his helmet he would have certainly been killed.

We are just out for a rest or rather a sleep for it was impossible to sleep up there even if you had the time.

Well, I trust that I shall not meet with the same misfortune, so will close now.[8]

Joe Rowett was all right after his hit in the head and seems to have remained in the fighting. He too was friendly with Elsie, and they corresponded during the Ypres Offensive. Such scraps of contact with friends were important, because no one could know what lay ahead.

May Tilton's fiancé was somewhere in the line when he heard that No. 3 Casualty Clearing Station at Brandhoek had been shelled on 21 August. Four days later, after May had moved to a Canadian clearing station at St Omer, he appeared. He had ridden sixty kilometres on a bike he found by the roadside. Fearing for her safety, he managed to get thirty-six hours' leave to track her down. Desperately tired and in need of sleep, he found a bed in town and saw her the next day. That night the Germans came, making an 'awful racket' over St Omer. May, 'too anxious and scared' to rest in bed, walked about all night. Early the next morning her fiancé arrived, looking worried.

All that day, my poor dear seemed more than usually troubled, and fought hard to hide his feelings from me. At 7 p.m. he returned to the line. But his usual cheery manner before we parted was changed to a silence that frightened me to think what he was feeling. With my heart crying against the parting, I braced myself to regain the courage which had almost deserted me. To be strong was our only hope. He strode away, whistling a gay tune. Next day he wrote me all he could not say. My heart died as I read the words: 'Every man has a premonition of his fate up here, before the end.' I tried to keep before me, and remember, all the things he asked of me.[9]

May's mood was made heavier that night when it started raining; it poured for a week. She knew that thousands of men, waiting in their trenches for the expected hop over, would drown if they lay down to sleep. Some were buried in mud, and when dug out were found dead. But May could not afford to dwell on her fiancé's safety even if she wanted to; there was too much to do.

Some Australian divisions were resting behind the lines at Argues, three kilometres from St Omer, and they and the sisters took the chance to socialise. Many of the soldiers visited daily, and the sisters patched their clothes, knitted them socks and helped to cheer them up before they left in early September to march back to the line.

At Argues there was a hospital full of shell-shocked patients, but no sisters, and its commanding officer allowed May and her colleagues to visit and take the boys out. They would sit beside the canal, playing cards and reading, and dipping into hampers they took with them. Such respites were rare. The cobbled roads were crowded with arm-swinging and singing troops, and at night Fritz's planes came, loaded with bombs. Late one night, a bomb fell in the midst of the sisters' tents, leaving the canvas riddled with shrapnel holes big enough to put a fist through. Next morning May souvenired a jagged ten-centimetre piece of shrapnel, which she kept for the rest of her life.

In mid-September, May moved to No. 47 British Casualty Clearing Station at St Sixte in Belgium, as part of the preparations for the advance to capture Passchendaele, Polygon Wood and Broodseinde. The camp was huge and included two other clearing stations. After days of preliminary heavy shelling, the Germans were forced back on either side of the Ypres-Menin Road. By noon on the 20th, the Australians and British had won Menin Road and were at the edge of Polygon Wood. Some 5000 Australians were among the Allied casualty toll of up to 25,000. In a sea of mud, the Australians moved onto Polygon Wood which the 4th and 5th Divisions captured. The wounded poured into the three hospitals, 200 at a time. There was only time to attend to urgent dressings and make them as comfortable as possible.

For May Tilton, 21 September was a day she would always remember as dreadful and full of foreboding. 'I felt something had happened to spoil my life. I could not throw off the depression. Matron, chancing to notice my ghastly appearance, insisted on me going off duty for a couple of hours. I could not divulge my secret fear to her.' That night no one could sleep for the roaring of the guns. May and several of her colleagues were called at 3 a.m. to open a new ward to cope with the rush of patients. Explosions from an air raid taxed their nerves. Being up and doing something was a relief. As the raids continued, some of the wounded were too ill to take much notice, while others, so overwrought they could scarcely lie in their beds, cried out: 'Sister, give me an injection, quickly, before they come again. I can't stand any more tonight.'

It was left to the sisters' discretion whether to give morphia or stimulants. Unlike the general hospitals, the casualty clearing stations could order unlimited supplies of brandy, champagne and stout, and chicken—luxuries that the men loved. They deserved this at the very least, May thought. She had witnessed 'such frightened expressions' as she bent over them, working to relieve their pain, bathing their eyes with bicarbonate of soda and inserting cocaine solution to relieve the agony from mustard gas. Pads and bandages kept these patients in darkness. A sister worked continuously on each side of the ward, while yet more sisters tried to relieve patients' distressed breathing by administering oxygen for ten minutes every half hour. They were unable to work in the gas wards for long. Stooping over patients, the nurses soon became affected by inhaling the residual gas. Their throats grew sore, their eyes smarted and watered. The odour of the ward would stay in their nostrils for weeks.

In early October, May and the other Australian sisters were recalled to No. 3 Australian Casualty Clearing Station, which had been re-established at Nine Elms, ten kilometres from Ypres. For her friend Elsie Grant, there was a pleasant surprise at Ypres. Her brother, 2nd Lieutenant Allan Herbert Grant of the 40th Battalion, had arrived there two hours before her. He knew Elsie was in the general area, but had no more information until he saw a transport carrying Australian sisters with her unit colours late at night. As he asked if any of them knew where Elsie was, the car she was in stopped and the first person she saw was Allan. 'Really I thought to myself God must have sent him as a comfort after the day we had had. We all embraced him and the dear left at 5 a.m. next morning,' she wrote to a friend.[10] Allan had laughed at Elsie's fears and said he would be down to see her the first chance he got. In her letter, Elsie confided that she badly wanted 'to come home on transport but I really can't bring myself to leave Allan behind. That is the principle reason I don't come'. Two months later, on 20 October, Elsie received a letter from a sergeant in Allan's battalion.

> It is with regret I take up my pen to write these few lines telling you that your Brother A.H. Grant was killed in action on the 12:10:17; but Sister is it not just consolation to know that he died a grand and noble death fighting for his God; King; Country and dear ones. I had not met your brother prior to his joining our Battn (40th) but he was so jolly; full of sport; and good natured that he was soon known and loved by all the boys, in fact his platoon used to just idolise him and I too used to love to get a chat with him. The night prior to the Stunt which as it happened to be his last I was talking to him for quite a long while, and as I was being left out of the Stunt, he gave me his wallet, a letter and paper to you . . . He asked me as a favor if anything did happen [to] him to forward these articles on to you, which I am duly doing and trust the parcel will reach you safely . . . I know Sister it is hard to part with our dear loved ones, but still think what a grand and noble death his was and truly a better and braver Soldier than he could never be. He was loved by all and I ask you to accept our deepest sympathy in you great loss.[11]

Aged twenty-eight, Allan was shot in the head while attacking a German pillbox at Passchendaele. He was buried where he fell.

---

The advance up the line took a heavy toll. In the first twenty-four hours about 3000 patients were admitted to No. 3 Clearing Station. Hospital trains stood by and carried the wounded away as fast as the sisters could get them ready. They had time to attend only the worst cases. The resuscitation ward resembled a butcher's shop; those who were conscious smiled grimly, glad to be wounded and out of the fighting. Annie Shadforth was at No. 3 and shuddered at the sight of the terrible injuries. She thought she had 'seen horrific wounds and badly gassed patients until I looked on the [boys] at the CCS.' The 'poor boys died like flies . . . I felt that I must pull myself together otherwise I would be sent back to the base. I didn't want to go back. I was convinced it was a CCS that needed skilled women,' she recalled later.[12] The pressure on the sisters was immense.

Ordered to grab a few hours' rest, May Tilton and another sister were groping their way along the duckboards one rainy night when they slipped into what they thought was an empty ward. Tripping over a stretcher, they found the floor covered with a mass of wounded. Men were being sick, moaning in pain, or crying out for a drink. Many pleaded for their boots to be removed. The two sisters set to work, lifting the stretchers into some sort of order and searching for haemorrhage cases while other wounded men held torches to guide them. When their backs would hold up no longer, they sat on the floor and cut the boots and socks off the men's stone-cold and swollen feet, wrapping them in bundles of cotton wool and bandages. All the while, the guns roared, and 5.9-inch shells screamed overhead. On 4 October 1917, in the midst of the Battle of Broodseinde, May wrote:

We hated and dreaded the days that followed this incessant thundering, when the torn, bleeding and pitifully broken human beings were brought in, their eyes filled with horror and pain; those who could walk staggering dumbly, pitifully, in the wrong direction. Days later men were carried in who had been found lying in shell-holes, starved, cold, and pulseless, but, by some miracle, still alive. Many died of exposure and the dreaded gas gangrene.

That same day, 'Hughie' Hewish and 'Joe' Rowett were in the thick of the action at Broodseinde. Hughie and his ambulance unit were caught up in the fighting as they retrieved the wounded from the battlefield. He was killed, two months short of his twentieth birthday. Joe wrote at once to tell Elsie Eglinton the sad news. Ernest, she wrote home, 'was one of God's good men'.

---

May Tilton was assigned to theatre, where the staff worked the longest hours of any sisters. She went on duty at 8 p.m. and worked continuously during a 'stunt' until midday the following day, with ten minutes for supper at midnight and an hour for breakfast at 8 a.m. This brought her into contact with an American surgeon, Captain Philip Wilson, who had been working with the French Army since the war began, and more recently with the newly arrived Americans. He was quick and clever, and trusted May, telling her that in critical cases she should use a scalpel on the minor wounds, otherwise the patient would die. 'I trembled at the knees, for it meant using the scalpel—work I had never done before. When I told him, he replied: "I could not have a better or more capable assistant than you have proved to be. Forget yourself and think only of our patient." So I did, and we saved lots of lives.'[13] That month, the theatre team performed 1500 operations.

A Canadian airman who knew May and her colleagues wrote to them after he was shot down. 'We were bombed nightly, and I don't know how you stick it like you do—the sleepless life, the reeking atmosphere, and everything. I say, "Three cheers and a tiger for our brave little sisters." We know and appreciate the work you do, and love you for your bravery and endurance.'[14]

Endurance meant many things. As May walked along the duckboards after coming off duty following yet another heavy night, a dud shell fell less than two metres away, burying itself deep between the tent ropes. Two orderlies walking behind her gasped that it had been a close shave. 'Yes,' May replied, and walked on to her tent, wondering how she had escaped it. 'Too dead tired to notice the guns, I ceased to be worried by them. We learned to fit them into the back of our subconscious minds and forget them.'[15]

But there are experiences that push beyond endurance and war weariness, that challenge one's notion of fate. On 16 October 1917, May had just finished dinner and was waiting to go on duty when someone handed her a paper to read. Her first thought was the Casualty List.

The one name I feared to read was there under the big, black heading, 'Killed'. [It was her fiancé.] An overpowering sense of desolation swept through me. I felt I could endure no more. That night I wrestled with myself all alone in my tent, unable to face the work in the theatre. My team were able to carry on without a sister, and, fortunately, I could be spared from working that night.

Next morning, Captain Wilson came and sat beside me, and talked of things that made me realise my own selfishness in forgetting for a moment the needs of our poor men, dependent on us. The comforting kindness and consideration of those about me helped me to restore my balance again. But something had happened to my head, which was all tight inside.

Over the years, May's fiancé's name has been lost to history, but to her he was 'the one man in all the world'. They had made plans for the future.

Another of May's friends, twenty-seven-year-old Percy Wells, was a driver with the 2nd Brigade Australian Field Artillery. Hearing of the death of May's fiancé, he wrote to her. 'I am coming down to see how you are looking and to persuade you to go home after this.' But he never made it. He was killed taking ammunition to the front line on 30 October 1917 at Passchendaele. His body lay on the Menin Road for five days before it could be recovered. He was buried close to May's cousin, Gallipoli veteran Sergeant Norman Ellsworth, who had died of wounds on 31 July that year when the Third Battle of Ypres had begun.

Not long before she read of her fiancé's death, May had written that the war was cruel and senseless, 'but we knew we had to stick it, and sacrifice precious lives to win it'. Stoical she may have been, but this loss, coming after the death of Norman and compounded by the death of her friend Percy, was a sacrifice too far. A few weeks later, No. 3 Clearing Station was converted into a convalescent camp. Matron sent May and Elsie Grant, who was keenly suffering the loss of her brother, to Cannes, in the south of France, for a rest. It was soon apparent that they needed more than a holiday.

When they returned to No. 3 Australian General Hospital at Abbeville in January 1918, 'terrific headaches' prevented May from sleeping. Boils appeared on her arms and wrists. Elsie Grant fell prey to a nervous condition that caused painful swelling in her face. Believed to be headed for a breakdown, they were detailed for transport duty back to Australia. May left knowing that wherever she went or whatever she did in future, the best part of her would always remain at Passchendaele, which had been captured by the Australians but with terrible losses. In eight weeks of fighting, there had been 38,000 Australian casualties. Here lay many of the friends she loved best.

# 26

# SURVIVAL

As the war ground away inexorably at the spirits of May Tilton, Elise Grant and Alice Ross King, the realisation had long settled on sisters and soldiers that they had little control over life. A splinter of shrapnel in the midst of a bombardment, a bayonet charge over the top, or the wraith-like fog of mustard gas, and life could be wrecked or ended in a moment. So many friends had died, and so many hearts had been broken. No one had escaped the relentless ravages of war. On the Western Front in 1917, there was little of the carefree optimism and joyous romanticism of those early days in Egypt in 1915.

But many still tried. Eggs arrived for the patients, often from young women in England who attached notes with their addresses. At No. 13 Stationary Hospital correspondences that started this way were soon known as 'egg romances'. One patient was so upset when his 'real girl' failed to write that the Australian sisters suggested he get someone else to write and let her know he was very ill, with compound fractures of both arms, wounds in his head and chest, and his left eye gone. 'No,' he said. 'I am not going to chase any woman; they can chase me now.'[1] He was soon doing well under the sisters' care.

But they had more than their job to do. Hardest of all was writing to inform mothers of the death of a son. In 1917, this task fell to Ida O'Dwyer after the death at No. 3 Casualty Clearing Station of Private Donald Nicol, an eighteen-year-old from Bulli on the New South Wales south coast and a member of the 56th Battalion.

Mrs Nicol

Dear madam

I am writing to tell you about your son Pte D.B. Nicol 2453. He was brought into this hospital yesterday very collapsed and suffering from a very severe shell wound of both legs and shattered left arm. His condition was very low from shock and loss of blood, and though everything possible was done he did not rally at all and died in about 3 hours.

I am afraid it is not very much to tell you but it might be some comfort to you to know that he was in hospital where he had every care and attention and was relieved of all his pain.

He was buried this morning in a military cemetery at Nine Elms near Poperinghe and if there is anything further with regard to the grave that you wish to know you can write to the Officer in Charge G.R.U. War Office.

This unit is in charge of all the Soldiers' Graves in France. All his small personal belongings will eventually be sent on to you as his next of Kin.

Remain yours faithfully

Ida O'Dwyer

Sister in Charge[2]

Ida shielded Mrs Nicol from the full extent of her son's injuries. Besides the leg and arm wounds, his Army service file shows that he had also suffered a disfiguring gunshot wound to the mouth.

Nurses often had to fill the role of mothers, sisters and sweethearts. In an
Acute hut of forty beds at No. 3 Australian General Hospital at Le Treport in
Normandy, Anne Donnell had care of the badly injured from Bullecourt
and Vimy Ridge in May 1917. Many had their loved ones come over from
England to give what comfort they could before they died. This provided
some relief for the nurses. But there were some patients who had no one.

. . . there was one dear laddie in a corner bed with terrible wounds in
his back that my heart went out to, and his people had not yet come.
There was no time to special [the patients], one just did what one
could for each, and then it was, I thought, a case of the survival of the
fittest. The days were gone before you knew, and you felt you had
accomplished nothing. But this laddie in the corner, I thought, shall
have some special care, and matron had brought him some lovely
oranges that he fancied, so I quietly sat down and fed him and told
him he would be mine until his mother came. He gave me the
loveliest smile as he replied 'and I'll make you my special,' but quickly
added, 'You must forgive me, sister, I wouldn't have said that under
ordinary circumstances.' Next morning when I went on duty, his bed
was empty, just another one of the many there that made the supreme
sacrifice. His parents arrived—too late to see him, but I was so
thankful to be able to give them his last message of love.[3]

Later, Anne reflected on her role and what she represented to the wounded
men.

It's very terrible to see them coming in as they are, and it's a blessing
that one cannot stop to think or analyse things. I only know that I am
not a mere nurse, but represent to them for the time being their
dearest ones, and many a time I find myself going to the marquee flap
to hide the tears that will gather, and ask for strength to control a
distorted face, and go back.[4]

But their concern for the boys extended beyond this. What happened to them outside the hospitals, such as when they went on leave to London, also mattered. Inevitably prostitutes or factory and servant girls out for a good time targeted the boys around the Australian headquarters on Horseferry Road. Tev Davies' forbearance was tested by what she saw.

It is such a shame, such fearful women one sees tailing onto Australian boys, then again water finds its level, still the boys have such a bad time in France that one cannot well blame them when these women are kind and friendly to them. The Authorities could not have chosen a worse place [for Australian HQ], I simply dread going down there every time, one sees these awful creatures with men who have done such good work in France, but are spoiling it all in just a few days.[5]

Grace Wilson, by now temporary Matron-in-Chief at AIF headquarters, saw it first hand.

Men came to the Sisters for safety among pressing temptations. In many instances they were kept from women they wished to avoid by spending time in the Sisters' mess and by the Sisters going to dinner or to entertainments with them. Our men will have the society of women somehow. I think there was a big field of influence exercised here—that cannot very well be put into print.[6]

Friendships and relationships between sisters and soldiers were valued as much for the moment as for the future, especially when the future could be snuffed out in a second. Sisters and soldiers alike were young and in the prime of life. It was natural that attractions should develop. But the sisters also had a professional duty. On occasions, though, the distinction was blurred.

Fanny Speedy was working at Brockenhurst Hospital in England, where
New Zealand troops wounded in France were sent. She noted in her diary
that she would miss eight of the men who left to go home on the hospital
ship *Maheno*. One in particular, Cargill, had been there the longest. 'Have
been rather amused to find that the romance I fancied was growing could
only have been in my imagination for he is already engaged.'[7] Some friendships developed into discreet liaisons, perhaps like the one New Zealander
Erle Crawford was referring to when he recorded cryptically in his diary that
he had 'met Sister Whitta in Red Cross store room'.[8]

An insight into the bonds between soldiers and nurses, and the emotions
sometimes unsuspectingly aroused in the men, can be found in an anonymous letter mailed to the sisters living at Villa Marguerite in Dieppe in
November 1917. Among the recipients was Elsie Tranter, who recorded the
text in her diary:

Dear Sisters in seclusion sweet
Who live in Villa Marguerite
Whose time is given to good deeds
In ministering to heroes needs,
Who unsuspecting of all ill
Your daily task of love fulfil
Beware! Lest you should start a fire
In hearts which thought not to aspire
To charms like yours. Each martial breast
Whilst convalescing is at rest
From warlike thoughts, and open lies
Exposed to Cupid's darts. Keen eyes
Which undismayed looked oft on Death
Unflinching, have withstood the breath
Of battles' fiercest strain, now full
Abashed when challenged by the call

Of eye to eye. You know your power,
How great the strength of woman's dower
Be careful if ye would be wise!
For if you're not there may arise
Disaster dread. Nor place much trust
In men who promise when they must
Fulfil but only when they can
And have in show the faults of man.
Remember for each Marguerite
There is at least one Faust to me.[9]


Elsie Tranter knew both sides of the situation, for she was also engaged to a Digger. She had to put that to one side as she nursed the wounded. For the men lying in the beds, often dependent on the nurses to feed them, and in some cases for their very survival, the relationship was special. A South African soldier tried to capture it with a verse he sent Elsie in August 1917:

To Sister
Tommy is back for a lie in bed
To be patched and settled, nursed and fed,
Safe for a time from the distant storm,
Berthed in hospital smug and warm.
Sister has taken him under her wing,
She's a white capped, slender slip of a thing.
She has frank eyes and capable hands,
Sister is merry and fond of chaff.
But she knows when to pity and when to laugh.
She helps him through with his bit of pain,
And makes him feel his old self again,
She washes and brushes and makes him smart

Till the sight of him gladdens her orderly heart.

And Tommy's a good little boy once more

Though he stands six feet on the well scrubbed floor.

Special favours she grants to none.

She loves and mothers them every one.

And parts from her boys with real regret.

They don't say much but they won't forget.[10]

Earlier that year, after crossing the English Channel to Boulogne, Elsie Tranter travelled to Etaples to work at No. 26 British General Hospital. Her new matron had a succinct message about fraternisation for Elsie and the other sisters joining the staff. 'We left matron with a jingle of "<u>don'ts</u> for nurses" in our ears and feeling that if we met a boy pal and talked with him we would be about due for 6 months in the clink and if we walked with him it would mean sudden death. Of course it was not really as bad as that.'[11]

Sometimes, though, the affections of the bedridden patients were real, as May Tilton learned at No. 1 War Hospital, in Birmingham, in February 1916. 'A fine, hefty Canadian told me all about his ranch, and said he'd be doing a cowboy act when this "dust up" was over if I did not consent to his proposals, for he sure meant to collect me and to take me over there as his "souvenir of the war"—and not to forget it. He refused to accept the fact that I was already promised to an Aussie. "Poof!" he said. "All's fair in love and war. Just wait and see."' His mother wrote to May, saying she was waiting to welcome her. 'He went back to France and gave his life,' May lamented.[12]

Nurses in France who were to be married usually did so in England. When Elsie Eglinton arrived in France to join the quarantine camp outside Marseilles, there was a surprise gift waiting for her: a heavy tartan rug sent by the *Ionian*'s third engineer, George Mackay, whom she had got to know while sailing back and forth in the Mediterranean. When the *Ionian* docked in Marseilles, Matron Gould gave Elsie the afternoon off. She and George went to Marseilles and had tea, and Elsie gave him two beautifully carved emu eggs. The reunion was so memorable that Elsie coyly noted, 'A lovely thing happened today.'[13] And it wasn't just that she had been Mentioned in Despatches 'for gallant and distinguished services in the field' while working on hospital ships.

Later in 1916, Elsie was granted leave to travel to England. By the middle of the month, the *Ionian* had returned to London and George arranged to see her in Hertfordshire. Demurely, she noted, 'Mr Mackay came down to see me and brought me a beautiful ring.'[14] Elsie was engaged. Not long after, her joy was muted when she read in the morning paper that one of her old friends, a soldier, had been killed in action in France. 'It seems like yesterday to me that he was a little boy playing with his wooden dolls.'[15]

She did not want to leave No. 2 General Hospital in Wimereaux, but in April 1917 she was sent to England with pneumonia. Recovered, she went to No. 2 Australian Auxiliary Hospital at Southall. Four months later, Elsie and George Mackay married in London, after which she left the Army Nursing Service, as the regulations required, and worked for the Red Cross. Elsie noted that two of her friends and cabin mates on the *Kyarra*, Olive Haynes and Pete Peters, were coming to London to be married, 'so I shall not be lonely then'.

Less than three months after her marriage, the *Ionian* was torpedoed and several men drowned, but George Mackay survived the sinking and remained in the service. In April 1918, Elsie returned to Australia alone. She wondered how she would settle down 'especially when I think of the dangers my husband and our dear boys are facing . . . It will be like lying down to rest on a bed of pins and needles, don't be surprised if I come away back [to Europe] again.'[16]

At No. 2 Australian General Hospital in Boulogne, Olive Haynes was officially engaged to 2nd Lieutenant Pat Dooley, a law graduate from Melbourne University who was now an orderly. The moment they met the

previous year, they had clicked. Everyone admired the platinum engagement ring with three diamonds that Pat had sent from London. He wrote
to Olive that he was about to go to France with the 22nd Battalion and
hoped to see her. 'Still, even if I don't, I'm the luckiest guy on earth to
have such a great woman waiting and working for me to blow back,' he
added.[17] Olive wrote to her parents in Adelaide to ease their concerns about
whether Pat, who planned to become a clergyman, would be able to provide
for her. As an Anglican cleric himself, her father probably had his own
reasons for his doubts. Olive desperately wanted them to understand that it
would be all right. She told them that as soon as Pat could get leave they
would marry.

I know you all think we shouldn't, but you must see from our point
of view. Mine is that, if anything happened to Pat, I would never
forgive myself for not having done what he wanted, and you just have
to face things out here. You see, I know a bit of what they have to go
through and how awful it is up there, and we see so many go out and
never come back. It is with us all the time—and then Pat just wants it
so, and he wants to get me out of this joint, out of the rotten old
Military, and he knows we can't go on forever and how the Military
treat you when you are of no further use to them. Until you are down
and out, you can go on and on.[18]

By August, leave was proving hard to get. Olive, in particular, was
showing signs of frustration and rebelliousness. When Evelyn Conyers
visited Boulogne, Olive wrote sarcastically to her mother, 'Old Conyers . . .
is over here today, nosing around. I wouldn't mind her job—sitting up in
M. Headquarters in London most of the time and just touring France
occasionally, watching other people work.' The Australian Director of
Medical Services, General Neville Howse, did not escape her ire. 'General
Howse was here the other day and we were all ready to bail him up about

leave, but he must have got wind of it, because he kept well away—unless he was well-surrounded by Matron and the [officer commanding].'[19]

Pat managed to scrounge some time away from the front, found a bike at St Omer and rode sixty kilometres to Boulogne to see Olive. He could only stay for two hours, and as she was on duty, her friend Ruth Earl offered to take her place while she 'imsheed', or took time off unofficially. Pat had just two hours, and they managed dinner in town. Pat wrote when he got back to the division, hoping she thought it was worth it. 'Though we didn't have time for a heart-to-heart talk—nor perhaps the necessary mood, I think we're brought closer together, and have one more to add to our few but dear memories. Perhaps I have my own way of being in love—but then I have my own way of doing pretty well everything, and I can't help it!'[20] Pat asked the chaplain to find out whether it was possible for them to be married in France by an AIF chaplain—'or by the cove at the C. of E. [Church of England] in Boulogne'. Pat thought it should be possible, but did not know what formalities were necessary. 'Must the banns be read for three Sundays?'[21]

Just as Olive's friend Pete Peters was leaving for London to marry, Pat was wounded in the chest at Broodseinde. He was sent to the Anglo-American Hospital, near Boulogne. Olive was thankful that he was out of the action for a while. Indeed, she thought it was 'great' that he had been wounded. The boys, she noted, were having an awful time, and were up to their waists in mud as they advanced. 'Pat was lying in a shell hole for hours before he was carried in, and some of them have been in shell holes for days.'[22] For some, injury could be a mercy.

Pat was in hospital for five weeks, then sent to London to be boarded for Australia. Olive, meanwhile, was transferred to No. 3 Australian Auxiliary Hospital in Dartford, Kent. As November drew to a close Pat posted the banns at Oxford, where they married on 11 December 1917, at St Peter le Bailey church. They returned to their hotel for the wedding breakfast, Olive noting that there was 'no wedding cake, of course'. Her brother

Dal, who had farewelled her when she left Adelaide in November 1914 and was now a gunner, was Pat's best man. Olive watched as Dal kissed her bridesmaid, fellow Adelaide nurse Muriel Eddy, 'with great gusto in the Vestry'. The newlyweds honeymooned in Bournemouth and waited to return to Australia in 1918. Their war was almost over.

# 27

# GIFTS FOR FRANCE

Verdun was the prize Germany wanted. If France could be defeated at the fortress city, the psychological impact would be enormous. But the French were not going to give it up. '*Ils ne passeront pas!*' was their defiant pledge. The battle began on 21 February 1916, and would last until the week before Christmas that year. It would become the longest single battle of the war, with more than 377,000 casualties, including 162,000 men killed or missing. France's medical and nursing capabilities could not cope with the enormity of the carnage and were in danger of a complete breakdown.

Aware of this shortage, the New South Wales division of the Red Cross offered its sister organisation, the Croix-Rouge, twenty Australian nurses to be sent directly to military hospitals in France. The French readily accepted, but added that the sisters should speak French and be adaptable to 'primitive' conditions. Curiously, the Australian Jockey Club became a financial partner with the Red Cross in this venture. The club, under pressure to stop racing for the duration of the war, offered to support the nurses for six months.

Elsie Cook was one of eighty applicants. On her return from Egypt in March 1916 she had been placed on home service at No. 4 Australian General Hospital in Randwick. Her husband, Syd, was also in Sydney recovering from the gunshot wound to his head that had almost killed him at Lone Pine. He was close to returning to active duty. Knowing that the Australian Army Nursing Service held no future for her now she was married, Elsie was determined to find a way back to the war.

Thanks to her experience, she was among those chosen to go with the Red Cross contingent to France. In mid-1916 she resigned from the Army Nursing Service and, just five days later, sailed from Woolloomooloo on the Hospital Ship *Kanowna*, bound for England. The Defence Department granted the nurses free passage—with the stipulation that the sisters were totally in the care of the Red Cross, which had agreed to pay them at the same rate as Army staff nurses. The move was a cynical one, as it absolved the Commonwealth of all responsibility for the nurses on their return to Australia.[1]

The Red Cross sisters could be distinguished from their Army nursing colleagues by their uniform, a dark blue shirt and jacket with pale blue piping, and a dark blue hat. They quickly became known as the Bluebirds. A French teacher travelled with them, giving three lessons a day. The same month the Bluebirds left Sydney, *Kai Tiaki* in New Zealand noted their departure and reported press approval of the decision to send them, given the 'wonderful heroism' of the French soldiers in the face of the German battering at Verdun, which was 'draining the manhood of France'.

*Kai Tiaki* added that New Zealander Ella Cooke, now with the Imperial Military Nursing Service in Alexandria, had served with the French Flag Nursing Corps at Bernay. The matron in charge of the corps—which would later be taken over by the French Croix-Rouge—travelled up and down the Western Front seeing the nurses and smoothing out difficulties. Some Frenchmen thought the English nurses 'washed their patients too much . . . [Matron] explained the different national outlook to one doctor, saying that in England a bath was a daily necessity, in France an anniversary.'[2] Just what effect this assertion may have had on Anglo-French relations went unrecorded.

When the Bluebirds reached England in late August 1916, arrangements were made to send them to military hospitals in France. In London, Elsie's father-in-law, former Prime Minister Joe Cook, visited unexpectedly and took her to dinner at the fashionable restaurant Frescatis and to a show at the Palladium. Elsie arrived with Lillian Fraser Thompson. Fraser, as she was called, had long wanted to go to the war but appears to have believed that the Army Nursing Service would not be sending any more nurses for a while. She had come to this view after receiving a letter from her medical officer brother, Captain Clive Thompson, who had risked his life under a hail of bullets at Gallipoli to attend the mortally wounded General Bridges. He wrote that there was a belief among the medical corps in Egypt 'that no more nurses were to be brought from Australia for some time as there are more than are required here already'.[3] Fraser joined the Bluebirds instead.

No sooner had they arrived than Fraser was reunited with her Army medical officer fiancé, Captain Gordon 'Nubby' FitzHill. They decided to marry, and two days later drove to Salisbury for the wedding, in a quaint, ivy-covered Norman church. The wedding breakfast was no grand affair, just a simple lunch at a little country inn, but in the midst of a war it was something to be cherished.

The Bluebirds were posted in pairs, and Elsie and Fraser were sent to a convalescent hospital, No. 74 Hospital at Cannes, where they arrived on 12 September 1916. Like their fellow Bluebirds elsewhere in provincial France, they were unimpressed by what they saw. 'Very down hearted and depressed at the state of things here—our first dinner with the staff awful—had to quit hurriedly and go to the Hotel for dinner,' Elsie wrote.[4] Nellie Crommelin, a thirty-four-year-old nurse from Bombala on the New South Wales south coast, was another Bluebird who, too, was exasperated that the French authorities were yet to take their presence seriously. She had already experienced nursing in a war hospital in England at the outbreak of the war, before returning to Australia in late 1915. The Bluebirds gave her the opportunity to return to the war. Posted to Auxiliary Hospital 117 at Les Andelys, west of Paris, she was immediately at home among the French, if not the administration of the hospital system. While she liked the patients under her care, there were nonetheless some challenges.

[The men] are very dear and good—like to be fussed over and petted and spoiled and coaxed just like our English Tommies and they are of course naturally very polite and nice in their manner—though I'm sorry to say they don't seem to know the use of baths, toothbrushes etc. Also they expectorate profusely just wherever they happen to be—especially in the ward—for they sit round one anothers [*sic*] beds playing cards and the floor for yards all round beggars description. [5]

If the conditions in the wards were dirty, the administration was another issue altogether. Nellie noted that there was 'absolutely no method—no management. No order in any one single department. It is deplorable. Everything is so dirty it sickens you and of course we've no authority to make anything clean. I wish they'd turn the place over to us. It would give us a chance of proving our work to our Red X.'[6]

Elsie Cook was dismayed by the backwardness of the French system, with its cold and unclean hospitals lacking the sanitary standards of Australian hospitals. 'French hospitals are very queer and amazingly badly off for properly trained people.' Elsie had sixty patients in her ward and found her 'lack of the French tongue most trying'.

Language aside, they were not as challenged as they wanted to be. They felt frustrated being so far from the fighting on the Western Front. Elsie told the French War Office and the Croix-Rouge president that she and Fraser wanted to be sent north into the Army zone. In Australia, the Red Cross executive committee met to consider the Bluebirds' predicament and decided to cable London. The Croix-Rouge immediately agreed to transfer Elsie and Fraser to a hospital in Paris, but they were still not satisfied. Elsie cabled back insisting that she and Fraser be sent to the front.

Soon afterwards, a phone call summoned them to the War Office, where they were given orders to a French officers' hospital in Amiens, Hospital 108. Their arrival coincided with an Allied push, from the end of January 1917, in which several important ridges and towns near Bapaume were won back from the Germans. Raids by German aircraft were frequent around Amiens, and even the hospital courtyard had been bombed. Elsie noted that sandbags were everywhere, in case of bombardment.

Elsie had a rude introduction to life near the front that first night. 'About 4 a.m. we were awakened by the firing of our anti-aircraft guns and two bombs were dropped—we arose affrighted and hastily donned a cloak and slippers and fled to the cellar—where after a long cold wait, things passed and we retired to bed.'[7] They went on duty in two wards, each with thirty-two officers under her care. Initially not very busy, they waited to begin work in the operating theatre when the next push began to drive the Germans from Bapaume. Serendipitously, Australian troops were based nearby at Fricourt, and Syd Cook was among them. He made a surprise visit on a twenty-four-hour leave pass. It had been nearly nine months since he and Elsie had last seen each other in Sydney. 'Perfectly splendid to see him again,' she enthused.[8]

Two weeks later, despite the risk of shelling and gas, Elsie wanted to go to the front line. Driving through Albert, thirty kilometres away, she witnessed the damage caused by German bombardment and shelling only a few days earlier. The drive ended at Fricourt, and Elsie found to her 'delight and surprise' that Syd was just out of the lines. 'Gave him a great surprise—had lunch in his hut.'[9] Syd organised another day's leave and they set off for Amiens to the sound of guns booming and flashing, and shellbursts lighting the horizon. Elsie had been about seven kilometres from the Australian front-line trenches and about eight from Bapaume. Perhaps Syd's presence had momentarily inured her to the danger, for she concluded that 6 March had been 'a lovely day'.

Elsie was conscious that her husband twice had been wounded at Gallipoli and that without her personal intervention he might well have died. Now they were both in France on the Western Front. Except for their honeymoon in September 1914, they had not been together for any length of time. Since the euphoria of joining up, there had been nothing in their lives but war. Their naïve belief that it would be over quickly was long forgotten. Now, there seemed no end to it. The war had become a way of life, with its own patterns and pressures, madness and mayhem. Amid the chaos they had to create their own version of normalcy, and that required ingenuity, luck and determination. Above all, it required commitment from them both. At a time when communications were haphazard, there were few certainties Elsie and Syd could rely on to keep the flame alive.

For Syd, the opportunity to stay with Elsie in her lodgings in Amiens must have seemed like an extraordinary luxury after the rats, mud and death of the trenches. Elsie and Fraser had decorated the flat with pictures, made lampshades and pasted new wallpaper. On 26 March 1917, Syd arrived on twenty-four-hours' leave and in time for lunch. He and Elsie sat by the fire placing photos in an album. They shopped for that night's meal 'and had a lovely party in our ménage, the fire in the middle of the dinner'. Five days later Syd arrived again and announced that he was being sent to England. With Syd gone, Elsie and two Australian nurses from No. 2 General Hospital at Boulogne, and two fellow Bluebirds, had supper together. Even though they were in different services, the barriers did not diminish old friendships.

The Battle of Bullecourt in mid-April resulted in huge losses for the Australian troops involved. The attack was hastily planned and mounted, with the two brigades of the Australian 4th Division that carried out the attack, the 4th and 12th, suffering more than 3300 casualties and losing nearly 1200 men as prisoners of war. The battle also brought 1500 wounded French troops to Amiens. Elsie's hospital was full. Nearby, Hospital 111 needed more nurses, and Elsie and Fraser were sent. They had 250 patients to look after, and worked all day doing dressings. Another 100 wounded came the next day. The work did not stop. Nellie Crommelin at Les Andelys wrote to her mother that sometimes when the new men came in she could not 'see their wounds thro' my tears—for it breaks my heart to see them suffering so simply from neglect—yards of dressings plastered on in any kind of fashion and underneath filthy hands or feet and nails which have not been cleaned or cut'.[10] In rectifying this, the Bluebirds brought a professionalism that was in sharp contrast to the semi-trained and even untrained women who staffed the hospitals.

After some initial ambivalence about the Bluebirds, the Red Cross wrote to Elsie and Fraser to renew their contracts. Neither would have had it any other way. Elsie applied for a month's leave in England, where she joined Syd. They rented a flat, rode bikes through Dorset, Devon and Cornwall in the early English summer and, for one of the few times since their honeymoon, had a chance to enjoy, if only briefly, something approaching normal life. It was a 'sad day' when their leave ended. Back in Amiens, Elsie did not find it easy to settle back into being Sister Cook again, but Fraser had organised new lodgings and friends were soon calling.

A week of lectures on the Carrel-Dakin treatment of wounds was followed by the 5th Divisional Sports day at Henencourt Woods on 4 July. 'Ever so many people we knew there,' Elsie noted. Among them were General Pompey Elliott, Generals Smith, Tivey and Hopkirk, Captain Hamilton and the entire 14th Field Ambulance. 'We were presented to General Birdwood, had tea, guests of 14th Brigade and General Hopkirk.' She also noted that several sisters from No. 3 Casualty Clearing Station were there. If meeting Birdwood was an honour for Elsie and her fellow Bluebirds, there was another in store. Eight days later, at the Artillery and 5th Division Sports, again at Henencourt, they were presented to King George V. In England, Syd saw a newspaper photo of Elsie with the King and sent her a cutting. In a letter to the *Sydney Morning Herald*, Elsie said the King had shaken hands with her, Fraser Thompson, Frida Warner and Fanny Harris and asked how it was that they were working in French hospitals. 'So we explained that as France needed trained nurses, the New South Wales Branch of the Australian Red Cross had sent us as a gift to France to nurse the French wounded.'[11]

What made all of this socialising possible was that, as Elsie observed, the hospital was 'still very empty and [there was] practically nothing to do'.[12] Despite the heavy work after the Battle of Bullecourt, she was frustrated and wanted to be doing more. Perhaps she knew that further north, the Australian casualty clearing stations were struggling under the weight of German air raids. 'We are so tired of not having proper work to do,' she complained. 'So we called on Mr Pascard—Principal MO of the region—to ask for a transfer to a casualty clearing station, or somewhere where we will have work.'[13]

Just three months earlier, the issue of the Bluebirds' work had been the subject of a terse communication between the New South Wales Red Cross and the Croix-Rouge. The Red Cross Commissioner in London noted that the Croix-Rouge seemed 'intensely irritated' over the whole matter. The chairman of the New South Wales Red Cross, aware of the discontent among the nurses, replied that while he did not want to 'revive any old controversy now, I will only say that if a first rate nurse is doing a tenth rate job it seems to me a pitiable waste of good nursing skill'.[14] This was a sentiment that all the Bluebirds could agree with, not least Nellie Crommelin, who wrote to her mother that there was an 'awful waste of skill and experience'.

There isn't a case here that V.A.D.s [Voluntary Aid Detachment staff] couldn't do and in fact did before we arrived and you can imagine the result ... The papers and the W.O. [War Office] are continually asking for more doctors yet they haven't utilised their well trained nurses. Given one decent Dr and a staff of well trained practical nurses instead of the dozens of semi or untrained women and our hospitals would do much better work than at present.[15]

It seems that the French authorities took notice of the discontent. The posting of two fellow Bluebirds—Fanny Harris and Frida Warner—to Zuydcoote in Belgium, closer to the line, fired up Elsie and Fraser to reassert their demands. They got what they wanted. 'Offered a hospital in the Belgian frontier and accepted, as it seems to be a good chance of going to a casualty clearing station, near the Front.'[16] Four more Bluebirds—Sisters Hilda Loxton, Lynette Crozier, Winifred Hough and Helen Wallace—were already at the frontline. They had been stationed at the Hopital Chirurgicale, Mobile no 1 in Belgium, a hospital funded by wealthy American women for the French. They were only ten kilometres from the Front, and were now exposed to the full danger of the war, with frequent air raids and gas attacks, which forced them to wear gas masks. The bombs and the continual barrage of guns and anti-aircraft guns gave them constant headaches. Hilda Loxton kept a fragment from one of the bombs as a memento.[17]

As they waited for the postings, Elsie and Fraser hired bikes and made the 100-km round trip from Amiens to Abbeville to call on Australian sisters they knew at No. 3 General Hospital. They were also given leave to go to England. Elsie wanted to surprise Syd on their imminent wedding anniversary. Early on 19 September she drove to Fovant Camp, 'where I found Syd not yet up and gave him a great surprise at my unexpected appearance'. After breakfast they drove to the thatched farmhouse that Elsie had rented. It was 'a very delightful' anniversary.

A fortnight later Elsie and Fraser returned to Amiens to find orders instructing them to go to Zuydcoote immediately. Making their way to the hospital, they met Fanny Harris and Frida Warner but had to give Warner the upsetting news that her nephew had been killed. The hospital, previously a large sanatorium on the sea front, was enormous. Right beside it were two British casualty clearing stations. They were twenty kilometres from the front-line trenches and just eight kilometres from Dunkirk, which was under heavy attack. But they were much more satisfied with their greater responsibilities.

By now, Nellie Crommelin and her colleague Alice Robinson had been moved to a hospital at Revigny, about fifty kilometres behind the line at Verdun, and in the 'Zone of the Armies'. While the German offensive had been stopped at Verdun, a doctor told Nellie before she left Les Andelys that Revigny was where there were 'many Zeppelins'. She soon experienced an air raid there. It happened while she was in the village. A piece of jagged shrapnel, the length and thickness of a forefinger, fell at her feet. 'Not until some officers came hurrying down the street and told us to take shelter and a huge piece fell through the roof of a house nearby and I could hear tinkle tinkle all around me, did I think of the danger of being hit,' she told her mother. In the letter, she drew an outline of the shrapnel that had come close to wounding her.[17]

Elsie and Fraser received the troops straight from the field ambulances and aid posts within a few hours of their being wounded, and were soon dealing with big convoys. Death was all around, in the hospital and at Dunkirk, as German aircraft attacked frequently. Three bombs fell on the hospital, killing eight orderlies. Among the wounded was a nurse. The Germans unleashed gas, and the impact was immediate. Elsie was on night duty when hundreds of gassed troops were admitted. 'I spend much time in the admission room, bathing eyes and helping them get fixed up. They were quite blinded and suffering—fresh ambulances kept on arriving— 550 gassed cases were admitted from Nieuport.'[18]

As Christmas 1917 approached, Elsie observed that there was no let-up in the German attacks on Dunkirk, which were inflicting massive damage on the old town. 'Again tonight Dunkirk is getting a doing from the long distance guns at Nieuport—we can hear the shells screaming over our hospital and land with a dull thud in poor old Dunkirk.'[19] Many civilians were killed. Elsie and Fraser made a flying visit to Dunkirk, and 'just left in time—started to get hot and strong at 4 p.m'. With Christmas only two days away, they were intrigued when a French surgeon at the hospital asked for them to accompany him to a new hospital near the front. 'He and his fracture doctors are to go and we "Anglaises" all excited and bucked about it specially as it is so vague and therefore so many startlingly excited rumours are afloat.'[20] Elsie and Fraser also had another reason to be pleased—both had been awarded the French Médaille de Reconnaissance for their services.

Despite the war, Christmas preparations went ahead. In a snowstorm on Christmas Eve, Elsie and Fraser donned their cloaks and, armed with sharp knives, walked to the dunes to cut some heather, gathering large armfuls to decorate the ward. They sat up by the fire making little baskets for sweets and a gift for each patient. Waking early, they hurried to the kitchen to heat up a special treat of chocolate instead of the daily ration of black coffee for breakfast. They gave each man his packet—stationery, tobacco, pipe, matches, cigarettes and a box of chocolates—and carried their decorations into the ward 'amidst the cheers and pleasant surprised comments of the blessés', who were overjoyed with the presents. Wine was served with Christmas dinner, followed by plum pudding aflame. The patients sent the sisters a 'very sweet letter of thanks and appreciation'. They were 'quite touched by their funny little letter of thanks'.

Elsie and the other sisters saved their celebration until evening. Syd was not far from Elsie's thoughts. He had been with the 2nd Battalion at Hazebrouck for the previous seven weeks and, although he had sent her a brooch to mark the third anniversary of their engagement, she had not seen him since 13 November.

We lit our fire and spread out our cushions and rug and lazed about and opened our own little parcels. I wrote a Xmas letter to Syd—poor old dear—sitting about almost frozen in the trenches, perhaps whilst I'm cosily seated by this fire, my thoughts are with you all day, my dear old soldier man.[21]

Two days after Christmas a letter from Syd arrived. Its mood struck Elsie as 'miserable'. She thought of Syd 'writing on his knee with a candle on his tin helmet, in a ruin of an old chateau freezing with cold—poor old chap and going into the line, I can well guess. I'm feeling consequently very "blue".[22] Yet another New Year's Eve was upon her. She and Fraser sat by the fire and reviewed past New Years of the war. 'Mine 1st on the *Kyarra* en route to Egypt, 2nd at Ghezireh Palace Hospital in Cairo, 3rd at Cannes, and the fourth one here on the Belgian frontier—and the next? Where? How? What retrospection and introspection a New Year's Eve calls forth. Tomorrow starts a new diary.'[23]

In more than three years at the war, Elsie and Syd had met only sporadically. But they had managed to capture fragments of the normality that belonged to ordinary married couples. These shared moments were precious, theirs alone to understand and remember, and they helped them both survive. In the harshest and most unpredictable circumstances imaginable, they were building a relationship.

# 28

# CONSCRIPTION

The nurses faced a collective hurt as they watched a generation of their countrymen being maimed and killed on the Western Front. Confronted with hideous wounds and suffering beyond the imagination of ordinary people back home, they tried their best to keep the boys going. Often their efforts were to the detriment of their own health. But they felt as one with the troops. It was their job to patch them up and to keep them alive. They watched in anguish as the numbers of healthy men continued to slide and the burden fell on fewer shoulders because of blunders like Fromelles. Even earlier, Matron Grace Wilson had made clear her views about the men who did not sign up. She had just lost her brother at the Dardanelles.

> My opinion of any man who stays unless <u>absolutely prevented</u> from going isn't much—that is to say unmarried men—the others can do their duty otherwise—several wounded men said to me, 'You don't know what we say about the chaps who could come and won't or don't.'[1]

At first, there had been no shortage of men wanting to go to the war, but as the enormity of Australian and New Zealand casualties on the Western

Front emerged at home, the number of volunteers fell steadily. With no quick end to the war in sight, there was sustained British pressure on the Australian and New Zealand governments to keep troop numbers up. In January 1916, Britain introduced conscription for eighteen-year-olds, and as the year progressed, it was argued that Australia needed to provide 5500 new recruits per month to keep its forces overseas at operational level. Advertising campaigns were failing to achieve this.

Although they badly needed reinforcements, the troops were divided on conscription, many not wanting in their regiments the 'slackers and cold-footers' who had avoided voluntary enlistment. The sisters did not necessarily agree. They felt so keenly for the boys, who were often sent back into the line again and again—until they didn't come back. To rectify the shortage of men, Prime Minister William Morris 'Billy' Hughes decided to hold a plebiscite on whether men should be compelled to undergo training for service overseas. The date was set for 28 October 1916. Australians would be asked: 'Are you in favour of the Government having, in this grave emergency, the same compulsory powers over citizens in regard to requiring their military service, for the term of this War, outside the Commonwealth, as it now has in regard to military service within the Commonwealth?'

The government already had the power under the Defence Act to conscript men. This, however, was only for service in Australia—they could not be sent overseas to fight. To overcome that proviso, all the government needed to do was to change the Defence Act to extend the conscription power from home service to overseas service. But that was Hughes's problem. He knew that while he had enough supporters among Labor and Liberal MPs to secure a majority in the House of Representatives, he was a few short of a majority in the Senate.

The campaign split the nation and took on a personal significance for those with relatives and friends who were already serving overseas or would be eligible for conscription. Anti-conscriptionists, such as the Australian Women's Peace Army, mobilised against the plebiscite. They were especially active in Melbourne, where large crowds filled the Exhibition Building five weeks before the vote. In the next fortnight, 30,000 people crowded the Yarra Bank for a Sunday meeting, followed a week later by another crowd of 25,000. The Melbourne *Age* reported that an immense parade of women, promoted by the United Women's No-Conscription Committee, gathered in Swanston Street between Guild Hall and Princes Bridge, and for 'upwards of an hour the street was a surging area of humanity'. An anti-conscription stop-work meeting called by five trade unions on 4 October attracted 15,000 people.

The issue deeply divided the Labor Party. Ministers such as Hughes and George Pearce strongly pushed the case for conscription even though it was contrary to the ALP platform. Hughes denounced anti-conscriptionists as traitors. A climate of bitter sectarianism developed, with most Catholics opposing conscription and most Protestants supporting it. This was fanned by the aftermath of the 1916 Easter Uprising in Ireland and the brutal treatment of the rebels by the British.

One of those embroiled in the conscription debate was Colonel William Bolton, who had had brief command of the 2nd Australian Infantry Brigade at the Battle of Krithia at Gallipoli in early May 1915. His health and nerves had failed and he had been repatriated to Australia. Despite his experiences, Bolton supported conscription. However, the vote was lost, with 1,087,557 in favour and 1,160,033 against.

The nurses, too, cast their votes. In England, Anne Donnell observed, 'This morning we voted for Conscription—or against it.'[2] The sisters were, she added, 'the first women in England who have voted on a national question'. There was no doubt about where many of them stood. After the result became known, Alice Ross King wrote in her diary, 'Voting in Australia unsatisfactory.'[3] Tev Davies, now in Peshawar, India, agreed. 'Poor Australia being shown up by those agitators and Trades Hall people after so many brave men falling for the cause.'[4] She believed the government should have made the change 'without putting it to the vote, anyhow none of us in India had a vote but the Labor Party make me tired'.

In New Zealand, a Military Services Bill introducing conscription was enacted in May 1916. Only four MPs opposed it. One of them, Peter Fraser, who had played a leading role in forming the Labour Party and would become Prime Minister during World War II, was arrested for sedition for advocating the repeal of conscription. He served a full year in jail. Conscription was initially confined to New Zealanders of European ancestry, but it was extended to Maori in June 1917. More than 30,000 conscripts joined the New Zealand Expeditionary Force by the end of the war.

In Australia, recruitment continued to lag. Pressure for conscription increased when in 1917 Britain sought a sixth Australian division for active service. With emotions still running hot, pro-conscriptionists gave white feathers to eligible men, either sending them through the post or handing them out in person. There was no greater shame. Anticipating a no-confidence vote, Hughes crossed the floor with about half of the parliamentary Labor Party and became Prime Minister of a conservative Nationalist government. Hughes invited Colonel Bolton to join his new party, and he was elected to the Senate at the May 1917 federal election, which the Nationalists won.

---

In Amara, Mesopotamia—modern-day Iraq—Sister Narelle Hobbes, thirty-six, the former matron of Brewarrina Hospital in northwestern New South Wales, took a special interest in the debate, even though she was on a posting with Queen Alexandra's Imperial Military Nursing Reserve. She had travelled to England to join up in May 1915, and after working in Malta now found herself involved in a conversation with 'a nice old colonel' from Scotland. He was unhappy with the outcome of the vote on conscription. He told her:

My brigade fought side by side with the Australians at Anzac, I was proud of it, I've seen the Australians going into action and it was one of the finest sights God ever allowed me to see . . . I longed to be in command of them, taken on the whole they are the finest lot of men I've ever seen, as I watched them make one of their many charges I just said, 'God I'll stake my all, my very life on those men,' and then his voice rose and he said, 'and what are you doing, what are the people in Australia doing, that they are not sticking by their men, what are they doing that they are not sticking to their splendid dead, why are they allowing one of the finest armies we have helping us, to have to shorten their front in France for want of reinforcements. I said I would stake my very life on those men, so I would, on that first army of men at Anzac, but of Australians, no, they've gone back on their men who have made history, they have gone back on their dead.'[5]

Narelle mostly agreed with him, but felt she had to defend Australia. 'I knew it was true of the people who voted "No" but I wasn't going to let him condemn the Australians because of those cowards, so I just gave him a few remarks to go on with, and especially about the W.W. [International Workers of the World] people.' But the colonel refused to be mollified.

Sister, I know you are an Australian, and I admire them and I salute the men from Gallipoli, but the people who went against conscription I would <u>never</u> forgive, just as I a Scotchman, will never forgive the Clyde strikers, or the people in the Irish rebellion, for doing these things at a time when <u>every man</u> is wanted, when it means that the war is prolonged, for the want of more and more men, and men of your fine Australian type, 'the finest thing God ever made'.[6]

Narelle was sympathetic. 'Poor old chap, he goes back to the trenches today, quite an old man, has done 20 years in the army in India besides his home service. Oh dear <u>how</u> I wish Hughes had brought in conscription, you have absolutely no idea of the disappointment over his blunder, among the British people.'

The mood among the sisters ran strongly. In Salonika, Tasmanian Sister Laura Grubb could not understand the antiwar mood in Australia.

The strikes and general unrest all over Australia are doing a great deal of harm. I do wish one half of these agitators could be compelled to come out here and live under the conditions the men simply have to put up with—there would be no strikers, there would be no shirkers, it fairly makes one's blood boil to think of the grasping, callous crowd of men there living lives of positive luxury and armies of men out here.[7]

As 1917 came to an end, Hughes decided to hold another plebiscite on the issue. He wanted to give the people another chance to overcome what he saw as their great mistake. Again the campaign was bitter and divisive. Hughes proposed that voluntary enlistment should continue, but that any shortfall would be met by compulsory reinforcements of single men, widowers, and divorcees without dependents between twenty and forty-four years of age, who would be called up by ballot.

As the campaign proceeded, Sister Ada Mary Willis, from Crookwell in southern New South Wales, became increasingly angry. She had lost her younger brother, Frank, to a sniper's bullet while he was fighting with the 1st Australian Light Horse at the Battle of Romani in Egypt the previous year. A straight-speaking countrywoman who had been matron of Bega Hospital, Ada had wanted to do her bit like her brother, and was finally able to join the Army Nursing Service in September 1916, a month after Frank's death. After a posting in Egypt, she was sent to Salonika. In November 1917, she wrote to her mother about the reluctance of some people in Crookwell to enlist.

So they are still trying to get Dick G—to enlist! What an abomination and a blot on one's own town he and a few others are. Yet the 'microbes' are given work and no doubt are encouraged by individuals as mean-spirited as themselves.

Are the 'tin soldiers' at the brick-works still determined to bravely stay at home and keep the Germans out of Crookwell or have they weakened?[8]

On 20 December 1917, Australians voted on the question: 'Are you in favour of the proposal of the Commonwealth Government for reinforcing the Commonwealth Forces overseas?' After learning that the plebiscite had failed, with 1,015,159 votes in favour and 1,181,747 against, Ada wrote again to her family.

If I looked through the dictionary do not think I could find words exactly suitable to express the disgust I feel at the result of the conscription poll. I cannot say I expected much, did not dare hope it would be carried but did not think Crookwell would disgrace themselves so badly. It will be hard even after the war to forgive some of the people.

They don't understand in the smallest sense the meaning of patriotism. It is self, self all along the line and if we lose the war, and it's not finished yet by any means, they will be the first to squeal when the iron heel of Germany begins to crush us.[9]

In London, Elsie Eglinton spent Chistmas Day reflecting bitterly on the decision. 'We are feeling very sore about Australia turning down conscription. I am ashamed to mention it here.'[10]

May Tilton pondered the result not long before she returned to Australia in January 1918. She had voted at a convalescent home at Menton, near Monte Carlo on the Mediterranean coast, where arrangements had been made for all Australians in the south of France to cast their votes. As she did so, May thought back to the first plebiscite more

than a year earlier, and the many arguments that had been raised for
and against conscription.

> These naturally influenced our vote in the first instance, but they had
> no effect the second time, for we had seen men, wounded four and
> five times, return to the line again, until finally, in many cases, they
> died serving their country.
>
> During 1917, when every man was so badly needed, boys left our
> wards before they were fit to return to the line. Gunner A. S——, shot
> through the jaw, was sent back to France before he could properly
> masticate his food. Yet he never uttered a word of complaint at the
> decision. He, happily, came through safely.[11]

Sister Stella Colless, after two years' service in England, on hospital ships
and then in France, was exasperated.

> I wonder will they ever get conscription in Australia? I cannot see why
> so many of our noble boys should be killed, and the large number of
> eligibles left who are doing nothing towards defeating the Hun. There
> does not seem any chance of Australia being able to keep up the
> voluntary replacements at the present rate of casualties.[12]

As the votes in the plebiscite were being counted, Narelle Hobbes's health
deteriorated. Some months earlier, she had been bitten by a sandfly and had
become seriously ill. She developed a gastric ulcer, then had repeated attacks
of gastritis. Diagnosed with advanced liver cancer, she was put on the
hospital ship *Kanowna* when it docked in Bombay on its way to Alexandria
to take on more wounded before heading back to Australia. With her was
her sister Elsie, who had travelled from Australia to take her home. In May
1918, just four days out from Fremantle, Narelle died and was buried at
sea.[13] Conscription, likewise, was buried for the rest of the war.

# 29

# IT'S SOMETHING
# BIG, SISTER

———————

Anne Donnell was 'white, limp and helpless', shuddering as yet another shell
from an air raid exploded a few metres from her room. It was September
1917, and as the Ypres Offensive ground on, nerves were fraying. The Calais
townsfolk could seek shelter in cellars, but the sisters at No. 38 Stationary
Hospital had no protection at all. Their patients were terrified. Many said
they would rather be up in the front lines under artillery barrage than at
Calais, for there they would have some protection in their dugouts. Anne
and her fellow nurses took to sleeping under the bed when the German aircraft came. 'Once Matron came along with some whiskey that one of the
Captains had kindly sent over. I popped my head out gingerly from under
the bed and refused, the more I refused the more she insisted it would do
me good. I said, "Truly, Matron, I am not frightened." She quickly replied,
"What are you doing under the bed for then?"'[1]

Anne hated the nights. If she went to sleep, there were only nightmares
of guns, bombs and aeroplanes. She thought it silly to be so afraid but she
would not believe anyone who said they were not. The nightly air raids wore
her down and she became more fatalistic. 'We are powerless. This is how

I feel as soon as I know Fritz is above and the guns start. I seem to lose all my strength, a band tightens around my head, my senses are annulled, whether from the noise or fear I cannot say.'[2] To work under such circumstances clearly required an inner strength that Anne began to doubt in herself. Each night she awaited her fate 'midst the tumultuous noise of bombs and shells'. She survived Calais, but admitted that the experience 'has taken it out of me a bit'.

Now, in November 1917, as the dreadful slaughter of the offensive drew to a close after months of bitter fighting in deep mud, Anne waited in Abbeville for final orders to go to No. 48 Casualty Clearing Station, eighty kilometres from Amiens. With time to spare, she walked to No. 3 General Hospital to catch up with friends. 'Most of them envied me for going to the CCS, but I never was enthusiastic over a CCS, still less since the raids at Calais.'[3] She would never forget the drive out in an ambulance from Amiens, and the 'real waste, devastation and desolation' that brought home the full meaning of war. There was faint moonlight as her driver took her kilometre after kilometre to the town of Albert. 'Thence on, the ruins become worse and worse—the true havoc of war—not a tree left of the once beautiful avenues. Only the torn ragged stumps remain, and they are touched with whitewash so as to guide the traffic on dark nights.'[4]

The closer they got to the front, the less light there was. The headlights on her ambulance were turned off, the only light coming occasionally from the torches of sentries who stood in the middle of the road and demanded, 'Who goes there?' The vehicle would stop and then be given the signal to carry on. Little white crosses dotted the roadside to the right and left. This to Anne was sacred ground. 'I became silent, my heart ached, for this is a part of the vast valley of the Somme, where lie so many of our own heroes who have fought and fallen. Some things are too sacred for words.'[5] She drove past abandoned tanks and aeroplanes, past craters and past the devastation of Bapaume, then another sixteen kilometres to the clearing station, which lay between the ruined villages of Etres and Etrecourt, just eight kilometres from the line.

The clearing station became a centre of intense activity during the Battle of Cambrai, a town that by 1917 had become one of the Germans' most important railheads and command sites. After the British 3rd Army had forced the Germans back some six kilometres to Cambrai and pierced the three trench systems of the Hindenburg Line for the first time in the war, the Germans counterattacked and drove back through the British gains on 30 November 1917. At 7 a.m., as she dressed, Anne thought that a fiercer barrage than normal was going on. Three hours later the matron ordered her to get her respirator and helmet. Outside the tent, she watched as a British observation balloon was shot down. The Germans were only five kilometres away, and Anne fancied 'all at once that I can see the Germans swarming over the ridge'.[6] She hastened back to the boys on the stretchers to get them ready for evacuation, before throwing a few personal possessions—a purse, a few handkerchiefs, a comb and hairpins—into a suitcase. She saw the irony of it all, for the wounded and the gassed were making their way in streams towards the clearing station.

I shall never forget it, the expressions on those dear boys' faces as they come pouring in with their frightened, anxious, hunted look, combined with the suffering of fear, pain, and shock. Those who could see led queues of bandaged blind, each one placing his hands on another's shoulders, and thus feeling the way. Very soon every available space under cover is packed, and not only inside but outside as well. I leave my wounded men and go over to the gas side, where Matron soon joins in to help, also another Sister and as many order-lies as can . . . and there we go on hour after hour, putting cocaine in these poor smarting eyes, then sodi-bicarb pads and a bandage.[7]

Orders were given for the nurses to stay as long as the place itself was not being shelled. The Germans effectively had the casualty clearing station caught inside a horseshoe. That night, after the British began to check the

German advance, a colonel told Anne's tent-mate how close they had come to being taken prisoner.

Little changed over the next month; not even Christmas Eve brought a halt to the big guns' firing. At 2.30 a.m. on New Year's Eve the sound of close shelling suddenly awakened Anne, and she quickly detected 'a faint sweetish scent like pineapple'. The Germans were sending over gas shells, and Anne was told to have her respirator ready. 'I jumped up, as did most of us, and got dressed, shivered and shook and coughed, and I thought I never should manipulate that mask.'[8] With relief she signed out 1917 with 'Mafeesh' (Egyptian Arabic for 'all gone').

Besides the threat of Fritz, there was the bitter cold, ice and snow. After two months Anne's strength gave out. She was sent to the sick sisters' quarters at Abbeville and then to the warmer climate of Cannes. She would not return to the Western Front. Instead, she went to nurse in England. As she left France there were more than 100,000 men in hospitals—almost double the numbers of 1916. More than 1.6 million sick and wounded had been admitted to hospitals during 1917. The year's campaigns at Arras, Messines, Bullecourt, Passchendaele and Cambrai had cost the French, British, Australian, New Zealand and Canadian forces dearly.

———

Performing surgery on wounded troops required anaesthesia. Even during the Battle of the Somme in 1916 the demand for anaesthetists was so acute that at one casualty clearing station the padre spent most of his time in the operating theatre administering anaesthesia. In her diary, Alice Ross King recorded in August 1916 that the commanding officer at No. 1 Australian General Hospital in Rouen, known to her from the early days of the war, had taught her to give anaesthetics. This, Alice noted, saved 'one [medical officer] in our hut . . . Most of the big dressings in my ward have to be done over chloroform. I am giving chloroform most of the mornings.'[9] At a hospital in Cannes in late 1916, Elsie Cook also gave anaesthesia using Novocain—a drug that numbs the body but does not cause loss of consciousness. One surgical episode, using Novocain for an amputation, stayed in Elsie's memory. 'So uncanny to see the man sitting smiling and talking all the time his leg was being sawed off. Leg buried this afternoon.'[10] She continued giving anaesthetics.

In late 1917, British medical authorities followed the Canadian Armed Forces' lead of using nurses to administer anaesthetics, which had been their practice since 1915. The Americans also used nurse anaesthetists after entering the war. Nine Australians, including Elsie Tranter, and seven New Zealand nurses completed the training. At No. 10 Casualty Clearing Station near Dunkirk, New Zealander Margaret Davies noted that she and two other New Zealand sisters 'gave all the anaesthetics' and 'the surgeons seemed quite satisfied'. She was 'just loving the work', but the German air raids meant disturbed nights and taking cover in dugouts.[11] She was later attached as an anaesthetist to a surgical team and moved north with the casualty clearing stations, attending to a 'continuous stream' of wounded.

———

Three years of war and numerous offensives had failed to break the stalemate. The Allies had spent 1917 bludgeoning themselves on the German defences but had little to show for it. That was about to change as the war entered a decisive phase. On 21 March 1918, the Germans attempted to break the deadlock with Operation Michael. With Russia collapsing in revolution in the east, the Germans were able to release crack battalions of highly trained troops from the eastern front and prepare an all-out offensive across the old Somme battlefields that they hoped would win them the war before American troops reached Europe in force. The fear for the British was that their armies were dangerously under strength, and thus vulnerable.

The thunderous attack opened with an unprecedented 6600-gun barrage followed by trench mortars, flame throwers and a lethal gas attack. Diving deep into a weakened sector of the front held by the British 3rd and 5th Armies, from south of Saint-Quentin to Arras, the Germans reached Villers-Bretonneux, some fifty kilometres to the west and near the crucial Allied communications centre of Amiens. In just four hours they fired one million shells. Nothing above ground stood a chance in the inferno. Even survival underground was problematic. Men in dugouts ten metres below the surface watched in horror as rafters cracked and the earth heaved. The Germans' astonishing advance destroyed the 5th Army. Overwhelmed, the British began a retreat that ended ten days later at Amiens.

Nellie Crommelin was at a French temporary hospital at Villers-Cotterets when the offensive began. The Germans were soon within nine kilometres of the town. 'I was awakened in the night by the cannonade of the big guns and I felt it in my bones—the approach of some new danger. At 4 a.m. it reached its most violent force and everybody in their beds asked themselves the same question. All day long we hear the rumble in the forest, look at each other and sigh, or hold our breath for a moment—when a specially violent concussion shakes us.'[12]

Over the next five days the 'roar and thunder of the cannon' remained constant. Doors rattled, windows shook and houses trembled night and day as the fighting came nearer. Surrounding villages were evacuated, but Nellie remained defiant. 'We shall remain with our men, proud to be amongst them, and if the Hun should come we hope our Red Cross and our work for any that are wounded shall be our protection.'[13]

Allied intelligence had known beyond doubt that the Germans would mount the offensive, and that it would occur on the French and British sectors in the northwest of the front line. The only question was when. When the Germans had retired to the Hindenburg Line more than a year earlier, the casualty clearing stations and some stationary hospitals had moved forward. Now they would have to prepare to move back at short notice. Such a move was a complex matter, requiring anything from fifty to a hundred lorries to take all equipment, tents and personnel. This took time. When the attack came, it was clear that the British had miscalculated. The Germans' main thrust was at the front held by the 5th Army, where emergency arrangements to protect clearing stations were weakest.[14]

Alice Ross King had started 1918 with a promotion to head sister at No. 1 General Hospital, Rouen. In March, she wrote with alarm that the Germans were breaking through, and British plans for the removal of the clearing stations had collapsed because of poor planning.

> They have captured our CCS and all the good work the boys put in. The five Sisters were sent away early. I hear the boys saved most of the theatre equipment. We can hear the guns getting louder. The 5th Army broke—mostly Irish and Lancashires. They have been flooding into Rouen on any trucks. The trains are full and they are riding on top. They are walking into hospital with no tickets. One chap came into my ward. I said, 'Where are you wounded?' He showed me a broken blister on his hand. He said, 'I'm not going to stay up there to be shot.' The Sisters have orders to have a suitcase packed ready for evacuation. Things are very bad.[15]

They did not improve. The Germans advanced sixty kilometres in eight days, and the allies suffered 200,000 casualties.

> We hear the Aussies are in action. Round the town the POW are very cheeky. Command has cut their rations. We had a fatigue party of POW making a path outside my ward. When the orderly put the tin of slush from plates and tea dregs outside the kitchen door I saw them rush up and scoop the stuff up in their hands and eat it. They are starving but they still give cheek. They can hear the guns getting closer. No picnics in the woods these days. I'm frightened really.[16]

Until now, an indefatigable quality had enabled Alice to withstand the relentless grind of war. Now it was beginning to fail. She had good reason to be afraid.

After working in London, twenty-nine-year-old Sister Florence James-Wallace was one of three Australians sent to No. 61 British Casualty Clearing Station during the German March offensive. The station was in Ham, near Peronne, about ten minutes' walk from the railway station, and a siding ran right up to the hospital. On night duty at about 3 a.m. on 21 March, she heard the engines of German planes overhead but could see nothing because of fog. An hour later 'a terrific bombardment' began. It reminded her of 'continuous thunder rolling . . . Then I could distinguish shells screeching through the air and guns going off with a deafening crash, the whole place shook and trembled. I had never heard anything like it before, felt quite excited. The orderlies said, "It's something big, Sister".'17

When the medical officers appeared at 6:30 a.m. instead of 9 a.m., wearing tin hats and tearing around excitedly, it was clear that something was up. They began emptying wards and filling the hangars with walking patients. That night, exhausted from work, Florence 'slept soundly, too tired to be disturbed by noise'. About 2 p.m. the next day, she was woken by the cry, 'Girls! Get up quickly, you have to be dressed in 10 minutes.' Matron followed up with, 'Are you up, girls? The Germans are advancing, we have to leave everything. Train goes in 20 minutes, take what you can carry.'

The thirty-four sisters left carrying suitcases, boots, rugs and rucksacks. Troops, wagons, lorries, ambulances, gun carriages and pack-mules were all clattering down the road past the hospital as the guns crashed and shells whistled. Some medical officers met them as they tramped to the station, 'feeling very disgusted at being sent off when we feel the patients need us'. Florence and her colleagues waited for the train. What followed fascinated her.

Crash! A shell bursts about 200 yards away. French and English soldiers rush to see where it fell, then another crash a little nearer. Our two guns continue to fire. Crash! Crash! An earsplitting sound seemingly beside us, black dust rises in the air just behind the station shed, some falls on our hats. The RTO hurls himself out of his office and shouts to us to run to the other side of the line, which the soldiers have already proceeded to do, we grab our suitcases, haversacks, rugs, etc., and struggle over the line, in a few seconds the platform only holds our pile of luggage. I don't expect to see my collection of treasures any more. More shells fall round the station, we are told to walk down the line to meet the train. We proceed very hampered with our heavy suitcases, the men come to our rescue and help to carry them. Suddenly five Bosche [*sic*] planes come in sight. Our Archies [anti-aircraft guns] open up. We are told to go in the dugouts along the line, but very few do, most of us sit on our luggage and watch the fun. They seem to be trying to find our two big guns, they go again after dropping a few bombs.

The rail line to the hospital was hit and three men were killed not far from the sisters. By now it was nearly 6 p.m., but there was no sign of the train. The commanding officer of No. 47 Clearing Station suddenly appeared with five lorries to take all the nurses to Rosières, halfway to Amiens. On the way they passed two dead Germans lying in a ditch near a crashed plane. They arrived at No. 47 at 10 p.m. to find wounded men streaming in.

The next day Matron Baird took seven of the sisters by rail to Villers-Bretonneux, where they were billeted in a large school along with refugees. A day later there were about 500 patients, stretchers and walking cases waiting for them. They fed them all and dressed the worst wounds, bringing the abdominal and chest cases inside and leaving the rest in the open. However, a day later the number of wounded had swollen to about 8000 and was still growing. Stretcher cases lay on the ground for hundreds of metres around. Soon about 10,000 had been through the clearing station, and still they came. That night, in bright moonlight, the Germans began bombing the town. 'We were nearly home when one seemed to fall beside us with a deafening splitting sound,' Florence recounted. 'We dived into an archway, the air seemed full of fumes and gas, two other Sisters behind us fell flat on the pavement. However none of us were hit and we got to the school.'

And still came the wounded, thirsty, dirty and covered with blood. Hospital trains arrived but could not cope with the numbers. The nurses heard a shout that the train was leaving and ran down the hill, passing through the hut where the worst cases were, to grab their haversacks. The harrowing scene that followed etched itself on Florence's memory.

We were too hurried to think of the effect our leaving would have on them. I will never forget the expression on their faces when they saw we were going. 'Oh they are leaving us,' 'They are going,' I heard one man say. I went back to tell him we were going on a truck train and they would be going as soon as the hospital train arrived. It didn't seem to comfort him much. They looked as if they thought their last hope had gone, poor things, we hated leaving them, and it made us realise our being there meant more than the actual work we did.

They scrambled into the van. The train, which was full of walking wounded, travelled slowly and stopped just after nightfall in brilliant moonlight. They tried to sleep, but at about 10 p.m. the Germans were overhead. A traumatic night of bombing followed.

Fritz was over us, and driven off by Archies and back again and driven off and back, so on all night. A lot of the men went out in the fields. A dud dropped beside us, the line blown up in front of us. We heard in the morning we were in a cutting just out of Amiens and the town was bombed severely that night. It certainly was the most nerve-racking thing we had been through, to hear Fritz's engines above us all night. It was a relief to hear the bark of the Archies and the sing of the shells through the air. We could hear the bombs explode, they seemed all round us.

They passed through Amiens about 11 a.m. on the 27th and saw telegraph wires smashed, splintered building frames and broken glass everywhere. The train pulled up, and the boys found a goods train loaded with food. 'They helped themselves, but did not forget us,' Florence recalled, 'we were presented with bread, oranges, figs, milk, cheese, apples. We had tea and sugar which we gave the boys.' Relieved, they drew breath as the boys 'made their tea at the engine'.

There was little relief elsewhere. At No. 1 Australian General Hospital at Rouen, Annie Shadforth 'had the wind up horribly'. There was no time to rest. She was on night duty in a forty-bed ward that received acute gas patients during the German push. She and her orderly 'spent the best part of the night administering oxygen to patients and trying to keep delirious ones in bed'.[18] All lights went out in an air raid, leading to 'a dreadfully anxious few hours' during which Annie paced up and down 'in the dark with the aid of a hurricane lamp trying to calm delirious patients' who were trying to get out of bed.

At No. 3 Canadian Stationary Hospital, Doullens, Elsie Tranter was soon using her new skill in giving anaesthesia. There were four operating tables in constant use, 'and poor fellows lying on stretchers on the theatre floor, waiting till we could attend to them'. One soldier walked in 'with half his jaw blown away', supported by two wounded comrades. Elsie was in the theatre from 7 a.m. till 8 p.m. Then she worked in the chapel attending to the new admissions till early morning.

She had already survived a bombing raid in which 'a fairly large piece of shell ripped my tent, grazed past my face and passed right between my hands, tearing the kit bag and various things that were in it and burying itself in the bag'. And she had taken on an important task. 'I have many "last" letters to write now to mothers in Australia and New Zealand.

Many of the boys have entrusted me with their precious messages. They are game to the end.'[19]

By 24 April Elsie had administered anaesthetics to 227 patients. 'It is very tiring and trying work, for most of the men are badly wounded and give us a lot of anxiety.' A month later, shortly after being sent to Dieppe, she recalled her last night at Doullens as dreadful, with sixty-four bombs dropped in the vicinity. At Dieppe Elsie learned that the Australian Director-General of Medical Services, Major General Neville Howse, had forbidden Army Nursing Service members to work or be trained as anaesthetists. No explanation was given, but it is believed Australian doctors had insisted that only they should be permitted to perform anaesthesia.[20]

Despite her disappointment, Elsie kept toiling. One day a dog, a setter, came in with the walking wounded. It 'seemed almost human' and had a shrapnel wound in its forepaw. It waited with the men, then followed on to where a sister was dressing wounds. 'When she found time she dressed him and he seemed so grateful. The quartermaster has taken charge of him and every morning the dear doggie makes his way to the dressing station and waits till someone has time to attend to him. He is nearly well now but still limps rather badly.'[21]

Tev Davies was at No. 25 General Hospital on the coast at Hardelot, south of Boulogne, professionally satisfied to be in the thick of things after finding work in England too quiet. She wrote to her mother about the German offensive.

We are getting in gassed cases now, Mum, such cruel stuff it is, burns their skin causing blisters, causing inflammation of the eyes, and all mucous membranes, chokes up the lungs and irritates the stomach causing vomiting besides which, it has a depressing effect on the patient, the treatment is chiefly with alkalies, then one runs all day with inhalations, gargles, douches, eye baths, Mercy me! Fritz. Is fiendish alright [sic]. Not warfare at all, it is slaughter absolutely.[22]

The gassed men, Tev found, needed constant attention. 'Nearly all lose their voices, poor old things whisper away. You have to bend right down to hear what they say, then you get the gas down your own throat, my voice gets quite husky at times.'[23]

For some sisters it meant taking their chances away from the protection of air raid shelters. Among them was Sister Hilda Steele, a thirty-year-old Auckland nurse who was one of the original twelve New Zealand nurses who had gone off to war in March 1915 with the Australian sisters. Like the others, Hilda was in the unique position of being a member of both the Australian and New Zealand army nursing services. Now, in the midst of the German offensive, she found herself serving at No. 3 Australian General Hospital at Abbeville, a large tented hospital caring for battle casualties. Raids were common, and Hilda was caught in one in late May 1918. She had been asked to stay with a sick nurse who could not be moved from her quarters as the Germans attacked. Throughout the raid the two talked about their experiences and were almost oblivious to the screams of falling bombs. Next morning they learnt that nine young Women's Army Auxiliary Corps members (WAACs) stationed nearby were killed when their trench was obliterated by a direct hit.[24]

No one, not even those in hospitals, could escape the effects of the German offensive. Paris was no longer safe.

# 30

# THE STRUGGLE ENDS

The German onslaught headed towards Paris, where Elsie Cook and Fraser Thompson were working. Big guns pounded the city from 120 kilometres away. Parisians were startled, and Elsie joined the thousands who took refuge in bomb shelters.

> Paris shelled by long-range guns! All Paris awakened this morning to read this astounding news. So that all yesterday's mysterious regular explosions, which popular opinion decided had come from the 'new invisible aircraft', had been shells dropping in from more than 75 miles away. And still coming in—again, early at 7 a.m., a loud explosion proclaimed another day's bombardment and every quarter of an hour these explosions occurred, sometimes quite near—five fell around the hospital, several people killed, but the shells fall without much force and are not doing much damage.

The shelling resumed next day at 7 a.m. 'Germans trying a big push for Amiens,' Elsie noted. 'Things grave, but everybody calm and confident.' After six days of fighting, with the line now east of Albert and Roye, she wrote,

'It seems awful to think of the Germans being there, there where we used to walk and ride and see such a long way behind the lines.'[1]

The Allies halted the offensive in late March, leading the Germans to change strategy from a single massive attack to a three-prong attack, including a thrust south of the Somme to separate the British and French armies. Another attack came on the southern flank, and a third on the northern flank towards the sea. Nellie Crommelin witnessed long lines of French troops marching to the front.

> Up they went cheerfully knowing full well the awful task in front of them and there on arrival tired, dust covered, hungry thirsty they went straight into battle. They fought and died in thousands and those who escaped wounded came down to us in the middle of the night in their hundreds. What a night we had, but oh how happy we are to be doing this work. It makes us feel we are helping just a little bit, and the wonderful self denial and courage of them all the time, all the time!!![2]

Shifted to a temporary hospital with the French Army, Nellie was becoming more emotionally involved and, in the space of a few days, said she now saw herself as 'Military in every sense of the word'.

> I feel a little bit prouder to think I am really so much nearer it makes us feel we are sharing the dangers to be a little bit closer to our men, nearer to comfort them, nearer to help them, nearer to prove to them that we also can play our little part. And yet women seem useless, so helpless, against the awful strain of the present. I feel that if only all our millions could be transformed into men—real men. I mean, those who would not want to stay behind with the old people and children, and used to stem the avalanche of brutes that presses so relentlessly against our sorely tried troops, how gladly many of us would answer the call to help.[3]

The situation grim, the Croix-Rouge quickly assigned Elsie Cook and Fraser Thompson to a hospital at Compiègne, northeast of Paris and half-way to Amiens. But the hospital was burnt down by an incendiary bomb before they left Paris. As they awaited new orders, five German shells landed on a nearby church, killing seventy-five people and wounding ninety. The shelling came near the hospital where Elsie and Fraser worked, but they were not there long: they had been assigned to a specialist fracture hospital at Senlis, between Paris and Compiègne.

They arrived to find a lack of food, poor sleeping quarters and wards full of 'very sick and miserable looking wounded'. With no food to eat, they breakfasted 'on a soup plate of half cold coffee' and were kept busy 'washing the patients and making beds and trying to get things clean and in order generally'. They were given a tent to sleep in, furnished with duckboards, a stove and some partitions made from sheets. 'Green grass and daisies form a virginal carpet, our beds, with upturned packing cases, make up the furniture,' Elsie noted wryly.[4]

Elsie struggled to cope with the stream of broken bodies as the Germans mounted their last desperate efforts to win the war. Fear and heartbreak were everywhere. She noted that all the hospitals between Senlis and the front were being evacuated. Refugees were passing along in front of her hospital, driving their cattle and carrying odds and ends of family possessions on carts. 'Wounded pouring in by the hundreds—the receiving room full to overflowing—one long line of ambulances outside the hospital, disgorging and tearing off, others flying in at the gates, covered in dust. Up all night going hard.'[5]

Amid the din of air raids and the boom of long-range guns, Elsie and Fraser frantically dressed wounds, hearing rumours that they themselves would soon have to evacuate 'as the Bosch are getting so near'. The work-load was heavy for a fortnight. Thirty kilometres away at Villers-Cotterets, Nellie Crommelin, could hear the thunder of the cannon coming nearer and 'the hateful purring of the Gothas' during 27 to 28 May. Sleep was impossible. In a letter scrawled to her mother, she wrote:

Be brave little mother and all dear ones. Remember I shall never be taken prisoner by the Bosches and if I die it is for the sake of beautiful France and her suffering soldiers and the honour of our own dear Australia. God bless you all and keep you safe and well and unafraid. Long live Australia and Vive la France.[6]

In a later letter, Nellie explained that quite suddenly the hospital was inundated with stretchers and limping men: men with arms in slings, men with heads bound up, men covered with mud and blood. There were torn, mangled and quivering bodies everywhere. 'We put them on the beds at first and we bound up their dressings afresh waiting for the surgeon to come or the X Ray man to examine them. Later we put them on the floor, into the corridors and still they came. All night we worked and the morning found us in a sea of disorder and filth indescribable.'

In the midst of this, Nellie wrote how she was caught in a bombing raid one evening. Visiting a seamstress in town, she heard the Gothas overhead. It was too late to run from the house into the street because she knew she would be in greater danger.

I descended the stairs with a beating heart and creepey [sic] feeling down my back. I turned the light as low as possible and tried to occupy myself with tidying up in the little kitchen, but I was too scared to move almost. Bang! One-two very quickly three and four a few seconds later and the house seemed to rock. The panes splintered into fragments all the ornaments fell off the shelves and tables upstairs.

I was hurled against the wall, no damage. I didn't feel very happy and I certainly wasn't brave for my knees suddenly changed to rubber and crumpled up stupidly. Other bombs fell all around, some near, some further away, and finally I heard the droning less distinctly and decided to make a run for the hospital.

With shaky hands I locked the door and the gate leading into the street and just turned from the latter when I heard the noise approaching again this time very low.

I couldn't go back, it was too risky and too dark to see the key hole. No. I must go on. With a drunkards gait I kept close to the walls and longed for a steel helmet. One after another that dreadful rain of bombs fell and just as I turned the corner there was a terrific explosion. I fell into the shelter of an iron doorway just in time to escape the shower of tiles, glass, plaster etc which fell all around me.

In my hand I carried those big yellow leather bags given us by the French Australian League and I covered my head with that each time I heard the whistle of a bomb or saw the trail of light which followed its decent [sic]. It was the most horrible thing I have ever experienced and I really thought I should be killed. How I escaped I really do not know. Nearly an hour I remained in the streets taking shot runs from the shelter of one friendly doorway to another whenever the avions seemed to move away and the noise of their engines less distinct.[7]

Not long after, Nellie was given leave to recover in Marseille.

———◆◆◆———

In early June a letter from Syd Cook to Elsie arrived from the front with the news that he expected to finally get leave. He planned to travel to London to meet his father, Sir Joseph, who had just arrived. The letter raised a difficult dilemma for Elsie—whether to ask for leave herself to meet Syd in London, or stay where she was needed. Her conscience was troubled, but 'Although I shouldn't, I asked for leave to go to England tomorrow—don't know what Fraser will do, poor little thing, as with both of us it's like hell.'[8]

She worked until midnight, then got her things ready to leave early the next morning. 'Simply felt very mean leaving Fraser and the hospital at such time as this, but must go as Syd hasn't had leave for a year.'[9] They had two weeks together, during which they went to a performance of *Chu Chin Chow* and holidayed amid the picturesque firths and lochs of Scotland.

With the Germans focusing on Paris in one last desperate offensive, the Second Battle of the Marne began. The Germans established a bridgehead across the river before their attack was blunted by British divisions from the north. Just as the Marne had proved the high-water mark of German success in 1914, so it was now. But for the next few weeks their assault continued, and Elsie returned to work in the midst of it. 'Air raid tonight, the Boshe [*sic*] dropped a bomb about 100 yards from our sleeping quarters, but only knocked down a tree—made a big hole,' she noted in mid-July.[10]

Orders came to evacuate as many patients as possible, as every bed would soon be needed. 'So every one who can possibly travel is being sent off—poor broken legs taken down out of apparatus and put in plaster or splints of voyage and sent off this evening and thro' the night.'[11] The next day Elsie was relieved that a French-American attack around Soissons and Château-Thierry had started successfully. Wounded Americans and Frenchmen flooded in. Every bed and stretcher was soon full, and those who could not find a bed lay on stretchers on the floors. Tents were hastily erected and soon packed with the worst cases. Time to attend to them was at a premium.

> After we finished our work we went into one tent and found it full of wounded who hadn't had anything to eat or drink for three days. Another tent—our old sleeping quarters—were full of cases who couldn't live long—weren't even operated on. In our old room lay a German officer and private, side by side and at one rank in illness and captivity. We made cocoa and with bread, took it around—it was eagerly swallowed.[12]

Among the wounded was an American 'with the worst fractured femur' Elsie had ever seen. Amputation was likely. She wrote to the mother of a 'nice little Scotch officer' who was very ill with a leg amputated, an arm broken and several other wounds.

By 17 July, it was apparent to the German High Command that the offensive had failed. American forces were arriving in France at the rate of 300,000 a month, while German reinforcements and resources were at breaking point. The arrival of the Americans had boosted British and French morale and delivered a body blow to the Germans.

On 18 July the Allies attacked and advanced at Château-Thierry. The pressure on the hospital staff intensified. 'Wounded pouring in daily and hourly. Baraques full and reception rooms full—they are waiting hours— the lesser cases—Germans, days to be operated on. Wards overflowing.'[13] By now there was no room inside the tents, and stretchers were placed on the ground outside. In the midst of this, Elsie received a letter from Syd 'complaining of a scarcity of letters from me'. If she was feeling put out by his letter and her endurance was being tested by the never-ending convoys of the wounded, a 'perfectly lovely' parcel from her mother-in-law eased the situation, with 'good things to eat—plum pudding and jam, camp pie, sugar and cheese'. It provided 'such a party'.

The Germans were now steadily pulling back, and the Australian 1st Division, with Syd's involvement, had taken the Menin Road. Despite the 'excellent war news' that the Germans had been driven back across the Marne and were still retreating, there was no let-up. On the last day of July, Elsie noted that the hospital was 'very full and wounded still arriving'. There had been an air raid the previous night. 'Another bomb dropped in the hospital park—another good tree spoilt, and our sleep disturbed.' She and Fraser and another nurse discovered a dugout near their hut, built for three, and planned 'to repair there on a real lively raid'. A few days later the Allies recaptured Soissons, but Elsie's joy was dampened when, not long after, 'the poor little Scotchman died and a Yorkshire boy' also. Elsie attended the funeral, at which a 'pathetic old guard of honour of ancient French territorials' lined up to fire a volley over the graves. The news continued to improve: more towns and villages were recaptured from the Germans, and tens of thousands of prisoners of war and guns were taken.

———

On 2 June 1918, Pearl Corkhill arrived at No. 38 British Casualty Clearing Station at Longvillers, between Abbeville and Doullens, in the Somme. War work for her was not just a matter of nursing, but also of keeping track of her brother Norm, a lieutenant in the 30th Battalion in France, and her cousin Fred, who was in Flanders in the thick of the action. She was determined to look after their interests and keep them provided, where possible, with fresh clothes. They wrote to each other as much as they could. She had passed on news of Norm's progress to her mother. There was a rumour that he had been wounded.

> Got your letter yesterday telling me about the news you had heard of Norman. Now there is no need to take any notice of anything you hear, if anything happens to Norman I will cable to you anyhow. There is no need to go and worry yourself sick and imagine all the time that something is going to happen. Why I don't even do that and I've got Fred up there as well, and I know far more what they are going through than you do, when they are in the lines and when they are out but it does not make things a bit better by worrying, so now you just leave it off and be a bit happy.[14]

If the two boys were in the thick of it, so was Pearl. On 19 July the Germans raided the clearing station at night, dropping three bombs. One fell in the middle of the camp and destroyed the sterilising room. Pearl saw the panic among her patients. She ignored the alarm to take shelter and, with her orderly, dashed around the hospital putting the sick and wounded under their beds. She knew her actions would not have saved lives if a bomb had hit the wards, but she maintained that they gave the patients 'that feeling of safety'.[15] Nine days later she was notified that she had been awarded the Military Medal for her coolness and presence of mind. The citation read: 'For courage and devotion to duty on the occasion of an enemy air-raid. She continued to attend to the wounded without any regard to her own safety, though enemy aircraft were overhead. Her example was of the greatest value in allaying the alarm of the patients.'[16]

With some modesty, Pearl wrote to her mother about it.

No doubt before you get this letter you will have heard of my good fortune. I suppose I may call it good fortune. I told you our hospital had been bombed one night while I've been on night duty, and I'm in charge of the place at night. Whatever night sister is on duty is in charge of the place. Well the CO recommended me for the Military Medal and today word came that I had been awarded the MM. Well the CO sent over a bottle of champagne and they all drank my health and now the MOs are giving me a dinner in honour of the event. I think it's awfully nice of them. I can't see what I've done to deserve it, but when I said that, the only answer I got was that lots had got it for far less, but the part I don't like is having to face [King] George and [Queen] Mary to get the medal. It will cost me a new mess dress, but I suppose I should not grumble at that. I'm still wearing the one I left Australia in and it is about worn out now. Although I had received a few hints that I had been recommended, it came as a great surprise, especially as they are so quick about it, it generally takes much longer.[17]

A few weeks later Pearl was promoted to Sister. Her Military Medal brought to eight the total number awarded to Australian nurses during the war—seven of them members of the Australian Army Nursing Service.

By August 1918, just as the Allies were beginning to gain the upper hand, a new enemy appeared. The so-called Spanish flu was indiscriminate and spread like wildfire. In the spring of 1918 large numbers of soldiers in the trenches became ill, complaining of sore throats, headaches and loss of appetite. Although it appeared to be highly infectious, recovery was rapid and doctors dubbed it 'three-day fever'. In the British Expeditionary Force the flu first appeared in April 1918, and by May it was rampant in the British, French and German armies. It was noticed at the end of April at the various Allied bases in Rouen, Le Havre and Marseilles, and early in May at Boulogne and Calais.

At first doctors were unable to identify the illness but eventually they concluded that it was a new strain of influenza. The soldiers called it Spanish flu, but it is now generally accepted that the disease was brought to the Western Front by a group of American soldiers from Kansas. By the end of 1920 it had killed an estimated 50 million people worldwide.

At first there were few fatalities among the infected troops. But in the summer of 1918, symptoms became much more severe. About one in five victims developed bronchial pneumonia or septicaemic blood poisoning, and many died. This second wave of the epidemic spread quickly. Men became delirious, with high temperatures and severe headaches. In one sector of the Western Front more than 70,000 American troops were hospitalised and nearly one-third of them died. Rows of corpses filled mortuary tents, dead from a sickness doctors were powerless to halt.

The Australian troops were just as hard hit. By the end of September, No. 3 General Hospital, Abbeville, had 1647 flu patients. By October, two more large wards were filled with flu cases. No one worked harder than the nurses who now faced a quite different challenge from the war injuries they had been treating. Anne Donnell was working at No. 1 Australian Auxiliary Hospital, Harefield Park, England, when the pandemic took hold. 'During our busiest time the influenza swept over us, involving extra work for those who kept well.'[18]

Not all did keep well. In mid-1918, one of Anne's colleagues, Ruby Dickinson, from Sydney, came down with the flu. She died on 23 June, aged thirty-two. Anne was saddened. 'When the worst was over more help came, but I shall always think that it came too late and at the price of life; for Sister Dickenson [*sic*]—a dear comrade who was with us on Lemnos and who felt she couldn't give in—died, one might say, at her post, for she was on duty the day previous and died of pneumonia the next day. It was a sad shock to us all. She was buried in our peaceful corner with our own hero boys.'[19]

Four months later, Matron Jean Miles Walker also died. She was thirty-nine and had been awarded the Royal Red Cross (1st Class). Anne Donnell thought her 'such a fine woman, and all we Nursing Sisters abroad have indeed lost a friend . . . Matron and I have just returned from her funeral at Sutton Veny. The coffin was draped with the Union Jack, but when I saw her red cape and white cap lying on top of the beautiful wreath of flowers it fairly broke me up.'[20] The flu went on to claim the lives of another nine Australian nurses.

New Zealand Sister Bertha Taylor, at No. 1 New Zealand Stationary Hospital in France, noted in September that nothing seemed able to save the French soldiers infected with a particularly virulent strain of the flu.[21] *Kai Tiaki* reported in October that the flu was rampant and mortality high, owing chiefly to lung complications. In November, it claimed the life of nurse Mabel Whishaw at Featherston Camp in New Zealand.

In France, another New Zealand nurse, thirty-five-year-old Ellen Brown, who had joined the Australian Army Nursing Service in 1915, developed a simple therapy that helped ensure none of her flu patients died. All men brought into her hospital were given oxygen until their blue cheeks assumed a natural colour. Thereafter they were moved to wards upstairs, where careful nursing and plenty of whisky effected a cure. 'Octopuses' were set up in the wards: an oxygen bottle stood in the centre and hoses took the gas to the patients' breathing masks.

In August 1918, the troopship *Tahiti* was transporting New Zealand soldiers of the 40th Reinforcements to England when the Spanish flu struck, apparently brought on board by coal loaders when the ship docked in Sierra Leone. Two days later eighty-four men were ill. The ten nurses and two medical officers were soon overloaded with work. One of the nurses described the epidemic in a letter to *Kai Tiaki*. The ship's hospital being so small and able to take only the worst cases, the men had to be nursed on their own decks. Two sisters soon joined the sick, while others struggled to stay on duty. 'Sister Evans should really have been off duty, but managed to keep going to ward the attack off,' the nurse wrote. 'She still has a nasty cough, but each night we hear less coughing amongst the girls, so I hope before long coughing will be an unheard of thing in our ward.'[22] It had been a 'lucky thing', she said, 'that a few of us kept up'. Within a week, the ship had 800 influenza cases, including both the doctors, and thirty-three men were dead.

They responded to no treatment whatever—stimulate and nourish them as we would—they went downhill rapidly, and this was the worst time of all. To see the poor boys die on our hands, one after the other, was terrible, but I must say that all that could be done for them was done. It was hard for us to see them go, but harder, I think, for their mates. Such a number of them were quite lads, about twenty. Having no lights on the decks made it twenty times harder for us, and one night almost every way we turned we found men, who a few moments before had seemed fairly well lying in a collapsed condition, dying about an hour later.[23]

By the time the *Tahiti* reached Plymouth, seventy-six men were dead and many were still sick. Ten more died on special trains that took the ill to hospitals. Among them was nurse Esther Tubman, from Dunedin, who was put into an isolation ward. Next morning she seemed better and brighter, but by afternoon her temperature had risen sharply. 'She raved terribly all night and next morning became unconscious,' *Kai Tiaki* reported.[24] She died two weeks later, on 18 September. Almost a year earlier, her brother had been killed in action in France.

# 31

# THE FIFTH NEW YEAR

On 8 August 1918, combined French and British forces stunned the Germans with an attack along an eighty-kilometre front, from the River Oise in the south to the River Ancre, on the old Somme front, in the north. The Allies had recovered far more quickly than they thought possible from their losses in the spring. The preparations were made in complete secrecy, and when the attack was launched—with prominent Australian involvement—the Germans gave way. Their big guns were captured and many prisoners taken. The German Commander, General Erich von Ludendorff, described it as the black day of the German Army.

The Spanish flu epidemic only added to Germany's problems. More than 400,000 German civilians died of the disease in 1918, making it impossible to replace sick, wounded and dying soldiers. German morale crumbled, both in the Army and at home, where the effects of the Allied blockade had reduced people to subsistence living. They wanted an end to the war. The Kaiser's control was collapsing.

Everyone had had enough of the war, including twenty-seven-year-old Sister Frances Laird, from Mount Gambier, South Australia. She was working in the 'head ward' at No. 2 General Hospital in Boulogne, otherwise

known as 'hell ward . . . It was a very sad place,' she remembered. 'It was
the head ward that just about fixed me. I was doing night duty there and
these head cases, they took such a long time to die.'[1] The situation worsened
when troop shortages made it necessary to send trained orderlies into battle.
This left just a skeleton staff for the head ward, including a boy sent from the
laboratory to help. He was shaking when he asked Frances if anyone would
die that night. Frances replied, 'I know three who won't be here in the
morning.' Resigning himself to the work ahead, the boy asked Frances just
to tell him what he had to do.

One morning her colleagues asked what sort of a night she'd had.
'I jumped up in the middle of my breakfast and I said, "I can't stand another
five minutes of it." I wrote out an application for transport duty to Australia.'
The endless misery was made worse by men beseeching her to get them on
a transport because 'I only want to die in Australia'. At the end of July 1918,
Frances returned to Adelaide on transport duty, relieved to be home after
three years away.

Nowhere was safe. But the tide of war was turning, and a new American
song about nurses captured the imagination of troops everywhere. *The Rose
of No Man's Land* would be heard on phonographs in the wards, performed
at concerts, and sung, hummed and whistled by the troops.

> There's a Rose that grows in No Man's Land,
> And it's wonderful to see.
> Tho' it's sprayed with tears,
> It will live for years
> In my garden of memory.
> It's the one red rose
> The soldier knows,
> It's the work of the Master's Hand;
> In the War's great curse stands the Red Cross Nurse,
> She's the Rose of No Man's Land.

Although heavily sentimental, the lyrics captured the feelings of the troops. The nurses who had spent four years caring for them were now revered by the men. Nowhere was this truer than in the relationship between the Diggers and the Anzac sisters. In a hospital in England, Private John Hardie wrote to his mother:

I would never have got across here if it hadn't been for one of the nurses in our ward, who was an Australian. She used to do her best to get all the Aussies across. There seems to be a great difference between our nurses and the others [British nurses]. Of course they are all very kind, but I would rather be in an Australian hospital at any time.[2]

The times were changing. With fewer wounded and less pressure, a more relaxed atmosphere developed. Early in September, Syd Cook unexpectedly arrived at Senlis with eight days' leave for Paris. As he waited for Elsie to join him, he reacquainted himself with hospital life. 'Syd wandered around the ward and watched a few of the dressings being done, which filled him with horror,' Elsie wrote, amused.[3] An ambulance taking wounded men into Senlis conveyed the couple on to Paris, where they booked a hotel room overlooking the Tuileries Gardens in full bloom.

They dined at the Folies Bergère. 'Rather "*un peu forte*" the review,' Elsie commented about the show, which was clearly a little too risqué for her liking. '*C'est Paris*,' she wrote. They slept late, strolled in the gardens, toured the 'squat, over-decorated iced cake' that was the Palace of Versailles, bought each other wedding anniversary gifts, and fell in love with the city. In the Bois de Boulogne, Elsie was entranced by the 'lovely Parisiennes, looking chic and very elegant, with their latest young man of leave, or a very ridiculous little tiny dog, with a great big bow, and a very long chain'.

Returning to Senlis to become 'Sister Cook once more', she was soon inundated with work. 'There's no doubt that a fracture hospital never cools down and fractures always are much work.' On 19 September, she reflected that in four years of marriage she and Syd had 'very nearly' managed to celebrate all their anniversaries together. This year, however, Syd was near St Quentin, attacking the Hindenburg Line. Elsie was alone and melancholy.

He won't have much time to be thinking of anniversaries and reminiscences. Each year I look forward and think that perhaps the next anniversary will see us back in our own little home in Australia, but each anniversary sees us still pegging away. If we had realised that day, four years ago, that in four years time we should still be here, the war still going on, I'm afraid our hearts would have quailed and our hopes and spirits not so high as they were on that brief honeymoon at the 'Pacific' [Hotel]. However, this year things certainly do look much brighter and hopeful for a finish and I feel sure that next anniversary will be spent at home—how strange to be in our home![4]

The war news continued to improve. Bulgaria asked for peace, and the Allies launched a major advance at Cambrai. It and St Quentin were soon in their hands, clearing the way for yet more towns and villages to be wrested from the Germans. The British took Lille, and Belgian troops with their King and Queen, entered Ostend just two hours after the Germans had retreated. Bruges followed, as the Allies advanced rapidly. Syd wrote to say that his battalion had taken more prisoners than it had men. As Germany, Austria and Turkey sought peace talks in October, Syd was sent to England for military training.

The workload at the Senlis hospital wound down, and at the end of October, twenty lorries came at daybreak to move the hospital to Laon, an old fortress city thirty-six kilometres southeast of St Quentin. With time on their hands, Elsie and Fraser Thompson travelled to Paris, exultation building as the end of the war loomed. They had their hair done, lunched at Au Printemps, had clothes made, and visited Montmartre. They returned to the hospital at Laon via Soissons, 100 kilometres northeast of Paris.

Here the town was literally levelled to the ground, the houses just one heap of stones, streets neatly cleaned up and debris thrown back from the roadside. The lovely cathedral was just a shell—a great gaping hole torn in the roof, nearly all its walls blown out, just a tall graceful column left standing here and there, and a piece of a beautiful braced Gothic window frame. We sat in the ruins of the Cathedral to have lunch. Then set off to get on the road to Laon.[5]

They passed the Chemin des Dames battlefield, where the French Army had been broken in April 1917 in the Second Battle of the Aisne, which cost 187,000 casualties and sparked mutiny among the troops. Fighting on the historic battlefield had erupted again between August and October 1918.

It was indescribable, just one mass of heaving tortured earth, shell holes and mine craters of enormous size, old trenches and dugouts, blown up roadways. One could only recognise where a village had once stood by the white coloured dust and brick dust and small pieces of ironwork. For miles this expanse of awful ruin and shell torn earth stretched, thickly interspersed by graves—German and French, a helmet to mark the nationality from afar. The road we travelled over was very bad, still broken up at frequent intervals by shell holes and craters, some mines were still going up that day.[6]

She and Fraser were not at the Laon hospital for long. After just two days, they said their final goodbyes and set out for Paris, on their way to London. There Syd met Elsie and took her back to the military town of Aldershot, where he was based. Soon they heard the news that had taken four years to come.

The war was over.

It was time to celebrate. Some found it hard to do so. Not so Elsie Cook. She recorded the sheer joy and excitement of 11 November 1918:

Armistice Day!!

About 11.15 am bells began to ring, and sirens blow—the news that the Germans had accepted and signed our armistice terms—great excitement. Syd and I sallied forth, people began to hang out flags and bunting, the aeroplanes from the aerodrome opposite arose and circled and dived and made merry in air. We went to the mess where Syd learnt that he had four days leave, so we decided to rush off to London—packed hastily and caught the midday train to Charing Cross. Found London in a state of great rejoicing and merry making. Processions, in which Australians seemed to be taking a leading part, were in full swing along the Strand—we couldn't move, only by inches, finally arrived at the Savoy, where the gaiety was in high form—found the Pater [Sir Joseph, who had been appointed High Commissioner] out, couldn't get any lunch, sat in his sitting room awhile—went over to the Strand Palace, where Syd had managed to reserve a table in the grillroom. Had a very nice dinner, celebrated the great occasion by a bottle of fizz. Couldn't get a room in town anywhere, so went out to Golders Green and stayed with [friends].

After dinner we went over to the Savoy where a fearful din was going on—dancing in full swing—lots of crockery smashed, officers playing tug'o'war with the tablecloths—others raided the kitchen and returned wearing the cook's caps and aprons, cake baskets on their heads a la helmets. We had quite a good dance in the ballroom in spite of the fact that the orchestra would only play one steps and fox trots.[7]

The couple continued their celebrations over the next few weeks, often accompanied by Sir Joseph, with dinner at the Strand Palace, lunch at the Savoy Hotel, where he was staying, and visits to the theatre. Elsie bought some long evening gloves 'at a ridiculous price', and with Syd attended a dance at the Grafton Galleries. Fraser and her husband, Nubby, were there, too. That night they 'slept the sleep of the just'.

At Harefield Park, Anne Donnell heard the guns go off at midday to mark the Armistice. 'Sister, the Kaiser has chucked his job and the war's over,' one of her patients told her, waving a copy of the *Daily Mail*.[8] For Anne, the news that the war was over seemed almost too much for words.

There is a certain amount of quiet excitement with most of us. Some are overjoyed and I wish I could feel as they do, but I am terribly depressed. When I went over to the home for morning tea the Sisters seemed very happy and excited and anticipating pleasure and freedom once more. It's wonderful, really but I can't take in all that it means. I think of the gladness, then follows the sadness, and in the gladness I am saddest because I think of those who have lost, the mothers at home whose sunny boys are not going back to make them glad.[9]

The signing of the Armistice buoyed human spirits that had hung on grimly, trying merely to survive until victory was achieved. Now it was here, and few could hold back their exhilaration. In London, Anne saw people doing 'the maddest things . . . Two or three of our Sisters stood up on a table in one of the crowded restaurants and coo-eed, and the coo-ees that followed from the Aussies around just deafened everything else for awhile. They repeated it again in the centre of Piccadilly Circus, and had great fun.'[10] Two other sisters saw a 'big tall Aussie without any teeth who said, "Here I am, the war's over and not any of the girls kissing me."'

In Paris, crowds massed on the Champs-Elysées and the Place de la Concorde, climbing over captured German guns and cheering, dancing and singing as the *Marseillaise* and *God Save the King* rang out. Flags were everywhere. Men climbed on rooftops, aviators performed stunts, and the city erupted in wild celebrations.

In Boulogne, South Australian Sister Dora Birks watched the patients' instant joy. 'I was on duty on the morning of the peace day when a tall

American boy, a convalescent patient, managed to get his boots, which were usually hidden, and he danced down the ward in his big heavy boots,' Dora recalled.[11] That afternoon she walked into Boulogne, where the streets were crammed with people singing and dancing and holding hands. At night the hospital staff celebrated with 'a joyful evening meal, everybody talking hard'.

For Elsie Tranter, the celebrations were muted.

Church bells pealed, bugles were blown, guns boomed and France went mad with joy. Pourquoi? The joy of the people was beyond bounds. Little children and adults dance in the streets. Flags were flying from all the windows; adults kissing everyone, first one cheek, then the other.

Sunny Jim [a patient] finished his battle towards evening. He was barely eighteen years of age [when he died]. We were so fond of him, we did not feel able to enter fully into the Armistice.[12]

Several unnamed New Zealand sisters wrote to *Kai Tiaki* describing exultant scenes. One wrote:

London was crazy with joy. Some New Zealand company Engineers were seen with Union Jacks down each side of their trousers, cowboy fashion, and the French flag round their waists. They wended their way happily, but slightly unsteadily, down the centre of the streets, not hurrying or moving for any one, and the traffic was held up for them several times.[13]

There were bonfires in Trafalgar Square, which, like the Strand, was a seething mass of people. 'Folks dancing on the footpaths, singing, shouting, waving flags; loaded lorries and motor cars going up and down the crowded thoroughfares laden with excited creatures, half mad . . . The officers were as bad as the men.'[14]

Fanny Speedy had been about to go to France, but an accident had prevented her. The Wellington matron was recovering at the sisters' convalescent hospital at Brighton when the war ended. 'The bells rang at 11 a.m. and soon we knew that the Armistice had been signed. The streets are thronged here and flags and bunting in all directions with shouting and singing . . . The whole thing seems too big to realise and too sad to understand.'[15]

At the New Zealand Stationary Hospital at Wisques, near Calais, the end of the war brought a heartfelt letter to Matron Eva Brooke from two French officers on behalf of the French patients.

Dear Matron,

Will you please accept on behalf of yourself and the Nursing Staff, our very respectful thanks for the excellent reception shown to us, and for the perfect care which we have received in your fine hospital. We have met with every kindness and attention from all with whom we have come in contact; you have all seemed to know just exactly what we required, and your sympathy is appreciated very much.

We all carry away with us to our various homes many happy remembrances of our stay with you at a time when the great day of victory arrived to the cause of the Allies.

We trust that you may soon return to your far distant New Zealand, which, through your kindness, has become very dear to us, and we wish to carry to your dominion our kind thoughts and well wishes.[16]

At No. 1 Australian General Hospital, Rouen, the announcement of the Armistice etched itself into Annie Shadforth's memory. 'It was delightful to see the dear old boys who had not taken any interest in anything in weeks, buck up and become enthusiastic once again,' she recalled.[17] Alice Ross King was also at No. 1. She had come to believe that the war was not going to end, and had been depressed and frightened. But Armistice Day restored her spirits. It was 'a wonderful day', she wrote.

> People were dancing in the street. Just a skeleton staff in the wards. John Prior and Blue came out for me to see the town. One very drunk Australian soldier came up to me leading a white draught horse he had pinched from a Frenchie's cart. It had a red collar on it. He said, 'Here you are Sister, I won't want this horse again. I'm going back to Australia.' I said, 'Is it your horse?' He said, 'No! But you can have it.' And I was left with a horse![18]

In Salonika, Ada Willis captured the scene for her family back home in Crookwell. 'Tonight there is more noise than usual, people cheering here and there, a bagpipe skirling over the back somewhere, some of the girls having some music and singing and unofficial dancing over in the sitting room and every now and then roars from the orderlies quarters where there is a whist drive in progress.'[19]

Syd Cook returned to camp at Aldershot after the celebrations and, farewelling him at Charing Cross Station, Elsie was struck by the difference. Now that the war was over she could acknowledge something to herself that she had been loath to admit before. 'Not so bad seeing him off now, not the feeling that I mightn't be seeing him any more, which makes all the difference.'[20] Elsie and Fraser wanted to return to France. They arrived in Paris on New Year's Eve. That night, Elsie wrote her last diary entry for the war. 'And so endeth another year, but now it is really the last year of the war—the fifth New Year's Eve, in which I have kept my diary, and in which I have wondered if it were really the last year of war.' She and Syd had made it through.

# 32

# THE AFTERMATH

War forever changed the lives of the nurses and troops who were part of it. Youthful exuberance at the chance of a Great Adventure was sobered by the experience. In 1919, General Sir Douglas Haig wrote of the nurses' contribution in the First World War, noting particularly the part played by those who served with the British armies in France. He thanked sisters from Canada, Australia, New Zealand, South Africa and the United States for 'cheerfully enduring fatigue in times of stress and gallantly facing danger and death'.[1] Few thanked Haig: his military leadership had seen too many unnecessary deaths, and too many men hospitalised and maimed.

Australia and New Zealand now beckoned, but like the troops, many nurses wondered how easy it would be fitting back into civilian life. The readjustment for many would be painful. Some nurses found themselves unable to let go of the commitment to caring for their patients. Others were treated shabbily by governments on their return. Adelaide sister Dora Birks, who served at Boulogne, recalled the story of a colleague who declined a suitor's offers of marriage and served overseas. On her return, she worked at a military hospital where she nursed a man who was paralysed from the shoulders down.

He used to get his pals to bring him drink secretly, and when he left
hospital she went with him, and married him. To the relief of all of us
who knew her he died in two years. She never married again. She was
a lovely girl, and we all loved her. She was a really good sport, and
I grieved when I knew she had married this man in Adelaide.[2]

*Marquette* survivor Sister Gladys Metherell had served four years in
Alexandria and then England before returning to Christchurch in April
1919. Two months after her return to New Zealand, she wrote to Brigadier-
General G.S. Richardson, drawing his attention to discrimination against
returned nurses compared with returned soldiers in relation to financial
help such as housing loans. Gladys wanted to build a house for her widowed
mother.

> I must apologise for troubling you, but upon arrival home I was dis-
> appointed to find that the privileges to soldiers with regard to money
> lent for building etc was not extended to members of the Army
> Nursing Service.
>
> So I thought I would write to you before Parliament sits to ask if
> you could have this law altered to include the Sisters.
>
> I know it is generally understood that women have no responsibil-
> ities, but I know of several like myself whose life-long ambition it has
> been to erect a house for the mother who was left a widow in their
> infancy, and you can imagine my feelings when after a four years'
> absence, I return to find boys with only a few months' service to their
> credit in some instances, enjoying these privileges.
>
> Thanking you in anticipation for your attention.[3]

Her request was turned down. She spent the rest of her life sharing a
house with her sister, and they had to take in a boarder to supplement
their income.

In New Zealand, planning started early to commemorate the *Marquette* nurses. In 1927 the Nurses' Memorial Chapel was opened in the grounds of Christchurch Hospital, dedicated to their memory. The Nurses Chapel with its *Marquette* museum and stained glass windows dedicated to nurses has survived attempts to have it demolished and is the country's only memorial built in memory of New Zealand nurses killed in war. Australia was slow to acknowledge the nurses who served in the war. This was belatedly rectified in October 1999 when a memorial to Australian nurses who served in all wars was unveiled on Anzac Parade in Canberra.

For the Bluebirds, the post-war period left a sour taste from the discrimination they experienced. Fifteen of the twenty had renewed their contracts for the final six months of the war, but they were afforded shoddy treatment when the war finished. To their dismay, they had to work their passage home as duty nurses caring for AIF wives and babies on ships. The same treatment was given to nurses who married, including Olive Haynes and Elsie Eglinton, while Charles Laffin had to find the fare to bring his wife Nell Pike home to Australia while knowing that the government was paying the fares of English war brides. To rub salt into the wound, Prime Minister Billy Hughes decreed that the returning soldiers on the ships had 'done their duty [and] should be amply provided with games [and] books . . . in short, they must be treated with that consideration which their great deeds and many hardships have earned'.

The Bluebirds also found themselves denied the government's war gratuity, paid at a flat rate of 1s 6d from the date of embarkation to the signing of the Treaty of Versailles on 21 June 1919. In contrast, the gratuity was ultimately awarded to the 129 Australian nurses who worked with the Queen Alexandra's Imperial Military Nursing Service. Because the Bluebirds had also seen active service, various approaches were made to win them the gratuity, but the Government refused to budge, worried that such a payment could open the floodgates to all volunteers. The Government argued that the Bluebirds were given a free passage on the proviso that the Commonwealth accepted no liability for them on their return to Australia.

This left the responsibility with the Red Cross, which paid the fifteen who returned to Australia a 25 pound bonus, and resolved that no further action be taken, even though several became ill as a result of their work. One, Sister Annie Jamieson, was committed to an asylum and struck off the nursing register as insane in 1928. Historian Dr Melanie Oppenheimer points out that Annie had spent nearly a year nursing in a mobile hospital near the front and had been gassed several times. 'It is reasonable to assume that her war work could have contributed to her later mental illness,' Oppenheimer says.[4]

For all the returned nurses in this early post-war period, it was soon clear that they remained invisible from the emerging Anzac legend, which comprised only men. This was a product of the times, when women were still regarded as dependents of men. Authorities in Australia saw the nurses' role as secondary to that of the soldier.

Yet despite early resistance from some medical officers, Australian and New Zealand nurses had quickly proven their competence and won acceptance. It was the soldiers who were in the best position to understand the Army nurses' achievements and give them the respect they deserved. To them, they were the other Anzacs. Sister Elizabeth Rothery enlisted in 1914 and served on hospital ships and in hospitals for the wounded overseas. In June 1918, while home on leave, she died in Beechworth, Victoria, of peritonitis. Her brother Henry had died in action at Gallipoli in November 1915. Their grief-stricken father wrote to military authorities that even though he had given his only son and one of his daughters 'to the cause', and had made no financial claim on the Commonwealth, the military had failed to return a single item of either Elizabeth's or Henry's possessions.[5]

The local paper reported that Sister Rothery's last thoughts had been of the boys overseas. The returned servicemen of Beechworth gave her a military funeral. The coffin, draped with the Union Jack and her uniform laid on top, was carried through the streets by six veterans as a large crowd stood in silence. Other veterans stood at the graveside with rifles reversed.

Three volleys were fired over the grave, and the Last Post was played.[6] The funeral had been arranged entirely by the ex-servicemen and civic leaders; Army officials had no hand in it. Elizabeth Rothery, like her nursing colleagues in Australia and New Zealand, had won recognition and respect from those who mattered.

And that respect continued. In the 1930s Nell Pike took her children to several Anzac Day marches in Sydney, watching from the George Street footpath. Nell's daughter Daphne remembers men breaking away from the columns of ex-diggers to embrace her mother, crying, 'Little Sister, Little Sister!'

For some nurses, their experiences in the war were so overwhelming that they felt compelled to leave the profession. Tev Davies was one. 'I have finished with nursing Mum,' Tev wrote from England. 'I don't want to work all my life. It is too funny to hear all the girls talking, some are going to make sweets, others take flats and sub-let them, others tea rooms, we are all sick of having women over us and will do anything to be independent. I think the government will advance money at easy rates to returned people.'[7]

Olive Haynes headed back to Australia in February 1918, a month after her husband, Pat, who had been medically boarded to also return. Before she left, she wrote to her mother about one of the wounded. 'There is a poor old Aussie over here with both arms off, both legs off, and both eyes out. He got someone to write to the King, asking to be put out of his misery, but the King refused—wasn't it terrible, to save him in the first place?'[8] Olive and Pat had seven children. Until their deaths in 1978, Olive and Pat remained close friends with Pete Peters and her husband Norm, who had married in England shortly after them.

Before Pearl Corkhill left England in late January 1919, she attended an afternoon tea in London. One of the nurses had married a medical officer.

The day before I gave the boys in my ward a party, most of them are returning to Australia on the hospital ship which may go next week,

Sister and I wanted to give them something before they went. So we had a very nice spread and music and singing. Then one of the boys invited us to step forward, and made a speech and presented us both with a beautiful silver manicure set. They were so delighted that they had sprung such a surprise on us. They are grand kids and I will miss them horribly.[9]

During World War II, Pearl was matron of a home for limbless soldiers in Sydney. After the war, she returned to the New South Wales south coast to become Senior Sister at Bega District Hospital. She never married, and died in 1985. It later emerged that she had been engaged to a soldier in 1915, but he had been killed.

After returning to Australia, Elsie Tranter married William Cumming, who had served with the 13th Field Ambulance in Egypt and on the Western Front. They lived in Launceston and had two daughters. Elsie died in 1968.

May Tilton returned to Melbourne on transport duty in March 1918 and, after a period at the Caulfield Military Hospital, worked for nineteen years as a welfare sister with Prahran Council. She also became a trustee of the Edith Cavell Trust Fund. She never married and died in 1964, aged eighty.

Daisy Richmond did not marry either. According to family folkore, her fiancé died in the war. She was awarded the Royal Red Cross, became matron of Wollongong Hospital and supervisor of nursing services in Tasmania, and was involved with the Bush Nursing Service. She was invested with the MBE in 1964 for her service to the community, and died in 1969.

In May 1918, Kath King gave birth to a daughter, Betty. She and Gordon Carter returned to Australia in April 1919, and settled at Roseville in Sydney. Less than a year later, baby Betty took ill with blood poisoning. Kath wrote in her diary, 'We lost our little girlie at 10.30 p.m.'[10] After so much death and loss, Kath and Gordon were emotionally spent.

Three sons followed, and one more daughter, Shirley. Gordon became the New South Wales government's chief electrical engineer and later, mayor of

Kuringai, which kept Kath busy as lady mayoress. In World War II their sons joined up, and in April 1944 one went missing while returning from enemy territory near Dunkirk. He was never found. On 24 April, Kath wrote in her diary: 'John is now presumed dead and there really seems very little hope.' In July 1946, when her two surviving sons and daughter were demobbed, Kath wrote with relief, 'Thank goodness.' Gordon died in 1963, and Kath in 1972.

After the war, Elsie and Syd Cook moved to Perth, where he was appointed Commonwealth Works Director for Western Australia. In 1940 he was transferred to Sydney in the same position, and was responsible for federal defence works such as the Garden Island dock and defence roads to Darwin airfield. In Sydney, Elsie opened an antiques store and named it after the London establishment where she'd celebrated the end of the war—the Grafton Galleries. In later years, their grandchildren would run their fingers over the groove on Syd's scalp left by the bullet at Lone Pine. Both Elsie and Syd died in 1972.

Before the war was quite over, Elsie Eglinton returned to a hero's welcome at Murray Bridge, South Australia. 'Although it was damp and foggy I might say half the town was on the station and when the band struck up "Home Sweet Home" we nearly all cried and could scarcely listen to any of the speeches.'[11] Some time later, she wrote of her experiences in the first few years after the war.

The next twelve months was the hardest time I have ever put in, to feel so far away from what had been part of one's life. It would have been quite a different home coming had the war been won, but even in July, 1918 were none [*sic*] too sure how it would all end.

If only I could have gone to sleep and slept until 11th November all would have been well.

But to go out and meet people and try and talk about your experiences, for they all took an interest in you and expected you to talk, was just unbearable at times.

And the quiet Australian life, after the rush and bustle of the other side was maddening.

Well it is all over and past now and the *Euripides* brought me back my Scotchman. So now I am happy and have nothing to grumble about (unless a few butt ends and a few dead matches) but consider myself very fortunate to have served in the most terrible war the world has ever known.

It seems like a long past dreadful dream now and I really can't imagine it was part of my life for such a long period.

My dear little boy and girl sometimes hear their father and I talking of the war and later when we are alone will beg—'do tell us some of the stories about the war Mummie, I'm just going to be a soldier when I grow up.'

I pray God that never as long as the world may last will there ever be such a dreadful slaughter.[12]


As Anne Donnell discovered, returning home had its lighter yet poignant moments. On board the troopship when she sailed from England in January 1919 was a 'dear little Pomeranian doggie' that was being smuggled back to Australia. When it was discovered, the officer commanding ordered that it could not be taken ashore and would have to be put down. The senior medical officer intervened and won a reprieve. The dog's future became the focus of the passengers' conversation.


Last night I was talking to some of the boys about it and I gathered this, that if the doggie does go overboard the OC will soon follow it. The boys (they say) keep a guard of twelve to fourteen over it night and day, and I can see they are determined to take it to Australia. They tell me the doggie's history and I do admire our boys' sentiment. A soldier brought it from Australia as a pet, and it was with him until he was killed in France. The boy's mate then looked after it and vowed that if he lived he would take the doggie back with him and give it to the boy's mother. So from France it went to England, and in the camp at Weymouth it became a great pet. The boy taught it to run into a kit bag without a murmur until it was let out, and that's how this little thing came on board—in a kit bag. I don't know how the OC got to know of it being here, but unfortunately he does.[13]

Anne talked to the commanding officer, but her pleading for the dog was unsuccessful. He told her it would be impossible to let the dog land in Australia because it was strictly against the law and he would be fined £50. Anne offered to take up a collection, confident that she would soon raise such an amount. 'Just then I caught a look from one of the officers sitting opposite, and later on he said, "Sister, the dog is all right, don't you worry over it". Then with a wink he whispered, "It's officially dead".'[14] When she landed in Melbourne, Anne heard the following remark: 'Mother, see that little doggie running about, I saw it jump out of one of the soldiers' kit bags.'

Annie Shadforth returned to Australia in October 1919 and caught up with her childhood friend from Ballarat, John Hughes, who arrived back from the war in December 1918. They married in 1924. Their grandson, Des Ryan, suspects from his research into the family history that they had 'quite a remarkable wartime love story'. There were at least four occasions when their paths could have crossed: at Heliopolis in early 1916; at Rouen hospital in May 1917, when John was being treated for shell shock; at Rouen in July 1918, after he was gassed; and again at Rouen in August, after he was shot in the arm. The period July–August 1918 provided more occasions to catch up, possibly while Annie was treating John in hospital. It seems too coincidental that she took leave in London in October 1918 while he was convalescing.

Annie died in 1948, aged sixty, and John in 1969, aged seventy-eight. His war memories turned into demons, and he spent his declining years as an alcoholic in a nursing home in Geelong. 'He would go missing and be found drunk among the wool stores near Corio Bay. For all the trouble he must have caused, the woman who ran the nursing home never sent a bill to the family. She understood,' Des Ryan said.[15]

Elsie Grant returned to Queensland, married and had four children. Post-traumatic stress, complicated by undiagnosed post-natal depression, coupled with the loss of her brother Allan finally overwhelmed her. In September 1927, as the tenth anniversary of his death approached, she suicided.

In February 1919 Alice Ross King returned to Australia on the transport *City of York*. Not in the mood to begin a new diary, she nonetheless found things she wanted to record. She jotted down her thoughts on bits of paper on the ship and continued to do so after she arrived home. Alice had wanted to take leave and sightsee in England, but was denied permission. Senior nurses like herself were needed back in Australia to organise re-patriation hospitals, she was told. 'I don't care anyhow,' Alice wrote, in her despondent mood.

She was put in charge of the ship's hospital, and it pleased her that there was not much sickness on board. This meant she only had to roster herself on for two hours a day. It was 'a generally happy crowd', but that happiness was not something she was always in a mood to share. 'If only Harry could be here!' she lamented. After she landed in Australia, Alice visited Harry Moffitt's mother. She needed to share her grief.

But she grieved anew when she heard that her friend Topsy Tyson had died in April 1919, at the age of twenty-eight. According to military records, she died of a cerebral haemorrhage, although Alice believed it was a con-sequence of Spanish flu. Topsy was buried at Sutton Veny in Wiltshire. There was a touch of bitterness in Alice's sorrow. 'The English sent her off to an infectious hospital and she was away from us. If they had only returned her to her unit we would have specialled her.'[16]

On the voyage Alice had become friends with the ship's medical officer, Major Sydney Appleford. He had been posted overseas in 1916 and served in Egypt and France as an MO. Alice thought he was 'not bad'. He was 'engaged to a girl in Geelong and feels he doesn't want to marry her'. Sydney called off the engagement to his Geelong fiancée because he felt she would never be able to understand what he had experienced in the war.

In August 1919, Alice and Sydney married. They were both war weary and, wanting a quiet life, settled at Lang Lang, in Gippsland, Victoria, where Sydney ran a medical practice with Alice's help. They raised four children. In the late 1930s, as the threat of war loomed again, Alice began training young women as members of Voluntary Aid Detachments. When war began, both she and Sydney joined up. Sydney was an Army medical officer, eventually becoming a lieutenant-colonel, and Alice was assistant controller of the Voluntary Aid Detachments in Victoria, with the rank of Major.

Alice was responsible for some 1900 servicewomen, 300 of whom were sent overseas. She played a leading role in organising appeals and raising funds for the Red Cross and other causes. In May 1949, the International Red Cross awarded her the Florence Nightingale Medal—bestowed only every second year on no more than thirty-six women from all countries with a Red Cross organisation. The citation read: 'No one who came in contact with Major Appleford could fail to recognise her as a leader of women. Her sense of duty, her sterling solidity of character, her humanity, sincerity, and kindliness of heart set for others a very high example.' Alice resigned from the Army in 1950 and returned to helping Sydney in his practice until his death in 1958. Following her death in 1968, the Australian Army Medical Women's Service established the Alice Appleford Memorial Award, presented annually to a member of the Royal Australian Army Nursing Corps. In March 2008, her work and service were recognised when her name was added to the Victorian Women's Honour Roll.

Alice led a full and accomplished life, both professionally and personally in a loving relationship. However, there was a part of her that stored a private grief for Harry Moffitt. Each year on the anniversary of his death, she would spend the day quietly, retiring to her bedroom for a time. After her death her children discovered a shoebox under the bed in which she kept her most personal possessions. Inside was Harry's last letter.

# AUSTRALIAN WORLD WAR I
# NURSES HONOUR ROLL

———◆◆◆———

NAME
PLACE OF BIRTH
CAUSE OF DEATH/DATE
BURIED
AGE (where known)

BICKNELL, Louisa Annie, Sister
Abbotsford, Vic
Septic infection, 25 Jun. 1915
Cairo, Egypt
35

BLAKE, Edith, QAIMNS Sister
Sans Souci, NSW
Drowned, Hospital Ship *Glenart Castle*
26 Feb. 1918

CLARE, Emily, Sister
Footscray, Vic
Influenza, 17 Oct. 1918
Deolali, India
28

DICKINSON, Ruby, Sister
Forbes, NSW
Influenza, 23 Jun. 1918
Harefield, Middlesex
32

GOODMAN, Pearl, Sister
Millthorpe, NSW
Influenza, 8 Mar. 1919
Sydney, NSW
34

HENNESSY, May, Sister
Castlemaine, Vic
Malaria/dysentery, 9 Apr. 1919
Bendigo, Vic
25

HOBBES, Narelle, Matron
Brewarrina Hospital
Cancer, 10 May 1918
At sea
39

KNOX, Hilda Mary, Sister
Benalla, Vic
Cerebral disease, 17 Feb. 1917
Rouen, France
33

MCPHAIL, Irene, Staff Nurse
Echuca, Vic
TB, 4 Aug. 1920
Brighton General Cemetery, Vic
27

MILES-WALKER, Jean, Matron
Tasmania
Influenza, 30 Oct. 1918
Sutton Veny Churchyard, UK
39

MOORHOUSE, Edith Ann, Sister
Undera, Vic
Influenza, 24 Nov. 1918
Lille Southern Cemetery, France
33

MORETON, Letetia Gladys, Sister
Brim, Vic
Enteric, 11 Nov. 1916
Quetta Govt Cemetery, India
26

MOWBRAY, Norma Violet, Staff Nurse
St George, Qld
Influenza, 21 Jan. 1916
Cairo War Memorial Cemetery, Egypt
32

MUNRO, Gertrude Evelyn, Sister
Ballarat, Vic
Influenza, 10 Sep. 1918
Mikra British Cemetery, Salonika, Greece
36

NUGENT, Lily, Staff Nurse
Wagga Wagga, NSW
Phthisis, 21 Feb. 1918
St Vincent's Hospital, NSW

O'GRADY, Amy Veda, Sister
Castlemaine, Vic
Cholera, 12 Aug. 1916
Bombay, India
41

O'KANE, Rosa, Sister
Charters Towers, Qld
Influenza, 21 Dec. 1918
Woodmans Point, WA
27

PORTER, Katherine Lawrence, Sister
Milton, NSW
Influenza, 16 Jul. 1919
Waverley Cemetery, NSW
34

POWER, Kathleen, Sister
Ireland, enlisted Cairo
Cholera, 13 Aug. 1918
Bombay (Sewri) Cemetery, India
28

RIDGWAY, Doris Alice, Sister
Salters Springs, SA
Influenza, 6 Jan. 1919
Woodmans Point, WA
27

ROTHERY, Elizabeth, Sister
Whitehaven, UK
Pneumonia, 15 Jun. 1918
Beechworth, Vic
33

STAFFORD, Mary Florence, Sister
Nyngan, NSW
Leukaemia, 20 Mar. 1919
Adelaide, SA
26

THOMPSON, Ada Mildred, Sister
Dubbo, NSW
Influenza, 1 Jan. 1919
Western Australia
33

TYSON, Fanny Isobel Catherine, Sister
Balranald, NSW
Cerebral, 20 Apr. 1919
Sutton Veny Churchyard, UK
28

WATSON, Beatrice Middleton, Sister
Elsternwick, Vic
Cerebral, 2 Jun. 1916
Ismalia War Memorial Cemetery, Egypt
34

WILLIAMS, Blodwyn Elizabeth, Sister
Ballarat, Vic
Pneumonia, 24 May. 1920
Caulfield/ Ballarat Cemetery, Vic
38

WILLIAMS, Hilda Grace, Sister
Victoria
Influenza, 4 Jan. 1919
Quarantine Station, Woodmans Point, WA
26

WILSON, Myrtle, Sister, QAIMNS
Queensland
23 Dec. 1915
Wimereux Cemetery, France
38

# NEW ZEALAND WORLD WAR I
# NURSES HONOUR ROLL

NAME
PLACE OF BIRTH
CAUSE OF DEATH/DATE
BURIED
AGE (where known)

BROWN, Marion Sinclair, Staff Nurse*
Riverton
Drowned, 23 Oct. 1915
Mikra Memorial, Greece

CLARK, Isabel, Staff Nurse*
Oamaru
Drowned, 23 Oct. 1915
Mikra Memorial, Greece
30

COOKE, Ella, Staff Nurse
French Red Cross and QAIMNSR
Accidentally killed on active service, 8 Sep. 1917
Alexandria (Hadra) War Memorial Cemetery, Egypt
30

FOX, Catherine Anne, Staff Nurse*
Dunedin
Drowned, 23 Oct. 1915
Mikra Memorial, Greece

GORMAN, Mary, Staff Nurse*
Waimate
Drowned, 23 Oct. 1915
Mikra Memorial, Greece


HAWKEN, Ada Gilbert, Staff Nurse
Auckland
Enteric fever, No 19 Gen Hospital, Alexandria, 28 Oct. 1915
Alexandria Military and War Memorial Cemetery, Egypt
29


HILDYARD, Nora Mildred, Staff Nurse*
Christchurch
Drowned, 23 Oct. 1915
Mikra Memorial, Greece
28


ISDELL, Helena Kathleen, Staff Nurse*
Kumara
Drowned, 23 Oct. 1915
Mikra Memorial, Greece


JAMIESON, Mabel Elizabeth, Staff Nurse*
Palmerston North
Drowned, 23 Oct. 1915
Mikra Memorial, Greece


KEMP, Dorothy, QAIMNS


LIND, Lily, French Flag Nursing Corps
Pulmonary tuberculosis, Dec. 1916
Buried at sea


RAE, Mary Helen, Staff Nurse*
Dunedin
Drowned, 23 Oct. 1915
Mikra Memorial, Greece
36


RATTRAY, Lorna Aylmer, Staff Nurse*
Christchurch
Drowned, 23 Oct. 1915
Mikra Memorial, Greece

ROGERS, Margaret, Staff Nurse*
Christchurch
Drowned, 23 Oct. 1915
Mikra Memorial, Greece

THOMPSON, Margaret Hepple, Staff Nurse
Dunedin
TB, 28 Feb. 1921
Christchurch
35

TUBMAN, Esther Maude, Staff Nurse
Dunedin
Cerebro Spinal Meningitis, Salisbury Hospital UK, 18 Sept. 1918
Tidworth Military Cemetery, Wiltshire, England
31

WHISHAW, Mabel, Sister
Wellington
Influenza, Featherston Camp, 10 Nov. 1918
Featherston Cemetery

* Sisters lost from the *Marquette*

# NOTES

━━━►●◄━━━

## INTRODUCTION

1. Sherayl Kendall and David Corbett, *New Zealand Military Nursing*, self-published, Auckland, 1990, p. 21.
2. Dr Kirsty Harris, *Sabretache*, Vol. 49 no. 1, March 2008.
3. Sherayl McNabb (nee Kendall), private correspondence.
4. Opinion of Crown Solicitor 1932, Australian War Memorial file 734/1/- and 826/1/7.
5. A First World War Nurse, *A War Nurse's Diary: Sketches from a Belgian Field Hospital*, Macmillan, N.Y. 1918.
6. *Australasian Nurses' Journal*, 15 December 1914.
7. The *Burrowa News*, 22 January 1915, National Library of Australia.
8. Gertrude Doherty, quoted in Ruth Rae, 'Operating in the Theatre of World War I: France', *Acorn*, Vol. 17 no. 2, 2004.
9. Sister Ida O'Dwyer, A descriptive narrative account of the conditions of nursing in an Australian CCS, Australian War Memorial.
10. Elsie Eglinton, letter, 2 July 1916, Australian War memorial.

## CHAPTER 1   THE BIG ADVENTURE

1. Elsie Eglinton, 16 January 1915 (incorrectly dated 6 January).
2. Elsie Eglinton, 16 January 1915.
3. Elsie Cook, diary, 13 January 1915, Australian War Memorial.
4. Elsie Cook, 15 January 1915.
4. Elsie Cook, 16 January 1915.
6. Nellie Crommelin, letter, 20 August 1916, Australian War Memorial.
7. Kath King, diary, 25 November 1914, Australian War Memorial.

8. Elsie Cook, 5 December 1914.
9. Elsie Eglinton, 27 November 1914.
10. Margaret Young, ed. *We are Here, Too: Diaries and Letters of Sister Olive L.C. Haynes*, Australian Down Syndrome Association, SA, 1991; 26 November 1914, p. 13.
11. Elsie Eglinton, 4 December 1914.
12. Elsie Eglinton, 10 December 1914.
13. Elsie Cook, 7 December 1914.
14. Elsie Cook, 9 December 1914.
15. Elsie Cook, 31 December 1914–1 January 1915.
16. Letter to *Kai Tiaki*, April 1915.
17. *Kai Tiaki*, April 1915.
18. *Kai Tiaki*, April 1915.

CHAPTER 2   RELATIVE RELATIONS
1. Because there was another Alice King from Tasmania in the AANS, the Army included her second Christian name, Ross.
2. Daisy Richmond, diary, 20 January 1915, Australian War Memorial.
3. Narrative of an anonymous sister, AWM 41, Australian War Memorial.
4. Alice Ross King, diary, 22 January 1915, Australian War Memorial.
5. Kath King, 28 January 1915.
6. Olive Haynes in *We are Here . . .*, p. 30.
7. Kath King, 30 January 1915.
8. H.G. Carter, letter, 31 January 1915, Australian War Memorial.
9. Kath King, 3 February 1915.
10. Elsie Cook, 20 January 1915.
11. Elsie Cook, 13 February 1915.
12. Elsie Cook, 22 February 1915.
13. Elsie Cook, 1 February 1915.

CHAPTER 3   DIFFERENT RULES
1. Alice Ross King, 15 March 1915.
2. Kath King, 26 March 1915.
3. Alice Ross King, 25 March 1915.
4. Alice Ross King, 24 April 1915.
5. Alice Ross King, 10 March 1915.
6. Alice Ross King, 1915, no date.
7. Alice Ross King, 2 February 1915.
8. Alice Ross King, 30 January, 1915.
9. Alice Ross King, 1 February 1915.

10. Alice Ross King, 6 February 1915.
11. Alice Ross King, 7 February 1915.
12. Charles Bean, 'Australian hospitals at the front watch a Turkish attack', Cairo, 22 February 1915, AWM 3DRL 8039/6.
13. Alice Ross King, 19 February 1915.
14. Alice Ross King, 20 February 1915.
15. Alice Ross King, 24 February 1915.
16. Alice Ross King, 2 March 1915.
17. Alice Ross King, 13 March 1915.
18. Alice Ross King, 8 April 1915.
19. Alice Ross King, 10 April 1915.
20. Alice Ross King, 7 March 1915.

CHAPTER 4   THE PRELUDE
1. Elsie Cook, 19 March 1915.
2. A.B. Facey, *A Fortunate Life*, Penguin Books, Ringwood, Victoria, 1981, p. 248.
3. A.G. Butler, *Official History of the Australian Army Medical Services, 1914–1918*, vol. 1, p. 76. Australian War Memorial, Melbourne, 1938.
4. Letter, 27 December 1914, quoted in *The Australian Army Medical Corps in Egypt*, James Barrett and Lieut. P.E. Deane, M.K. Lewis and Co., London, 1918, pp. 117–18.
5. Elsie Eglinton, 8 February 1915.
6. Evelyn Davies, diary, 10 April 1916, Australian War Memorial.
7. Alice Ross King, 1 March 1915.
8. Alice Ross King, 7 March 1915.
9. Daisy Richmond, 2 April 1915 (incorrectly dated 1 April).
10. Alice Ross King, 2 April 1915.
11. Alice Ross King, 3 April 1915.
12. Alice Ross King, 4 April 1915.
13. Elsie Cook, 3 April 1915.
14. Alice Ross King, 18 April 1915.
15. Alice Ross King, 24 April 1915.
16. Alice Ross King, 25 April 1915.

CHAPTER 5   GALLIPOLI
1. Ellis Ashmead-Bartlett, Hobart *Mercury*, 8 May 1915.
2. H.G. Carter, diary, Carter family.
3. Kath King, 25 April, 1915.
4. Kath King, 25 April, 1915.
5. Daisy Richmond, quoted in the *Auckland Star*. Undated article published June 1964 after she was awarded the MBE for service to the community.
6. George Mackay, statement, Australian War Memorial.

7. Kath King, 26 April, 1915.
8. Kath King, 27 April, 1915.
9. Kath King, 28 April, 1915.
10. Hester Maclean, *Nursing in New Zealand*, Tolan Printing Company, Wellington, 1932, p. 157.
11. Kath King, 28 April, 1915.
12. J.E.F. Deakin, 'Some experiences with the No. 2 Australian Stationary Hospital', *Medical Journal of Australia*, 27 January 1917, p. 77.
13. J.E.F. Deakin, 'Some experiences . . .'
14. J.E.F. Deakin, 'Some experiences . . .'

CHAPTER 6   BLOODED
1. Kath King, 29 April to 5 May, 1915.
2. Narrative of an anonymous sister, Australian War Memorial, 41.
3. Elsie Eglinton, 2 May 1915.
4. Olive Haynes in *We are Here* . . ., 30 April 1915, p. 39.
5. Sister Emma Cuthbert, quoted in Ruth Rae, *Scarlet Poppies*, College of Nursing, Burwood, NSW, 2004.
6. Sister Emma Cuthbert, in *Scarlet Poppies*.
7. Quoted in Patsy Adam-Smith, *The Anzacs*, Thomas Nelson, Melbourne, 1978, p. 76.
8. Quoted in Patsy Adam-Smith, *The Anzacs*.
9. Daisy Richmond, 4 May 1915.
10. Daisy Richmond, 6 May 1915.
11. Alice Ross King, 8 May 1915.

CHAPTER 7   NOT MUCH COMFORT TO A MOTHER
1. Gordon Carter, letter 30 April 1915. Held by Carter Family.
2. Kath King, 5 May 1915.
3. Elsie Cook, 29 April 1915.
4. Elsie Cook, 30 April 1915.
5. Elsie Cook, 1 May 1915.
6. Elsie Cook, 1 May 1915.
7. Elsie Cook, 7 May 1915.
8. Elsie Cook, 7 May 1915.
9. Elsie Cook, 13 May 1915.
10. Elsie Cook, 3 May 1915.
11. Kath King, 13 May 1915.
12. Daisy Richmond, 16 May, 1915.
13. Kath King, 14 May 1915.
14. Kath King, 20 May 1915.
15. Kath King, 21 May 1915.
16. Kath King, 23 May 1915.

17. Daisy Richmond, 25 May 1915.
18. Ion Idriess, *The Desert Column*, Angus & Robertson, 1985, p. 27.
19. Alice Ross King, 20 May 1915.
20. Elsie Eglinton, 23 May 1915.
21. Elsie Eglinton, 23 May 1915.
22. Alice Ross King, 22 May 1915.
23. Alice Ross King, 10 May 1915.
24. Alice Ross King, 10 May 1915.
25. Alice Ross King, 25 May 1915.
26. Alice Ross King, 26 May 1915.
27. Alice Ross King, 28 May 1915.
28. Alice Ross King, 29 May 1915.
29. Elsie Cook, 18 May 1915.
30. Elsie Cook, 19 May 1915.

CHAPTER 8   HEARTILY SICK OF IT
1. Lieutenant-Colonel Dr Percival Fenwick, *Gallipoli Diary*, Auckland Museum, p. 31.
2. Kath King, 10 June 1915.
3. Kath King, 16 June 1915.
4. Elsie Cook, 31 May 1915.
5. Elsie Cook, 15 June 1915.
6. Elsie Cook, 26 June 1915.
7. Elsie Cook, 27 June 1915.
8. Elsie Cook, 27 June 1915.
9. Elsie Cook, 27 June 1915.
10. Alice Ross King, 2 June 1915.
11. Alice Ross King, 3 June 1915.
12. Alice Ross King, 6 June 1915.
13. Alice Ross King, 8 June 1915.
14. Alice Ross King, 13 June 1915.
15. Alice Ross King, 14 June 1915.
16. Alice Ross King, 15 June 1915.
17. Alice Ross King, 20 June 1915.
18. Alice Ross King, 16 June 1915.
19. Alice Ross King, 28 June 1915.
20. Olive Haynes in *We are Here . . .*, 5 June 1915.
21. Elsie Eglinton, 4–6 June 1915.
22. Elsie Eglinton, 1 July 1915.
23. Elsie Eglinton, 11 July 1915.
24. Olive Haynes in *We are Here . . .*, 10 July 1915.
25. May Tilton, *The Grey Battalion*, Angus & Robertson, Sydney, 1933.

26. Daisy Richmond, 29 June 1915.
27. Kath King, 16 June 1915.
28. Kath King, 20 June 1915.
29. Evelyn Davies, 20 May 1915.
30. Evelyn Davies, 24 June 1915.


CHAPTER 9   THE KIWIS ARRIVE
 1. Le Gallais family papers, 1870–1920, Auckland War Memorial Library, ms 95/11, folders 3 and 6.
 2. Hester Maclean, *Nursing in New Zealand*, p. 131.
 3. Hester Maclean, *Nursing in New Zealand*, p. 131.
 4. Hester Maclean, *Nursing in New Zealand*, p. 143.
 5. Hester Maclean, *Nursing in New Zealand*, p. 163.
 6. Hester Maclean, *Nursing in New Zealand*, p. 165.
 7. Hester Maclean, *Nursing in New Zealand*, p. 168.
 8. Ida Willis, *A Nurse Remembers*, A.K. Wilson, Lower Hutt, New Zealand [no date], p. 33.
 9. Sir Fred Bowerbank, *A Doctor's Story*, Wingfield Press, Wellington, 1958, pp. 107–8.
10. Anna Rogers, *While You're Away*, Auckland University Press, Auckland, 2003, pp. 64–5.
11. Anna Rogers, *While You're Away*, pp. 64–5.
12. Hester Maclean, *Nursing in New Zealand*, pp. 168–9.
13. Le Gallais family papers, no date.
14. Le Gallais family papers, 22 August 1915.
15. Le Gallais family papers, 22 August 1915.


CHAPTER 10   NONE OF THE OLD SMALLNESS IN IT
 1. Alice Ross King, 3 July–14 August 1915.
 2. William Kinsey Bolton, National Archives of Australia, serial number B2455, barcode 3097255.
 3. Alice Ross King, 3 July–14 August 1915.
 4. Alice Ross King, 3 July–14 August 1915.
 5. Alice Ross King, 3 July–14 August 1915.
 6. Alice Ross King, 3 July–14 August 1915.
 7. Alice Ross King, 3 July–14 August 1915.
 8. Alice Ross King, 3 July–14 August 1915.
 9. Alice Ross King, 3 July–14 August 1915.
10. Alice Ross King, 3 July–14 August 1915.
11. Alice Ross King, 3 July–14 August 1915.
12. Alice Ross King, 3 July–14 August 1915.
13. Alice Ross King, 3 July–14 August 1915.
14. Alice Ross King, 3 July–14 August 1915.

15. Alice Ross King, 1 September 1915.
16. Alice Ross King, 30 August 1915.
17. Alice Ross King, 3 September 1915.
18. Alice Ross King, 4 September 1915.
19. Alice Ross King, 6 September 1915.
20. Alice Ross King, 8 September 1915.
21. Alice Ross King, 11 September 1915.
22. Alice Ross King, 18 September 1915.
23. Alice Ross King, 18 September 1915.
24. Alice Ross King, 14 October 1915.
25. Alice Ross King, 14 October 1915.

CHAPTER 11    BROKEN BODIES
1. Quoted in Les Carlyon, *Gallipoli*, Macmillan, Sydney, 2002, p. 326.
2. Les Carlyon, *Gallipoli*, p. 329.
3. Kath King, 23 July 1915.
4. H.G. Carter, 11 August, 1915; private family records.
5. H.G. Carter, 16 August 1915.
6. H.G. Carter, 30 August 1915.
7. Kath King, 29 September 1915.
8. Elsie Eglinton, 15 August 1915.
9. Elsie Eglinton, 2 August 1915.
10. Elsie Eglinton, 2 August 1915.
11. Elsie Eglinton, 6 August 1915.
12. Daisy Richmond, 11–12 August 1915.
13. Elsie Eglinton, 13 August 1915.
14. Elsie Eglinton, 13 August 1915.
15. Elsie Eglinton, 15 August 1915.

CHAPTER 12    TEARS IN THE DARK
1. Elsie Cook, 12 August 1915.
2. Undated story attached to a letter from the *Lithgow Mercury* to Syd Cook;
   Cook family records.
3. Elsie Cook, 14 August 1915.
4. Elsie Cook, 14 August 1915.
5. Elsie Cook, 15 August 1915.
6. Elsie Cook, 19 August 1915.
7. Elsie Cook, 7 September 1915.
8. Elsie Cook, 15 September 1915.
9. Daisy Richmond, 15 September 1915.
10. Le Gallais family papers, 13 September 1915.
11. Le Gallais family papers, 13 September 1915.
12. Le Gallais family papers, 8–15 October 1915.

## CHAPTER 13   THE SHABBY SISTERS

1. Cited in John Laffin, *Damn the Dardanelles*, Sun Books, Melbourne, 1985, p. 168.
2. Elsie Eglinton, 13 August 1915.
3. Grace Wilson, letter, 6 August 1915, Australian War Memorial.
4. Grace Wilson, 6 August 1915.
5. Cited in Rupert Goodman, *Our War Nurses*, Boolarong Publications, Brisbane, 1988, p. 42.
6. A.G. Butler, *Official History . . .*, vol. 1, p. 395.
7. A.G. Butler, *Official History . . .*, vol. 1, p. 375.
8. Fetherston Report, Australian National Archives, Melbourne, p. 59.
9. Olive Haynes in *We are Here . . .*, 10 October 1915.
10. Evelyn Davies, 9 September 1915.
11. Evelyn Davies, 9 September 1915.
12. John Laffin, *Damn the Dardanelles*, p. 168.
13. Evelyn Davies, 12 November 1915.
14. Evelyn Davies, 12 November 1915.
15. Alison Alexander, *A Wealth of Women*, Duffy & Snellgrove, Sydney, 2002, p. 119; see also Percival Fenwick, *Gallipoli Diary*, p. 99.
16. Anne Donnell, *Letters of an Army Sister*, Angus & Robertson, Sydney, 1920; 10 November 1915.
17. Olive Haynes in *We are Here . . .*, 29 September 1915.
18. Nellie Morrice, narrative, Australian War Memorial, 41 1013, pp. 7–8.
19. Grace Wilson, 17 August 1915.
20. Fetherston Report, p. 34.
21. Fetherston Report, p. 34.
22. A.G. Butler, *Official History . . .*, vol. 1, p. 392.
23. Anne Donnell, *Letters of an Army Sister*, 6 December 1915.
24. Anne Donnell, *Letters of an Army Sister*, p. 69.
25. Evelyn Davies, 15 January 1916.
26. Olive Haynes in *We are Here . . .*, 15 January 1916.
27. Anne Donnell, *Letters of an Army Sister*, 21 January 1916.
28. *Medical Journal of Australia*, 27 January 1917, p. 76.
29. Anne Donnell, *Letters of an Army Sister*, 23 March 1916.
30. Sister Selwyn-Smith, quoted in Rupert Goodman, *Our War Nurses*, p.44.

## CHAPTER 14   ALONE IN THE AEGEAN

1. Edith Popplewell, letter to *Kai Tiaki*, January 1916.
2. John Meredith Smith, *Cloud Over Marquette*, Fiesta Products, 1990, p. 60.
3. Letter, Canterbury Museum, Christchurch, vol. 1, Regimental No. 22/71.
4. John Meredith Smith, *Cloud Over Marquette*, p. 63.
5. Vic Nicholson, unpublished interview with Christopher Pugsley, Palmerston, NZ, 1984.

6. Vic Nicholson, unpublished interview.
7. John Meredith Smith, *Cloud Over Marquette*, p. 67.
8. John Meredith Smith, *Cloud Over Marquette*, p. 65.
9. Edith Wilkin, letter, 7 November 1915, Nurses' Chapel, Christchurch.
10. Joan Rattray, *Great Days in New Zealand Nursing*, A.H. & A.W. Reed, Wellington, 1961, p. 137.
11. British National Archives, cable no. 2042 E.
12. *Kai Tiaki*, January 1916.
13. Joan Rattray, *Great Days . . .*, p. 137.
14. John Meredith Smith, *Cloud Over Marquette*, p. 25.
15. Court of Inquiry report, 1916, p. 290.
16. Court of Inquiry report, p. 290.
17. *Oamaru Mail*, undated.
18. Edith Wilkin, letter.
19. Vic Nicholson, unpublished interview.
20. Court of Inquiry report, p. 290.
21. Sister Mary Damian, *Growl You May But Go You Must*, A.H. & A.W. Reed, Wellington, 1968, p. 52.
22. *The Press*, Christchurch, 23 October 1965, p. 5.
23. Court of Inquiry report, p. 290.
24. *Kai Tiaki*, January 1916, p. 9.
25. John Meredith Smith, *Cloud Over Marquette*, p. 25.
26. John Meredith Smith, *Cloud Over Marquette*, p. 25.
27. Fanny Abbott, letter, 30 October 1915, Nurses' Chapel, Christchurch.
28. John Meredith Smith, *Cloud Over Marquette*, p. 36.
29. John Meredith Smith, *Cloud Over Marquette*, p. 36.
30. *Oamaru Mail*, undated.
31. William Tennant, letter, Nurses' Chapel, Christchurch.
32. John Meredith Smith, *Cloud Over Marquette*, p. 36.
33. Mary Damian, *Growl You May . . .*, p. 54.

CHAPTER 15   'WE THOUGHT THEY WOULD LET US DIE!'

1. Court of Inquiry report, p. 292.
2. Len Wilson statement, Wilson family records.
3. Court of Inquiry report, p. 292.
4. Court of Inquiry report, p. 292.
5. Court of Inquiry report, p. 342.
6. Court of Inquiry report, p. 291.
7. Cameron family communication.
8. Court of Inquiry report, p. 339.
9. Court of Inquiry report, p. 292.
10. Court of Inquiry report, p. 292.

11. John Meredith Smith, *Cloud Over Marquette*, p. 32.
12. John Meredith Smith, *Cloud Over Marquette*, pp. 26–7.
13. *Kai Tiaki*, January 1916, p. 11.
14. John Meredith Smith, *Cloud Over Marquette*, pp. 29–30.
15. John Meredith Smith, *Cloud Over Marquette*, pp. 30–1.
16. Mary Beswick, *Oamaru Mail*.
17. *New Zealand Nursing Review*, December 2001, p. 10.
18. *New Zealand Nursing Review*, December 2001, p. 10.

CHAPTER 16   NO TIME FOR MOCK MODESTY
 1. John Meredith Smith, *Cloud Over Marquette*, p. 138.
 2. Court of Inquiry report, p. 290.
 3. Court of Inquiry report, p. 293.
 4. Len Wilson, statement.
 5. Anna Rogers, *While You're Away*, p. 101.
 6. Edith Popplewell, letter.
 7. Nicholas Boyack and Jane Tolerton, eds, *In the Shadow of War*, Penguin, Auckland, 1990, pp. 88–9.
 8. *NZ Nursing Review*, p. 10.
 9. Mary Damian, *Growl You May . . .*, p. 57.
10. Edith Wilkin, letter.
11. Fanny Abbott, letter.
12. Ina Coster, letter, 31 October 1918
13. *Star*, 1 October 1965, Nurses' Chapel, Christchurch.
14. Kath King, 23 October 1915.
15. Anna Rogers, *While You're Away*, p. 104.
16. Anna Rogers, *While You're Away*, p. 106.
17. Mary Damian, *Growl You May . . .*, p. 58.
18. Le Gallais family papers, letter, 17 November 1915.
19. Le Gallais family papers, letter, 17 November 1915.
20. *Kai Tiaki*, January 1916, p. 9.
21. *Kai Tiaki*, January 1916, p. 9.

CHAPTER 17   THE PRICE OF SACRIFICE
 1. Olive Haynes in *We are Here . . .*, 25 October 1915.
 2. *Argus*, 29 November 1915.
 3. *Star*, 3 November 1915; Nurses' Chapel, Christchurch.
 4. Edith Wilkin, letter.
 5. Edith Wilkin, letter.
 6. May Tilton, *The Grey Battalion*, pp. 44–5.
 7. Ida Willis, *A Nurse Remembers*, p. 34.
 8. *Kai Tiaki*, January 1916.

9. Hester Maclean, *Nursing in New Zealand*, pp. 187–9.

10. Arthur Judge, transcript of interview, February 1979, Nurses' Chapel, Christchurch.

11. Undated, unnamed newspaper file, Nurses' Chapel, Christchurch.

12. *Kai Tiaki*, January 1916.

13. Court of Inquiry report, p. 300.

14. Kath King, 13–29 October 1915.

15. Statement, Royal New Zealand Army Medical Corps Museum, Burnham Camp, Christchurch.

16. John Meredith Smith, *Cloud Over Marquette*, p. 190.

17. Court of Inquiry report, p. 344.

18. Court of Inquiry report, p. 347.

19. Anna Rogers, *While You're Away*, p. 111.

20. Anna Rogers, *While You're Away*, p. 108.

21. Hester Maclean, *Nursing in New Zealand*, p. 194.

22. Anna Rogers, *While You're Away*, p. 109.

23. La Gallais family papers, letter, 14 April 1915.

CHAPTER 18   THE FIRST ANZAC SERVICE

1. Alice Ross King, 1 January 1916.

2. Alice Ross King, 10 January 1916.

3. Elsie Cook, 31 December 1915.

4. Elsie Eglinton, 10 November 1915.

5. Kath King, 11 February 1916.

6. Kath King, 11 February 1916.

7. *The Leader*, Orange, 18 February 1916.

8. Elsie Cook, 22 April 1916.

9. Alice Ross King, 30 January 1916.

10. Alice Ross King, 12 February 1916.

11. Alice Ross King, 14 February 1916.

12. A.G. Butler, *Official History . . .*, vol. 2, Australian War Memorial, Melbourne, 1940, p. 376.

13. Alice Ross King, no date.

14. Pearl Corkhill, letter, 17 April 1916, Australian War Memorial.

15. Alice Ross King, no date.

16. Statement to the assistant collator, medical history, Ryan family records.

17. Pearl Corkhill, 28 April 1916.

18. Olive Haynes in *We are Here . . .*, 8 April 1916, p. 135.

19. Olive Haynes in *We are Here . . .*, 8 April 1916, p. 135.

20. Olive Haynes in *We are Here . . .*, 14 April 1916, p. 136.

21. Olive Haynes in *We are Here . . .*, 21 April 1916, p. 137.

22. *Kai Tiaki*, October 1916.

23. *Kai Tiaki*, July 1916.

24. Kath King, 25 April 1916.
25. Anne Donnell, *Letters of an Army Sister*, 25 April 1915, p. 95.
26. May Tilton, *The Grey Battalion*, 25 April 1916, p. 100.
27. Pearl Corkhill, 28 April 1916.


CHAPTER 19   WAITING FOR HARRY
 1. H.G. Carter, diary, 11 June 1916.
 2. Kath King, 11 June 1916.
 3. H.G. Carter, 11 June 1916.
 4. Alice Ross King, 9 May 1916.
 5. Alice Ross King, 16 May 1916.
 6. Alice Ross King, 18 May 1916.
 7. Alice Ross King, 17 May 1916.
 8. Alice Ross King, 20 May 1916.
 9. Alice Ross King, 31 May 1916.
10. Alice Ross King, 1 June 1916.
11. Alice Ross King, 2 June 1916.
12. Alice Ross King, 7 June 1916.
13. Alice Ross King, 10 June 1916.
14. Alice Ross King, 13 June 1916.
15. Alice Ross King, 13 June 1916.
16. Alice Ross King, 15 June 1916.
17. Alice Ross King, 18 June 1916.
18. Alice Ross King, 27 June 1916.
19. Alice Ross King, 30 June 1916.
20. Alice Ross King, 1 July 1916.
21. Sister Fairland, *The Australasian Nurses' Journal*, April 1917, p. 122
22. Philip Gibbs, *Now It Can Be Told*, Project Gutenberg, http://gutenberg.org/
    etext/3317.
23. Annie Shadforth, statement to assistant collator, Ryan family records.
24. Alice Ross King, 3 July 1916.
25. Alice Ross King, 6 July 1916.
26. Alice Ross King, 9 July 1916.
27. Alice Ross King, 11 July 1916.
28. Alice Ross King, 12 July 1916.
29. Alice Ross King, 14 July 1916.
30. Alice Ross King, 17 July 1916.


CHAPTER 20   HARRY'S LETTER
 1. Ross McMullin 'Disaster at Fromelles', *Wartime*, Issue 36, Australian War
    Memorial, Canberra, 2006.
 2. W.H. 'Jimmy' Downing, quoted in McMullin 'Distaster at Fermelles'

3. W.H. 'Jimmy' Downing, quoted in McMullin 'Distaster at Fermelles'.
4. C.E.W. Bean, *Official History of Australia in the War, Vol. III: The Australian Imperial Force in France, 1916*, 12th edition, 1941, p. 437.
5. Robin Corfield, *Don't Forget Me Cobber*, Corfield & Company, Rossana, Victoria, 2000, p. 260.
6. Les Carlyon, *The Great War*, pp. 50–1.
7. Australian Imperial Force unit war diaries, 1914–18 war, item Number 1/50/5/part 3, Australian War Memorial.
8. Yvonne McEwen, *It's a Long Way to Tipperary*, Cualann Press, Dunfermline, 2006, p. 131.
9. *Canberra Times*, 13 March 2005.
10. Robin Corfield, *Don't Forget Me Cobber*, p. 147.
11. Australian Red Cross Society Wounded and Missing Enquiry Bureau files, 1914–18 War, 1 DRL/0428, Australian War Memorial.
12. Australian Red Cross Society . . .
13. Letter held by Marion Sanders.
14. Alice Ross King, 4 August 1916.
15. Alice Ross King, 12 August 1916.
16. Alice Ross King, 23 August 1916.

CHAPTER 21   GRASPING FOR HOPE
1. Alice Ross King, 20 August 1916.
2. Alice Ross King, 6 September 1916.
3. Alice Ross King, 13 August 1916.
4. Alice Ross King, 14 August 1916.
5. Alice Ross King, 24 September 1916.
6. Alice Ross King, 25 September 1916.
7. Alice Ross King, 25 September 1916.
8. Alice Ross King, 26 September 1916.
9. Alice Ross King, 29 September 1916.
10. Alice Ross King, 2 October 1916.
11. Alice Ross King, 3 October 1916.
12. Alice Ross King, 5 October 1916.
13. Alice Ross King, 7 October 1916.
14. Alice Ross King, 10 October 1916.
15. Ida O'Dwyer, A descriptive narrative account . . .
16. Ida O'Dwyer, A descriptive narrative account . . .
17. Ida O'Dwyer, A descriptive narrative account . . .
18. Ida O'Dwyer, A descriptive narrative account . . .
19. Ida O'Dwyer, A descriptive narrative account . . .
20. Olive Haynes in *We are Here . . .*, 25 August 1916, p. 159.
21. Olive Haynes in *We are Here . . .*, 29 August 1916, p. 161.

22. Olive Haynes in *We are Here* . . ., 12 September 1916, p. 164.
23. Olive Haynes in *We are Here* . . ., 26 September 1916, p. 165.
24. Olive Haynes in *We are Here* . . ., 5 August 1916, p. 158.
25. Ida Willis, *A Nurse Remembers*, p. 39.
26. Matron Mary Finlay, quoted in Rupert Goodman, *Our War Nurses*, p. 60.
27. Ida Willis, *A Nurse Remembers*, pp. 38–9.
28. *Kai Tiaki*, January 1917.

CHAPTER 22    THE CHILL OF WAR
1. Australian Red Cross Society . . .
2. Australian Red Cross Society . . .
3. Australian Red Cross Society . . .
4. Alice Ross King, 21 January 1917.
5. Australian Red Cross Society . . .
6. Alice Ross King, 21 January 1917.
7. Australian Red Cross Society . . .
8. Alice Ross King, 15 February 1917.
9. Alice Ross King, 15 February 1917.
10. Alice Ross King, 29 March 1917.
11. *Kai Tiaki*, July 1917, pp. 133–4.
12. Lyn MacDonald, *The Roses of No Man's Land*, Penguin, London, 1980, p. 83.
13. Pearl Corkhill, 24 November 1916.
14. Alice Ross King, 23 January 1917.
15. Elsie Eglinton, 29 November 1916.
16. Elsie Eglinton, 4 January 1917.
17. Elsie Eglinton, 14 January 1917.
18. Olive Haynes in *We are Here* . . ., 15 January 1917, p. 182.
19. Elsie Eglinton, 8 February 1917.
20. *M.O., Church of England Messenger*, 4 April 1919, p. 790.
21. Gordon Carter, 17 February 1917.

CHAPTER 23    NO PLACE TO HIDE
1. *UNA*, Journal of the Victorian Collage of Nursing, 30 October 1917, p. 244.
2. Elsie Eglinton, 17 March 1917.
3. Ida Willis, *A Nurse Remembers*, p. 40.
4. Elsie May Tranter, diary, 17 August 1916, Australian War Memorial.
5. Elsie May Tranter, 2 March 1917.
6. Elsie May Tranter, 5 March 1917.
7. *The Leader*, Melbourne, 2 May 1931.
8. Ida Willis, *A Nurse Remembers*, pp. 39–40.
9. Elsie May Tranter, 2 May 1917.
10. Elsie May Tranter, 5 May 1917.

11. Elsie May Tranter, 12 May 1917.
12. Elsie May Tranter, 3 April 1917.
13. Elsie May Tranter, 3 April 1917.
14. Elsie May Tranter, 4 April 1917.
15. Elsie May Tranter, 2 May 1917.
16. Elsie May Tranter, 5 May 1917.
17. Gordon Carter, 2 June 1918.
18. Report by Miss Wilson, 22 May 1933, Australian War Memorial.
19. Ada Smith quoted in Ruth Rae, *Operating in the Theatre of World War I*.
20. Ada Smith quoted in Ruth Rae, *Operating in the Theatre of World War I*.
21. Anne Donnell, *Letters of an Army Sister*, 5 July 1917, p. 169.
22. Gertrude Doherty, letter, 15 July 1917, Australian War Memorial.
23. Elsie May Tranter, 19 June 1917.
24. Elsie May Tranter, 24 June 1917.

CHAPTER 24    BOMBS AND BASINS
 1. Ida O'Dwyer, A descriptive narrative account . . .
 2. Alice Ross King, undated entry.
 3. Alice Ross King, 25 July 1917.
 4. *UNA*, Melbourne, 30 October 1917.
 5. Letter held by Marion Sanders.
 6. Alice Ross King, 4 August 1917.
 7. Alice Ross King, 9 August 1917.
 8. *British Journal of Nursing*, 2 February 1918.
 9. Rupert Goodman, *Our War Nurses*, p. 67.
10. Rachael Pratt, National Archives of Australia, barcode 8018638, series no. B2455.
11. Ida O'Dwyer, A descriptive account . . .
12. May Tilton, *The Grey Battalion*, 21 August 1917, p. 235.
13. May Tilton, *The Grey Battalion*, 21 August 1917, p. 235.
14. G.C. Munschamp, letter, *UNA*, 30 November 1917, vol. 15, no. 9, p. 277.
15. G.C. Munschamp, letter.

CHAPTER 25    DESOLATION
 1. Alice Ross King, 27 August 1917.
 2. Alice Ross King, 4 August 1917.
 3. Alice Ross King, 4 August 1917.
 4. Alice Ross King, undated.
 5. Alice Ross King, 10 December 1917.
 6. Elsie Eglinton, 19 October 1915.
 7. Elsie Eglinton, 9 November 1916.
 8. Letter, Ernest Hewish, quoted by Elsie Eglinton, 29 June 1917.
 9. May Tilton, *The Grey Battalion*, 25 August 1917.

10. Elsie Grant letter, 23 August 1917, Australian War Memorial.
11. Letter to Elsie Grant, 20 October 1917, Australian War Memorial.
12. Annie Shadforth, statement.
13. May Tilton, *The Grey Battalion*, 4 October 1917.
14. May Tilton, *The Grey Battalion*, 25 August 1917.
15. May Tilton, *The Grey Battalion*, 1 November 1917.


CHAPTER 26   SURVIVAL
 1. Olive Haynes in *We are Here . . .*, 19 July 1917, p. 154.
 2. Ida O'Dwyer, letter to mother of Pte D.B. Nicol, 16 October 1917, Australian War Memorial.
 3. Anne Donnell, *Letters of an Army Sister*, 5 July 1917, p. 170.
 4. Anne Donnell, *Letters of an Army Sister*, 1 May 1918, p. 218.
 5. Evelyn Davies, 8 March 1917.
 6. Report by Grace Wilson.
 7. Anna Rogers, *While You're Away*, p. 152.
 8. Anna Rogers, *While You're Away*, p. 152.
 9. Elsie Tranter, 17 November 1917.
10. Elsie Tranter, 1 August 1917.
11. Elsie Tranter, 2 March 1917.
12. May Tilton, *The Grey Battalion*, no date, p. 177.
13. Elsie Eglinton, 22 May 1916.
14. Elsie Eglinton, 14 September 1916.
15. Elsie Eglinton, 28 September 1916.
16. Elsie Eglinton, 30 April 1918.
17. Olive Haynes in *We are Here . . .*, 1 August 1917, p. 215.
18. Olive Haynes in *We are Here . . .*, 24 July 1917, pp. 215–16.
19. Olive Haynes in *We are Here . . .*, 9 August 1917, p. 223.
20. Olive Haynes in *We are Here . . .*, 20 August 1917, p. 225.
21. Olive Haynes in *We are Here . . .*, 22 August 1917, p. 226.
22. Olive Haynes in *We are Here . . .*, 16 October 1917, p. 237.


CHAPTER 27   GIFTS FOR FRANCE
 1. M. Oppenheimer, 'Gifts for France: Australian Red Cross nurses in France, 1916–1919', *Journal of Australian Studies*, no. 39 (Dec 1993), pp. 65–78.
 2. *Kai Tiaki*, July 1916, p. 160.
 3. Thompson family records, letter, 22 January 1916.
 4. Elsie Cook, 12 September 1916.
 5. Nellie Crommelin, letter, 6 October 1916, Australian War Memorial.
 6. Nellie Crommelin, letter, 21 October 1916.
 7. Elsie Cook, 15 February 1917.

8. Elsie Cook, 23 February 1917.
9. Elsie Cook, 6 March 1917.
10. Nellie Crommelin, letter, 26 October 1916.
11. Elsie Cook, *The Australasian Nurses' Journal*, 15 September 1917.
12. Elsie Cook, 14 July 1917.
13. Elsie Cook, 31 July 1917.
14. Quoted in M. Oppenheimer, 'Gifts from France . . .', p. 70.
15. Nellie Crommelin letter, 6 October 1916.
16. Elsie Cook, 25 August 1917.
17. Nellie Crommelin letter, 11 June 1917.
18. Elsie Cook, 12 December 1917.
19. Elsie Cook, 19 December 1917.
20. Elsie Cook, 23 December 1917.
21. Elsie Cook, 25 December 1917.
22. Elsie Cook, 27 December 1917.
23. Elsie Cook, 31 December 1917.

CHAPTER 28   CONSCRIPTION

1. Grace Wilson, 6 August 1915.
2. Anne Donnell, *Letters of an Army Sister*, 21 October 1916, p. 125.
3. Alice Ross King, 2 November 1916.
4. Evelyn Davies, 24 November 1916.
5. Narelle Hobbes, letter, 22 March 1917, Australian War Memorial.
6. Narelle Hobbes, 22 March 1917.
7. Laura Grubb, letter, 14 November 1917, Australian War Memorial.
8. Ada Willis, letter, 9 November 1917, Stibbs family records.
9. Ada Willis, 14 February 1918.
10. Elsie Eglinton, 25 December 1917.
11. May Tilton, *The Grey Battalion*, pp. 281–2.
12. *Nepean Times*, undated.
13. Melanie Oppenheimer, *Oceans of Love*, ABC Books, Sydney, 2006, pp. 253–6.

CHAPTER 29   IT'S SOMETHING BIG, SISTER

1. Anne Donnell, *Letters of an Army Sister*, 5 September 1917, pp. 192.
2. Anne Donnell, *Letters of an Army Sister*, 6 September 1917, pp. 195.
3. Anne Donnell, *Letters of an Army Sister*, 7 November 1917, pp. 205–6.
4. Anne Donnell, *Letters of an Army Sister*, 22 November 1917, pp. 208–9.
5. Anne Donnell, *Letters of an Army Sister*, 22 November 1917, p. 209.
6. Anne Donnell, *Letters of an Army Sister*, 8 February 1918, p. 215.
7. Anne Donnell, *Letters of an Army Sister*, 8 February 1918, p. 216.
8. Anne Donnell, *Letters of an Army Sister*, 31 December 1917, p. 226.
9. Alice Ross King, 5 August 1916.
10. Elsie Cook, 23 December 1916.

11. *Kai Tiaki*, January 1919.
12. Nellie Crommelin letter, 22 March 1918.
13. Nellie Crommelin letter, 27 March 1918.
14. Lyn MacDonald, *The Roses of No Man's Land*, p. 271.
15. Alice Ross King, undated entry.
16. Alice Ross King, undated entry.
17. A.G. Butler, *Official History . . .*, vol. 3, pp. 559–63. All following quotations from this citation.
18. Annie Shadforth, statement.
19. Elsie May Tranter, 1 April 1918.
20. Kirsty Harris, 'Giving the dope: Australian Army nurse anaesthetists during World War I', *Australian Military Medicine*, vol. 12, no. 3, December 2003.
21. Elsie May Tranter, 19 April 1918.
22. Evelyn Davies, 31 March 1918.
23. Evelyn Davies, 17 May 1918.
24. Hilda Steele, National Archives of Australia, Series no. B2455, Item barcode 11609811; See also: http://throughtheselines.com.au/research/abbeville.

CHAPTER 30    THE STRUGGLE ENDS

1. Elsie Cook, 27 March 1918.
2. Nellie Crommelin, 3 April 1918.
3. Nellie Crommelin, 14 April 1918.
4. Elsie Cook, 16 April 1918.
5. Elsie Cook, 30 May 1918.
6. Nellie Crommelin letter, 1 June 1918.
7. Nellie Crommelin letter, 10 September 1918.
8. Elsie Cook, 14 June 1918.
9. Elsie Cook, 15 June 1918.
10. Elsie Cook, 12 July 1918.
11. Elsie Cook, 14 July 1918.
12. Elsie Cook, 16 July 1918.
13. Elsie Cook, 19 July 1918.
14. Pearl Corkhill, 8 April 1917.
15. Norm Hoyer, Private interview, 13 September 2004.
16. Private family records.
17. Pearl Corkhill, 29 July 1918.
18. Anne Donnell, *Letters of an Army Sister*, 9 May 1918, p. 249.
19. Anne Donnell, *Letters of an Army Sister*, 9 May 1918, p. 249.
20. Anne Donnell, *Letters of an Army Sister*, 5 November 1918, p. 241.
21. Anna Rogers, *While You're Away*, p. 177.
22. *Kai Tiaki*, January 1919, p. 15.
23. *Kai Tiaki*, January 1919, p. 16.
24. *Kai Tiaki*, January 1919.

CHAPTER 31   THE FIFTH NEW YEAR

1. Frances Laird, interview with Beth Robertson, J.D. Somerville oral history collection, Mortlock Library of South Australia.
2. Pte J. Hardie, letter, 30 October 1917, Australian War Memorial.
3. Elsie Cook, 3 September 1918.
4. Elsie Cook, 19 September 1918.
5. Elsie Cook, 29 October 1918.
6. Elsie Cook, 29 October 1918.
7. Elsie Cook, 11 November 1918.
8. Anne Donnell, *Letters of an Army Sister*, 11 November 1918, p. 272.
9. Anne Donnell, *Letters of an Army Sister*, 11 November 1918, pp. 272–3.
10. Anne Donnell, *Letters of an Army Sister*, 11 November 1918, p. 273.
11. Dora Birks, interview, oral evidence no. 36, December 1982, Mortlock Library of South Australia.
12. Elsie Tranter.
13. *Kai Tiaki*, January 1919.
14. *Kai Tiaki*, January 1919.
15. Anna Rogers, *While You're Away*, p. 175.
16. *Kai Tiaki*, January 1919.
17. Annie Shadforth, statement.
18. Alice Ross King.
19. Ada Willis, 11 November 1918.
20. Elsie Cook, 29 December 1918.


CHAPTER 32   THE AFTERMATH

1. Yvonne McEwen, p. 188.
2. Dora Birks, interview.
3. Letter held by Ivon Teague, family of Gladys Metherell, Christchurch.
4. Melanie Oppenheimer, 'Gifts for France: Australian Red Cross Nurses in France, 1916–1919', *Journal of Australian Studies*, no. 39, December 1993, p. 76.
5. Letter, Elizabeth Rothery file, Australian National Archives.
6. John McQuilton, 'Enlistment for the First World War in rural Australia: The case of north-eastern Victoria, 1914–1918', *Journal of the AWM*, issue 33, 2000.
7. Evelyn Davies, undated, 1919.
8. Olive Haynes in *We are Here . . .*, 6 February 1918, p. 257.
9. Pearl Corkhill, 7 December 1918.
10. Kath King, 3 March 1920.
11. Elsie Eglinton, 20 June 1918.
12. Elsie Eglinton, 20 June 1918.
13. Anne Donnell, *Letters of an Army Sister*, 24 January 1919, p. 280.
14. Anne Donnell, *Letters of an Army Sister*, 25 January 1919, p. 280.
15. Personal communication with Des Ryan.
16. Alice Ross King, February 1919.

# BIBLIOGRAPHY

---

## BOOKS

Adam-Smith, Patsy *The Anzacs*, Thomas Nelson, Melbourne, 1978.

—— *Australian Women at War*, Thomas Nelson, Melbourne, 1984.

Alexander, Alison *A Wealth of Women*, Duffy & Snellgrove, Sydney, 2002.

Armstrong, Dorothy Mary *The First Fifty Years*, Royal Prince Alfred Hospital Graduate Nurses' Association, Sydney, 1965.

Barker, Marianne *Nightingales in the Mud*, Allen & Unwin, Sydney, 1989.

Barrett, James and Deane, Lieut. P.E. *The Australian Army Medical Corps in Egypt*, M.K. Lewis and Co., London 1918

Bassett, Jan *Guns and Brooches: Australian Army Nursing from the Boer War to the Gulf*, Oxford, 1997.

Bean, C.E.W. *Official Histories, First World War: The Australian Imperial Force in France, 1916*, vol. 3, 12th edition, Australian War Memorial, Canberra, 1941.

Bowerbank, Sir Fred *A Doctor's Story*, Wingfield Press, Wellington, 1958.

Boyack, Nicholas and Tolerton, Jane (eds) *In the Shadow of War*, Penguin, Auckland, 1990.

Broadbent, Harvey *Gallipoli: The Fatal Shore*, Viking, Melbourne, 2005.

Butler, A.G. *Official History of the Australian Army Medical Services*, Australian War Memorial Melbourne, editions 1938 and 1940.

Carlyon, Les *The Great War*, Macmillan, Sydney, 2006.

—— *Gallipoli*, Macmillan, Sydney, 2002.

Corfield, Robin *Don't Forget Me, Cobber*, Corfield & Company, Rosana, Victoria, 2000.

Cowley, Robert (ed.) *The Great War*, Pimlico, London, 2004.

Damian, Sister Mary *Growl You May But Go You Must*, A.H. & A.W. Reed, Wellington, 1968.

Deacon, L.A. *Beyond the Call*, Regal Press, Launceston.

Donnell, Anne *Letters of an Army Sister*, Angus & Robertson, Sydney, 1920.

Facey, A.B. *A Fortunate Life*, Penguin Books, Ringwood Victoria, 1981.

Fenwick, Lieutenant-Colonel Dr Percival *Gallipoli Diary*, Auckland Museum.

Ferguson, Peter *Darkness in Paris*, Scribe Publications, Melbourne, 2005.

A First World War Nurse *A War Nurse's Diary: Sketches from a Belgian Field Hospital*, Macmillan, New York, 1918.

Goodman, Rupert *Our War Nurses*, Boolarong Publications, Brisbane, 1988.

Huxtable, Charles *From the Somme to Singapore*, Kangaroo Press, Kenthurst, NSW, 1987.

Idriess, Ion *The Desert Column*, Angus & Robertson, Sydney, reprinted 1985.

Kendall, Sherayl and Corbett, David *New Zealand Military Nursing*, self-published, Auckland, 1990.

Laffin, John *Damn the Dardanelles*, Sun Books, Melbourne, 1985.

MacDonald, Lyn *The Roses of No Man's Land*, Penguin, London, 1980.

Maclean, Hester *Nursing in New Zealand*, Tolan Printing Company, Wellington, 1932.

McEwen, Yvonne *It's a Long Way to Tipperary*, Cualann Press, Dunfermline, 2006.

Oppenheimer, Melanie *Oceans of Love, Narelle: An Australian Nurse in World War I*, ABC Books, Sydney, 2006.

Pugsley, Christopher *Gallipoli: The New Zealand Story*, Reed Publishing, Auckland, 1998.

Rae, Ruth *Scarlet Poppies*, The College of Nursing, Burwood, NSW, 2004.

Rattray, Joan *Great Days in New Zealand Nursing*, A.H. & A.W. Reed, Wellington, 1961.

Rawstron, R.E. *A Unique Nursing Group: New Zealand Army Nurse Anaesthetists of WWI*, The Printery, Massey University, 2005.

Reid, Richard *Just Wanted to Be There: Australian Service Nurses 1899–1999*, Commonwealth of Australia, 1999.

Rogers, Anna *While You're Away: New Zealand Nurses at War 1899–1948*, Auckland University Press, Auckland, 2003.

Scates, Bruce and Francis, Raelene *Women and the Great War*, Cambridge University Press, Cambridge, 1997.

Smith, John Meredith *Cloud Over Marquette*, Fiesta Products Ltd, Christchurch, 1990.

Tilton, May *The Grey Battalion*, Angus & Robertson, Sydney, 1933.

Tyquin, Michael *Gallipoli: The Medical War*, New South Wales University Press, Sydney, 1993.

Tyquin, Michael *Madness and the Military*, Australian Military History Publications, Loftus, 2006.

Willis, Ida *A Nurse Remembers*, A.K. Wilson, Lower Hutt, NZ [no date]

Young, Margaret (ed.) *We Are Here, Too: Diaries and Letters of Sister Olive. L.C. Haynes*, Australian Down Syndrome Association Incorporated, SA, 1991.

## NEWSPAPERS AND JOURNALS

Ellis Ashmead-Bartlett, *Mercury,* Hobart, 8 May 1915.

*Australasian Nurses' Journal,* 15 December 1914.

*British Journal of Nursing,* 2 February 1918.

*Canberra Times,* 13 March 2005.

Gibbs, Philip *Now It Can be Told,* Project Gutenberg, http://gutenberg.org/etext/3317.

*Kai Tiaki, 1914–1919.*

Kirsty Harris, 'Giving the dope: Australian Army Nurse anaesthetists during World War I', *Australian Military Medicine,* vol. 12, no. 3, December 2003.

—— *Sabretache,* Vol. 49 no.1, March 2008.

Ross Mcmullin 'Disaster at Fromelles', *Wartime,* Issue 36, Australian War Memorial, Canberra, 2006.

John McQuilton, 'Enlistment for the First World War in rural Australia: The case of north-eastern Victoria, 1914–1918', *Journal of the AWM,* issue 33, 2000.

*Medical Journal of Australia,* 27 January 1917.

*M.O., Church of England Messenger,* 4 April 1919.

*Nepean Times,* undated.

*New Zealand Nursing Review.*

*Oamaru Mail.*

Melanie Oppenheimer, 'Gifts for France: Australian Red Cross Nurses in France, 1916–1919', *Journal of Australian Studies,* no. 39 December 1993.

Ruth Rae, 'Operating in the theatre of World War I: France', *Acorn,* vol. 17, no. 2, 2004.

*The Burrowa News,* 22 January 1915.

*The Leader,* Orange, 18 February 1916.

*The Press,* Christchurch, 23 October 1965.

*Star,* Christchurch, 1 October 1965.

*UNA,* 30 October 1917.


## DIARIES, STATEMENTS AND LETTERS

Fanny Abbott, letter, 30 October 1915; Nurses' Chapel, Christchurch.

Australian Imperial Force unit war diaries, 1914–18 war, AWM4 Item Number 1/50/5/part 3; Australian War Memorial.

Mary Beswick, letter, the *Oamaru Mail*; Nurses' Chapel, Christchurch.

Dora Birks, interview, oral evidence no. 36, December 1982; Mortlock Library of South Australia.

H.G. Carter, letters, AWM 1DRL/0192; Australian War Memorial.

H.G. Carter, private family records.

Elsie Cook, diaries, AWM 2DRL/1085; Australian War Memorial.

Elsie Cook, private family records.

Ina Coster, 162/78 letter (typescript), Manuscripts Department, Canterbury Museum, Christchurch, posted at www.rootsweb.com/~nzlscant/coster.htm

Nellie Crommelin, letters, AWM PR00065; Australian War Memorial.

Evelyn Davies, diary, AWM 3DRL/3398(B); Australian War Memorial.

Elsie Eglinton, letters, AWM PR86/068; Australian War Memorial.

Elsie Grant, letters, AWM PR00596; Australian War Memorial.

Mary Gorman, private family records.

Laura Grubb, letters, AWM PR83/040; Australian War Memorial.

John Hardie Pte, letters, AWM PR 00519; Australian War Memorial.

Narelle Hobbes, letters, AWM 2DRL/0162; Australian War Memorial.

Lydia Kathleen King, diary, AWM, 3DRL/6040; Australian War Memorial.

Lydia Kathleen King, private family records.

Frances Laird, interview with Beth Robertson, J.D. Somerville oral history collection; Mortlock Library of South Australia.

Lottie Le Gallais, Le Gallais family papers, 1870–1920 MS 95/11, folders 3 and 6; Auckland War Memorial Museum Library.

Hilda Loxton, letters, AWM 2DRL/1172; Australian War Memorial.

George Mackay, statement, AWM PR86/068; Australian War Memorial.

Nellie Morrice, narrative, AWM 41 1013, 3DRL/2000; Australian War Memorial.

G.C. Munschamp, letter, UNA, vol. 15, no. 9, 30 November 1917, p. 277.

Vic Nicholson, unpublished interview with Christopher Pugsley, Palmerston, 1984.

Ida O'Dwyer, A descriptive narrative account of the conditions of nursing in an Australian CCS, AWM 25 173/9; Australian War Memorial.

Ida O'Dwyer, letter from Sister Ida O'Dwyer to Pte D.B. Nicol's mother, AWM PR89/061; Australian War Memorial.

Rachael Pratt, barcode 8018638, series no. B2455; National Archives of Australia.

Daisy Richmond, diary, AWM 2DRL/0783; Australian War Memorial.

Alice Ross King, diary, AWM PR02082; Australian War Memorial.

Elizabeth Rothery file, Australian National Archives, series number B2455, barcode 8038563.

Annie Shadforth, statement to the assistant collator, medical history; Ryan family records.

William Tennant, letter; Nurses' Chapel, Christchurch.

May Tilton, typescript of manuscript, The Grey Battalion, sent to C.E.W. Bean, AWM 41 1075; Australian War Memorial.

Elsie Tranter, diary, AWM 3DRL/4081(A); Australian War Memorial.

Edith Wilkin, letter, 7 November 1915; Nurses' Chapel, Christchurch.

Ada Willis, letters; Stibbs family records.

Grace Wilson, letters, AWM PR01870; Australian War Memorial.

Grace Wilson, report, 22 May 1933, AWM 41 1073; Australian War Memorial.

Len Wilson, statement; Wilson family records.

## OFFICIAL RECORDS AND REPORTS

Australian Red Cross Society Wounded and Missing Enquiry Bureau files, 1914–1918 War, I DRL/0428, Australian War Memorial.

William Kinsey Bolton, serial number B2455, barcode 3097255; National Archives of Australia.

Cable no. 2042 E; British National Archives.

Court of Inquiry report, ADM 137 3132; British National Archives.

Opinion of Crown Solicitor 1932, AWM file 734/1/- and 826/1/7; Australian War Memorial.

Fetherston Report, Series B539 AIF 239/8/88; Australian National Archives, Melbourne.

Papers of C.E.W. Bean, AWM 3DRL 8039/6.

# ACKNOWLEDGEMENTS

There are many people who have generously shared their knowledge, documents and time during my research for this book. Special thanks go to Marion Sanders, the daughter of Alice Ross King. Through Marion it was possible to get more than just a glimpse of her mother. Marion generously shared her private records and photos which help show just what a remarkable woman Alice was and were crucial to understanding the effect of the war on her in particular, and nurses in general.

John Carter, grandson of Kath King, has provided great help with records and photos of Kath and her husband, Gordon Carter. I'd also like to thank Kath's son, Ted Carter, and her niece, Sue Myers, for additional help.

Hartley Cook, grandson of Elsie and Syd Cook, kindly shared Elsie's photo album—which he only found in 2006 while moving premises. It was a great find.

Norm Hoyer knew Pearl Corkhill and was ever-willing to share his memories of her and their conversations. Gay Lane also contributed information about her great aunt Pearl and her engagement ring.

Rae Richmond was in the unique position of being related to two of the nurses in this narrative—Daisy Richmond and Marie Cameron. Rae and his late wife, Molly, were only too happy to share their records and recollections. Thanks also go to July Bailey and Maggie White for help with photos, and for their generous decision to donate Marie Cameron's medals to the Nurses' Chapel in Christchurch.

Many others have helped out in important ways. John Tilton and Judy Dyer shared their knowledge of May Tilton, while Margaret van Schaijik and Andrew Talbot were very helpful with family history records and photos relating to Tev Davies.

Thanks go to Bill Thompson, in Bathurst, for sharing his records on Lillian Fraser Thompson, and to Patricia Williams and Daphne Tongue for providing information and records relating to their mother, Nell Pike.

Thanks also go to Des Ryan for generously sharing his family history research on Annie Shadforth, and to Margaret Stibbs for sharing her records and photos relating to Ada Willis. I'd also like to thank Yvonne Sangster for material provided.

At the Australian War Memorial, I would especially like to thank Robyn van Dyk and Jeremy Richter, while at the Red Cross, Noel Barrow and Shirley Wood went to some effort to provide me with records relating to the Bluebirds. Thanks are also due to Iain McInnes for sharing photos and memorabilia of Ada Moore.

Helen Croll, of the Royal Prince Alfred Hospital Museum in Sydney, helped with Kath King's records and photos. Thanks are also due to Caitlin Rees and Tim Langford for their help in relation to photos and records.

In New Zealand, I am indebted to the tireless Lorraine Shannon who provided wonderful help in research into the *Marquette* disaster. Lorraine had boxes of documents ready for my arrival in Christchurch and went out of her way to help follow up extra leads.

Thanks are due to Martin Collett, Manuscripts Librarian at the Auckland War Memorial Museum, for his help in sourcing the letters of Lottie Le Gallais and her brother, Leddra. Michael Gorman kindly provided letters of his aunt, Mary Gorman.

Ivon Teague, Ian Wilson and Barbara Collie generously provided me with copies of family records relating to the *Marquette* nurses, while I am indebted to Linda Stopforth of the New Zealand Nurses Organisation for providing me with copies of *Kai Tiaki* published during the World War I. Thanks are also due to eminent New Zealand historian Christopher Pugsley for allowing me to publish an interview he recorded with one of the *Marquette* survivors.

Thanks are also due to Chris Bryett for his invaluable help on the Battle of Fromelles, Alan Kitchen of the Western Front Association, and to Chris Wesley and David Bartlett, of Bartlett's Tours, for their insights into the Australian experience on the Western Front.

Nursing historian and author Dr Ruth Rae generously shared her knowledge of the Australian First World War nurses. Christchurch historian and author Anna Rogers helped me understand the New Zealand perspective.

I'd also like to thank Sherayl McNab for her updated research on the number of New Zealand nurses who went to the war, and similarly acknowledge the work of Dr Kirsty Harris in updating the number of Australian nurses who served overseas. I'd also like to acknowledge Dr Melanie Oppenheimer's research on the Bluebirds and, in particular, the poor treatment they received on their return home.

For the fourth time around, I have been fortunate to be under the wing of Rebecca Kaiser, my publisher at Allen & Unwin, who has influenced this book from start to finish, suggesting changes with clarity, delicacy and tact—and all with her usual humour. Thanks are also due to copyeditor Liz Keenan for her helpful suggestions, and to proofreader Alex Nahlous for her forensic eye.

And lastly, no words can do justice to the wonderful support, encouragement and suggestions that Sue Langford provided during the research and again as the manuscript took shape.

# INDEX

Individual nurse entries are indicated in **bold**